WAVES OF BELONGING

WAVES OF BELONGING

Edited by Lydia Heberling,
David Kamper, and Jess Ponting

INDIGENEITY, RACE, AND GENDER IN THE SURFING LINEUP

University of Washington Press *Seattle*

Design by Mindy Basinger Hill

Composed in Minion Pro and Gilroy

UNIVERSITY OF WASHINGTON PRESS *uwapress.uw.edu*

LIBRARY OF CONGRESS CATALOGING-IN-PUBLICATION DATA

Names: Heberling, Lydia, editor. | Kamper, David, editor. | Ponting, Jess, editor.

Title: Waves of belonging : indigeneity, race, and gender in the surfing lineup / edited by Lydia Heberling, David Kamper, and Jess Ponting.

Description: Seattle : University of Washington Press, 2025. | Includes bibliographical references and index.

Identifiers: LCCN 2024019706 | ISBN 9780295753409 (hardcover) | ISBN 9780295753416 (paperback) | ISBN 9780295753423 (ebook)

Subjects: LCSH: Surfing—Social aspects. | Surfing—Cross-cultural studies. | Indigenous peoples—Social life and customs.

Classification: LCC GV839.5 .W38 2024 | DDC 306.4/83—dc23/eng/20240903

LC record available at https://lccn.loc.gov/2024019706

∞ This paper meets the requirements of ANSI/NISO Z39.48-1992 (Permanence of Paper).

Contents

Acknowledgments

The editors of this collection would like to thank our contributors, for their excellent work and for their patience as we navigated the creation of this project through the COVID-19 global pandemic. As it goes, these projects always take longer than we anticipate, but the stresses of these last few years certainly amplified all the various ways that edited collections can get bogged down. The kind of collaborative work required for a project as ambitious as this one was restricted by our lack of mobility and capacity to gather (and surf!) together in person. We express our full-hearted gratitude to each of you for your willingness to see this book through.

We also thank the communities of all the contributors. We know that writing never happens in isolation, and that moreover writing about such a relational and situated practice like surfing means that each contributor was thinking, writing, dreaming, and scheming about belonging in their own entangled networks of relations, interlocutors, families, and lands and waters. The work in this book is upheld and generated out of many vast and diverse networks of relations.

Finally, we thank our own communities for supporting us through this process. We are also embedded in our own local relations—in surfing communities, in tribal communities, in activist communities from San Diego to San Luis Obispo, California, and beyond. We are grateful to the San

Diego State University Surf/Skate Studies Collaborative, a multi-institutional organization of scholars who are purposefully creating space for the intersection between surfing, skating, and scholarship in the United States and beyond. The 2019 conference, "Impact Zones and Liminal Spaces: The Culture and History of Surfing," is the origin for this project, and we are grateful to those who organized that conference and brought together a generative community of surfers and scholars.

Thank you, finally, to our families and friends who always held space for us to think through this project with them. We are forever grateful for your support, encouragement, and love.

WAVES OF BELONGING

Introduction

Changing Tides and Shifting Swells

LYDIA HEBERLING, DAVID KAMPER,
AND JESS PONTING

Waves of Belonging: Indigeneity, Race, and Gender in the Surfing Lineup is a collection of essays about surfing, by surfers, that acknowledge the intimacies between surfing, storytelling, power, and relationships. Surfing is a salient and provocative method of engaging with how power is constructed in place. This book animates the possibilities for how surfing, as a practice and an analytic, serves as a productive space to reflect on the contemporary politics of our worlds. Surfing illustrates how Black, Indigenous, Latinx, queer and trans, and female-identifying communities, among others, navigate global spaces and politics and transform surfing culture into boarder-lands of possibilities for new imagined relations and belonging.

The authors showcased in this book are only a few of the many surfers, academics, community organizers, and activists who are interrogating the implications of, among other global contexts, the COVID-19 pandemic and twenty-first-century racial protest movements as they manifest in surfing communities, geographies, and cultures across the world. In this stage of late capitalism and its co-constitutive rise of fascism and authoritarianism around the world, these authors illustrate the deeply relevant stakes of surfing as sport and leisure activity.[1] The title of this collection, *Waves of Belonging: Indigeneity, Race, and Gender in the Surfing Lineup*, distills the core of these stakes: hope and (an affirmation of) belonging animate these projects of resistance to and refusal of a structural politics of settler colonialism, heteronormative patriarchy, and capitalism. The essays contained in this book emerge out of surfing spaces where questions of power and identity shape relations in and around waves with a fundamental desire for surfing futures that dream beyond the limitations of current relations and power dynamics.

We choose to center these ideas, themes, and histories here in the introduction to this collection because Indigeneity opens productive, if not difficult, conversations about land—whose is it, who should have access to it, who should steward it, what should happen on it and to it. Surfing, always, occurs on Indigenous lands. Within the context of surfing and surf studies, "land" is an expansive term to think about coastal zones that include oceanic waters, river mouths and deltas, and any space where surfing and surf culture is performed and articulated. While surfing communities have a long-standing reputation for their commitments to environmental conservation and protection, environmentalism and conservation structures that do not account for Indigenous peoples and Indigenous sovereignty reproduce settler colonial dispossession. Place names, health, legal determination, safety, equity, and sovereignty all become crucial topics in the ongoing expansion of the field of critical surf studies. This includes previous work by scholars such as Colleen McGloin, whose work in the 2017 *Critical Surf Studies Reader* situates "indigenous surfing" as a crucial "pedagogical force [that] disrupts dominant discourses of national identity" and "recenters indigenous knowledges, *epistemes*, histories, and spatiotemporalities."[2] As this volume will illustrate, there are diverse discourses around Indigeneity, settler colonialism, and surfing that construct dynamic constellations of relations, knowledges, and responsibilities, in the field of surfing studies and in our own local communities. Directly or indirectly, the essays within this book address these place-based relationalities and can be read productively with this rubric in mind.

While this book primarily centers North American geographic and disciplinary and cultural thought around critical surfing studies, the global flows of such practices and thought are rich with regionally specific knowledges and sociocultural formations of surfing communities and ideologies outside of North America (and the Global North more broadly). Critical surfing studies has many sites of energetic convergence within the academy and across global cartographies—scholars have published works on surfing in the blue humanities, leisure and tourism studies, outdoor recreation studies, ocean studies, sports studies, gender and sexuality studies, settler colonial studies, and Indigenous and ethnic studies, to name a few. One reason for this energetic and multisited growing body of work is that surfing and surfing studies contribute one of many possible formal processes for navigating the flows, tides, shoals, and oceanic boundary zones (where currents converge) that decenter traditional notions of power. The global diversity of surfing's participants has allowed for and necessitated conversations around who can be in what waters, where, and when. Engaging in critical surfing studies commits us to the idea that the affect of surfing—pleasure and joy, or, in surfing lingo, the "stoke"—translates into material and relational practices of living in better relations to place and each other. The ocean as both place and idea invites those who approach and enter it into a relational space of humility and respect and the promise of reorganizing power.

In this collection we activate these broader interdisciplinary surfing studies discourses around race and gender through the lens of Indigeneity. We take, as our point of departure, a question raised by Colville scholar Dina Gilio-Whitaker, who, in the context of environmental justice, asks, "What does environmental justice look like when Indigenous peoples are at the center?" We extend this question to the topic of surfing (Gilio-Whitaker also happens to be a critical surfing studies scholar and is included in this collection) to ask, What does surfing and critical surfing studies look like with Indigeneity at the center?[3] Hence, Indigeneity functions as an *analytic*. That is, Indigeneity is a framework or rubric that makes legible the sets of concerns Indigenous peoples have with regards to their rights to land, language, education, health, and political and legal self-determination.[4] When we center the Indigenous, these relations emerge and invite us into a set of privileges and responsibilities that animate how we move through the world. Applied in this way, "Indigeneity" leverages a political right to (re)claim and (re)center the sovereign rights of Indigenous peoples to define the terms of their existence within and beyond the settler colonial regimes that have produced their oppression for hundreds of years.[5] This analytic seems salient, given that at its heart surfing is an Indigenous activity that was co-opted by settlers and then refracted through modernity to provide settlers with purported unmediated and intimate access to nature, all while disregarding the historical and material conditions of colonialism and capitalism.[6] By centering Indigeneity in critical surf studies, the editors of this collection argue for the responsibilities, relationships, and forms of respect that such a reframing entails. As Wheaton, Waiti, Olive, and Kearns have argued, "Drawing on Indigenous knowledges is ethical and necessary in how we understand, care for, and develop relationships with blue spaces and marine ecosystems."[7] The better we understand the structures and processes of settler colonialism and how they manifest over time in surfing and surf culture, the more potentially transformative the space of surfing.

Surfing as an act and an idea has expanded far beyond the conventional narrative of its Hawaiian origins. And in fact, while surfing is popularly conceived as having Hawaiian origins, scholars such as Kevin Dawson and Colleen McGloin affirm that wave riding occurred prior to its modern iteration in a range of places, from Africa to Australia and beyond.[8] As a metaphor, it has taken on specific cultural connotations related to acts of gliding, skimming, or riding through both physical and virtual spaces and is invoked as both "a lifestyle and a structure of feeling," as well as "a language for imagining contemporary global mobility [that] suggests pleasurable, creative, and freeing outcomes."[9] From sidewalk surfing (or skateboarding) to surfing the world wide web, the idea and act of surfing transgress its discrete physical origins and embodiment—that is, the ocean and the body—and circulate as a multisited cultural idiom, a "globalist trope" that implies "the social possibilities generated by the circulation of international capital, new information technologies, and people in transit."[10] Loosened from its origins in this way, surfing has become a cultural signifier for twenty-first-century cultural routes—that is, how we travel and move through space and time, whether down the face of a wave, across an asphalt parking lot, or through the multidimensional spaces of virtual reality—as well as roots—how we locate ourselves in cultural and physical geographies, storying cartographies and animating relationships. Routes and roots have served as productive homophonic relatives in cultural studies. Specifically, here we are thinking with Vicente M. Diaz's insightful analysis of Chamorro and Central Carolinian seafaring traditions in which cultural practices of voyaging and wayfinding—routing—are roots of knowledge and identity. Diaz compellingly argues, "To view the mobility of the canoe as a cultural foundation as well as to understand foundational culture in fluidic ways is to capture through strategic mixing of metaphors the dialogic and generative tensions between cultural forces of routing and historical process of rooting indigenous identity and tradition."[11] Scholars such as Diaz who work on Pacific Indigenous oceanic and seafaring traditions are crucial intellectual forebearers to those of us working in critical surfing studies, and especially those working at the intersection of Indigenous and critical surfing studies.

Entangled in this complex and multidimensional signification is the reality that surfing has, like the shorelines and coastal spaces where it occurs, also long been occupied by Westerners. Its Indigenous origins have been mostly vacated except for the most romanticized gauzy mythologies of its tropical origins. The origins of surfing's popular histories in the Western world are rooted in narrative practices of what Jean O'Brien might describe as "firsting": white settler men, at the turn of the twentieth century, rehabilitate surfing from the "last" vestiges of Kanaka Māoli surf traditions after European contact systemically constructs barriers for Hawaiians to continue surfing—and catalyze a new era of surfing culture built on structures of racism and colonialism for primarily white affluent men.[12] While these firsting narratives often gesture to the roles that key Kanaka Māoli figures such as Duke Kahanamoku and George Freeth played in the development of modern surfing culture, they are usually tokenized figures at best.[13] Modern surfing origin stories sublimate the legacy of Kanaka Māoli and other Pacific Indigenous wave-riding peoples in favor of centering white (male) ownership of the sport and the lands and waters where it happens. The result is a strong prevalence of white male surfers dominating surfing spaces and producing surfing's modern-day narratives.[14]

That said, this collection is not exclusively an Indigenous studies project. In purposefully centering Indigenous peoples and Indigenous studies *first*, this collection then expands outward to think *with* issues of race, gender, and sexuality across geographies and cultures. We find it incredibly productive to be thinking with the generative scholarship of thinkers such as Tiffany Lethabo King, whose work in *The Black Shoals* animates the geologic formation of the shoal—an underwater sandbar or structure—as an intellectual form that "disrupts nautical and oceanic coherence" and "enables other modes of thinking about Blackness that opens up other kinds of potentialities, materialities, and forms."[15] King applies this potential to thinking about the intersections of Black and Indigenous thought, arguing that each is a productive shoal to the other. King is herself building on a long tradition in Black thought that draws metaphoric and rhetorical arguments from oceanic materiality. For example, Edward Kamau Brathwaite's invocation of "tidalectics"—the productive blending of *tidal* with *dialectic*—understands Black diasporic cultural practices in terms of goings out and comings in, emphasizing the constant change and flow of Black diasporic cultural practices. Likewise, we see this collection contributing to voices such as Jesús Estrada Milán and Luis Escala Rabadán, whose work on transborder surfing at the US-Mexico border between Tijuana and San Diego illuminates how surfing is a space for analyzing "tremendous power and economic imbalances" that shape our understanding of "identities, nationalism, the cultural production of surfing spaces next to or near national borders" as well as the "rivalries and affinities that . . . exist among surfers of different countries."[16] In purposefully considering borders as multiply determined—geopolitical borders, geographical boundaries, and ocean-land convergence sites—Estrada Milán and Escala Rabadán implicitly work with Walker's theorization of "boarder-lands" and resituate an analysis of surfing on Chicana scholar Gloria Anzaldúa's theoretical site, the geographical area between what is now the United States and Mexico where identity and power become muddled, and reorganized, in the ambiguity of these border regions. And of course Kanaka Māoli historian Isaiah Walker then innovates the concept of the "boarder-lands" in relation to Anzaldúa's borderlands in his 2011 monograph, *Waves of Resistance:*

Surfing and History in Twentieth-Century Hawai'i, as a way of extending the idea of these spaces into the surf zone. While Walker is specifically describing surfing politics and social structures for Indigenous Hawaiians, the concept of the "boarder-lands" applies productively beyond the social and geographical spaces of Hawai'i, and surfing studies scholars situate this theoretical concept in global geographies in diverse and dynamic ways.

Gender and sexuality studies scholars have fundamentally shaped the field of critical surfing studies. Ian Masterson has persuasively argued, "In the root culture of surfing—throughout Polynesian history, women were held in the highest esteem as surfers, respected and acknowledged by men and women alike."[17] Informed *first* by the gendered relations of Indigenous surfers prior to and/or outside of colonialism, Masterson establishes a framework for thinking from this orientation about gendered social relations within surfing culture more broadly. lisahunter affirms that sex, gender, and sexuality in surfing are "categories that are socially constructed" and "do particular work through perception, cognition, action and interaction. They interact with other subject positions, identities and practices that mark and position individuals and groups. In conjunction with identities such as race, ethnicity, religion, age, ability, size, experience, wealth and many other markers used to discriminate between people, sex, gender and sexuality are used to socially position people, or to define who one 'is' and what ones 'does.'"[18] Indeed, a diverse range of scholars are working hard to understand how heteronormative patriarchy and racial power manifest in surfing's sociopolitical realms. The issues of race, gender, and sexuality within surfing culture have emerged in publications worldwide, affirming the claim this book makes here that surfing and surfing culture are productive sites of analysis when it comes to power, identity, and belonging.[19]

This collection's title, *Waves of Belonging*, invokes both the material wave—those rolling, peeling shoulders of water breaking along global shorelines—and the metaphorical work of the term *wave* within academic discourse. In academic circles the word *wave* is perhaps most often associated with feminism and the three waves of feminist thought. Years before critical surfing studies was considered an academic field or discipline, Kanaka Māoli scholar Hokulani Aikau invoked the act of surfing and surfers' ability to read waves as an entry point for disentangling what feminist scholars mean when referring to "waves" of feminist thought.[20] She writes, referring to herself in the third person,

> As she sat on the beach reading the literature on third wave feminism, she listened to and watched the waves roll onto shore and wondered about the materiality of the wave metaphor. Where do waves come from? How do they operate? When she sat and watched wave after wave roll onto shore she wondered, how can we tell when one wave begins and another ends? According to surfers, waves come in at least three sets of three with the third wave being the ideal one to catch and ride to shore. The first two waves allow the surfer to read the size and speed of the waves that will follow. The surfer does not worry if she does not catch the third wave or if the set fades out before reaching shore because she knows that more will be coming on the horizon. Surfers turn their back to the shore and look to the horizon in eager anticipation of the next set of waves.[21]

Here Aikau describes in detail the knowledge surfers possess about the behavior of waves, the way they travel in sets of approximately three, even as they appear rather continuous in nature. She also describes what surfers come to know—that of these waves, it is wise to "read" the first two before taking off and riding the third. Applying this embodied knowledge to her field of feminist studies, she draws a productive juxtaposition between the materiality of waves and sets, in terms of how surfers literally "read" the ocean's energy, and the energetic flow of feminist theories. Long before the emergence of critical surfing studies as an academic field, Aikau is disentangling the temporal waves and generations of feminist thought through an Indigenous epistemology of waves, establishing a crucial precedence that amplifies the reality that for Indigenous Hawaiians the ocean has always been a site of knowledge production and a way of making sense of the world.

Kanaka Māoli scholar Karin Amimoto Ingersoll more recently affirms the centrality of oceanic epistemologies for Kanaka sovereignty. Her 2019 book, *Waves of Knowing: A Seascape Epistemology*, which draws on "oceanic potential," argues that surfing (*he'e nalu*) embodies the potential for Kanaka Māoli to transform Indigenous knowledges into political praxis. She writes,

> Kanaka empirical experiences encountered in the world, experiences such as he'e nalu [surfing], connect to a politicization of Hawaiian knowledge and place that involves interconnection, flexibility, and movement. There is a potentiality for Kanaka Māoli to turn ocean-based knowledges and practices into a politics and ethics (oceanic literacy is not political or ethical on its own) because ka moana is mixed into Native Hawaiian genealogy, place, and history, and thus helps lay the foundation for articulating Kanaka theories and other ways of knowing that arise from a connection to 'āina. As a political and ethical act, he'e nalu re-creates patterns already set in motion by our ancestors.[22]

Ingersoll directly links the activity of *he'e nalu* with decolonial politics precisely because it is an ethical act grounded in ancestral knowledge. The first part of her title, *Waves of Knowing*, participates in a longer practice of titling surfing scholarship along with Walker's book *Waves of Resistance* (as well as this book), as it draws on that ambiguity between the materiality and temporality of waves and the metaphorical waves of political and decolonial thought in twenty-first-century Hawai'i. Her emphasis on *knowing* in this case centers her focus on building an epistemology grounded in oceanic knowledges that are entangled in Indigenous epistemologies of Hawai'i and the Pacific.

Our book, which we confess we titled strategically to invoke this tradition of punning with and complicating the material and metaphorical wave, is meant to expand this tradition of wave analysis by centering conceptualizations of belonging that are grounded in a sense of hope, or a kind of futurity. We draw our working definition of *hope* from Teresa Shewry, settler scholar of Pacific and oceanic literatures and cultural production, who defines hope in relation to the Pacific Ocean, specifically, as "a relationship with the future that involves attunement to environmental change and more specifically to the ocean" and argues for "the relevance of hope as a creative and critical engagement with present and past environmental constraints, including myriad forms of loss."[23] Hope, as "a psychic, political, and social mode of engaging the future in terms of specific aspirations and imagined pathways," animates cultural production.[24] We argue that hope serves as a useful frame for belonging in surfing studies, as surfers/scholars engage with surfing to articulate a political, psychic, and social engagement with their own versions of hope.

We see the concept of hope as existing in intimate relation with the notion of dreaming, as articulated by Athabascan poet and scholar Dian Million. Million, an Indigenous feminist scholar dedicated to the acts of creativity and acts of scholarship that imagine Indigenous futures, describes dreaming as "the effort to make sense of relations in the worlds we live, dreaming and empathizing intensely our relations with past and present and the future without the boundaries of linear time. Dreaming is a communicative sacred activity. Dreaming often allows us to creatively sidestep all the neat little boxes that obscure larger relations and syntheses of imagination."[25] Dreaming, in other words, bypasses the restrictions and limitations of settler colonial realities and draws on long-standing relationships that supersede the boundaries of temporality and animate visions of a future that is other than the settler colonial (and oppressive) present. We might begin the process of dreaming by asking, "What are the relations of our knowing? What and who does our acts of making meaning serve?"[26] While Million writes specifically for and about Indigenous peoples, surfers and scholars of critical surfing studies would be wise to allow such questions to animate our questions. How does surfing shape our relationships? What we know? Who do we serve when we show up in surf zones and surfing communities?

Surfing is known for its exclusivity, its intense localisms, its gender-based discrimination, and often its socioeconomic limitations for participation. In centering belonging in the title of this book and inviting our contributors and readers to think with these concepts of hope and dreaming, we challenge these histories of exclusivity and signal to readers that the scholarship included here is intentional in its articulations of belonging in place. Many of the chapters in this book detail how surfing's counterculture reputation is reoperationalized by Black, Indigenous, and LGBTQ+ peoples to construct spaces of belonging. The writers in this collection illustrate how they think with surfing, instructing readers how to think and move with surfing to imagine different political futures, community futures, futures of belonging. Hence, surfing can be viewed as a method for decolonizing, righting historical wrongs, restoring relationship with and to lands and waters, and as a praxis for language learning. Surfing is a vehicle for storytelling, reimagining histories, and restoring agency. In this collection every contributing scholar acknowledges and accounts for Indigenous land theft and names the colonial conditions by which surfing has emerged in the contemporary world as a sport dominated by white Westerners. This is certainly not (yet) the norm in surfing communities and cultures, but these scholars, who are also teachers and professors and community members, are all working in academic and community spaces to normalize the reality that we live and surf on Indigenous lands. One of our hopes for this collection is that it animates questions of identity and belonging in our readers. Whether you are a scholar, a surfer, a boarder, an outdoor recreator, or some combination of these, we prompt you to consider what, *for you*, becomes visible in your spaces of recreation, leisure, and study with Indigenous peoples at the center.

This volume also attends to the fact that as surfing studies develops, our scholarship needs to chart our methodologies and theoretical approaches into and through the waters of the field. We encouraged contributors to explicitly signal their unique entry points, narrate how they are reading the waters of surfing studies as they paddle out into it, and define and describe the equipment they use to situate themselves in the waters of surfing studies. Many of these projects are responsive to community needs and ethics that operate outside of traditional, or Western, disciplinary traditions, and so it is crucial that we explain our methodologies, responsibilities, and relationship positionalities as we go. We are delighted by how personal so many of these essays are. Methodologically, surfing studies has a high prevalence of autoethnographic approaches (understandable, given how individualized the act of surfing is in the first place).

Indeed, the critical attention on research methodologies as embodied, when we are engaged as practitioners, is an ongoing conversation across global critical surfing studies and sports studies spaces. The key is not whether we approach our study "as a past or present (non)active participant" or whether we conduct "interviews, focus groups, observations or discourse analysis." As Olive and others have stated, "Instead it is about the reflexivity of the researcher in terms of how their dynamic position in the action sports culture *and* the academy, and their movement between these fields, influences their research questions, methodological choices, and theoretical approaches and representational styles, at various stages during their project."[27] These are our experiences as surfers, but also as Indigenous people, people of color, and allies and collaborators: surfing animates and articulates broader conversations about identity and belonging, and the scholars in this book model how to work from this kind of personal experience or praxis. The importance of autoethnographic, autobiographical projects reveals vibrant and significant possibilities of theorizing from diverse identity positions.[28] Dian Million is adamant that "story is theory," and that especially for Indigenous peoples, stories illustrate complex relationships and responsibilities that animate how one is to move through the world. Within critical ethnic studies and gender studies, the project of autoethnographic theorizing is grounded in theories of knowing in place, knowing from the undercommons.[29]

Lastly, this volume acknowledges and integrates the ways surfing has intersected with contemporary social, political, and economic events since 2017.[30] The announcement in 2019 that surfing would be included in the 2020 Olympic games raised timely questions around Hawaiian political sovereignty and whether Hawai'i would be able to compete as its own nation in the Games (as Isaiah Walker writes about in this collection). The 2020 COVID-19 global pandemic brought surf tourism to a crawl and amplified racial tensions. Social protest movements such as the Black Lives Matter protests of 2020, catalyzed by the violent police killings of George Floyd and Breonna Taylor, garnered attention in the global surfing community. Paddle-outs—where groups congregate in the ocean on surfboards, kayaks, paddleboards, and other seafaring technologies, typically to memorialize a person—were organized, bringing a surfing tradition typically practiced as memorial into the realm of political protest. Activists also continued to tie important ocean legislation for local and state governments to community-based issues for surfers and Indigenous peoples alike. In short, the last six years has seen a robust growth in the political consciousness of the global surfing community, and surfers and surf scholars alike are generating provocative bodies of knowledge around the intersection of these events and the ways in which surfing mediates, intervenes on, and provides a productive critical lens for thinking with these events as community.

The academy and academic publishing are inherently colonial spaces, and the act of centering Indigenous knowledges, writers, and analytics in this space does not "decolonize" anything, per se. And as three non-Indigenous editors, we further understand that we operate from specific social locations that preclude us from claiming to create decolonial knowledge-making projects.[31] As we organized this volume, we placed Indigenous writers at the beginning of each part of the book as an invitation to readers to understand how Indigeneity, Indigenous knowledges, and Indigenous writing (re)frame and (re)orient approaches to surfing studies. Rather than assert a philosophical claim to decolonizing the field, we invite readers, surfers, and community members to allow your own beliefs, values, social locations, and practices of surfing and surfing scholarship to be shaped through the knowledges and values of the diverse writers included here.

Part 1, "From Local to Global," locates readers within a range of approaches to critical surfing studies that affirms Indigenous origin stories and demonstrates the possibilities of routing surfing as both practice and relation *from* these local relations and logics. It opens with Kanaka Māoli scholar Isaiah Walker with a piece on Hawaiian sovereignty and its political status as an independent nation in the context of the Olympics. Walker reflects on the way the introduction to surfing in the Olympics has opened an opportunity for Hawai'i's sovereignty as an independent entity to be recognized, with the potential of Olympic athletes representing Hawai'i in competition. Walker's piece draws surfing's Hawaiian origins into the contemporary sociopolitical moment to illustrate how the sport of surfing conveys the sociopolitical stakes of Indigeneity. Kevin Dawson then brilliantly reminds us that surfing has multiple origin stories and expands on our understanding of Africa as a site of wave riding, ocean leisure, and communal storytelling around the act of surfing. Together, Walker's and Dawson's essays affirm multiple local sites of surfing development across the globe and implicitly invite us to consider the multiple Indigenous communities who locate at least aspects of their sense of place and relationality in surf zones.

Tara Ruttenberg and Peter Brosius's piece illustrates the contemporary politics of surf tourism by locating the problem of localism in origin myths of surfing that have been superseded by the surf tourism industrial complex. In other words, their essay offers an illuminating framework for understanding how surfing has been co-opted, delinked from its Indigenous origins, and retrafficked as a neocolonial project of capital and patriarchy. Krista Comer's keynote speech from the 2017 Surf Studies Conference, held at San Diego State University, concludes this part by linking growing global manifestations of fascism and authoritarianism to forms of heteropatriarchy. She then amplifies the way surfeminism "brings to light problems of accessing ocean and beach spaces and accessing surf economies" and that a lack of access "shows racial injustice, blindness to Indigenous sovereignty, homophobia, and inequality in competitive surf purses, sponsorship, surf livelihoods, and the lineup."

Part 2, "Bo(a)rderlands," is meant to invoke the multiple significations of the words *board*, *border*, *boarder*, and *borderlands*. In this part the essays extend beyond the sport of surfing to engage with and include skateboarding and snowboarding. Ojibwe scholar Nicholas Reo's beautiful meditation on surfing opens with the route he takes to surfing via skateboarding and snowboarding, or "snurfing" (a colloquial, neological blend of *snowboarding* and *surfing*). His essay then turns to the productive relationship between learning how to surf and learning how to speak Ojibwe, and how the two learning journeys mutually support each other. Anishinaabe artist, curator, and writer Jaimie Isaac reflects on her experience curating the *Boarder X* art exhibition, which featured artistic works related to acts of Indigenous surfing, skateboarding, and snowboarding as expressions of sovereign identities and sovereign relationships to occupied Canadian lands and waters. This exhibition opened in Winnipeg and traveled west across several Canadian art institutions, finishing in Vancouver. The traveling nature of the exhibition allowed Isaac to connect with local Indigenous boarding communities and affirm the importance of rooted connections between communities, places, and board sports cultures.

Chase Bucklew and David Kamper's essay maintains the energetic momentum generated by Reo and Isaac with their provocative rereading of *Dogtown and Z-Boys*, the seminal 2001 skateboarding documentary that cemented the link between skate, surf, and counterculture in the Santa Monica/Venice Beach neighborhoods of Los Angeles. A retelling of the origin story of modern skateboarding, *Dogtown and Z-Boys* chronicles the emergence of counterculture radicalism in predominantly white, masculine skating communities. Bucklew and Kamper question the legacy of these purported countercultural heroes as canonized by both the film and the original imaginary created by Craig Stecyk's "Dogtown" articles and the extent to which this radicalism has become commodified or even overstated in the first. Through a rereading of the history of the "Dogtown" area, they suggest that a productive place to locate inheritors of this counterculture radicalism is in contemporary communities of American Indian skaters and BIPOC surfers. Writing from the same Los Angeles coastal communities, Cassie Comley then asks us to consider local representations of surfing at LA's beaches and how Mexican American surfers are changing the surfscapes. Comley argues that the popular discourse around surfing has limited the recognition of surfers of color to Indigenous Hawaiians and to a lesser extent Brazilian or occasionally Mexican national surfers. Comley asks us to consider more disruptive Brown bodies, those of Chicanx surfers in Southern California. Comley illustrates how Mexican American surfers are coded as outsiders to coastal environments and notes that this segregation is compounded by the fact that many white surfers see themselves as "color-blind" and therefore struggle to see their own involvement in preserving an oppressive racial politics.

"Bo(a)rderlands" concludes with lisahunter's move to queer the surfing lineup and resituate this space as a dynamic borderland of queer identity formation. Returning to Gloria Anzaldúa's formulation of the borderland, lisahunter's essay challenges the rigid formulas of identity and power in surfing spaces and suggests that a proliferation of identities within surfing communities, rather than a critique of or breakdown of existing identity categories, performs a radical act of reimagining belonging in the surf zone. Together, these bo(a)rderland narratives illustrate the vastly diverse and exciting methodological approaches to and interventions on popular narratives of surfing and surfing cultures.

The essays in the third and final part of this book, "Intersections and Relations," illustrate the dynamic possibilities of centering surfing as an analytic in a range of topics and conversations. Writing on topics from California state politics to literary studies to the racial and gendered politics of California's beaches, the scholars included here demonstrate the possibilities for making theory, policy, and protest on a surfboard and from a situated space. Indigenous scholar Dina Gilio-Whitaker (Colville) and settler scholar Krista Comer productively model a feminist approach to surfing scholarship and activism that is grounded in their respective positions as Indigenous and settler feminists and surfers. Their essay, "Being Good Relatives: A Story of Indigenous and Settler Surfeminist Collaboration and Legislated Land Acknowledgments," illustrates how surfeminism opens common ground for female-identifying scholars from diverse identity positions to mobilize political activism to amplify Indigenous sovereignty. Their essay chronicles their campaign to pass Assembly Bill (AB) 1782—a bill that would designate surfing as the official state sport of California—*with* an acknowledgment of surfing's Indigenous roots.

Asako Yonan's essay, "In the Name of Public Safety: Gendered Surveillance and Sexual Violence within Southern California Beach Lifeguarding Culture," interrogates the power structures of California's beach lifeguarding complex, which is grounded in a politics of militarism and heteropatriarchy that alienates Indigenous, nonwhite, female, and queer bodies in California beach spaces. An autoethnographic tale of discrimination within the lifeguarding-"paramilitary" complex, Yonan's essay theorizes the concept of "patch privilege" and frames lifeguarding "as an institution bound by values and traditions modeled after military and law enforcement institutions" to reveal the way it violently restricts and penalizes nonconforming bodies. Yonan utilizes a queer of color feminist critique to call out lifeguarding as a site of gender and racial violence in California.

Lydia Heberling's essay, "Totally Tubular Aesthetics: Surfing, Seafaring, and Storytelling in *News from Native California*," examines one California Indian storyteller's invocation of surfing in the quarterly publication *News from Native California* as an entryway for thinking about how surfing, and then seafaring, are powerful sites of sovereignty for California Indian peoples within California's coastal spaces. She argues that surfing, as a trans-Indigenous activity, amplifies the importance of ocean-going material cultures for decolonial relations in California's hypersaturated coastal regions. Elizabeth Sine concludes this collection with a meditation on the ways that the events of 2020 have fundamentally shaped surfing discourses and communities. Sine contextualizes her essay in the intersecting and overlapping social crises of the COVID-19 pandemic, the police murders of George Floyd and Breonna Taylor, the killing of Ahmaud Arbery, the US-Mexico border crisis, and the Trump presidency, explaining that these events catalyzed open conversation about race and power in mainstream surfing. Sine then argues that these "new" fissures in the collective surfing consciousness created "fresh possibilities for advancing alternative visions of what surfing was and ought to be—visions that were anchored in efforts . . . long in the making" and lays out the longer history of race activism in California's surfing cultures. Sine concludes by suggesting that this particular sociopolitical moment catalyzes a renaissance in surfing, in terms of awareness and appreciation for surfers of color and Indigenous surfing, but one always-already grounded in women-, Black-, Brown-, Indigenous-, and queer-led activism.

These essays could have been organized into many different clusters to draw out a range of themes and topics that are relevant within surfing cultures and surfing studies right now. In the moment that this book is being published, we are moving past the immediacy of the 2020 era, and it remains to be seen what happens within discourses of "DEI" (diversity, equity, and inclusion), whether it will structurally reorganize American outdoor and surfing cultures or whether the "DEI industrial complex" will simply reify and uphold the supremacy of some and not others.

Currents are shifting, and new swells are being forecast in the deep waters of our collective moment. As critical surfing studies scholars and as surfers always entangled in constellations of relations, we remain attentive to the waves as they approach, mapping them, calculating their size, energy, and direction, and occasionally maneuvering into one, down and across its face, gliding with its dynamic energy as we move toward shore before turning around to paddle out for another. There are always waves; there is always space for belonging with them.

Notes

1 Authors in this collection are also inclusive of related sport and leisure activities that animate surfing cultures, such as skateboarding, snowboarding, and lifeguarding. Scholars of surf studies beyond those included here have included bodyboarding, swimming, canoeing, kayaking, and more into broader discussions of surfing, culture, and power. See Olive, "Swimming and Surfing in Ocean Ecologies," and Wheaton, Waiti, Olive, and Kearns, "Coastal Communities, Leisure and Wellbeing," as two of many examples of scholarship centering surfing and leisure studies, particularly from Oceania.

2 McGloin, "Indigenous Surfing," 197.

3 Gilio-Whitaker, *As Long as Grass Grows*, 13. We also consider the work of Chadwick Allen in his 2008 presidential address to the Native American and Indigenous Studies Association, which invites us to imagine the rubric of "Indigenous" "not simply as a collection of individuals, communities, tribes, and nations gathered together for events such as this conference, but as significantly *related*, with all the privileges, responsibilities, and hard work that reciprocal relationships entail." Allen, "2014 NAISA Presidential Address," 2.

4 Teves, Smith, and Raheja articulate the complex ways the ideas and politics of "Indigeneity" are operationalized by Indigenous peoples and within Indigenous studies in their essay, "Indigeneity," and we recommend their excellent essay in its entirety for a fuller understanding of the ways "Indigenous" and "Indigeneity" operate in various discourses.

5 Any time the prefix *re* is applied in this way, it acknowledges the work of Indigenous scholars such as Linda Tuhiwai Smith (Maori), Mishuana Goeman (Tonawanda Band of Seneca), and Cutcha Risling Baldy (Hupa, Yurok, and Karuk), who have, in multiple contexts over the last twenty-five years, the-

orized the complexity of actions involving "again" or "going back to" within ongoing structures of settler colonialism. Smith includes the projects of remembering, revitalizing, regenerating, representing, reframing, restoring, and returning in her "Twenty-Five Indigenous Projects," published in *Decolonizing Methodologies* back in 1999. In a literary studies context, Goeman argues that Indigenous women's stories "re-map" settler literary and geographic cartographies. Within the intersectional fields of anthropology and California Indian studies, Risling Baldy invokes the use of the parenthetical *(re)* to strategically describe the practice of women's coming-of-age ceremonies in northwestern California. Our use of the parenthetical *(re)* is meant to draw from these intellectual genealogies and affirm that Indigenous peoples have *always* had the right to claim and center their own sovereignty, even if and as they continue to take this power *back* from colonizer states.

6 For excellent further reads on these histories, we recommend Walker (Kanaka Māoli), *Waves of Resistance*; Laderman (settler), *Empire in Waves*; and the works of authors included in the 2017 collection *The Critical Surf Studies Reader*, edited by Hough-Snee and Eastman.

7 Wheaton, Waiti, Olive, and Kearns, "Coastal Communities, Leisure and Well-being," 450.

8 See Dawson's work *Undercurrents of Power*, as well as McGloin's essay "Indigenous Surfing."

9 Comer, *Surfer Girls in the New World Order*, 6.

10 Comer, *Surfer Girls*, 6, 12. Citing Comer here engages in a specific politics of citation that foregrounds our book's commitments to thinking about surfing through the evolution of its intellectual and disciplinary engagement. Comer was a founding settler surfeminist scholar and broke open the possibilities of surfing studies in the academy with her 2010 book. Her work inspired a generation of scholars to draw from our own multisitedness—as women, as surfers, as people of color, and as academics—and think with surfing as a productive site of critical analysis. We are thankful for Comer, who is included twice in this collection. We also acknowledge the shortcomings of white and settler feminist critiques within surfing studies, and many essays in this collection expand on the work begun by Comer to be more inclusive and center intentionally marginalized voices within surfing.

11 Diaz, "Voyaging for Anti-colonial Recovery," 22.

12 O'Brien, *Firsting and Lasting*, xii–xiii. In *Empire in Waves*, Laderman describes the effects of American colonization and Mormon missionization on

Kanaka Māoli relationships with and to surfing and the popular (yet untrue) belief that because Europeans began witnessing fewer Hawaiian surfers by the end of the nineteenth century, there must be no more Hawaiian surfers remaining. Laderman writes, "Those that continued to ride the waves were survivors of not only the biological onslaught introduced by white contact but also a radically different labor system and the concerted efforts of at least some white missionaries to demonize a pastime they associated with barbarism and sexual indecency." Laderman, *Empire in Waves*, 21–22. Isaiah Walker chronicles this same history "but from a Hawaiian perspective" in the first chapter of his 2011 book, *Waves of Resistance*, writing that Alexander Hume Ford's figuration of surfing as "extinct" was a fallacy designed to dispossess Native Hawaiians from the boarderlands.

13 Gilio-Whitaker's 2015 public work on George Freeth, "How American Surf Culture Was Built on a History of Indigenous Erasure," published in the popular surfing e-magazine, *The Inertia*, and Patrick Moser's 2022 book, *Surf and Rescue*, are both important critical works that show how power, race, and Indigeneity work to construct whiteness in early twentieth-century surfing.

14 It doesn't take a particularly astute scholar to survey the vast landscape of surfing media, including written publications and visual texts, to see that contemporary North American surf culture deeply favors and centers hetero-patriarchal, white, cisgender values.

15 King, *The Black Shoals*, 8.

16 Estrada Milán and Escala Rabadán, "Riding Waves on the Mexico-United States Border," 218.

17 Masterson, "Surfing Ali'i, Kahuna, Kupua and Akua," 206.

18 lisahunter, *Surfing, Sex, Genders and Sexualities*, 3.

19 Notable collections of surf studies scholarship that curate a robust range of critical thinking on these issues include Hough-Snee and Eastman's *Critical Surf Studies Reader*. Hough-Snee and Eastman's collection, like this one, also included innovative works on surfing, Indigeneity, and settler colonialism alongside the issues of race, gender, sexuality, and power, and we are indebted to their field-making work. lisahunter's edited collection, *Surfing, Sex, Genders and Sexualities*, similarly intentionally centers scholarship on the role of these issues in surfing culture.

20 If you are reading this and stop at the name Aikau and wonder if she related to Eddie Aikau, the Hawaiian big wave surfer and lifeguard who is famous for surfing Waimea Bay, sailing the Hōkūleʻa, and mysteriously disappearing

as he tried saving the Hōkūle'a, yes: Hokulani Aikau is the niece of Eddie and Clyde Aikau. And it matters that long before surfing studies was a field, Kanaka Māoli academics like Aikau were drawing from oceanic epistemologies to make sense of Western academic disciplines.

21 Aikau, Erickson, and Moore, "Three Women Writing/Riding Feminism's Third Wave," 398.

22 Ingersoll, *Waves of Knowing*, 10–11.

23 Shewry, *Hope at Sea*, 2.

24 Shewry, *Hope at Sea*, 3.

25 Million, "Intense Dreaming," 314–15.

26 Million, "Intense Dreaming," 314.

27 Olive et al., "Surfing Together," 47.

28 Linda Tuhiwai Smith theorized decolonizing research projects, including testimony, storytelling, remembering, intervening, and representing (among others), which all describe specific Indigenous practices of making knowledge, asserting visibility, and building relations.

29 We invoke Stefano Harney and Fred Moten's concept of the undercommons as they articulate in *The Undercommons*. They define the undercommons as the structures that uphold institutional power, such as the prison, universities, slave ships and settler colonialism, and systems of debt and credit. It is the space where Black, Brown, Indigenous, queer, colonized, and otherwise make common ground.

30 In 2017 Duke University Press published the first *Critical Surf Studies Reader*, and so we want to intentionally signal that this volume picks up where that volume leaves off.

31 David Kamper and Jess Ponting identify as cisgender heterosexual white men, Kamper from the United States and Ponting Australia. Lydia Heberling identifies as cisgender heterosexual white-passing Mexican American woman who has grappled humbly with how to navigate family stories of undocumented Yaqui ancestry and acknowledges the ways in which doing so publicly has shaped, reshaped, and transformed her responsibilities and relations. We are big fans of anticolonial knowledge projects, however! For more on the distinctions between decolonial and anticolonial projects, read la paperson's *Third University Is Possible.* They write, "Decolonization is, put bluntly, the rematriation of land, the regeneration of relations, and the forwarding of Indigenous and Black and queer futures—a process that requires countering what power seems to be up to" (xv).

Bibliography

Aikau, Hokulani, Karla Erickson, and Wendy Leo Moore. "Three Women Writing/Riding Feminism's Third Wave." *Qualitative Sociology* 26, no. 3 (2003): 397–425.

Allen, Chadwick. "2014 NAISA Presidential Address: Centering the 'I' in NAISA." *Native American and Indigenous Studies* 2, no. 1 (2015): 1–14.

Comer, Krista. *Surfer Girls in the New World Order*. Durham, NC: Duke University Press, 2010.

Dawson, Kevin. *Undercurrents of Power: Aquatic Culture in the African Diaspora*. Philadelphia: University of Pennsylvania Press, 2018.

Diaz, Vicente M. "Voyaging for Anti-colonial Recovery: Austronesian Seafaring, Archipelagic Rethinking, and the Re-mapping of Indigeneity." *Pacific Asia Inquiry* 2, no. 1 (2011): 21–32.

Estrada Milán, J., and L. Escala Rabadán. "Riding Waves on the Mexico–United States Border: Beaches, Local Surfers and Cross-Border Processes." *Journal of Sport and Social Issues* 45, no. 2 (2021): 217–32.

Gilio-Whitaker, Dina. *As Long as Grass Grows: The Indigenous Fight for Environmental Justice, from Colonization to Standing Rock*. Boston: Beacon Press, 2019.

———. "How American Surf Culture Was Built on a History of Indigenous Erasure." *The Inertia*. December 1, 2015. www.theinertia.com/surf/how-american-surf-culture-was-built-on-a-history-of-indigenous-erasure.

Goeman, Mishuana. *Mark My Words: Native Women Mapping Our Nations*. Minneapolis: University of Minnesota Press, 2013.

Harney, Stefano, and Fred Moten. *The Undercommons: Fugitive Planning and Black Study*. London: Minor Compositions, 2013.

Hough-Snee, Dexter Zavalza, and Alexander Sotelo Eastman. *The Critical Surf Studies Reader*. Durham, NC: Duke University Press, 2017.

Ingersoll, Karin Amimoto. *Waves of Knowing: A Seascape Epistemology*. Durham, NC: Duke University Press, 2016.

King, Tiffany Lethabo. *The Black Shoals: Offshore Formations of Black and Native Studies*. Durham, NC: Duke University Press, 2019.

la paperson. *A Third University Is Possible*. Minneapolis: University of Minnesota Press, 2017.

Laderman, Scott. *Empire in Waves: A Political History of Surfing*. Berkeley: University of California Press, 2014.

lisahunter, ed. *Surfing, Sex, Genders and Sexualities*. Abingdon: Routledge, 2018.

Masterson, Ian ʻAkahi. "Surfing Ali'i, Kahuna, Kupua and Akua." In *Surfing, Sex, Genders and Sexualities*, edited by lisahunter, 191–207. Abingdon: Routledge, 2018.

McGloin, Colleen. "Indigenous Surfing: Pedagogy, Pleasure, and Decolonial Practice." In *The Critical Surf Studies Reader*, edited by Dexter Zavalza Hough-Snee and Alexander Sotero Eastman, 196–213. Durham, NC: Duke University Press, 2017.

Million, Dian. "Intense Dreaming: Theories, Narratives, and Our Search for Home." *American Indian Quarterly* 35, no. 3 (2011): 313–33.

Moser, Patrick. *Surf and Rescue: George Freeth and the Birth of California Surf Culture*. Champaign: University of Illinois Press, 2022.

O'Brien, Jean M. *Firsting and Lasting: Writing Indians out of Existence in New England*. Minneapolis: University of Minnesota Press, 2010.

Olive, Rebecca. "Swimming and Surfing in Ocean Ecologies: Encounter and Vulnerability in Nature-Based Sport and Physical Activity." *Leisure Studies* 42, no. 5 (2023): 679–92.

Olive, Rebecca, Holly Thorp, Georgina Roy, Mihi Nemani, lisahunter, Belinda Wheaton, and Barbara Humberstone. "Surfing Together: Exploring the Potential of a Collaborative Ethnographic Moment." In *Women in Action Sport Cultures*, edited by Holly Thorpe and Rebecca Olive, 45–68. London: Palgrave Macmillan, 2016.

Risling Baldy, Cutcha. *We Are Dancing for You: Native Feminisms and the Revitalization of Women's Coming-of-Age Ceremonies*. Seattle: University of Washington Press, 2018.

Shewry, Tess. *Hope at Sea: Possible Ecologies in Oceanic Literature*. Minneapolis: University of Minnesota Press, 2015.

Smith, Linda Tuhiwai. *Decolonizing Methodologies*. 2nd ed. London: Bloomsbury Press, 2012.

Teves, Stephanie Nohelani, Andrea Smith, and Michelle Raheja. "Indigeneity." In *Native Studies Keywords*, edited by Stephanie Nohelani Teves, Andrea Smith, and Michelle Raheja, 109–18. Tucson: Arizona University Press, 2015.

Walker, Isaiah Helekunihi. *Waves of Resistance: Surfing and History in Twentieth-Century Hawai'i*. Honolulu: University of Hawai'i Press, 2011.

Wheaton, B., J. T. A. Waiti, R. Olive, and R. Kearns. "Coastal Communities, Leisure and Wellbeing: Advancing a Trans-disciplinary Agenda for Understanding Ocean-Human Relationships in Aotearoa New Zealand." *International Journal of Environmental Research and Public Health* 18, no. 2 (2021): 450–70.

PART I

FROM LOCAL TO GLOBAL

1

Hawaiians in the Olympics

Autonomy in Progress

ISAIAH HELEKUNIHI WALKER

On August 4, 2016, the International Olympic Committee (IOC) announced that surfing would be an Olympic sport in the 2020 Tokyo Games. Months before, at the Critical Surf Studies Conference hosted by the University of Waikato, a conference presenter confidently announced that the IOC would admit surfing into the Olympics soon. While much of my research, including the paper I was presenting at that conference, explored the empowering nature of recognized Hawaiian autonomy in surfing, this news had a direct impact on my scholarship. So, in a knee-jerk response, I asked, "Do you think Hawai'i will have an Olympic team?"[1] Unfortunately, I already knew the answer was no. As that set in, I was increasingly troubled by the thought of Hawai'i not having representation in a surfing event as prominent as the Olympics. But eventually, my disappointment turned into a motivation to creatively establish a Hawaiian Olympic surfing team.

The first step was to bring the right people together to organize a Hawaiian national Olympic committee, a Hawaiian surfing federation, and a Hawaiian surf club. The next step was to complete all the necessary steps to submit an official application to the International Olympic Committee in Geneva, Switzerland—which happened on March 18, 2018. In this chapter, I will illuminate the efforts taken by those who advocated for a Hawaiian surf team in the 2020 Olympics. Although the IOC did not approve the application in 2018, Hawai'i was still represented in the 2020

Olympic games through Native Hawaiian athletes like Carissa Moore and the media's interest in surfing's Native Hawaiian origins.

While news media often wrote about Carissa Moore and her cultural connection to the history of surfing in Hawai'i in 2020 and 2021, they also highlighted the twentieth-century Hawaiian icon: Olympic gold medalist swimmer and father of modern-day surfing, Duke Kahanamoku. Through stories about these Native Hawaiians, the media beamed a spotlight on the cultural importance of surfing, the complexity of Hawaiian history, and the Hawaiian application to the IOC. This attention helped strengthen a Hawaiian cause by raising awareness of the possibility of Hawaiian autonomy. Through this experience, we find that surfing is an effective vehicle for expanding global awareness toward international recognition of Hawai'i's contested political status.

He'e nalu and the Hawaiian Kingdom National Olympic Committee

He'e nalu, or surfing, is a Hawaiian art, sport, and cultural practice. Though wave riding on various crafts existed in precolonial Africa, South America, and other regions, the tradition of riding waves on wood planks has roots dating back hundreds, and possibly thousands, of years in Polynesia. But in Hawai'i, surfing's roots run deepest. Here, surfing developed as an intricate practice in the ancient world, encompassing the art of standing on surfboards, established surfing competitions, and elaborate stories of surfing. Nineteenth-century historian David Malo described surfing as a Hawaiian national pastime practiced by most people, regardless of age or gender.[2]

However, *he'e nalu* is not only a traditional Hawaiian cultural practice; it has endured and persevered across different eras, including times of occupation and denationalization. From Hawai'i, surfing proliferated to the rest of the world at the turn of the twentieth century, propagated by Hawaiians like Jonah Kuhio, David Kawananakoa, George Freeth, Duke Kahanamoku, and numerous others.

While surfing spread to places like the United States, Australia, South

America, and beyond, it continued to grow and thrive in Hawai'i, even as surfing evolved into contemporary forms. In essence, Hawaiian surfers have consistently been at the forefront of the evolution of modern-day surfing, contributing to changes in equipment and technique and excelling in competition. As an enduring Hawaiian practice, surfing also serves as an artifact upon which Native identities and nationalities are bolstered.[3] Thus, surfing is a great source of pride for Hawaiians. Representation in professional competition has also served as a vehicle for advancing, promoting, and proliferating such pride and identity. This was a key motivating factor for the Hawaiian surfing community to support the representation of Hawai'i in the Olympics.

On December 12, 2017, advocates for a Hawaiian Olympic surfing team formed the Hawaiian Kingdom National Olympic Committee (HKNOC) with the hopes that the IOC would recognize Hawai'i as its own country. According to the Olympic Charter, a "national sports organization applying for recognition as a NOC [national Olympic committee] shall file an application with the IOC demonstrating that the applicant fulfills all conditions prescribed by the Olympic Charter."[4] HKNOC executive officers include Alika Desha, president; Willy Kauai, PhD, vice president; Isaiah Walker, PhD, secretary general; and Nalani Balutski, secretary-treasurer. Desha explained the nature and objective of the application: "Our request to be recognized by the IOC is not tied to any kind of sovereignty movement or other politics. We just realized that we do meet all the criteria outlined in the Olympic Charter. We are following the IOC guidelines and hope they will take us seriously. If our application is given careful consideration, they will see that we meet the criteria."[5]

Although it seemed like a long shot to some, the IOC has historically admitted unconventional countries into the Olympics. For example, several non-self-governing territories have had Olympic teams in the past (Puerto Rico [since 1948], Guam [since 1988], American Samoa [since 1988]), and the IOC even recognized a refugee Olympic team in 2016. Our key goal was to align our application's definition of *country* with the IOC's since they define *country* in unique and specific ways. The term *country* in the Olympic Charter "means an independent State recognized by the international community."[6] Under this definition, we believe that Hawai'i technically meets the criteria.

Two months after the HKNOC submitted an official application to the IOC, Ms. Schiliuk from the office of the IOC sports director communicated to HKNOC attorney Federico Lenzerini in Italy that the IOC received our application and would pass it on to an IOC competent body soon. The communication stopped after that point. The hope was for the IOC to review our document with open-mindedness. While the application provides extensive legal history and other documentation, we were essentially asking the IOC to acknowledge that Hawai'i has been recognized as an independent state by the international community. Although that sounds outlandish to those who know little of Hawai'i's political history, scholars of international law and Hawaiian history have shown that the Hawaiian Kingdom technically still exists as a nation-state.

Our starting point as to the Hawaiian Kingdom being an internationally recognized independent state is in the *Larsen v. Hawaiian Kingdom* arbitration case held at the Permanent Court of Arbitration (PCA) from 1999 to 2001.[7] In this arbitration, the PCA did not deny the continued existence of the Hawaiian Kingdom as an independent state. The idea of recognition has been gaining attention with scholars of international law and UN officials more recently. While serving as the United Nations independent expert for the officer for the commissioner of human rights, Dr. Alfred M. deZayas acknowledged that "the lawful political status of the Hawaiian Islands is that of a nation-state in continuity; but a nation-state that is under a strange form of occupation by the United States resulting from an illegal military occupation and a fraudulent annexation."[8]

In 2001, the Hawaiian Kingdom's status as an independent state in the 1800s was also reaffirmed by the PCA in the Hague.[9] The international tribunal stated, "In the nineteenth century the Hawaiian Kingdom existed as an independent State recognized as such by the United States of America, the United Kingdom, and various other States, including by exchanges of diplomatic or consular representatives and the conclusion of treaties."[10] The Hawaiian Kingdom also established itself as a neutral country and was the first non-European country admitted into the family of nations.[11] On January 1, 1882, the Hawaiian Kingdom became a member of the Universal Postal Union and maintained over ninety legations and consulates throughout the world.[12]

It is indisputable that the Hawaiian Kingdom was an independent state and recognized by the international community before its government was illegally overthrown by the United States in 1893. This incursion began on January 16, when United States troops, by order of the US diplomat John Stevens, invaded the Hawaiian Kingdom without the support of the US Congress or the president. President Grover Cleveland called it "an act of war, committed with the participation of a diplomatic representative of the United States and without authority of Congress," by which "the Government of a feeble but friendly and confiding people has been overthrown."[13] Although President Cleveland formally agreed to reinstate Hawaiʻi's Queen Liliʻuokalani as the executive monarch on December 18, 1893, he wasn't able to carry out that commitment because of political wrangling in Congress, whose members wanted to secure Pearl Harbor as a naval base and turn the Hawaiian Islands into a military outpost. The culprits who overthrew the Hawaiian monarchy then submitted a treaty to the US Congress requesting annexation. Fortunately for Hawaiians, that treaty was killed in Congress in 1897—in part because of petitions signed by thousands of Hawaiians who opposed it.[14] The annexation treaty never passed.

Hawaiian celebrations of victory were interrupted by the election of expansionist president William McKinley and the outbreak of the Spanish American War in 1898. Anxious to use Hawaiʻi as a military outpost for future advances in Asia (the Philippines in particular), the new administration moved to take Hawaiʻi. To expedite the process, they enacted Congressional laws, which are limited in authority to United States territory, to purportedly annex Hawaiʻi in 1898. Use of these domestic laws violated international law and would be the equivalent of Congress annexing Canada today by enacting a law in Washington, DC. Annexation requires a signed treaty.

Can the Hawaiian Kingdom still exist as an independent state today even though its government was illegally overthrown over 125 years ago? This is where international law, since the nineteenth century, separates the government from the state. According to international law pioneer, Professor Quincy Wright, "International law distinguishes between a government and the state it governs."[15] And Professor Sheldon Cohen explains that the "state must be distinguished from the government. The state, not the government, is the major player, the legal person, in international law."[16] Our application used this context to validate the Hawaiian Kingdom National Olympic Committee and to argue that a Hawaiian Olympic surf team is technically justified.

In addition to forming an Olympic committee, we also organized the Hawaiian Surfing Federation (HSF) and the Hawaiian Surfing Club (HSC) on January 18, 2018, at a meeting held at the Volcom house located at Ehukai Beach on the North Shore of O'ahu. The HSF was recognized by the HKNOC for the sport of surfing in the Hawaiian Islands. HSF executive officers include Brian Keaulana, president; James Kimo Leong, secretary; Haunani Kane, treasurer. Executive officers of the HSC include Rainos Hayes, president; Jason Shibata, secretary; and Geodee Clark, treasurer. The HSC was to be responsible for working under the HSF and directly with the Olympic athletes. As with the HKNOC, these entities were also established with constitutions and bylaws. These organizations were organized by highly respected surfers, scholars, and ocean experts. From professors to former professional surfers, each individual is renowned internationally. HSF president Brian Keaulana is the son of legendary Makaha surfer Buffalo Keaulana and one of the world's top ocean rescue and safety experts. Seen as an icon in the sport of surfing, Keaulana led the HSF because "surfing's roots are deeply Hawaiian. It is a key part of my culture and a central piece of my family. It is huge to think that surfing could be the vehicle for advancing the status of Hawaiians internationally. It would be huge! So I wanted to be part of it."[17]

Former professional surfer Rainos Hayes is one of Hawai'i's premier surf coaches and was anxious to coach Hawaiian athletes in the Olympics. Over the last twenty years, Hayes has been coaching Hawai'i's exceptional young surfers, particularly for Hawai'i's International Surfing Association (ISA)

World Junior Teams. Hayes has helped Hawai'i win several gold medals and is recognized as one of the world's top surf coaches. He explains, "I have been proud to wave the Hawaiian flag internationally with team Hawai'i over the years. Hawai'i has always been recognized as its own country in these events. Now that I understand the IOC guidelines and Hawai'i's background as an independent state, I look forward to seeing Hawai'i represented in the 2020 Olympics."[18]

Hawaiian Club surfers rank among the world's top professionals. Former professional surfer and treasurer of the HSC Geodee Clark explains, "Hawaiian surfers are anxious to represent Hawai'i in the 2020 Olympics because *he'e nalu* [surfing] is a deep part of their identity, history, and culture. Surfing is an ancient sport originated by our *kupuna* [ancestors] hundreds and hundreds of years ago. It is only fitting that Hawai'i is included. Also, Hawai'i surfers today are the elite of the elite. It would only raise the level of competition to include these athletes."[19] In addition to others previously mentioned, those willing to participate in the Hawaiian Surfing Club include Ezekiel Lau, Imaikalani DeVault, Seth Moniz, Malia Manuel, Coco Ho, and several other top surfing professionals. Each of these athletes was highly ranked by the World Surf League. In 2019, the ISA announced that the top WSL Championship Tour rankings would determine who qualified for the 2020 Olympic Games. Essentially, the two highest-ranked men and women from their respective countries may qualify. In 2019, there were four men and three women from Hawai'i on the championship tour. Based on that criterion, if the IOC recognized the HKNOC, Hawai'i would have had four surfers qualify. This would have also benefited the United States. For example, of the four athletes competing for the United States in the 2020 Olympics, two of them were from Hawai'i (John Florence and Carissa Moore). Had a Hawaiian team been recognized, it would have opened the door for more surfers from the United States to participate in the Olympics. For example, if John Florence surfed for Hawai'i in the 2020 Olympics, the United States would have added the greatest surfer of all time, Kelly Slater (the surfer next in line to qualify) to their roster.

Carissa Moore and the Media

Carissa Moore is one of the most accomplished athletes in surfing's history. To date, she holds five WSL world championship titles and an Olympic gold medal in surfing. Months before her foray into the 2020 Olympics, I met up with her father, Chris, while giving a lecture on the cultural significance of surfing at the ʻIolani Palace.[20] In the discussion afterward, he explained that Carissa was searching for "her why" in the upcoming Olympics. Since she spent her entire career representing Hawaiʻi as an athlete, surfing under the stars and stripes was a new experience, a somewhat foreign identity that Carissa was working to negotiate. As we explored ways for Carissa to still feel connected to her Hawaiian roots as an American athlete, Chris became intrigued by the various Hawaiian coats of arms displayed at ʻIolani Palace. Since Carissa could not represent Hawaiʻi with a Hawaiian flag, he hoped she could use another, a similar symbol, to represent her Native Hawaiian identity.

Over the next several weeks, we teamed up with Hawaiian artist Jack Soren to produce a custom coat of arms that reflected Carissa's identity. Based on a traditional Hawaiian coat of arms, Carissa's symbol used imagery and icons that were tailored to her more specifically. For example, instead of Kamehameha's twin warriors as central figures, she chose two Hawaiian surfing icons in her design, Rell Sunn and Duke Kahanamoku. The ribbon with Hawaiʻi's national motto, "Ua Mau Ke Ea o Ka ʻAina i Ka Pono" (the life/sovereignty of the land is perpetuated in uprightness/righteousness), became the crest of a breaking wave. The four hibiscus flowers represented her four world titles at that time, and the *pohuehue* vines reference a Hawaiian chant used for summoning large waves.

Happy with the outcome, and hopeful that she could discreetly use this image on her surfboard, she ordered a quiver of boards with it laminated on the bottom of each one, just above her fins. Despite an initial nod by team USA surfing, they eventually decided that the logo wasn't allowable in the Olympics. Despite this decision, Carissa still found ample opportunity to express her identity as a Native Hawaiian in various media stories leading up to the Olympics.

Starting with an NBC story titled "Surfer Carissa Moore Discusses Hawaiian Roots Heading to the Olympics," media outlets became fascinated with the story of both surfing's and Carissa's Native roots in 2020 and 2021. By the time she won her Olympic gold medal, stories about Carissa and her Native Hawaiian roots were everywhere in the mainstream media (including the Associate Press, NBC News, Fox News, *Sports Illustrated*, *New York Times*, the *Washington Post*, and many others). These stories about Carissa almost always emphasized her genealogical connection to surfing as a Native Hawaiian. Most stories recognized that she would have normally represented Hawaiʻi as a professional surfer. For example, the *Washington Post* explained, "When she surfs in international tournaments, Moore wears the Hawaiian flag on her sleeve. Out of deference to Hawaiʻi's status as the birthplace of surfing and recognition of its independence, before it became a US state, the World Surf League recognizes Hawaiʻi as its own sovereign entity. In those events, Moore chooses to compete under her native banner."[21] Other stories went a bit further to discuss the significance of surfing as a cultural marker of Hawaiian identity. These stories discussed surfing as a Native sport, something that Carissa identified with culturally. Some contextualized surfing as an Indigenous cultural practice, a sport that empowered Hawaiians in an era of colonization. Greg Bishop from *Sports Illustrated* highlighted this point. After pointing out that both Carissa Moore and John Florence would have preferred to surf for Hawaiʻi instead of being "forced to surf under the US Flag," he explained that most in Hawaiʻi "see surfing as the strongest way to bond their life before and after colonization, to protect what it means to be Hawaiian, in spirit, in soul." He continued, "They believed the ocean was a sort of sanctuary, with autonomy and history and an important preservation of cultural identity at stake."[22]

I was delighted to watch mainstream media emphasize surfing as a cultural identity marker for Hawaiians and as a sanctuary for Kanaka Māoli during an era of displacement and political occupation. The focus of my scholarship over the last two decades centered on emphasizing this perspective. In *Waves of Resistance*, I argued that the surf zone was a refuge and a borderland "where Hawaiians felt free, developed Native identities, and thwarted foreign domination." It was also a space where "Native surfers secured a position atop a social hierarchy" despite facing marginalization on land.[23] Furthermore, I have elsewhere explained the history of Hawai'i's independence in competitive surfing.[24] It is fascinating that Hawai'i has been recognized as an independent nation by the surfing world, and I was happy to see mainstream media recognize this phenomenon. Hawai'i's independence in surfing is not new but has been around since the inception of professional surfing. Hawai'i is also recognized as independent in amateur events around the world. These are all important topics that strengthen the application to the IOC. The Olympics provided a platform for conversations about these important topics, especially as they focused on contextualizing Hawaiian athletes like Carissa Moore.

Some journalists focused on our Hawaiian Kingdom National Olympic Committee's application to the IOC. In an NBC News article titled "Team Hawaiian Kingdom? Activists Want Some US Olympians to Surf for a Different Homeland," Clair Wang interviewed members of our committee to contextualize our story. Although the author erroneously referred to us as sovereignty activists, the article did provide our perspective, reasoning, and process for applying to the IOC. Unlike most others, this article discussed the complexity of Hawai'i's political history, noting that "the treaty of annexation was never ratified by congress."[25] Sally Ho, from the Associated Press, wrote a more extensive story touching briefly on almost all of the topics mentioned above—discussing surfing's roots, Carissa Moore as Native Hawaiian surfing under the American flag, and our application to the IOC.[26] Although this story covered a lot of issues, the particular wording "whitewashed Native Hawaiian Roots" opened the door to some negative criticism and misrepresentation of our agenda. For example, Bill Maher on HBO's *Real Time with Bill Maher* attacked this specific AP story for several minutes—his criticism was based primarily on the author's use of the word *whitewashed*. Here, Bill Maher criticized the "woke Olympics" and the Associated Press for falsely claiming cultural appropriation in surfing. Over the next several minutes, he harped on the idea of cultural appropriation in surfing, assuming that Hawaiians were upset about surfing being allowed in the Olympics.[27] Although the AP story had its flaws, the story was not about Hawaiians withholding surfing, or cultural appropriation. While this negative attention had a bad taste to it, I suppose the adage "all news is still good news" may apply to us in this situation.

Although celebrations were stymied by COVID restrictions in 2021, Carissa was still celebrated as a hero when she returned home to Hawai'i. While the global media's attention on Carissa slowed, Hawai'i still celebrated Carissa's accomplishments in creative ways. Perhaps most notable among these was the 150-foot mural of Carissa painted on the side of a large Honolulu building. Local artist Kamea Hadar spent twenty-five days painting a massive mural celebrating the Hawaiian Olympian. Carissa is depicted in two images. First is a massive portrait of her with a flower in her ear, wearing her gold medal, draped in the Hawaiian flag. Below that is a smaller image of her surfing, hitting the lip of a blue wave. Perhaps the most revealing sentiment in this mural is his choice of flag. The fact that she is painted with a Hawaiian flag draped around her reflects a common sentiment, that she surfed for Hawai'i. In many ways, this mural serves as a kind of rectifying element, a revisionist history, where Hawaiians rewrote themselves into the 2020 Olympics. But Carissa wasn't the only Olympian painted into Hawai'i's Olympic history in this mural. Duke Kahanamoku, the original Hawaiian Olympic *moho* (champion), is depicted on the mural as well.

Duke Kahanamoku: Reemphasized

The inclusion of surfing in the Olympics rekindled an interest in the life story of Duke Kahanamoku. For example, during the Olympics, most of the news stories on surfing in the Olympics and Carissa Moore also wrote about Kahanamoku. In addition to all these stories, in 2022, PBS broadcast *Waterman*, a full-length feature documentary on Kahanamoku. By revisiting Duke's story in the wake of surfing's first Olympics, a brighter spotlight beamed on Hawai'i's tainted political history. Often referred to as the father of modern-day surfing, Kahanamoku was also a multi-gold medalist Olympic swimmer, winning medals in 1912, 1920, and 1924. But he was also a Native Hawaiian whose life spanned a traumatic period of change in Hawaiʻi, including the overthrow of the Hawaiian Kingdom, the denationalization of Hawaiian identities through an anti-Hawaiian curriculum in schools, the dissuasion of speaking Hawaiian, and the displacement and militarization of his own family's neighborhood in Kalia, Waikiki.

Duke Kahanamoku was two years old when Queen Liliʻuokalani was illegally overthrown. Since his family was connected to the royal family, the Kahanamokus moved from Honolulu to his mom's family property in Kalia, in part, to get away from the political disruption in Honolulu. Since the surf zone was an overlooked realm to colonial authorities, Waikiki was a place for his family to feel at home, at ease, and still in charge. While change was often imposed on Kahanamoku, he was also an agent of change on the world—including the resurgence and global proliferation of surfing, the establishment of water safety and water rescue programs, the development of successful beachboy entertainment and concessions, and even the establishment of professional surfing (one of the first professional events named after him). But he was also known as the world's fastest swimmer in the early twentieth century.

While Kahanamoku competed in Olympic relay races and also on the US water polo team, he was most known for his prowess in the hundred-meter sprint, beating the world record in 1912. By this time, the Olympics had become more egalitarian; for example, the 1912 Olympics included women in swimming for the first time. The United States also had several athletes of color who dominated their respective divisions. Most notable among them was Native American Jim Thorpe (of the Sac and Fox Nation), who dominated in land sports. Thorpe and Kahanamoku were friends who broke color lines in American sports history during America's Jim Crow era. Although Duke was successful in breaking many color lines, racism still had a prominent impact on Kahanamoku, who often struggled to find balance in the early twentieth century.

Kahanamoku gained fame as an Olympic swimmer, but he became a global phenomenon as a surfer. As Kahanamoku traveled the world en route to decades of Olympic Games, he hit celebrity status at his surfing exhibitions. New Zealand, Australia, New Jersey, and many other communities hosted Duke's surfing shows. At each exhibition, he was cheered by throngs of spectators as the Hawaiian celebrity who walked on water. Known as soft-spoken on land, Kahanamoku was a superstar in the surf. This was also true of his *hui nalu* peers in Waikiki; together they moonlighted as Waikiki beachboys. These Hawaiians were entertainers, surf instructors, and beach celebrities in the early years of Hawaiʻi's tourism. Duke profoundly influenced the lives of people in Waikiki as a beachboy and through his embodiment of aloha. However, Duke has been undermined by the misuse and misinterpretation of his expression of aloha.

Many have labeled Duke as tourism's ambassador of aloha who was unscathed by racism, exploitation, or Native dispossession. In my opinion, this is one of the most troubling misrepresentations of Duke. Certainly, Kahanamoku was an example of Hawaiian generosity and he shared his humble attribute of aloha with many—both Hawaiian and malihini (visitors) alike. However, this does not mean he was immune or passive to racism, colonialism, or Native displacement. Despite portrayals of him being aloof to issues of colonialism, Duke was quite aware of Native Hawaiian struggles in the wake of the overthrow, including the dispossession of his family, his nation, and his people from Native lands and political power. Ironically labeled the father of modern-day surfing, Duke wasn't always a fan of modern life in Hawaiʻi. When asked which time he would prefer to live, Duke swiftly answered that he longed to live in Old Hawaiʻi, before all the change brought by occupation and development.[28] Although film and other media coverage shared Duke's story to millions of viewers and raised new awareness of Hawaiʻi's complex history in the wake of the 2020 Olympics, some stories sugarcoated the difficult parts of Duke's life—particularly the impact of change that Hawaiians like the Kahanamokus experienced in the twentieth century, particularly regarding his relationship to racism, tourism, and the military.

Unfortunately, throughout most of his adult life, he watched his family's former Hawaiian village in Kalia transform from a Hawaiian ocean-based community into hotel development and a US Army R&R center called Fort DeRussy. While most Native Hawaiian families were displaced in the twentieth century by land speculators, many Kalia residents lost their land to the US Army when they condemned family-owned properties in

Waikiki with eminent domain. Although the army said they needed Kalia to help protect the island, they instead used the area to rest and recuperate servicemen. In the early and mid-1900s, one of Kalia's R&R center's activities was sanctioned prostitution.[29] Duke and many fellow Hawaiian men resented the exploitation of Hawaiian women in Waikiki. There are several legendary stories of fights between Hawaiian surfers and military men in Waikiki throughout the 1900s.[30] The displacement of his family from Kalia contributed to his struggle in his later life.

Kahanamoku's life was an amalgam of success and struggle. Although world-famous as an athlete and a surfing icon, Duke, like most Hawaiians of his time, faced financial hardship. He eventually purchased his own home in Hawai'i, but only through the help of the Hawaiian community and wealthy and influential friends, like American billionaire tobacco heiress Doris Duke. His struggle to survive in the modern Hawaiian economy was inhibited by the Olympics in many ways. Back then the Olympics had strict rules about not using your athletic skills as a profession. It prohibited Duke from making money from his greatest strength, swimming. So he tried his hand at acting in Hollywood films.

Kahanamoku appeared in a variety of Hollywood films, but mostly in minor roles. Despite the fact many revered him as an icon of Hawaiian strength, he was often overshadowed by Hollywood stars in many of these films. For example, in the 1954 film *Wake of the Red Witch*, John Wayne's character, Captain Ralls, swam deep underwater to kill a giant octopus. Meanwhile, Kahanamoku's character stood on the bank of the water, unable to dive down and do the same. As the island's chief, Kahanamoku then rewards Ralls with a giant chest of pearls, their greatest treasure. Elsewhere, I argue that these kinds of representations contributed to a collection of colonial discourse on Native men generally, but on Hawaiians in particular.[31] Essentially these kinds of established tropes helped viewers justify and normalize an unsettling and complex history of actual conquest. Such films helped promote the myth that Hawaiians needed to be saved and that they were happy to surrender their autonomy and their pearls (or Pearl Harbor) to their hero in return. But to Native Hawaiians, Duke Kahanamoku is an empowered icon, our *moho* (champion).[32] Not only was he powerful in the ocean, but also his prowess and masculinity shone as an example of strength and hope to a struggling Hawaiian *lahui* (people/nation). To us, he was a Hawaiian warrior who navigated a challenging time in our history.

Duke credited his surfing and swimming success to his race and ethnicity, which became a source of pride for Hawaiians. For example, when reporters asked Kahanamoku where he learned his winning swim technique, he gave credit to his Hawaiian blood or ancestry. He also mentioned that his father taught him to swim from a very young age. As Native Hawaiian power in social and political realms on land lessened in the twentieth century, many Native Hawaiians, as seen with the Kahanamoku family, found solace in the ocean as a traditional sanctuary during a challenging time in Hawaiian history. For some, the ocean waves became an escape from the hardships of colonial impacts, like the drastic depopulation of Hawaiians by foreign introduced diseases and the overthrow of the Hawaiian Kingdom. Because of this, surfing remains a prominent cultural identity marker for Native Hawaiians today, even in competitive surfing arenas.

Although the IOC has not yet recognized a Hawaiian national Olympic committee, the International Surfing Association (ISA) still recognizes Hawaiʻi as an independent nation in their Olympic qualifying events. For example, team Hawaiʻi dominated the 2022 ISA World Junior championships, in El Salvador. Competing against forty-five other countries, team Hawaiʻi won the overall team gold medal, with Australia winning silver and the USA bronze. Native Hawaiian surfer Eweleiʻula Wong won first place in the Girls under 18 division. A student in the Hawaiian Language Immersion Program, Ewe is well-versed in the Hawaiian language and culture. To her, surfing is a deep part of her family, culture, and identity as a Hawaiian. After winning gold, she explained, "I am so proud to represent Hawaiʻi. . . . It is an amazing feeling that Hawaiʻi has its own unique place at the ISA. I really wish Hawaiʻi had its own place at the Olympics. But I guess that is something for later on."[33]

The future looks bright for Hawaiʻi athletes, and their hopes for Hawaiian representation in the Olympics are still alive. Considering Hawaiʻi's cultural and political history, it seems viable that a Hawaiian surfing team could participate in the Olympic Games. Such recognition would not only allow Hawaiian athletes to continue surfing independently but also help overthrow a century-old misunderstanding about the political history of Hawai'i as an independent state. Hawai'i's top professional surfers and their coaches are anxious to have a Hawaiian national team in the Olympics. A Hawaiian national team would validate the historical origins of surfing, which was invented in Hawai'i over one thousand years ago. Hawaiians are hopeful that 2024 might see the recognition of a Hawaiian Kingdom National Olympic Committee by the IOC. Regardless of the IOC's response, Hawaiian surfers (as seen with Carissa Moore and Duke Kahanamoku) will nonetheless represent their *kupuna* (ancestors), their community, and their culture in future Olympic Games.

Notes

1 Later published as a chapter in *The Critical Surf Studies Reader*. See Walker, "Kai Ea."
2 Malo, *Hawaiian Antiquities*, 223.
3 See Walker, *Waves of Resistance*, 2–7.
4 Olympic Charter (August 2, 2015), 65.
5 Interview with the author, Hau'ula, Hawai'i, June 26, 2018.
6 Olympic Charter, 68.
7 Larsen v. Hawaiian Kingdom, Permanent Court of Arbitration, 2001, https://pca-cpa.org/en/cases/35.
8 Alfred M. deZayas, Memorandum was written to members of the Hawai'i State Judiciary, on February 25, 2018.
9 Larsen v. Hawaiian Kingdom.
10 "Larsen v. the Hawaiian Kingdom," *International Law Reports*, no. 119 (2001): 581 (hereafter "Larsen case").
11 Westlake, *Chapters on the Principles of International Law*, 81. In 1893, there were 44 independent and sovereign states in the family of nations: Argentina, Austria-Hungary, Belgium, Bolivia, Brazil, Bulgaria, Chile, Colombia, Costa Rica, Denmark, Ecuador, France, Germany, Great Britain, Greece, Guatemala, Hawaiian Kingdom, Haiti, Honduras, Italy, Liberia, Liechtenstein, Luxembourg, Netherlands, Mexico, Monaco, Montenegro, Nicaragua, Orange Free State (which was later annexed by Great Britain in 1900), Paraguay,

Peru, Portugal, Romania, Russia, San Domingo, San Salvador, Serbia, Spain, Sweden-Norway, Switzerland, Turkey, United States of America, Uruguay, and Venezuela. In 1945, there were 45 independent and sovereign states, and today there are 193.

12 Thrum, *Hawaiian Register and Directory for 1893*, 140–41.

13 Larsen case, Annexure 1, 608.

14 See Silva, *Aloha Betrayed*.

15 Wright, "The Status of Germany and the Peace Proclamation," 307.

16 Cohen, *Arms and Judgment*, 17.

17 Interview with the author, Sunset Beach, Hawai'i, June 8, 2018.

18 Interview with the author, Sunset Beach, Hawai'i, June 8, 2018.

19 Interview with the author, Hau'ula, Hawai'i, June 26, 2018.

20 Isaiah Walker, "Waves of Resistance," Na Mo'olelo Lecture Series, hosted by the 'Iolani Palace, February 6, 2020, https://youtu.be/8thKFaXRqG4.

21 Adam Kilgore, "For Carissa Moore, Surfing Brought the Ocean's Power and Glory to the Olympics," *Washington Post*, July 28, 2021, www.washingtonpost.com/sports/olympics/2021/07/28/carissa-moore-surfing-hawaii-gold-medal.

22 Greg Bishop, "Surfing's Spirit, Hawaiian History Embodied in Sport's First Olympic Gold Medalist," *Sports Illustrated*, July 28, 2021, www.si.com/olympics/2021/07/29/carissa-moore-tokyo-olympics-gold-medal-hawaii.

23 Walker, *Waves of Resistance*, 2.

24 Walker, "Kai Ea."

25 Clair Wang, "Team Hawaiian Kingdom? Activists Want Some US Olympians to Surf for a Different Homeland," NBC News, July 26, 2021, www.nbcnews.com/news/asian-america/team-hawaiian-kingdom-activists-want-us-olympians-surf-different-homel-rcna1503.

26 Sally Ho, "Olympic Surfing Exposes Whitewashed Native Hawaiian Roots," Associated Press, July 13, 2021, https://apnews.com/article/2020-tokyo-olympics-games-racial-injustice-hawaii-surfing-5048591ab4620f8796a08ff54331feco.

27 *Real Time with Bill Maher*, "New Rule: The Woke Olympics," HBO, July 29, 2021, https://youtu.be/anUlV6umjqM.

28 *This Is Your Life: Duke Kahanamoku (Father of Surfing)* was originally broadcast on NBC, on February 20, 1957. https://youtu.be/XQgcSXota_U.

29 Ferguson and Turnbull, *Oh, Say, Can You See*.

30 See Walker, *Waves of Resistance*, 75–77.

31 See Walker, *Waves of Resistance*, 92–99.

32 Cliff Kapono, Daniel Ito, and others released an animated short story during the Olympics that reflected a contemporary Hawaiian perspective of Duke Kahanamoku as a surfing icon. See mohothemovie.com.

33 "Billy V Interviews: Ewe Wong and Luke Swanson," YouTube, June 13, 2022, https://youtu.be/ahaz1872Aws.

Bibliography

Cohen, Sheldon M. *Arms and Judgment: Law, Morality, and the Conduct of War in the Twentieth Century*. London: Routledge Taylor and Francis Group, 1989.

Ferguson, Kathy E., and Phillis Turnbull. *Oh, Say, Can You See: The Semiotics of the Military in Hawai'i*. Duluth: University of Minnesota Press, 1998.

Malo, David. *Hawaiian Antiquities: Mo'olelo Hawaii*. Honolulu: Bishop Museum, 1951.

Silva, Noenoe. *Aloha Betrayed: Native Hawaiian Resistance to American Colonialism*. Durham, NC: Duke University Press, 2004.

Thrum, Thomas. *Hawaiian Register and Directory for 1893*. Honolulu: Palala Press, 2016.

Walker, Isaiah. "*Kai Ea*: Rising Waves of National and Ethnic Identities." In *The Critical Surf Studies Reader*, edited by Dexter Zavalza Hough-Snee and Alexander Sotelo Eastman, 62–83. Durham, NC: Duke University Press, 2017.

———. *Waves of Resistance: Surfing and History in Twentieth-Century Hawai'i*. Honolulu: University of Hawai'i Press, 2011.

Westlake, John. *Chapters on the Principles of International Law*. Cambridge: University Press, 1894.

Wright, Quincy. "The Status of Germany and the Peace Proclamation." *American Journal of International Law* 46, no. 2 (April 1952): 299–308.

2

Surfing and Surf-Canoeing in Atlantic Africa

KEVIN DAWSON

Atlantic Africans invented surfing probably a thousand years ago, or more. Yet, most people do not associate surfing with Black people, while historical and cultural erasures and racialized assumptions conspire to obscure understandings of African surfing. History is made and remade as each generation weighs its values against past circumstances and present realities. Memories are formed, ignored, willfully forgotten, rediscovered, and reimagined. Histories advances particular narratives, mythologies, and biased monologues. Settler colonial countries have created historical memories about their inception: their real and imagined origins and how they came to possess that land. Popular histories are typically flat, myopic, unnuanced, triumphant, and filled with fabricated memories that willfully ignore *unpleasantries.*

The popular history of surfing, as told by surfers turned amateur historians, like the popular histories of settler colonialism, centers white men and rarely includes the accomplishments of people of color and women, regardless of race. As the story goes, by the late nineteenth century, flood tides of colonialism and Christianity drove Hawaiian surfing to near extinction. Surfing-illiterates Jack London and Alexander Hume Ford moved from inland California and South Carolina, respectively, to Oʻahu, where Hawaiian surfer George Freeth (1883–1919) taught them to surf. They founded the segregated Outrigger Canoe Club (1908) and profited by using surfing and racism to promote Hawai'i as a tourist destination, which facilitated surfing's spread to North America and Australia. Early twentieth-century haoles (non-Hawaiians, usually white people), relegated nonstanding forms of surfing as wave riding, making them less attractive to scholarly deliberation. Such tropes seek to unseat Hawaiians as the founders of modern surfing by deifying blond-haired surfers, forging myths that white surfers perfected and spread surfing by going on surfaris to uncivilized places. Borrowing prose from the myth that Christopher Columbus "discovered" and colonists civilized the *new world* by clearing it of savage people and savage forests to establish European-style farms and towns, surf histories claim that intrepid Californians and Australians discovered unridden surf, civilizing it with modern surfboards.[1] Fortunately, a generation of scholars, especially Kanaka Māoli, or Indigenous Hawaiians, like Isaiah Helekunihi Walker, Tom Pohaku Stone, and Karen Amimoto Ingersoll, have dipped their pens in Oceania's deep cultural waters to write Hawaiians back into the narrative as *central figures* who gifted modern surfing to humanity.[2] Recognizing that Atlantic Africans independently invented surfing does not diminish Hawaiians' cultural contributions to humanity; rather, it charts new seas of human experiences.

This chapter provides a countervailing discourse by considering what has been ignored, reconsidering what we know and what we thought we knew, while examining what we did not know. Sources suggest surfing became a widely held skill in many coastal societies throughout Atlantic Africa, which stretches some from Senegal, in the north, to Angola, in the south. Atlantic Africa possesses few natural harbors, with waves breaking along much of its six-thousand-mile coastline. This essay argues that even as early modern (ca. 1440–ca. 1860) Atlantic Africans found surfing pleasurable, it was primarily a *pragmatic* solution to environmental challenges that enabled them to understand how to navigate surf-canoes. To reach fisheries and shipping lanes that connected coastal societies to each other, Africans first had to successfully navigate surf zones—the dynamic space where waves break. Surfing required youth to use their senses of sight, sound, and feeling to understand hydrography (marine geography, including the seafloor, and effects of tides, winds, and currents on waterways), wavelengths (the distance between waves), the physics of breakers, that waves form in sets with several-minute intervals between sets, and that to catch a wave one has to match the wave's speed, something Westerners did not realize until the late nineteenth century.[3] Sources suggest that perhaps one thousand years ago, Atlantic Africans developed surf-canoes, which are dugout canoes designed to surf waves as they beached and to slice through waves as they launched from beaches. In an age with few energy sources—when societies harnessed only wind, animal, and human power—Atlantic Africans used wave energy to slingshot surf-canoes laden with tons of cargo ashore. While Oceanians surfed waves in outrigger canoes, Atlantic Africans are the only known peoples to bridle wave energy as part of their daily productive labor.

Unfortunately, early modern historical accounts preclude a gendered consideration of surfing. Sources were written primarily by men who apparently assumed that African maritime activities, like Western traditions, was masculine, causing them to largely ignore female aquatics. Accounts mention girls and young women surfing, while some say "children," without being gender specific. Unfortunately, no known sources provide the details necessary for sustained gender analyses.

Surfing in Atlantic Africa

Scholars have scoured the archives of Oceania for the first written account of surfing. European accounts of African surfing predate those of Oceania by 130 years. This does not suggest that written sources are superior to much older Hawaiian oral traditions or that it legitimizes African surfing, rather, it illustrates how long African surfing has been ignored. The first known European source to document African surfing was transcribed by German merchant-adventurer Michael Hemmersam during the 1640s at Cape Coast, located on the Gold Coast in what is now Ghana. Believing he was watching Fante girls and boys learn to swim, he wrote that parents "tie their children to boards and throw them into the water."[4] Seven miles away, French slave trader Jean Barbot similarly penned, in 1679, that Fante "boys and girls" at Elmina learned "to swim, on bits of boards, or small bundles of rushes, fasten'd under their stomachs, which is a good diversion to the spectators."[5]

Later accounts are unambiguous. In 1823, John Adams illustrated the link between surfing and surf-canoeing when describing how wood from unseaworthy dugouts was carved into surfboards, writing that Fante "children" in coastal villages around Cape Coast

> obtain pieces of broken canoes, which they launch, and paddle outside of the surf, when, watching a proper opportunity, they place their frail barks [boards] on the tops of high waves, which, in their progress to the shore, carry them along with great velocity; and the principal art of these young canoe-men consists in preserving their seats while thus hurried along, and which they can only do by steering the plank with such precision, as to prevent them broaching to; for when that occurs, they are washed off, and have to swim to regain them, while their more dexterous companions reach the shore amidst the plaudits of the spectators, who are assembled on the beach to witness their dexterity.[6]

In 1834, while at Accra, James Alexander wrote, "From the beach, meanwhile, might be seen boys swimming into the sea, with light boards under their stomachs. They waited for a surf; and came rolling like a cloud on top of it."[7]

Members of many ethnic groups surfed in small, surfboard-size canoes. For instance, in 1861, Thomas Hutchinson observed surfing in southern Cameroon. Fishermen rode canoes "no more than six feet in length, fourteen to sixteen inches in width, and from four to six inches in depth" and "made of light wood." Describing how work turned to play, Hutchinson penned:

> During my few days stay at Batanga, I observed that from the more serious and industrial occupation of fishing they would turn to racing on the tops of the surging billows which broke on the sea shore; at one spot more particularly, which, owing to the presence of an extensive reef, seemed to be the very place for a continuous swell of

> several hundred yards in length. Four or six of them go out steadily, dodging the rollers as they come on, and mounting atop of them with the nimbleness and security of ducks. Reaching the outermost roller, they turn the canoes stems shoreward with a single stroke of the paddle, and mounted on the top of the wave, they are borne towards the shore.[8]

Bodysurfing equally provided understandings of surf zones, with an Englishman noting the correlation between bodysurfing and surf-canoeing. In 1887, while at Accra, he watched a man named Sua, saying he was as at home "in his element, dancing up and down and doing fancy performances with the rollers, as if he had lived since his infancy as much in the water as on dry land." As a wave approached, "he turns his face to the shore and rising on to the top of it he strikes out vigorously with it towards land, and is carried dashing in at a tremendous speed *after the same manner as the surf-boats [surf-canoes] beach themselves.*"[9]

African surfboards varied in size. Many were three to five feet long and fourteen to twenty inches wide, though some were six to eight feet long. Most were made from a single plank of wood, though some from the Congo/Angola region were crafted from three or four boards that joined together to make surfboards eighteen to twenty-six inches wide. Sources suggest that most people surfed in a prone position or while kneeling on one knee, though some stood.[10]

The movie *The Lost Wave* (2007) claims to have found "Indigenous" surfing, on São Tomé. Instead, it unknowingly documented enslaved Africans' ability to transplant surfing, known as *corre barra*, which means wave-running, in one of the island's Portuguese-based creole languages. The islands of São Tomé and Príncipe, located off equatorial West Africa, were uninhabited until the Portuguese colonized them during the fifteenth century and imported enslaved Africans from what is now Ghana, Togo, Benin, Nigeria, and primarily Congo/Angola to produce sugar for European markets. Captives from Ghana and Congo/Angola probably introduced surfing, including the single-plank and multiplank surfboards seen in the movie.[11]

Hawaiians and Atlantic Africans took surfing in different directions. Hawaiian surfing took on spiritual, cultural, social, and political underpinnings.[12] Atlantic African surfing had a different purpose, following a different trajectory. Atlantic Africans are unique in that they used surfing to float entire economies, including the export of ivory, gold, and the Atlantic slave trade, with documents suggesting that surf-canoemen transported many of the twelve million enslaved people exported out of Africa to slave ships. European rowboats were slow and cumbersome, often floundering and capsizing in surf, causing Europeans to conceptualize Africans' spaces of pleasure and profit as a "surf-bound coast" and barriers of fear where Europeans drowned or were eaten by sharks. In 1774, William Smith of the Royal Africa Company described England's reliance on "dexterous Canoe-men" to "carry the Passengers and Goods ashore," through breakers, "which to me seem'd large enough to founder our Ship." Conveying European fears, Smith expressed it was "barely possible, that a [white] Man may, if [a canoe] overset here, save his Life by swimming, but it is not very probable, for there are such numbers of Sharks here."[13]

Surf-canoes are innovative watercrafts. Responsive, fast, lightweight, and agile, they had a shallow draft, meaning they could pass through waters only a few inches deep while carrying several times their weight and were durable enough to withstand waves twisting their hulls and slamming them onto beaches. Unlike Western framed vessels, dugouts would not sink, even if filled with water. Professional canoe-makers used iron tools to craft surf-canoes, thinning hulls to as little as half an inch thick, using their hands as calipers to calculate the hull's consistent thickness, assuring a balanced craft. The surf-canoes had flat or semirounded bottoms, which improved stability and allowed them to sit flat when beached.[14]

Surfing and surf-canoeing were proficiencies absent in Westerners' maritime lexicon, with slave trader John Atkins explaining, in 1735, that African waves were "a natural Prohibition to Strangers [Europeans], and whence it follows in respect to Trade, that Ships are obliged to send their Boats with Goods near Shore, where the Natives meet them, and barter for Slaves, Gold, and Ivory." Knowing surf zones were difficult passages for ships' boats, prudent travelers, including racist slave traders and mariners, accepted their reliance on African maritime technology and expertise. In 1860, even as an American naval officer racialized Africans, he was forced to admit the supremacy of Fante surf-canoemen and surf-canoes, saying "Uncle Sam's boats are not built for beaching, we have to trust ourselves again to a big dug-out and a dozen noisy paddlers to bear us through the surf; for which we pay an English shilling, or an American quarter, each."[15] Ship captains regularly replaced rowboats with surf-canoes and hired surf-canoemen to crew them. French botanist Michel Adanson noted this practice in 1749, writing, "Our European boats appearing to me too heavy and cumbersome, to make use of them every day in passing" through the surf that breaks across the mouth of "that [Senegal] river; I therefore thought to exchange them for a kind of Negro canoo."[16] This dependence continued into the twentieth century. Nineteenth- and twentieth-century navigational guides published by the British and American navies repeatedly warned ship captains that landings "must not be attempted in a ship's boat" and should only be done by canoemen in surf-canoes. Prior to the construction of modern seaports during the 1950s, surf-canoes transported most of the goods and people conveyed between ship and shore.[17]

Canoe-Making

Watercrafts, the world over, represent more than modes of transport, and a canoe's value was not solely determined by construction costs. Unlike other material possessions, boats preserved users' lives while providing incomes, causing mariners and their communities to form cultural and spiritual relationships with vessels. Surf-canoes articulated generational wisdom and values that reinforced communal bonds. Surf-canoes were not simply made; they were born into societies. Canoemen from many ethnic groups performed welcoming ceremonies for newly purchased canoes, often calling them brides to signify their symbiotic bonds. Their sides were highly ornamented with brightly painted high and low relief carvings that were expressions of belonging, denoting kinship, clan, lineage, ethnicity, and affiliations with other social groups, all of which possessed powerful spiritual underpinnings.[18]

Surf-canoes were sacred, carved from revered silk cottonwood trees, while waterscapes remain spiritual places. Tall, majestic cottonwoods, with their spreading canopies and wide buttress roots, connected the heavens and earth, with some societies believing the souls of children waiting to be born resided within them. They had a gender that determined how they surfed, while cottonwood's soul dwelt within them, communicating with water spirits. Members of many societies believed ancestral spirits and other deities lived in waterways, while the realm of the dead lay across or at the bottom of the ocean or another large body of water. Canoemen plied sacred waters in dugouts layered in spiritual beliefs, making sacrifices to surf-canoes, aquatic deities, and ancestral spirits who guided them to shoals of fish and rewarded them with safe passages and prosperous voyages. People from Senegal to South Africa and as far inland as Mali believed in deities that were half-woman, half-fish. Mami Wata, meaning "Mother Water" or "Mother of all Waters," became the most widely celebrated of these finned divinities. Shapeshifting between a woman and half-woman, half-fish, Mami Wata slipped between discrete elements and circumstances: water and earth, the real and surreal, the present and future, safeguarding followers from drowning, rewarding them with enhanced spiritual understandings, good health, and success. Waters possessing distinguishing characteristics, like surf zones and waterfalls, are the favorite abode of water spirits, with the sound of moving waters echoing spirits' voices.[19]

Surfing was the intergenerational transmission of wisdom, transforming surf zones into "waves of knowing" and central places of learning where youth holistically *experienced* the ocean. Mothers taught their children to swim after they learned to walk at about ten to fourteen months old or after they were weaned at approximately two to three years of age.[20] Sources suggest that many children began surfing when roughly four years old, transforming turbulence into thrilling, but safe, playgrounds. Youth learned about surf zones by *seeing* and *feeling* how the ocean pushed and pulled their bodies. At Elmina, Barbot watched "several hundred . . . boys and girls sporting together before the beach, and in many places among the rolling and breaking waves, learning to swim" and surf, concluding African dexterities "proceed from their being brought up, both men and women from their infancy, to swim like fishes; and that, with the constant exercise renders them so dexterous."[21]

Youthful surfing experiences benefited canoemen. For instance, people knew waves form in sets, thus surf-canoemen "count the Seas [waves], and know when to paddle safely on or off."[22] Similarly, surf-canoemen understood how to ride the back of waves too large to surf. Surf-canoes typically surfed the face, or front, of waves up to roughly eight feet high. Instead of paddling hard enough to catch waves larger than that, they paddled less forcefully, until atop a wave, then rapidly paddled so the breaking wave pulled, rather than pushed, them. At times, they set their paddles as brakes or paddled backward, so they would not be pulled over the crest of the breaking waves, causing them to capsize. Danish merchant Ludewig Rømer documented this at Accra, penning, "It looks dangerous when you are sitting or lying in these Negro vessels among those breakers. These waves come rolling as high as bell towers. You can see when the wave will break, and the black boatmen (*remadorer*) must then see to it that the canoes ride on top of the wave before it breaks, or, in all haste, row their vessels back, letting the wave break first."[23]

Surf-canoemen's ability to conduct trade would have been diminished without ports to facilitate commercial exchanges, compelling coastal communities to derive an innovative environmental solution for Africa's lack of natural harbors. Africans developed surf ports, which provided the same functions as seaports but required vessels to pass through surf zones. Thus, Africans transformed beaches into wharves and docks, making them important places of commercial and cultural exchange.

African beach cultures informed societal relationships with surrounding seas, transforming the ocean into a sea of possibilities. Considerable scholarly attention has been devoted to European and American seaports as hubs of communication, economic exchange, and connectivity. Virtually no attention has been devoted to how Africans developed surf ports to connect themselves to prospects within and beyond their horizons. Most scholars do not recognize that surf-canoemen enabled Western merchants to trade with Africans by lightering Western goods to continental Africa and African goods to Western ships. African beaches were, and still are, community gathering places. At surf ports, beached surf-canoes were meeting places and marketplaces where people of diverse ethnicities met, goods were sold, and maritime techniques discussed and exchanged. Here, children played in canoes, the sand, and the surf, with all understanding how surf-canoes were central in creating a community of communities, stitched together by commercial and cultural exchange.[24]

As Europeans ventured down the African coast during the fifteenth century, fishermen narrowed overseas horizons by luring them to home surf ports by bringing markets to sailors. When Duarte Pacheco Pereira sailed down the Grain or Pepper Coast (Liberia) during the 1490s, fishermen paddled out to sell melegueta pepper, glorified as the "grains of paradise," writing, "The negroes of all this coast bring pepper for barter to the ships in the canoes in which they go out fishing."[25] As Willem Bosman cruised the Ivory Coast during the 1680s, "*Negroes* in three Canoa's laden with Elephant's Teeth came on Board."[26]

As surf-canoemen engaged in trade with members of other societies and, later, Europeans, they blended diverse African and European traditions, creating composite crafts that retained surf-canoes' speed and maneuverability while strengthening their hulls. Planks called weatherboards were added to gunwales (top edge of canoe's sides), which kept water out and increased cargo capacity. Bows were further raised to keep water from splashing in when launching, as were sterns to keep waves that were being surfed from pushing water into them.[27] Traditional surf-canoes sometimes had cross thwarts, wave breakers, and keels. Surf-canoes were cut in half lengthwise and had inserted keels, which did not extend below the bottom of the bottom of the dugout, to strengthen hulls while expanding their width. Wave breakers are wedge-shaped timbers running down the bow to deflect oncoming waves. Cross thwarts strengthened hulls and provided brackets for securing cargo. All these elements became ubiquitous on hybrid surf-canoes, as did knees, which were adopted from ship designs. Knees are curved rib-like braces radiating from the keel and up the interior sides, further strengthening the hull. In 1693, slave ship captain Thomas Phillips reported on African and European collaborations, saying he "set our canoemen and carpenters to" modify surf-canoes purchased from the Fante at Winneba (Gold Coast) for use on the Slave Coast: "The canoos we buy on the Gold Coast, and strengthen them with knees and weather-boards for and aft, to keep the sea out, they plunging very deep when they go against a sea [wave]."[28] English Royal Africa Company records indicate that late seventeenth-century Ahanta canoe-makers and canoemen of the Gold Coast similarly collaborated with ship carpenters, as did other peoples. As European merchants transported canoes and canoemen throughout Africa, they further disseminated these modifications to mariners who internalized these alterations.[29]

While many coastal people developed Indigenous surf cultures, members of some ethnic groups, especially the Fante, Ahanta, Kru, Lebu, and Wolof-speaking peoples, are more extensively described in written sources. The Fante and Ahanta, who are both part of the Akan language/cultural group, were influential in the development of large surf-canoes. The Fante Confederation stretched roughly 140 miles along the coast of what is now Ghana with Cape Coast and then Elmina being their most important surf ports. The Ahanta are their eastern neighbors and established several surf ports, including Komenda, Takoradi, and Boutri. Prior to European contact, Fante and Ahanta mariners engaged in short- and long-distance commerce, traveling upward of 1,500 miles. Members of both groups had exchanged design elements, which intensified as seventeenth-century canoe-makers determined how to construct larger dugouts.[30] Jean Barbot noted that Gold Coast canoemen "transport their cattle and merchandise from one place to another, taking them over the breakers loaded as they are. This sort can be found at Juda [Ouidah] and Ardra [Allada], [roughly 240 miles away in Benin] and at many places on the Gold Coast. Such canoes are so safe that they travel from the Gold Coast to all parts of the Gulf of Ethiopia [Guinea], and beyond that to Angola."[31]

Fante fishermen established ethnic enclaves in other communities, sharing designs with surf-canoemen of different ethnicities and introducing surfing and surf-canoeing to those who were unversed. For example, oral histories indicate that they introduced both to the Ga. Ga, Gã, Gan, or Ga-Dangbe/Gã-Daŋbɛ are an ethnic group who reside primarily in the greater Accra region of Ghana. Traditionally, they were farmers and freshwater canoeists, with many moving during the sixteenth century to the coast, where they established the six independent, inland-oriented towns of La (Labadi), Accra (Ga Mashie), Osu, Teshi, Tema, and Nungua. The Fante inspired the Ga to surf and surf-canoe. "Long ago" two Fante men arrived at Accra with nets and a surf-canoe, teaching the Ga to use both. The Ga of La similarly "had nothing to do with the sea" until mid-eighteenth-century Fante fishermen introduced them to surfing and surf-canoeing. Likewise, the Fante, Ahanta, Kru, and other peoples introduced surf-canoeing to societies east of the Gold Coast, along the Slave Coast, now Togo, Benin, and Nigeria, as peoples there traditionally plied the calm waters of a vast lagoon system.[32]

Distinctive-looking Senegambian surf-canoes, commonly called pirogues, were apparently first developed by Niuminka (also Nyominka or Niumi) and other Wolof-speaking mariners living north of the Gambia River, with Lebu (also Lebou and Lébou) from the Cape Verde Peninsula in Senegal making important contributions. Senegambian surf-canoemen traveled some four hundred miles from the Cape Verde Peninsula to the Casamance River.[33] Elaborating upon preexisting designs, canoe-makers began developing pirogues, during the late fifteenth century, by increasing traditional surf-canoes' lengths and widths, so pirogues ranged from ten to thirty-five feet long and were upward of eight feet wide. Hulls were reinforced with knees and cross thwarts. Exaggerated bowsprits and aftsprits extended from the front and back while pronounced wave breakers extended below bowsprits, with these features giving pirogues their unique profiles.[34]

"Kru canoes" of Liberia, Côte d'Ivoire (Ivory Coast), and Sierra Leone are another type of surf-canoe, similar to those crafted by Batangans and members of other ethnicities. Kru was a not an ethnicity but more a language/cultural/labor group that evolved into an ethnicity during the nineteenth century. By the late eighteenth century, canoeists identified as "Kroomen," "Kroo," "Crou," and other variants routinely paddled surf-canoes to newly arrived ships to sell goods or boarded them to serve as coastal pilots and auxiliary sailors, pulling their dugouts aboard.[35]

Kru canoes were one- to three-person surf-canoes approximately fourteen to twenty feet long, sixteen inches wide, and twelve inches deep. They were designed to traverse large waves and rough seas, with anthropologist James Hornell completing a study of them in 1929. Hewn from cottonwoods, they were "thinned down to a thickness of about half an inch."[36] Traditionally used for fishing, they remained relatively unchanged after European contact, sources suggest. Members of other ethnicities adopted their designs, while early accounts from Liberia indicate that Kru speakers had a long history of surf-canoeing. In 1599, Johann von Lübelfing wrote, "Two Moors came to our ship in a tiny boat, consisting of merely a tree trunk, pointed at both ends and about 2 spans wide, so they had just enough room to sit inside on their knees . . . they rowed so swiftly that we soon lost sight of them. . . . One would not have thought it possible to travel on the sea in such a tiny boat (which I could easily carry in my hands); [yet] they came so far out to us that we could no longer see the land."[37]

Surf-canoemen's paddles further illustrate their ability to derive environmental solutions. They were designed to provide rapid acceleration necessary to catch waves while minimizing resistance when the blade accidentally struck chop during the forward stroke. While space precludes a lengthy discussion, Fante and Kru paddles illustrate innovative solutions. The Fante developed an array of paddles, including the distinctive three-pronged, trident-shaped paddle. While there are numerous variations to this paddle, its three slightly spread fingers increase the blade's surface area, as little water passes between the figures when paddled rapidly.[38] Most paddles seemingly had long, narrow blades that widened dramatically near the handle. For instance, the bottom twenty-eight inches, or so, of Kru paddle blades was roughly six inches wide, broadening to about eighteen inches near the handle. During the eighteenth and nineteenth centuries, the Fante paddle became widely disseminated, with many Kru adopting it.[39]

There were probably hundreds of variations of surf-canoes, with most distinct enough to warrant their own names. We might group surf-canoes into three broad categories: pirogues, the large type surfed from Sierra to Angola, with the third being smaller one- to three-person surf-canoes. Those crafted from roughly the Ivory Coast to Cameroon were designed to surf two- to eight-foot-high rollers that were rarely vertical. Pirogues were designed to surf the larger, steeper, hollow waves (meaning they form tubes) breaking along much of the coastline from Senegal to Liberia. Within these groupings, design nuances were informed by fishing techniques, like line fishing or drift netting; types of fish caught, like shark versus herring; and local variables, like the size, shape, and power of waves. For instance, Ga fishermen of Labadi used three types of surf-canoes along a couple miles of beachfront. The *Ali lele* was fast, stable, "rides the surf well" even when heavily loaded, and was fitted with a mast that was lowered in surf zones. In 1947, a colonial fishery official concluded that no "other type of boat would answer to local conditions so well as she does. The fishermen are seamen worthy of their boat." *Fa lele* means "river canoe," and was similar to *Ali*, though not fitted with a mast. *Tfani lele* were heavily built, used for beach seining, and could surf only small waves. Seines are long rectangular fishing nets with floats on one of the rectangle's longer sides and weights on the other long side, so they hang vertically in the water. A canoe took one of end a seine out to sea in a sweeping semicircle, and as it was hauled ashore, the weighted side dragged the ocean bottom, ensnaring everything within its embrace.[40]

Erasing African Surfers

Several factors inhibit our understanding of African surfing. Most early modern European-descended travelers to Africa were poor swimmers and afraid of sharks, remaining outlanders who rarely entered African waters and did not extensively document surfing. White people felt waves transformed otherwise calm waters where they might cool off into life-threatening turbulence, as illustrated, in 1920, when an English sailor lamented, "We could frolic on the fringe of the surf, but not being born that way, could never go so far as to swim in it."[41]

The 1860s witnessed a shift in how Westerners perceived Africa. Just as Westerners were taking a concerted interest in Hawaiian surfing, the Western eye shifted its focus from Africa's coast to the interior. Prior to the mid-nineteenth century, malaria caused West Africa to be deemed "the white man's grave." Thus, even though European steam ships could reach West Africa in a couple days, unlike Hawai'i, there was little desire to promote it as an exotic tourist destination. From the fifteenth through the mid-nineteenth century, coastal Africans prevented Westerners from going more than a couple miles into the interior, so they could control trade between the interior and overseas markets. Late nineteenth-century military technology permitted Europeans to undermine the power of coastal states, and quinine proved an effective malarial treatment, precipitating a rush to explore, document, and exploit the interior. Consequently, few travelers provided late nineteenth- and early twentieth-century accounts of African surfing that could be read alongside those of Oceania. Instead, explorers focused on the interior, painting Africa as the "dark continent," making false claims about savagery and cannibalism, to portray themselves as daring adventurers. Still, Westerners continued to observe and document Africans surfing into the late twentieth century.

Deliberate erasures and attempts to colonize historical narratives have, for generations, undercut considerations of African surfing, as illustrated by *The Endless Summer* (1966), the most influential surf movie ever made.[42] Produced by filmmaker Bruce Brown, *The Endless Summer* followed California surfers Robert August and Mike Hynson on a global trek to *discover* previously unsurfed waves, with the segment on Ghana being the most memorable. Unfortunately, Brown casually employs stereotypes while ignoring African surfers so he could claim to have introduced Africans to surfing.

In Ghana, they surfed at Labadi Village, a community within La, which was part of Accra, the national capital. While surfing, they were joined by fishermen in at least three surf-canoes. After some Ga youth rode the Americans' modern surfboards, Brown proclaimed they introduced surfing to Ghana. Yet, when viewers shift their focus from the two blond surfers, they will see African youth with at least six traditional surfboards hiding in plain sight. Rather than documenting African surfing, *Endless Summer* hid it behind what South African surf historian Glen Thompson called a "tyranny of blondness," allowing whites to assert ownership of African surfing.[43]

Twentieth-century Californians imagined themselves as *the* inheritors of

Hawaiian surfing. Positioning Hynson and August as the founding fathers of African surfing, Brown layered *Endless Summer* with colonialist prose, portraying the duo as colonizers who civilized savage unridden surf. "On the plane heading for Africa," they wondered, "Would they surf; would they catch malaria; would they be speared by a native?" Brown averred, "The people, of course, knew nothing about surfing and had never seen a surfboard." As adolescent males rode Hynson and August's surfboards, several kids ran home to retrieve traditional surfboards, which had been crafted for the purpose and can still be seen at Labadi. Despite their shape, Brown claimed kids ripped boards from their houses, asserting this was "the start of bellyboard surfing in Ghana."[44]

Brown's narrative was embroidered with blithe racialized idioms. Unable to resist unfounded jokes about cannibalism when commenting on trident-shaped surf-canoe paddles, Brown exclaimed, "When they go stroking out to sea in their big dugout canoe and you're sitting outside looking at them paddling toward you, you think they're coming out with their forks to have you for dinner."[45] In a scene shot in Orange County, California, and inserted into the movie as if it occurred in Nigeria, promoter R. Paul Allen donned blackface and "war paint" to portray himself as a savage bent on attacking the surfers.[46] These portrayals were well received by American audiences, with famed movie critic Roger Ebert chuckling that Brown's "sophomoric exaggeration and casual enthusiasm is just what the film needs," giving it three gold stars.[47]

We should not expect *Endless Summer* to critically analyze African surf history. Still Brown could have—*should have*—honestly presented the cultures he filmed. Instead, he embraced the deifying narrative that claimed white men perfected and disseminated surfing. Brown ignored youth riding traditional Ga surfboards. When two late adolescent men borrowed Hynson and August's boards, Brown, knowing it is difficult for adults to learn to surf, marveled at one man's ability to surf the first wave he paddled for, exclaiming, "It takes most beginners a long time to just catch a wave. In my years of surfing, I've never seen anything like this: the very first wave he tries." Perhaps the stereotype that Black people do not surf prevented Brown from considering that the man already knew how to surf.

Even after another man surfed, Brown refused to accept African surfing.

For generations, *Endless Summer* has been regarded as a carefree, self-liberating movie, inspiring white surfers, including the author's teenage friends, to depart on surfaris. For Black surfers, including the author, it was part of the racist juggernaut that normalized Black relegation in the histories of both surfing and surf zones. *Endless Summer* informed an exclusionary environment in which some 1970s surf shops redlined surf zones by discouraging Black people from buying surfboards. Simultaneously, some white surfers resorted to racial slurs and violence as a means of enforcing localism through de facto segregation, while others dubbed themselves "surf Nazis," emblazoned swastikas on surfboards and walls in spray paint and surf wax, and performed sieg heil gestures on beaches and in lineups to intimidate people of color by averring that "white supremacy lurked just beneath the surface of California beach culture."[48]

Conclusion

"Surfing and Surf-Canoeing in Atlantic Africa" unsettles assumptions about the past, about modernity, about what we think we know about Black people's relationship with the ocean and surfing. It asks us to stop defining surfing as early twentieth-century Western neophytes did, claiming it required one to stand while demoting traditional prone, kneeling, and sitting forms of African and Hawaiian surfing as "wave riding." This relegation unknowingly embraces colonialist tropes used to impose and perpetuate racial/gendered hierarchies of power while causing many scholars to treat nonstanding forms of surfing as intellectually insignificant.[49] This essay invites readers to expand perceptions and definitions of surfing beyond Western imperatives by examining surfing from African perspectives to consider how African surfers became surf-canoemen. Uniquely employing wave energy as part of their daily labor practices, surf-canoemen link land and sea, making themselves central to the development of Atlantic economies and cultures. In this vein, these histories compel readers to reassess assumptions regarding Western maritime supremacy by recognizing how surf-canoemen wove oceans and radiating rivers into a vast aqueous content long before they enabled European merchants to access African markets.

Standing on coastlines, Africans gazed past surf zones, past horizons to imagine, design, and craft surf-canoes capable of creating seas of opportunity. Surf-canoes and surf ports were Atlantic Africans' solution to environmental challenges, permitting them to link terrestrial and marine producers to distant markets. The first surf-canoe was made long ago. Yet, innovation was not frozen in time; canoe-making evolved to better surf particular types of waves while carrying increasingly heavy loads. There were hundreds of types of surf-canoes. Nuances in design features have largely gone unnoticed by scholars who do not perceive them or recognize how slight variations in maritime design profoundly inform performance. Westerners' ability to traverse deep blue oceans was important to global development; still they floundered in Africa's green liminal coastal waters between land and sea, relying on Africans to surf cargo ashore for some five hundred years.

Notes

1 The author intentionally uses the term *new world* in lowercase italics to draw attention to the problems with this term.

2 Isaiah Helekunihi Walker, *Waves of Resistance: Surfing and the History of Twentieth-Century Hawai'i* (Honolulu: University of Hawai'i Press, 2011); Karen Amimoto Ingersoll, *Waves of Knowing: A Seascape Epistemology* (Durham, NC: Duke University Press, 2016); Scott Laderman, *Empire in Waves: A Political History of Surfing* (Berkeley: University of California Press, 2014), 24. For civilizing spaces, see Kevin Dawson, *Undercurrents of Power: Aquatic Culture in the African Diaspora* (Philadelphia: University of Pennsylvania Press, 2018), 4, 12–13, 153–54.

3 John Dean Caton, "Surf Bathing at Hilo, on the Island of Hawaii," in *Miscellanies* (Boston: Houghton, Osgood and Company, 1880), 245.

4 Adam Jones, ed., *German Sources for West African History, 1599–1669* (Weisbaden: Franz Steiner, 1983), 98, 109.

5 P. E. H. Hair, Adam Jones, and Robin Law, eds., *Barbot on Guinea: The Writings of Jean Barbot on West Africa, 1678–1712* (London: Hakluyt Society, 1992), 2:532.

6 John Adams, *Remarks on the Country Extending from Cape Palmas to the River Congo* (London: W. B. Whittaker, 1823), 42–43. Adams is seemingly explaining that Africans carved unseaworthy canoes into surfboards.

7 James Edward Alexander, *Narrative of a Voyage of Observation among the Colonies of Western Africa* (London: Henry Colburn, 1837), 1:192; Kevin Dawson, "A Brief History of Surfing in Africa and the Diaspora," in *Afro Surf*, ed. Mami Wata (Cape Town: Mami Wata Surf Company, 2020), 23–26.

8 Thomas J. Hutchinson, *Ten Years' Wanderings among the Ethiopians: With Sketches of the Manners and Customs of the Civilized and Uncivilized Tribes, from Senegal to Gaboon* (London: Hurst and Blacket, 1861), 227–28.

9 Archer Crouch, *On a Surf-Bound Coast; Cable-Laying in the African Tropics* (London: Sampson Low, 1887), 295. Italics added.

10 C. Béart, "Jeux et Jouets de L'Oust African: VII. Le Surf-Riding," *Mémoires de L'Institut Français d'Afrique Noire* 1, no. 42 (1955): 329–31; author's observations while traveling throughout West Africa and based on conversations the author had with West Africans and American and British expatriates who had worked in the region between the 1950s and 1980s. Postcard: "Négres plongeant pour attraper des sous," "Negroes diving to catch money."

11 In Portuguese *corre barra* translates to "bar running," with "bar" referring to a wave breaking on a sandbar. A lagoon system paralleling the coast from Togo to Nigeria traditionally encouraged peoples to use those waterways for transportation and fishing, thus they rarely went to sea. Dawson, *Undercurrents of Power*, 100.

12 Kevin Dawson, "Surfing beyond Racial and Colonial Imperatives in Early Modern Atlantic Africa and Oceania," in *The Critical Surf Studies Reader*, ed. Dexter Zavalza Hough-Snee and Alexander Sotelo Eastman (Durham, NC: Duke University Press, 2017), 137–44.

13 William Smith, *A New Voyage to Guinea* (1774; London: John Nourse, 1967), 167.

14 Dawson, *Undercurrents of Power*, 101–3.

15 John Atkins, *Voyage to Guinea, Brasil, and the West-Indies* (London: Ward and Chandler, 1737), 69; Chas. Thomas, *Adventures and Observations* (New York: Derby & Jackson, 1860), vi, 80–83, 193, 212, 205, 321.

16 Michel Adanson, *A Voyage to Senegal, the Isle of Goree, and the River Gambia* (London: J. Nourse, 1759), 94; Dawson, *Undercurrents of Power*, 103–4.

17 Great Britain Hydrographic Office, *African Pilot* (London: Hydrographic Office, 1856), 148–49, esp. 160; Great Britain Hydrographic Office, *Africa Pilot*

(London: Hydrographic Office, 1893), 2:35–37, 42, 142, 181, 183, 208, esp. 181, 36, 37, 182, 183.

18 Dawson, *Undercurrents of Power*, 101–3, 117–20, 192–95.

19 Dawson, *Undercurrents of Power*, 104–5, 191–203; Kevin Dawson, "A Brief History of Surfing."

20 Ingersoll, *Waves of Knowing*; Dawson, *Undercurrents of Power*, 23–40.

21 Hair, Jones, and Law, eds., *Barbot on Guinea*, 2:532.

22 Atkins, *Voyage*, 69, 77–78; Robert Harms, *The Diligent: A Voyage through the Worlds of the Slave Trade* (New York: Basic Books, 2002), 228–30.

23 Ludewig Ferdinand Rømer, *A Reliable Account of the Coast of Guinea* (1760; Oxford: Oxford University Press, 2000), 192; author's observations.

24 Dawson, *Undercurrents of Power*. Beach culture is also based on author's West African and Caribbean observations.

25 Duarte Pacheco Pereira, *Esmeraldo de Situ Orbis*, trans. and ed. George H. T. Kimble (London: Hakluyt Society, 1937), 108, 113, 132.

26 Willem Bosman, *A New and Accurate Description of the Coast of Guinea, Divided inot the Gold, Slave, and Ivory Coasts* (London: James Knapton, 1705), 287.

27 Dawson, *Undercurrents of Power*, 100–117.

28 George Francis Dow, ed., *Slave Ships and Slaving* (Salem: Marine Research Society, 1927), 64, 72.

29 Dawson, *Undercurrents of Power*, 109–18.

30 Dawson, *Undercurrents of Power*, 125–26.

31 Hair, Jones, and Law, eds., *Barbot on Guinea*, 2:529.

32 A. B. Brown, "The Fishing Industry of the Labadi District," in F. R. Irvine, *The Fishes and Fisheries of the Gold Coast* (London: Crown Agents for the Colonies, 1947), 23–39; John Parker, *Making the Town: Ga State and Society in Early Colonial Accra* (Martlesham: Boydell & Brewer, 2000) 8; Dawson, *Undercurrents of Power*, 127.

33 George E. Brooks, *Eurafricans in Western Africa: Commerce, Social Status, Gender, and Religious Observance from the Sixteenth to the Eighteenth Century* (Athens: Ohio University Press, 2003), 5–7; George E. Brooks, *Landlords and Strangers: Ecology, Society, and Trade in Western Africa, 1000–1630* (London: Taylor and Francis, 1993), 210; Dawson, *Undercurrents of Power*, 117. The name *pirogue* is problematic as it derives from the Carib Indian word that became the French term for dugout canoe and was subsequently applied to a range of watercrafts.

34 Dawson, *Undercurrents of Power*, 115–17.

35 Dawson, *Undercurrents of Power*, 42, 58; Jeffrey Gunn, *Outsourcing African Labor: Kru Migratory Workers in Global Ports* (Berlin: De Gruyter, 2021), 15–70.

36 James Hornell, "The Kru Canoes of Sierra Leone," in *Mariner's Mirror: The Journal of the Society for Nautical Research* 15 (1929): 233–37.

37 Jones, ed., *German Sources*, 11; Dawson, *Undercurrents of Power*, 109–10.

38 Brown, "Fishing Industry," 25; Dawson, *Undercurrents of Power*, 114; author's observations.

39 Hornell, "Kru Canoes," 234–35, photograph, fig. 1; Louis Gustav Binger, *Du Niger au Golfe de Guinee par le pays de Kong et le Mossi* (Paris: Librairie Hachette, 1892), 2:311.

40 Brown, "Fishing Industry," 23–39.

41 Warren Henry, *The Confessions of a Tenderfoot "Coaster": A Trader's Chronicle of Life on the West African Coast* (London: H. F. & G., 1927), 109.

42 Keith Plocek, "The Secret History of the Endless Summer, the Most Influential Surf Movie Ever," *LA Weekly*, February 2016, www.laweekly.com/the-secret-history-of-the-endless-summer-the-most-influential-surf-movie-ever.

43 Bruce Brown, *The Endless Summer* (1964; Torrance, CA: A Bruce Brown Film, 1990); Glen Thompson, "Otelo Burning and Zulu Surfing Histories," *Journal of African Cultural Studies* 26, no. 3 (August 2014), esp. 325–26.

44 In *Endless Summer Revisited*, Brown backs down from this claim, stating, "The kids had their little bellyboards." *Endless Summer Revisited* (Torrance, CA: A Bruce Brown Film, 2000). Author surfed traditional surfboards at Labadi Beach.

45 In *Endless Summer Revisited*, Brown says the paddles looked like "salad forks."

46 Plocek, "Secret History."

47 Roger Ebert, review of *The Endless Summer*, June 12, 1967, www.rogerebert.com/reviews/the-endless-summer-1967.

48 Steve Estes, "Surfing the Sun Belt: An Oral History," *Journal of Southern History* 86, no. 4, (November 2020): 864–65; author's experiences from the 1970s to the present. During the 1970s, Southern California surf shops refused to sell the author's Black father surfboards, claiming he was too tall for them.

49 Glen Thompson considers how nonstanding forms of African surfing did not challenge white hegemony. Thompson, "Otelo Burning," 329.

3

Surfscapes of Entitlement, Localisms of Resistance

Toward a Critical Typology of Localisms in Occupied Surfing Territories

TARA RUTTENBERG AND PETE BROSIUS

The practice of localism is a contentious topic discussed often in both popular surf media and surf studies scholarship. Surf localism commonly refers to acts of aggression and expressions of dominance exerted by local surfers in the water and on land, with associated behaviors including threats and intimidation tactics, violent acts of retribution, abusive language, "locals-only" signage at surf spots, policing and regulating access to the surf, and asserting priority on waves irrespective of common surf etiquette (Fordham 2008; Usher and Kerstetter 2014; Usher and Gómez 2016). Critically, we can also understand surf localism as a pervasive phenomenon in which socio-ecological experiences of place (among the waves and in adjacent landscapes) and belonging (interpellated among gendered, (de) colonizing, and neoliberal cultural imaginaries) are negotiated via subjective positions of entitlement and resistance in the colonial-patriarchal "state of modern surfing" and its associated neoliberal "surf tourism industrial complex" (Hough-Snee and Eastman 2017b; Gilio-Whitaker 2017; Olive 2015; Evers 2004, 2008; Comer 2010). Through this lens of "critical localisms," we explore surf culture's propensity to make possible a new global/local, or "*translocal*," surfing politics of resistance, recognizing surfing subjects as connected to broader community struggles and social/gender justice movements at multiple scales (Comer 2010).

In speaking of imaginaries, we refer to the "conventional discourses" of modern surfing's cultural narratives that "tend toward abstraction, reification, and homogenization" while producing "concrete developments on the ground" (Schelhas et al. 2018; Strauss 2006, 2012). Hough-Snee and Eastman define the "state of modern surfing" as "'a semi-autonomous modern world of its own' under which the right to surf . . . is governed by pressures exerted by those seeking to institutionalize and profit from modern surfing . . . defining what surfing is, what surfing 'should' look like, and who can surf in different contexts" (2017a, 86–87). As a characteristic component of modern surf culture, critical surf scholars describe the "surf tourism industrial complex" as originating in early twentieth-century Hawai'i and persisting today through the industry-constructed travel-to-surf narrative that links "modern surfing and international exploration," implicating surf travel and associated developments in the cultural appropriation of surfing and "remaking of indigenous space into settler space" (Gilio-Whitaker 2017, 228; Hough-Snee and Eastman 2017a, 98; Ponting 2008). Surf localism, juxtaposed across the critical imaginaries of the state of modern surfing and surf tourism industrial complex, is thus made particularly complex where booming neoliberal real estate markets are redefining access and reproducing (neo)colonial entitlement in surfing destinations the world over, offering a compelling space of analysis for interrogating dynamics of surfscape occupation and exploring emancipatory possibilities in contemporary surf culture.

The premise for this chapter rests on the understanding that not all surf localisms are created equal, but rather they are navigated via surfers' differentiated subjection to the cultural imaginaries and geographical territories we describe as "surfscapes." Drawing on Ingersoll's (2016) discussion of "seascapes" as places of ocean-based knowing, we offer surfscapes as sites of study that link the geography of surf breaks and sea-adjacent landscapes with the politics of their related terrestrial zones of occupation, connoting both the legacies of colonial and military occupation, as well as ongoing processes of settler colonialism relevant to surf-related tourism and development (Westwick and Neushul 2013; Gilio-Whitaker 2017, 2019). We understand occupied surfscapes of entitlement to include claims to access, belonging, and ownership founded on both socio-demographic dynamics of systemic privilege built into modern surf culture imaginaries and land entitlement/ownership in real estate markets present in contemporary surfing locations as a legacy of colonization and neocolonial surf tourism development. Addressing surfscape entitlement as a function of the political ecology of real estate, we engage with critical surfscape ethnography as a research methodology for studying and typologizing diverse expressions of surf localism relative to the state of modern surfing and its occupied imaginaries. We situate this analysis among (a) *imaginaries of occupation* manifest in both surf tourism and coastal real estate markets in surfing's most iconic territories, (b) *the production of innocence* exemplified among settler communities in surfing locales, and (c) *the right to ignorance* espoused in occupied surfscapes built on histories of structural violence and genocidal erasure. This framework allows us to recognize instances of localism that serve to perpetuate neocolonial dynamics in modern surf culture, as well as critical localisms of resistance enacting a politics of emancipation in otherwise occupied surfscapes.

Surfer-Researcher Positionality

We come at this analysis in recognition of our subjectivities as insider-outsiders researching surf localism given our participation in surfing culture, experiences surfing in different surfscape territories, and embodied subjection to surfing's modern cultural imaginaries. Aligned with intersectional surfeminist research centering autoethnographic and reflexive discussions on positionality (Nemani 2015; Olive, Roy, and Wheaton 2018; Gilio-Whitaker 2019), our personal subject positions as surfer-researchers are situated at the intersections of critical surf studies and political ecology as they relate to questions of entitlement, neocolonialism, resistance, and emancipation. Together, we co-facilitate the University of Georgia's study abroad program Surfing and Sustainability: Political Ecology in Costa Rica, which encourages students to confront the critical relationships negotiated among tourism development, conservation, and surf culture, with localism as a focal point for analyzing trends in surf tourism–related real estate development.

Coauthor Brosius draws from a decades-long relationship with surf culture and localism dating from his youth in San Diego, California, in the 1960s, where he grew up in the neighborhood of Pacific Beach and identified as a local at Law Street, just north of Crystal Pier. Being a local surfer at Law Street meant participating in the mores of initiation and group membership, often by policing the surf break through shows of bravado and tactics of intimidation meant to keep nonlocal surfers (especially "inland kooks" who lived east of Interstate 5) from accessing the Law Street break. Subsequently, Brosius's coveted claim to local status was lost to circumstance, as his young adult life took him to live and surf in places like Santa Cruz in Northern California and as a transplanted haole in Hawai'i, and his academic pursuits brought him later to research and surf in Bali, Costa Rica, and Fiji. A local no longer, Brosius confronted firsthand the contradictions inherent in the conflict between surfing's foundational (however constructed) travel ethic and expressions of localism at increasingly crowded surf breaks, reflecting on his own participation as a kid, coming to terms with living the other side of that coin of entitlement. Brosius's political ecology lens on these and other subjective experiences offers an avenue for retrospective reflection on expressions of surf localism, including his own, in their propensity to perpetuate and/or resist neocolonial dynamics in occupied surfscapes.

Coauthor Ruttenberg draws from a range of multisited and gendered experiences with localism, given her positionality as a cisfemale-identifying surfer with eighteen years of surfing experience on six continents, and predominantly in Costa Rica, where she has lived as a foreign resident, researcher, and surfer for just as long. With an academic background in surfeminism and surf tourism studies, Ruttenberg experiences surfing life as a US-born woman surfer with no claims to a place-based locality, but rather she negotiates in awareness of her relative privilege/subjugation in relation to coloniality and patriarchy in the occupied surfscapes where she has lived and traveled. Intrigued by the concept of girl localism forwarded by surfeminist scholars, including Krista Comer (2010, 2017) and Rebecca Olive (2019), and inspired by the "undercommons" imaginary (Harney and Moten 2013) as an ideological space for conceiving of certain expressions of localism as acts of resistance or means of social emancipation, Ruttenberg approaches surf localism from among the bodies and imaginaries that have been otherwise refused, colonized, marginalized, objectified, subjugated, and silenced in occupied modern surfscapes. Inspired by black radical scholars Stefano Harney and Fred Moten's (2013) discussion of the undercommons as a "being together in homelessness" born of the "essential fugitivity" of nonconforming subject positions relative to colonial-capitalist modernity, we engage with the concept of the undercommons as a means of thinking through critical surf localisms as embodied subjectivities that challenge the state of modern surfing through modes of being that naturally destabilize, emancipate, and transform. Here we envisage a surfscape undercommons, perhaps aligned with critical surfing imaginaries and seascape epistemologies (Ingersoll 2016), and through which we might see certain instances of localism as representing a beyond-politics of emancipation in otherwise occupied surfscape imaginaries and territories. Expressions of girl localism, "blacksurfing" (Comer 2016), and networks forged among BIPOC surfing communities are relevant examples of the surfscape undercommons discussed in greater detail in our analysis. Co-author Ruttenberg's central question surrounds the potential spaces for camaraderie and coalition building among Global South localisms and girl localisms to contest surfscape occupation as subversive intersectional praxis of and in the surfscape undercommons.

Critical Surfscape Ethnography

Given that our research on surf localism is built from both decades of embodied surfing experience and a number of key theoretical developments in political ecology and, more recently, critical surf studies, we have come to understand the methodological framework for this analysis as *critical surfscape ethnography*. Engaging a "bricolage" approach to research (Denzin and Lincoln 2003; Derrida 1978; Lévi-Strauss 1962), this methodology combines a critical review of secondary sources with self-reflective and critical ethnography, drawing from different periods of multisited participant observation as surfer-researchers to ground our analysis in particular surfing territories, as well as in relation to surfing's pervasive cultural imaginaries (Stranger 2011; Koot 2016; Canniford 2005). This relatively "open" approach is often retrospectively autoethnographic (Koot 2016), reminiscent of Stranger's (2011, 11) "unorthodox ethnography" in the ways we make sense of the everyday "adaptations, resistance and critique" we have encountered in the occupied surfscapes we frequent and continue to inhabit as part of our "participant-observer" role in this research. In this way, critical surfscape ethnography "take[s] account of the relationship between the observer and the observed, but also the relationship between the . . . worlds they belong to" (Stranger 2011, 11), while also acknowledging an at least partial and temporal "unawareness" of our doing research on surf localism and surfscape imaginaries in the many instances we now recognize as informing the foundations of this analysis (Koot 2016).

As such, specific methods vary across the surfscapes we analyze here, given the availability of secondary sources as empirical reference, along with our personal experiences in each place and/or in relation to the cultural imaginaries with which we engage. Data sources include scholarly resources on surf localism, notes from critical ethnographic moments, memories from experiences in and among occupied surfscapes, semiformal and informal interviews with surfers and surfscape residents, surf films, magazine articles, surf studies conference discussions, and social media engagements. Together, our critical surfscape ethnographies in Hawai'i, California, Bali, Costa Rica, and Mexico provide contextual examples of surf localism as the basis for our analysis and typology of diverse localisms perpetuating and/or resisting surfscape occupation.

Political Ecology of Real Estate and the Production of Surfscapes

Surfing Macroeconomic Theory: Waves attract surfers. Surfing attracts energy. Energy attracts people. People attract capital. Investment attracts development. And so it goes. A quick survey from outer space would likely show an inordinate number of major coastal cities expanding outwards in concentric waves from a quality surf break.

STEVE BARILOTTI (2002)

Essential to our discussion of imaginaries and surfscape occupation, we draw from coauthor Brosius's recent work on the political ecology of real estate, linking the production of surfscapes to the legacies of enclosure and dispossession associated with the making of real estate markets (Brosius and Ruttenberg 2019). The productive imaginaries of desire created through paradise imagery and marketing the bohemian surfer lifestyle have driven coastal real estate booms in popular surfing destinations throughout the second half of the twentieth century, particularly in the places surfing claims in its origin stories—Hawai'i, California, Australia, South Africa—and now in a highly accelerated fashion through expanded tourism markets in places like Costa Rica and Indonesia. The production of surfscapes, analyzed through the lens of the political ecology of real estate, is founded on the same obscured histories of violence and colonial genocide implicated in modern surfing, grounding legacies of enclosure and dispossession into the fabric of settler colonialism, tourism development, and lucrative real estate markets in surfing's most iconic and most occupied surfing territories. Real estate imaginaries, built on the power dynamics inherent in politics of knowledge, translation, representation, memory, and scale, have become concretely institutionalized through legal legacies of racialized entitlement and the structural violence of property law, as well as technologies and epistemologies of investment and speculation foundational to the making of real estate markets (Rothstein 2017; Kahrl 2012). In the process, traditional precolonial or nonmodern modes of land tenure are functionally erased with the construct of paradise for sale through incommensurable means of enclosure and dispossession via privatization and land ownership entitlements operating at the levels of both real estate imaginaries and on-the-ground real estate developments.

Rothstein (2017) and Kahrl (2012) delineate the racialized legal legacies and structural violence of property law as the building blocks of contemporary coastal real estate markets, where both access and entitlement were legally codified as engines of dispossession through restrictive categories of land ownership. As we see across surfscapes of entitlement today, these legal legacies of racialized enclosure and settler colonial dispossession have resulted in the privileged whitewashing of coastal land access and a structuralized apartheid built into the production of real estate markets and imaginaries. Similarly, technologies and epistemologies of investment and speculation play a fundamental role in the expansion of tourism development and international real estate markets in Global South surfscapes. This process is institutionalized through a relatively routine set of measures "making the world safe for RE/MAX," requiring the neoliberalization of coastal landscapes through legal codes amenable to private property ownership, zoning, and land mapping according to real estate desirability, amenity development, infrastructure investment, and the introduction of security measures catering to Global North investment interests. These measures are often accompanied by tax incentives and financial deregulation to encourage foreign real estate investment as an important strategy to drive economic growth in states increasingly reliant on the global tourism and real estate development industries.

As real estate markets expand similarly and simultaneously across surfscapes of entitlement, neoliberal modes of property and land ownership are institutionalized in ways often incommensurable with traditional modes of land tenure and associated social organization, with devastating impact on local ways of life. Take, for example, the imposition of private property in nineteenth-century settler colonial Hawai'i and the loss of life, livelihood, and connection to land implicated in the constitutional transition away from the traditional *ahupua'a* system of communal/feudal land tenure through the purchase of Native land by settlers (Low 2013).[1] These sorts of property ownership incommensurabilities are paralleled in many other places around the world. While concepts of ownership cannot be thought of in commensurable ways across such vast ontological differences on modes of living with the land and sea, the political ecology of real estate reveals how the production of surfscapes entails structurally violent processes of dispossession while enclosing lands and access to resources vital to both the material and social survival of peoples in occupied surfing territories. Functionally, the legally codified rights of property owners in conjunction with governmental strategies of land transfer/dispossession (entitlement, mapping, taxation, etc.), create new vulnerabilities among "traditional" property owners vis-à-vis new property owners and investors, producing apartheids of exclusion, securitization, and surveillance, while institutionalizing structural relations of servitude disguised through accepted norms of neoliberalization and capitalist industry, namely tourism markets and related employment opportunities. For locals unwilling or unable to conform or participate, the result is continual marginalization, exclusion, dispossession, and erasure of cultures and livelihoods.

Much as "tourism imaginaries" link objectifying, seductive, and restrictive narratives on people and place to the production of sociocultural realities in tourism destinations (Salazar and Graburn 2014), real estate imaginaries function through the production of desire promulgated via media, realtors, government agencies, and other promoters who operate as agents of desire, transforming valorizations of land and sea spaces into desirable markets for residence and investment. The whitewashing constructs of paradise and exoticism function across surfscapes of entitlement to produce desire in investors, with marketing signage and strategic advertising catering to a gaze that buys into the fantasies being produced, while remaining blind to the political ecological realities of enclosure, dispossession, violence, and erasure that continue to characterize the real estate landscape. Through the incommensurable institution of neoliberalized modes of property ownership as a form of colonial dispossession, as well as via means of othering, racializing, or strategically deracializing places and people through careful marketing campaigns, real estate imaginaries built on obscured histories produce material realities that simultaneously reproduce those histories and make them increasingly less visible to those who benefit from not seeing them. Capitalizing on carefully constructed desire, the strategic erasure of colonial histories, the fetishization of paradise narratives, and the exoticization of cultures, real estate imaginaries are powerful means of producing a general innocence among travelers and investors, while allowing them the privilege of experiencing those constructed realities in tourist bubbles (Smith 1978) of ignorance as a privileged right of being in the world. As important epicenters of neocolonial dispossession and structural violence, Brosius and Ruttenberg (2019) flag the politics of memory, the production of innocence, and the right to ignorance as primary manifestations of entitlement in occupied surfscapes and real estate imaginaries by which the same violences obscured by these imaginaries continue to reproduce territories of occupation through the very subjects to whom these imaginaries appeal, and through whom they continue to function.

Finally, through this lens on the political ecology of real estate, we understand how surfscape entitlement functions in tandem with surfing's cultural imaginaries of occupation foundational to the state of modern surfing and surf tourism industrial complex. These imaginaries are identified by critical surf scholars as rooted in the whitewashing and appropriation of surfing's Native histories in Polynesia and transatlantic Africa (Wheaton 2017; Dawson 2017; Gilio-Whitaker 2017), implicated in the imperialist pursuits of dictatorial nation building and global capitalist empire (Laderman 2014), as well as mired in ongoing processes of settler colonialism displacing Indigenous, Mexican, and African American coastal communities through dispossession, gentrification, and legal entitlement frameworks privileging coastal real estate markets capitalizing on the promotion of the surfing lifestyle, particularly in California and Global South surfscapes (Westwick and Neushul 2013; Gilio-Whitaker 2019, 2017; Willard 2002; Jefferson 2020). As such, modern surfing's imaginaries of occupation represent an important point of departure for recognizing the ongoing violences of dispossession and (neo)colonization elided in both the development of surfscapes and the phenomenon of diverse surf localisms in occupied surfscapes (Strauss 2006, 2012; Salazar and Graburn 2014), to which we turn in the following section.

Surf Localism in Occupied Surfscapes

Scholarly discussions on surf localism are not new.[2] Existing literature emphasizes the ways native-to-place Global South locals defend their waves as territory by defining boundaries to access and use for local and nonlocal surfers and regulating behavior in the lineup (Usher and Kerstetter 2014; Usher and Gómez 2016; Ernst 2014). Other scholarship on Global South localism includes critical perspectives on localisms of resistance in Hawaiʻi and Bali contesting neocolonial encroachment by the modern surf industry and tourism overdevelopment (Walker 2011, 2017; Ernst 2014), localism in Peru as a mode of national identity-making separate from California's modern appropriation of Hawaiian surf culture (Hough-Snee 2015), and "girl localisms" navigating the violences of coloniality and patriarchy in modern surfscapes occupied by surfing culture's heteronormative and colonial-patriarchal imaginaries (Comer 2010, 2017; Olive 2019; Comley 2016, 2018).

Scholarship on localism in the Global North highlights the ways self-designated locals assert property rights, commodify wave resources, adopt masculinized and racialized localist identities, and/or form into small surf gangs as a means of policing and regulating surfscape access through violence and intimidation tactics to maintain exclusivity (Mixon and Caudill 2018; Scott 2003; Nazer 2004; Kaffine 2009; Anderson 2013; Mixon 2014, 2018).[3] While much of this scholarship portrays surf localism as a governance response to a common pool resource (CPR) dilemma or tragedy of the surfing commons due to overcrowding of wave resources (Mach and Ponting 2017, 2018; Mixon 2018), we have written alternatively on the utility of a multiple-perspective framework on the surfscape commons beyond the capitalocentric CPR management model (Brosius and Ruttenberg 2019). This framework is useful for recognizing power dynamics in Global North/Global South surfscapes in relation to neocolonialism and entitlement in the surf tourism industrial complex by identifying (a) instances of "commoning" surfscapes otherwise enclosed or occupied, (b) the defense of noncommodified surfscape commons against the threat of occupation, and (c) expressions of surfing's critical undercommons imaginary comprising nonconforming surfing bodies and subjectivities existing in essential fugitivity from the state of modern surfing. Here below, we draw from that study's critical surfscape ethnographies to highlight diverse instances of surf localism in particular surfing territories as central to our subsequent typological analysis.

CALIFORNIA

Much has been written on the localized surf gangs in California, most notably that of Lunada Bay on the Palos Verdes Peninsula, one of the most affluent communities in the Los Angeles area, where access to the surf is regulated by coded entry among mega-mansions and policed aggressively by the predominantly white male resident surfers who consider themselves local to that spot (Nazer 2004; Kaffine 2009; Mixon 2014, 2018; Carroll 2015). Similarly, coauthor Brosius's memories of his own 1960s Law Street surf gang include regular experiences patrolling the lineup with his peers, hierarches maintained, and masculinities tested, to prevent nonlocal, inland surfers from accessing the break. Understood in the historical context of segregation and colonization endemic to the production of California surfscapes, these instances of Global North localism represent acts of entitlement perpetuating settler colonial occupation rooted in a selective ignorance of both the dispossession of Latinx- and African American–owned coastal lands foundational to the whitewashed "California Dream" (Jefferson 2020) and genocide of California Indians "as a condition of possibility for surf culture to take root in California" (Gilio-Whitaker 2019, n.p.).

California has also become an epicenter for surfscape resistance, notably with paddle-out protests in 2020 affiliated with the Black Lives Matter movement centered at Bruce's Beach (Manhattan Beach) and the Bay Street "Inkwell" Beach (Santa Monica), historic leisure sites in California's African American history otherwise obscured in modern surfing culture (see Sine; Comley, this volume).[4] As we have noted elsewhere (Brosius and Ruttenberg 2019), the intersectional international networks being forged among surfing bodies and subjectivities regularly marginalized by the whitewashed imaginaries of the state of modern surfing can be seen as expressions of Global South localism reoccupying racialized and colonized surfscapes, while linking specific surfscape territories with *translocal* coalition-based movements for social justice (Comer 2010).

COSTA RICA

The other day I was surfing at the point and this local kid dropped in on me. So, I told him he needed to respect my waves, the waves I have been surfing here for longer than he's been alive. I've owned my house here for more than 15 years, before there were any local surfers. And that kid said: "This is my country. These are my waves." I couldn't believe it. So I said, "Yeah? Well, this is my sport." It's the truth.

MIKE | cishetero white male from California, beachfront property owner (pers. comm., October 2015)

I believe this place has made me who I am. It has shaped me. I'm one of the oldest locals here, so I have the responsibility . . . to protect my area . . . to defend and take care of it. . . . [But if people are going to keep disrespecting our place] we are going to have to respond more rigidly. More localism.

PABLO | local Costa Rican surfer/surf instructor (pers. comm., August 2019)

The localism when I first came here was much more gnarly than it is now. . . . They slashed tires, cut anyone's tents on the beach, stuffing all the crabs into the tent. [This place] was known as one of the gnarliest places to come. There weren't a lot of surfers here, but they were yelling at people in the water. You could barely get a wave. . . .

I've known all the other [Costa Rican] surfers . . . since they were kids . . . I don't have much of a problem with them. The worst . . . are guys from SoCal [Southern California] . . . the dudes who aren't from here. Sometimes I'll just wait, and then when a set passes, I just paddle right to the peak and just wait there, and then when they try to paddle past me, I'll just make it be known that isn't happening. I'll paddle with them shoulder to shoulder. Use the body. . . . You have to assert yourself as a woman. In general [this spot] doesn't have that many women who surf it, so it's usually a lot of testosterone. The locals respect me, not the tourists but the locals for sure.

AMANDA | US-born foreign resident white woman surfer and surfscape-adjacent property owner (pers. comm., August 2019)

These conversations, held with three different surfers in the same surfscape on Costa Rica's Pacific Coast, describe multiple expressions of surf localism from their distinct subject positions relative to the state of modern surfing's occupied surfscape territories and imaginaries.[5] The first statement describes both (a) an instance of place-based Global South localism ("this is my country, these are my waves") and (b) an assertion of Global North entitlement built on an appropriative sense of proprietary ownership over the practice of surfing itself ("this is my sport"). Through the lens of the political ecology of real estate, we might understand the expression of Global South localism as a means of renegotiating power dynamics, resisting neocolonial privilege, and reclaiming occupied space. By contrast, we can interpret the case of Global North localism described here as enacting modes of settler colonial cultural appropriation characteristic of modern surfing's occupied imaginaries, as well as reflecting the neocolonial consequences of neoliberal surf tourism–related development as they relate to entitlement in occupied surfscapes in Costa Rica and elsewhere (Ruttenberg and Brosius 2017, 2020).

The second statement reflects a sentiment about Global South localism as defending or protecting the local surfscape commons from misuse or disrespect, which Pablo qualified in terms of foreign visitors littering the beach or taking waves out of turn. In this instance, Global South locals defending surfscape territory by regulating use and access also includes an ethic of care for place, a nature-based connection to the land and sea places that this local surfer, in particular, feels a responsibility to protect from outsider occupation. We might differentiate this from the third statement, which references aggressive acts of localism employed specifically by foreign resident surfers/landowners from the Global North and engaging in localist behavior, slashing tires and beach tents, to maintain surfscape exclusivity, reminiscent of the California surf gangs discussed above. Here, we can understand Global North localism in Global South surfscapes as enacting modes of settler colonial entitlement perpetuating norms of surfscape occupation within the surf tourism industrial complex. Finally, the second part of the third statement above makes reference to both an expression of girl localism, a woman surfer using her body against Global North surfers to contest otherwise male-dominated space in surfing's occupied colonial-patriarchal imaginary, and a sentiment of camaraderie among women surfers, or "girl locals," and Global South locals, expressed as "respect" in Amanda's words.

OAXACA, MEXICO

Our critical surfscape ethnography of Barra de la Cruz in Oaxaca, Mexico, describes the connections among surf localism in the water and the town's unique community-based surf tourism governance model as a means of preventing the types of neocolonial encroachment experienced in other Global South surfscapes (Ruttenberg and Brosius, forthcoming). While local surfers dominate at the surf break, community-run cooperative enterprises, including a restaurant on the beach and beach access gate where surfers pay a nominal fee to enter, are linked to the autonomous Barra de la Cruz community assembly, which administers public services, community works projects, and a land rights framework prohibiting non-Natives from owning land or businesses. While Hough-Snee and Eastman (2017a, 99) describe Barra de la Cruz as a "neoliberal town centered around the surf industry" and Mach and Ponting (2018) identify the governance practices of Barra as "coopting" neoliberal governmentality, our research highlights Global South surf localism in Barra as a territorial extension of local surfers defending the communally governed surfscape against threats of neocolonial occupation common to the surf tourism industrial complex in other parts of the Global South.

We can compare this model of Global South localism with the neighboring Salina Cruz Surf Association, which runs exclusive surf camps and surf guide services under strict terms of access for nonlocals to area surf breaks. Foreigners can partner with locals in surf camp ownership but not own their own camps outright or surf the Salina Cruz spots without hiring a local guide. While the pay-to-play model applies to visiting surfers from both the Global North and Global South alike, surf camp stays and surf guide rates are price prohibitive, favoring wealthier surfers from the Global North to the exclusion of nonlocal Global South surfers on a budget, different from the nominal entry fees and relatively inexpensive accommodations options in neighboring Barra de la Cruz. As a result, while Global South localism in Salina Cruz may prevent the type of settler colonialism we see in other occupied surfscapes, it may do little else to subvert Global North entitlement in the state of modern surfing. Finally, it is worth noting that across Mexico, foreign ownership of coastal real estate is significantly limited by the country's legal framework on land entitlement, which has allowed for local communities and private landowners to benefit financially from owning and operating surf tourism businesses, while staving off tourism overdevelopment in many of Mexico's most frequented surf destinations, with the notable exception of Puerto Escondido.

HAWAIʻI

Surf historians have noted that surf localism in Hawaiʻi is linked to nineteenth-century settler colonialism, including the institutionalization of colonial property rights over the traditional *ahupuaʻa* land tenure system, described above (Low 2013; Walker 2011). This history parallels the neocolonial cultural appropriation of "authentic" Native Hawaiian history and imagery and its role in promoting tourism development associated with the modern surf industry as "complicit in larger, ongoing colonial projects to dispossess indigenous peoples—in this case, Kanaka Māoli—of their ancestral places and culture" (Gilio-Whitaker 2017, 228). Against this historical backdrop of colonization, dispossession, and cultural appropriation, Hawaiian surfer Dr. Cliff Kapono (2020, n.p.) describes how "surfing became this way to hold onto something," even while modern surfing's "renewable marketing iconographies" promoted through the surf tourism industrial complex enable "Westerners both to purportedly 'go native' and to recolonize the postcolonial world with blissful ignorance, surfboards under arm" (Hough-Snee and Eastman 2017a, 6).

In a similar vein, Walker (2011, 137) links Hawaiian surf localism in its multiple manifestations throughout the twentieth century—including displays of hierarchy and dominance in the surf, the formation of Native surf associations (huis), and political organizations contesting tourism and industry-related overdevelopment—to Hawaiian decolonial resistance against the surf industry, perceived by many Hawaiians as "an exploitative enterprise that marginalized Hawaiians and colonized their remote countryside." Understanding Hawaiʻi's occupied surfscape territories and imaginaries through the lens of the political ecology of real estate, we can interpret instances of Hawaiian surf localism as Global South resistance to colonization and neoliberal tourism development and as historical practices of decolonial subversion and ongoing struggles for emancipation versus settler colonialism in situ and via cultural appropriation in the state of modern surfing.

BALI

In Bali, the genocide of 1965–66 was a precursor to the establishment of Suharto's New Order, which actively promoted mass tourism as an economic development strategy. This genocide, and its subsequent historical erasure, is foundational to the island's sensationalized imagery as a peaceful and idyllic destination in both surfing's occupied imaginaries and the development of surf tourism in Bali. Just six years after the genocide, the iconic surf film *Morning of the Earth* (1972) featured Western surfers' discovery expeditions to Bali, full of pristine seascapes, uncrowded waves, and undeveloped coastlands. Essential to surf culture iconography at the time, *Morning of the Earth* fed into surfing's growing travel ethic, with Bali as an idyllic location. Nearly five decades later, Bali is now one of the world's most popular (surf) tourism destinations, with hyperdevelopment centering on the island's best surfing waves. While *Morning of the Earth* painted a picture of a peaceful paradise, unmarked burial sites and mass graves filled with skeletons from a violent past spanned the island's landscape and continue to reveal themselves on beaches adjacent to world-class waves in this paradise for sale.

As our ethnographic experiences confirm, surf localism in Bali is known to be heavy at standout spots, where Balinese surfers exert dominance over tourists and regulate the surf lineup, exhibiting control via aggressive policing tactics. Ernst (2014) chronicles the more recent phenomenon of Balinese surfers "blocking" for paying surf tourists as a "mutation of surf-guiding" and expression of place-based localism both resisting crowding by foreigners and supporting local surfer livelihoods.[6] Recognizing that "blocking presents an imperfect solution to wave-hoarding by tourists and overcrowding . . . merely one outgrowth of the larger issue of unchecked development on the island," Ernst (2014) quotes a local surf guide whose sentiments speak to the ways in which Global South localisms in Bali defend against surfscape occupation and also connect surf guides through an ethic of respect and communal camaraderie: "We started to be tough and angry. Tourists try to drop in on us. One, okay. Second time, no. So locals don't have a space to work sometimes. . . . With the locals we meet in the water, private guiding or private coaching, we respect each other. We'll talk about how many people we each have, and try to be fair and help each other." While Mach and Ponting (2018) identify blocking in Bali as "illustrative of a neoliberal governance mechanism" that "creates a new market for wave access priority," this description forecloses important space for recognizing the power dynamics of critical localisms as resisting and/or subverting neocolonial dynamics in Balinese surfscapes. Through the lens of the political ecology of real estate, we might differently understand these paid instances of blocking as a mode of localism which, however paradoxically, allows locals to reap financial benefit from tourists while simultaneously resisting their ongoing neocolonial/postgenocide encroachment by leveraging modes of commodified and privatized surfscape regulation.

Toward a Critical Typology of Diverse Localisms in Occupied Surfscapes

Based on the research and analysis presented here, we developed a foundation for typologizing diverse localisms in occupied surfscapes. Situating Global North, Global South, and girl localisms across a spectrum of entitlement/occupation and resistance/subversion, we categorize the expressions of localism discussed above based on their tendencies to perpetuate or contest colonial-patriarchal and neoliberal norms in surfscape territories and imaginaries. Typologizing diverse localisms along these categories allows us to engage with questions of power and positionality across multiple surfing subjectivities and identify potentially liberatory expressions of localism within an otherwise hegemonic state of modern surfing.

ENTITLEMENT/OCCUPATION

On the entitlement/occupation end of the spectrum, we identify enactments of localism related to race, class, and gender, as well as neighborhood-based localism, as representative of settler colonial imaginaries in Global North contexts. In occupied Global South surfscapes, we identify localisms of entitlement/occupation enacted by foreign residents versus short-term visitors or tourists, as well as against native locals and/or women surfers, including property-based entitlement by foreign landowners and those purporting to claim ownership over the practice of surfing itself ("this is my sport"). Together, these types of localism work to perpetuate colonial-patriarchal norms in occupied surfscape territories and imaginaries through settler colonial constructs determining access, ownership, and belonging through class-based, racialized, and gendered norms characteristic of the state of modern surfing.

RESISTANCE/SUBVERSION

Drawing on our case study examples, we observe native-to-place localisms as representing enactments of resistance and/or potential subversion in occupied surfscapes. We identify this category to include surf tourism management plans developed by local/native communities, as well as expressions of localism versus foreign visitors/tourists and foreign residents from the Global North. This category might also include native-to-place localism enacted against visitors from the Global South, with interesting implications related to the power dynamics of coloniality and class. We can also identify native-to-place localisms that give priority to foreigners paying for surf lessons and hired local surf guides "blocking" for visitors for a fee as in some ways resisting surfscape occupation, depending on whether these practices are working to strengthen neoliberal practices of commercializing surf tourism resources and/or contributing to communal surf tourism governance approaches with broader benefit for local communities. Unpaid blocking enacted by native-to-place locals for surfscape allies including friends and women (foreign/local) can also be included in the category of resistance/subversion, as well as girl localisms, which may represent the most subversive expressions of localism by contesting both coloniality and patriarchy in occupied surfscape territories and imaginaries across both Global North and Global South surfing contexts.

The categories in this typology are intended to distinguish critical localisms of resistance as spaces for surfing localism to redress, subvert, and transgress norms of settler colonialism, coloniality-patriarchy, and foreign-owned neoliberal tourism development endemic to the surf tourism industrial complex and related imaginaries of occupation ubiquitous in modern surfing culture.[7] Conclusions drawn from this analysis and typology speak to the potential for solidarity-in-coalition among localisms of resistance and subversion to enact an already-existing politics of emancipation contesting historical and ongoing occupation in the state of modern surfing.

Critical Localisms of Resistance as Emancipatory Politics in the Surfscape Undercommons

As a lens on surf localism as related to surfscape occupation, the political ecology of real estate provides a useful conceptual frame for categorizing Global North, Global South, and girl localisms along a spectrum of entitlement, resistance, and subversion in relation to modern surfing's occupied imaginaries foundational to the state of modern surfing and its associated surf tourism industrial complex. Drawn to this line of research from our distinct subject positions as surfer-researchers engaging with methods of what we propose as critical surfscape ethnography, we endeavored to analyze and typologize diverse expressions of surf localism in California, Costa Rica, Mexico, Hawai'i, and Bali. This analysis and typology focus on the ways in which Global North localism is often employed, through entitled surfers' rights to ignorance of colonizing histories of surfscape occupation, to reproduce the neocolonial power dynamics embedded within the dominant cultural imaginaries of the state of modern surfing. By contrast, we also provided examples of girl localism and Global South localisms in their multisited propensity to resist and renegotiate colonial-patriarchal power differentials in occupied surfscape territories and imaginaries.

These examples include BIPOC surfers in California creating an intersectional international movement for social justice and land acknowledgment/repatriation; local and women surfers in Costa Rica defending and protecting territory from further surfscape occupation while acting in solidarity through expressions of mutual respect; surf localism linked to community-based surf tourism governance frameworks and exclusionary land ownership laws preventing settler colonialism from occupying Mexican surfscapes; Hawaiian surfers resisting historical erasure and ongoing dispossession through "holding on" to their indigenous surf culture, connecting localism in the water to a politics of resistance against the modern surf industry and tourism overdevelopment; and Balinese locals reaping economic benefits from surfing tourism while using localism as a paradoxical means of resisting overcrowding related to surf tourism neocolonialism as an outcome of twentieth-century nation building in the wake of the 1965–66 genocide. While these localisms of resistance and subversion might be seen as disconnected expressions representing certain surfers' refusal to conform to, and/or an essential fugitivity from, modern surfing's dominant cultural imaginaries, we can also conceive of them, together, as enacting a meaningful politics of emancipation from surfscape occupation, past and present (Harney and Moten 2013). As such, we might also conceive of a surfscape undercommons comprising localisms of resistance and surfing subjectivities "being things which are not" (Harney and Moten 2013) in adherence to modern surfing's occupied imaginaries, and who, through solidarity-in-coalition linked to a translocal "decolonizing praxis in intersectional collaborative work" (Comer 2010; Gilio-Whitaker 2019, n.p.) and an already-existing emancipatory politics on multiple frontiers, are contesting and transgressing the colonial-patriarchal and neoliberal norms of the state of modern surfing and surf tourism industrial complex.

Notes

1 "Land tenure at that time was basically feudal. . . . Title to the land (meaning the right to use it) resided always in the king or paramount chief, who apportioned it to a group of high-ranked ali'i who, in turn, set aside small plots for the commoners, the maka'ainana. . . . The missionaries thought that freehold would create a nation of simple yeomen farmers like their own ancestors. . . . But only a few years after the passing of the new constitution, the flaw in that vision was evident. 'I am sorry to be obliged to say,' wrote Missionary Edward Johnson from his station in Hanalei, Kauai, 'that the people in this region have little confidence in what their rules say about the security of lands. They are told in the Constitution, as published some seven years since, that they, (the people) should have secured to them the right of holding their own house-lots and the fruits of the earth that their own hands had planted and reared up. Well, now, in the face and eyes of this sentiment of the Constitution, some twenty families in the single valley of Hanalei, are stripped of the fruit their own hands had planted; and not only that, but are now, some of them, being literally driven from the spot where they have always lived and were born. They are told that the white man has paid their king dollars, and therefore they must be content with their lot'" (Low 2013, 22–23).

2 We build on a growing body of literature that examines localism in surfing from a range of perspectives related to territoriality (Usher and Kerstetter 2014; Usher and Gómez 2016); social constructs of race, gender, and class (Evers 2004, 2008; Waitt 2008; Comer 2010); commons management, resource commodification, and surfscape governance (Hough-Snee and Eastman 2017b; Scheibel 1995; Kaffine 2009; Mach and Ponting 2018, 2017; Brosius and Ruttenberg 2019; Scott 2003; Nazer 2004; Anderson 2013; Mixon 2014, 2018); as well as gendered and anticolonial resistance to the state of modern surfing and surf tourism industrial complex (Comer 2010; Walker 2011, 2017; Olive 2019).

3 This literature also emphasizes surfers' translocal identities linked to terrestrial, littoral, and sociocultural surfing spaces, as in Anderson's (2013) exploration of localism in the UK, and Evers's (2008) discussion of hetero-patriarchal and racialized local surfer identities in Australian surfing culture. Another strand of scholarship portrays surf localism as a governance response to a common pool resource dilemma or tragedy of the surfing commons due to overcrowding of wave resources (Mach and Ponting 2017, 2018; Mixon 2018).

4 Importantly, these protests were met both simultaneously and successively with paddle-outs held in solidarity at more than sixty surfing beaches around the world, organized in large part by Black Girls Surf and their global network. More recently, the BIPOC surfing community around Los Angeles organized a series of paddle-outs in response to racialized violence against surfers of color. Remarkably, this community also supported a political movement pushing for the return of the occupied land around Bruce's Beach to the Bruce family from whom it was stolen, leading to a bill recently proposed to the California senate.

5 Names have been changed.

6 *Blocking* refers to the practice of surfers using their priority position in the lineup to "give" others access to waves.

7 We recognize that these categories often overlap and lean on each other as dynamic and multiple, rather than static, stand-alone, or otherwise "pure" examples of localism, particularly in the case of "girl localism(s)," which could be mapped alternatively across the entitlement/occupation-resistance spectrum in insightful ways. We encourage this type of fluid and critical engagement with the diverse localisms typology.

References

Anderson, J. 2013. "Surfing between the Local and the Global: Identifying Spatial Divisions in Surfing Practice." *Transactions of the Institute for British Geographers* 39, no. 2: 237–49.

Barilotti, S. 2002. "Lost Horizons: Surfer Colonialism in the 21st Century." *Surfer's Journal* 11, no. 3: 88–97.

Brosius, P., and T. Ruttenberg, T. 2019. "Surfscapes of Entitlement, Localisms of Resistance." Paper presented at "Impact Zones and Liminal Spaces: The Culture and History of Surfing." San Diego State University, April 28, 2019.

Canniford, R. 2005. "Moving Shadows: Suggestions for Ethnography in Globalised Cultures." *Qualitative Market Research: An International Journal* 8, no. 2: 204–18.

Carroll, R. 2015. "California's Surf Wars: Wave 'Warlords' Go to Extreme Lengths to Defend Their Turf." *Guardian*, May 18, 2015.

Comer, K. 2010. *Surfer Girls in the New World Order*. Durham, NC: Duke University Press.

———. 2016. "'We're Blacksurfing': Public History and Liberation Politics in *White Wash*." *Journal of American Ethnic History* 35, no. 2: 68–78.

———. 2017. "Surfeminism, Critical Regionalism, and Public Scholarship." In Hough-Snee and Eastman 2017, 235–63.

Comley, C. 2016. "'We Have to Establish Our Territory': How Women Surfers 'Carve Out' Gendered Spaces within Surfing." *Sport in Society* 19, no. 8/9: 1289–98.

———. 2018. "'Mexicans Don't Surf': An Intersectional Analysis of Mexican American's Experiences with Sport." In *Surfing, Sex, Genders and Sexualities*, edited by lisahunter, 91–109. New York: Routledge.

Dawson, K. 2017. "Surfing beyond Racial and Colonial Imperatives in Early Modern Atlantic Africa and Oceania." In Hough-Snee and Eastman 2017, 135–54.

Denzin, N., and Y. Lincoln, eds. 2003. *Collecting and Interpreting Qualitative Materials*. London: Sage.

Derrida, J. 1978. "Structure, Sign, and Play in the Discourse of the Human Sciences." *Writing and Difference*, trans. Alan Bass. London: Routledge: 278–94.

Ernst, M. 2014. "Crowdfunded: Surfing Is One of the Biggest Businesses on Bali and Blocking for a Client Is Good Business." *Surfer's Journal*.

Evers, C. 2004. "Men Who Surf." *Cultural Studies Review* 10, no. 1: 27–41.

———. 2008. "The Cronulla Race Riots: Safety Maps on an Australian Beach." *South Atlantic Quarterly* 107, no. 2. DOI: 10.1215/00382876-2007-074.

Fordham, M. 2008. *The Book of Surfing: The Killer Guide*. London: Bantam Press.

Gilio-Whitaker, D. 2017. "Appropriating Surfing and the Politics of Indigenous Authenticity." In Hough-Snee and Eastman 2017, 214–34.

———. 2019. "Being a Good Relative: Bringing an Indigenous Feminist Worldview to Surfing and Surf Culture." Paper presented at "Impact Zones and Liminal Spaces: The Culture and History of Surfing." San Diego State University, April 28, 2019.

Harney, S., and F. Moten. 2013. *The Undercommons: Fugitive Planning and Black Study*. Brooklyn: Autonomedia.

Hough-Snee, D. Z. 2015. "You Have the Right to Surf: Riding Waves of Decolonization, Modernity, and Nationalism in Peru." In *Sports and Nationalism in Latin/o America*, edited by H. F. L'Hoeste, R. M. Irwin, and J. Poblete, 201–23. New York: Palgrave Macmillan.

Hough-Snee, D. Z., and A. S. Eastman. 2017a. "Consolidation, Creativity, and (de)Colonization in the State of Modern Surfing." In Hough-Snee and Eastman 2017, 84–108.

———, eds. 2017b. *The Critical Surf Studies Reader*. Durham, NC: Duke University Press.

Ingersoll, K. A. 2016. *Waves of Knowing: A Seascape Epistemology*. Durham, NC: Duke University Press.
Jefferson, A. 2020. *Living the California Dream: African American Leisure Sites during the Jim Crow Era*. Lincoln: University of Nebraska Press.
Kaffine, D. 2009. "Quality and the Commons: The Surf Gangs of California." *Journal of Law and Economics* 52: 727–43.
Kahrl, A. W. 2012. *The Land Was Ours: How Black Beaches Became White Wealth in the Coastal South*. Chapel Hill: University of North Carolina Press.
Kapono, C. 2020. "Cliff Kapono: Tomorrow's Ancestors." *The Waterpeople Podcast*. September 2020.
Koot, S. 2016. "Perpetuating Power through Autoethnography: My Research Unawareness and Memories of Paternalism among the Indigenous Hai//om in Namibia." *Critical Arts* 30, no. 6: 840–54.
Laderman, S. 2014. *Empire in Waves: A Political History of Surfing*. Los Angeles: University of California Press.
Lévi-Strauss, C. 1962. *La pensée sauvage*. Paris: Plon.
Low, S. 2013. *Hawaiki Rising*. Waipahu: Island Heritage Publishing.
Mach, L., and J. Ponting. 2017. "A Nested Socio-ecological Systems Approach to Understanding the Implications of Changing Surf-Reef Governance Regimes." In *Lifestyle Sports and Public Policy*, edited by D. Turner, and S. Carnicelli. New York: Routledge.
———. 2018. "Governmentality and Surf Tourism Destination Governance." *Journal of Sustainable Tourism*. DOI: 10.1080/09669582.2018.1513008.
Mixon, F. 2014. "Bad Vibrations: New Evidence on Commons Quality and Localism at California's Surf Breaks." *International Review of Economics* 61: 379–97.
———. 2018. "Camaraderie, Common Pool Congestion, and the Optimal Size of Surf Gangs." *Economics of Governance*, no. 19: 381–96.
Mixon, F., and S. Caudill. 2018. "Guarding Giants: Resource Commons Quality and Informal Property Rights in Big-Wave Surfing." *Empirical Economics* 54: 1697–1715. https://doi.org/10.1007/s00181-017-1273-y2017.
Nazer, D. 2004. "The Tragicomedy of the Surfers' Commons." *Deakin Law Review* 9: 655–713.
Nemani, M. 2015. "Being a Brown Bodyboarder." In *Seascapes: Shaped by the Sea*, edited by B. Humberstone and M. Brown, 83–100. Farnham, Surrey: Ashgate.
Olive, R. 2015. "Surfing, Localism, Place-Based Pedagogies and Ecological Sensibilities in Australia." In *Routledge International Handbook of Outdoor Studies*,

edited by B. Humberstone, H. Prince, and K. Henderson, 501–10. London: Routledge.

———. 2019. "The Trouble with Newcomers: Women, Localism and the Politics of Surfing." *Journal of Australian Studies* 43, no. 1: 39–54. DOI: 10.1080/14443058.2019.1574861.

Olive, R., G. Roy, and B. Wheaton. 2018. "Stories of Surfing: Surfing, Space and Subjectivity/Intersectionality." In *Surfing, Sex, Genders and Sexualities*, edited by lisahunter, 148–67. New York: Routledge.

Ponting, J. 2008. "Consuming Nirvana: An Exploration of Surfing Tourist Space." PhD diss., University of Technology–Sydney.

Rothstein, R. 2017. *The Color of Law: A Forgotten History of How Our Government Segregated America*. New York: Liveright.

Ruttenberg, T., and P. Brosius. 2017. "Decolonizing Sustainable Surf Tourism." In Hough-Snee Eastman 2017, 109–34.

———. 2020. "Waves of Development: Surf Tourism on Trial in Costa Rica." In *The Ecolaboratory: Environmental Governance and Economic Development in Costa Rica*, edited by R. Fletcher et al., 204–16. Tucson: University of Arizona Press.

Salazar, N., and N. Graburn, eds. 2014. *Tourism Imaginaries: Anthropological Approaches*. New York: Berghahn Books.

Schelhas, J., S. Hitchner, and J. Brosius. 2018. "Envisioning and Implementing Sustainable Bioenergy Systems in the U.S. South." In *Handbook of Sustainability and Social Science Research*, edited by W. Leal Filho et al., 301–14. New York: Springer International.

Scott, P. 2003. "We Shall Fight on the Seas and the Oceans . . . We Shall: Commodification, Localism and Violence." *M/C: A Journal of Media and Culture* 6, no. 1.

Smith, V. L. 1978. "Introduction." In *Hosts and Guests: The Anthropology of Tourism*, edited by V. L. Smith, 1–14. Philadelphia: University of Pennsylvania Press.

Stranger, M. 2011. *Surfing Life: Surface, Substructure and the Commodification of the Sublime*. Farnham, Surrey: Ashgate.

Strauss, C. 2006. "The Imaginary." *Anthropological Theory*, no. 6: 322–44.

———. 2012. *Making Sense of Public Opinion: American Discourses about Immigration and Social Programs*. Cambridge, England: Cambridge University Press.

Usher, L., and E. Gómez. 2016. "Surf Localism in Costa Rica: Exploring Territoriality among Costa Rican and Foreign Resident Surfers." *Journal of Sport and Tourism* 20, nos. 3–4: 195–216. DOI: 10.1080/14775085.2016.1164068.

Usher, L., and D. Kerstetter. 2014. "Re-defining Localism: An Ethnography of Human Territoriality in the Surf." *International Journal of Tourism Anthropology* 4, no. 3: 286–302.

Waitt, G. 2008. "'Killing Waves': Surfing, Space, and Gender." *Social and Cultural Geography* 9, no. 1: 75–94.

Walker, I. 2011. *Waves of Resistance: Surfing and History in Twentieth-Century Hawai'i.* Honolulu: University of Hawai'i Press.

———. 2017. "*Kai Ea*: Rising Waves of National and Ethnic Hawaiian Identities." In Hough-Snee and Eastman 2017, 62–83.

Westwick, P., and P. Neushul. 2013. *The World in the Curl: An Unconventional History of Surfing.* New York: Crown.

Wheaton, B. 2017. "Space Invaders in Surfing's White Tribe: Exploring Surfing, Race, and Identity." In Hough-Snee and Eastman 2017, 177–95.

Willard, M. 2002. "Duke Kahanamoku's Body: Biography of Hawai'i." In *Sports Matters: Race, Recreation, and Culture*, edited by J. Bloom and M. Willard, 13–38. New York: New York University Press.

4

Surfeminist Responses to the Violence of Global Authoritarianism

KRISTA COMER

This keynote lecture for the San Diego State University conference "Impact Zones and Liminal Spaces" was delivered in April of 2019 at none other than San Diego's legendary Bird's Surf Shed. As a testimony to the collaborative spirit of the moment and in tribute to those who trekked across the world to attend, I have let the remarks stand largely as they were delivered, with some editing for publication. If specific historical events or actors have changed in the interim, the structure of political life and current challenges have not changed.

An accompanying slideshow that offered citations and additional details during the lecture now appears in endnotes with updates reflecting the burgeoning scholarship in surfeminist environmentalism. I am grateful to our conference hosts David Kamper, Jess Ponting, and Mike Roberts, who invited me to speak and invited, through the Institute for Women Surfers, a large feminist participant cohort. The unprecedented presence of our crew made a difference for the conference and for us. When I began working in surf studies, I never imagined such a varied audience would turn up for what I had to say, nor did I imagine in my wildest dreams the concept of "surfeminism." What an amazing privilege it was to give a lecture at the Surf Shed, and thanks to Bird Huffman for his service ethic. He always seems to be putting away chairs when others have gone home. Of the many extraordinary venues for conversation that my life with surfers has brought to me, I doubt I will ever again have a surfboard worktable as a keynote lectern!

I'm mindful about who is here, our audience, which is very mixed in terms of its communities. There seems to be a vision in play about how conferences producing new forms of surfing knowledge might work. The meeting hosted here tonight and featuring panels and talks over the weekend at San Diego State University brings together an international group of elected officials, scholars, artists, entrepreneurs, nonprofit people and foundation leaders, activists, surf journalists, surf artisans and board builders, pro surfers, and legendary surfers. Our meeting has much in common structurally with big meetings I've seen in other places—for instance, the 2018 Global Wave Conference in Santa Cruz, organized by Save the Wave Coalition and Surfrider Foundation. Or the Surf Social Summit that our Australian colleague Dr. lisahunter (present tonight from Monash University in Melbourne) co-organized in 2016 in Raglan, Aotearoa/New Zealand, with feminist scholars then at the University of Waikato, including Rebecca Olive, Belinda Wheaton, and Holly Thorpe. This San Diego conference shares structural similarity with the 2015 Surf for Social Good Summit in Bali, organized by the Irish big wave surfer and marine scientist Easkey Britton.

All of the above summits share similarities with the Institute for Women Surfers, cofounded in 2014 by champion surfer and well-known activist Cori Schumacher and me. Cori had read my book *Surfer Girls in the New World Order* and wanted to collaborate in activism. Other activists read it too and reached out. I was the last person who imagined such a future for that book. But how fortunate my life and research took that turn, and that I was encouraged by so many of you. Thank you. The Institute for Women Surfers has been generating new knowledges since with very diverse publics. We skill share as well as do feminist political education together and have gathered in California, Europe, and Oceania. lisahunter is a cofounder of IWS Oceania, someone with enormous integrity who is pushing the bounds of gender/sexuality systems in social life and in surf worlds. Lyndsey Stoodley, always up for elaborate road trips and pranks and laughs, is here from Wales and Cardiff University. Lyndsey cofounded the IWS Europe with the activist Dani Robertson, and introduced the IWS to the work of the World Surfing Reserves. We also have a lot of folks here in San Diego from all over California, activists, filmmakers, researchers. And Rhonda Harper has just returned from Senegal with the Senegalese pro surfer Khadjou Sambe and the Jamaican filmmaker Imani Wilmot. I will share some of the work from the institute tonight. Surf conferences, summits, and the IWS are attended not only, or even primarily, by university people. But we all, coming from wherever places in the world, are looking to do something with surfing that broadly contributes to and benefits the social good.

One priority for social good that surf worlds share is what we can start by calling "environment." Many of us here know a lot about the environment. We are here with people involved in the World Surfing Reserves, who show us how sophisticated the cross-sector and transnational collaborations about surf environmentalism can be. What a talent pool of international engineers, city planning officials, legal experts, investors, university researchers, tech innovators, all of whom are thinking through the ecological preservation and financial maintenance of the world's most revered surf breaks. By the same token, there are *a lot* of knowledges about environment. In this room there are a lot knowledges. These include especially Indigenous knowledges and expertise from traditional custodians of land. We heard today from Tom Pohaku Stone, Kevin Dawson, Isaiah Helekunihi Walker, and Lydia Heberling, and more to come tomorrow about Indigenized environmental justice and its relation to sovereignty from Dina Gilio-Whitaker and Angela Howe. We must continue learning to recognize "environment" itself as a complex concept with a fraught history. "Environment" does a lot of good work in surfing at the same time it carries immense colonial and settler colonial baggage.

My talk addresses three large points. The first has to do with authoritarianism and its relationship to planetary health and social violence. In an era of changed climate, authoritarianism is very bad for the Earth's health. It's also very bad for social life; it stokes violence between people.

What is important, for our discussion, is to link the two trends of violence, to link planetary and social violence. That's the first part of the talk. The second part thinks about feminist environmentalism as a philosophy and a politics that connects social with planetary violence. Specifically, how violence against women and against land, the oceans, and Earth reinforce one other—this is a serious insight. Last, I focus on building coalitions. We need coalitions that can fight for shared political goals, and the path is new relationships, understanding, and forms of kinship. Feminist work, at its most hopeful, is about coalitional politics.[1] Let me be sure to say immediately, because I get asked this question a fair amount, yes, definitely, men can be feminists. Women need male allies. Feminism is a politics, a theory about the way the world works. You don't need a female body to be a feminist, though I do grant women as having authority about women's lives.

Authoritarianism

What is "the Global Right"? What do I mean by "authoritarianism"? Why consider environment and misogyny in relation to these new forms of political governance?

In the US, political analysis in domestic media has understood the election of Donald Trump as a national referendum on working-class and white discontent. But taking a more international and less domestic view makes clear, as reporting by Peter Beinart of the *Atlantic* shows, that the election of Trump was part of a world political shift to the right. Turkey, Hungary, India, the Philippines, Brazil, Poland—all of these nations, in the last ten to fifteen years, have moved in hypernationalist and antidemocratic directions after electing hard-line men.[2] The wide-angle view, as National Public Radio reports, reveals "The Rise of the Far Right Threatens Democracy Worldwide."[3] Borders have closed to migrants, religious hatreds have worsened. Civil rights backlashes and racial hostilities have come out of hiding. Misogyny too. Across national contexts, expanding the powers of the executive branch at the expense of other branches of government or without regard to the rule of law has been the order of the day. Expansions of executive branch power and disregard for legal process, organized through the person of a central strongman, is the definition of an authoritarian regime.

Democratic cooperation between nations is the foundation of international climate change policy. Whatever its limits, without cooperation and diplomacy, climate problems worsen. It is widely accepted as fact by scholars, major international organizations like the United Nations, and big environmental foundations like Surfrider, that climate crises unevenly impact the world's people and places. Some people, some nations, are impacted far more than others. What is perhaps less apparent, because it is current and people are catching up to the impacts, is that authoritarianisms *accelerate* unevenly distributed climate crises. President Trump repudiated the Paris Climate Accord. Brazil's President Bolsonaro threw authoritarian fuel onto an already overwarm planet. New forms of authoritarianism can mobilize fears about the climate to seize power, justify antidemocratic reforms, and abandon policies of climate adaptation. I'm thinking about the former president of the Maldives (a "Climate King"), who used fears about subsidence and sinking islands to get elected, but then whose hyperdevelopment programs sped the rate of subsidence.[4]

Claims of climate change as a hoax or fake news, infamous Twitter topics of both Trump and Bolsonaro, were about far more than climate denial, as journalist Brandon Wu argues.[5] Antiscience policy has gone in hand with policy that exacerbates social inequality inside nations while it villainized migrants and refugees across nations. Cultures of fear, inequality, and xenophobia provide excuses to build walls, Wu points out, to divide people, and suppress dissent. Calls for border hardenings and harsher migrant detention policy come in an era when, as is often and wrenchingly reported, millions are on the global move because of war, economic precarity, and climate-related displacement. Millions more will join them sooner than later. Inter Press Service (News Agency) and United Nations University research predicts, at its most conservative, 250 million people climate-displaced by the year 2050.[6]

Hang on here, friends, there's a lot of bad news, it's unremittingly difficult, and in a moment, I will turn to surfeminism, which offers a brighter light.

Let's think about the gendered aspects of social inequality, because links between misogyny or the hatred of women and authoritarianism are even newer than those between climate acceleration and the rise of the Global Right. How to make sense of the gendered power orders of strongmen and Climate Kings? Is it coincidence that the Bolsonaros and Trumps are so explicit and public about their misogynies? This discussion and its disturbing details will be triggering for some, so be alert. The only point to restating such violent information is that it is dangerous to underestimate the battle faced by women, girls, and female-identifying people.

As I noted earlier, comparative analysis across the US, Brazil, Italy, Poland, Hungary, and the Philippines suggests that new authoritarian formations have not emerged exclusively from working-class and white discontent.[7] While not discounting these potent sources of political grievance politics, journalist Beinart shows that in countries where economic slowdowns are less a factor, where racial minorities in fact support strongmen, the shared source generating political consent for authoritarianism is male domination. Let's absorb that. Male domination. The glue holding together authoritarian political blocs in very different contexts operates through a resurgent patriarchal authority, curtailment of women's rights and power, and the humiliation of women leaders. Think of the humiliation of someone as eminently capable as Hillary Clinton. Or, as Charlotte Alter reported in *Time*, of Bolsonaro telling the Brazilian congresswoman Maria do Rosário, a human rights advocate, that he would not rape her because she was "not worthy of rape."[8] Bolsonaro delivered this comment on the floor of the Brazilian national legislature.

Beinart as well as other reporters detail how authoritarianism sanctions state violence in wars specifically against women in the Philippines, Poland, and Hungary. These forms of violence have many faces. The Philippine autocrat former president Duterte instructed state soldiers to "shoot [female] rebels in the vagina" as punishment for protest.[9] Mutilation was a better penalty for women opposing state rule than outright death, he proclaimed, because without a vagina, a woman was "useless." Infamous for so-called joking, Duterte boasted his regrets at not having had a chance to rape an Australian missionary who was gang-raped and murdered during a prison riot. He wanted to be the "first one" in line, he jested; "what a waste" he missed out on the chance, for the woman was very beautiful.[10] He also joked that under martial law, he would protect from prosecution soldiers who raped up to three women. In Poland, amid significant rollbacks of reproductive rights constraining women's sexual and reproductive autonomy, a public campaign waged in newspaper ads urged Polish women to increase the national birthrate by breeding "like rabbits."[11] In Hungary, a new social compact with women citizens offered debt-free education as a widespread so-called opportunity on the condition women bear at least three children.[12] In the US, the appointment of Brett Kavanaugh to the Supreme Court in 2018, regardless of multiple very public credible assault allegations against him, repeated the misogynist debacle of appointing Clarence Thomas to the court in 1991. In both instances, lawmakers protected these prominent men and put the weight of state power behind them. In effect, at the highest levels, sexual violence against women was sanctioned by the state. When states sanction violence, they enact political terror.

Feminist Environmentalisms

Given this deluge of catastrophe, how to keep facing the battles in front of us? What tools do we need, including especially the relationships that will help nurture the coalition building needed in this moment? One very reassuring development that stands against both the social violence of misogyny and planetary violence is the massive recent global presence of women and their allies in the street.

Feminist actions worldwide led opposition to the rise of the Global Right. Commencing with actions against abortion bans in Poland in October of 2016 (#BlackFriday), which spread to Argentina, Peru, Chile, Mexico, Brazil, Italy, Turkey, Europe, and the United States, feminist militancy has answered crises of misogyny, which, in real-time campaigns, brought out the environmental activists among them.[13] Mobilizing diverse constituencies, the feminist vision of combined independent organizations entwines reproductive justice with climate justice, the work of ending violence and bolstering gun control, access to health care, just immigration policy, feminist economics and livable wages, and the need to establish kin beyond heteronormative conformity.[14] The Global Women's Marches—begun on the first day of Donald Trump's US presidency and attended that day by some five-plus million people worldwide from thirty countries and all continents—brought together familiar constituents with new diverse coalitions. The marches continue, as do the policy formulations of the march organizers. In January of 2019, the march leadership debuted the first of its kind feminist national policy platform for US contexts. The 2020 election cycle, specifically called "The Women's Agenda," conceived its priorities through concepts of intersectionality and calls for sovereignty, climate and economic justice, racial justice, and an end to war.[15]

If the above actions did not name authoritarianism as motivation, the fact is that most were set in motion by rising Global Right attacks on women. In real time and social media, protests signaled a turning point in collective consciousness about the scale of violence against women, murdered and disappeared women, and ending the protection of perpetrators of sexual assault. Arising from Global South actions and US women of color feminisms (#MeToo, #Time'sUp, #NiUnaMenos, #VivasNosQueremos, #NoTeCalles), these protests caused the international public sphere to open in historic ways to feminist speak-outs and demands for accountability. The International Women's Strike movement, innovating trade union tactics, called for "feminist strikes" or female work stoppages to put into relief the fact that reproductive and productive labors of women are undervalued and often unpaid even though they make the world go 'round. Their lack of value impoverishes women and is the principle contributing factor to female economic injustice and maternal poverty (#WeStrike, #Feminism4the99%, #NosotrasParamos).[16] An astonishing five million women in Spain alone turned out for the #huelgafeminista on International Women's Day in 2018.[17]

How are strikes over women's undervalued labor linked to "environment issues"? One answer might be that the only reason there is a question about it is because "environmentalism" has been conceived in the West through traditions of nature appreciation, and then institutionalized in eco-advocacy organizations into campaigns that "protect" revered sites, historically wilderness.[18] Beginning from other starting places, however, allows for a different understanding. Feminist environmentalism teaches us that the inferior social status of women, Indigenous, and racialized people, and the natural world and nonhuman world, are connected inferiorities. Not the same, but ideologically linked. That is, the oppression of Others, the undervaluing of their labors and bodies and knowledges, and the domination of or "rape" of nature and free use of animal life, are related problems. To fix one, one must fix the others. To fight the climate emergency, activist worlds desperately need to operationalize insights about the multiple systems of power producing harm. To be sure, some organizations are ahead of the curve. Research-rich and very established groups like Women's Environment and Development Organization (WEDO), and Women Deliver, not to mention the UN Commissions on Women, have written volumes about how the climate emergency disproportionately affects women and their children as well as how women and girls are the world's "best bet" for a healthy planet.[19]

Why the "best bet"? Because women are close to problems of food insecurity and unhealthy water and land and might contribute solutions others have not considered. Also, because they are close to problems, they are incentivized toward solutions. Were we citing feminist scholarship on "ecofeminism" or "material feminism," I would travel through Vandana Shiva and Maria Mies, Silvia Federici, Stacy Alaimo, Greta Gaard, and bell hooks. In surfing work specifically, I would point to Cori Schumacher's thinking about immersion and queer ecological subjectivity. To Rebecca Olive, who is writing a great deal out of her wonderful new "Moving Oceans" project. As she puts it, in ecofeminist fashion, "People are part of ocean and coastal ecologies: our health is intertwined." I'm so grateful for how much she's given as a collaborator to both the Institute for Women Surfers Europe as well as Oceania. Barbara Humberstone too has shared research with institute audiences about surf, ageism, and sport across the lifecycle. And Belinda Wheaton's voluminous work considers issues of equity, sovereignty, sport, and human well-being in blue spaces. Finally, on topics of decolonial tourism, Tara Ruttenberg writes with such clarity from Costa Rica as participant/observer/theorist, and as you will see in minute, we'll turn to Dina Gilio-Whitaker.[20] Since this talk is for a public audience, I'm not parsing scholarly genealogies into schools of particular thought. Instead, I'm hoping to make a point about planetary violence and violence against women (comprising the majority of inferior-status people) as two sides of the same coin of patriarchal and capitalist control of bodies and natural resources. The political *solution* to environmental exploitation will require attention to women's liberation, across its complex diversities, in a way that most environmental organizations have not yet known they must prioritize.

Let's talk more about surfeminism. The term *surfeminist* emerged out of the collective energy of the first Institute for Women Surfers meeting in Oceanside, California, in 2014. Since then, it has evolved and continues to evolve in its meanings. Surfeminism functions as a network connecting people, ideas, particular coastal geographies, online and real-time communities, and the microeconomies of the multibillion-dollar global surf industry.[21] The network provides communication, across geographies, with other like-minded surfers. Women and girls aren't alone, they aren't (as gets worried aloud often) "crazy" or "overreacting" when they observe injustices.

As a politics, surfeminism has emerged across many of the world's coastal places at this same moment that witnesses the arrival of the Global Right and accelerated crises of climate and misogyny. It is one of many new innovative feminisms finding their ways into global public life speaking back to political extremism. Through action campaigns, artistic ventures, education projects, community building, and groundbreaking organizations and media presence, activist women and girls who surf band together in favor of a range of interconnected feminist issues. In all evolutions, though, surfeminism is an instance of feminist environmentalism. Environmental projects run through every other political project. There are not neat distinctions between, for instance, urban ecology education in Oakland for local girls of color, those same girls surfing on the beaches of Pacifica or Half Moon Bay, and the difficulty their women of color leaders face competing for permits with established white male commercial proprietors with long-standing businesses that sell surf lessons.

A surfeminist rallying point most of the world over is protest against the objectification of female surfers in global subcultural media and the typing of female surfers as blond and heterosexy. Why can't surf media get behind promoting visuals of diverse women actually surfing (not modeling)? Answer: profits from the sale of women's heterosexy images are prioritized over women's dignity and well-being. Nonmodeling visuals are extensively available in surfeminist photography, film, video, small magazines, art, and private Facebook pages, including archives of work created by some of us here. Elizabeth Pepin Silva alone has an archive twenty-five years deep.[22] Dayla Soul, the filmmaker, also here, created an instant classic in the film *It Ain't Pretty*. Welsh cold-water-loving women of Institute Europe created *Daughters of the Sea*. There are so many other examples.

By refusing, as surfeminists, to see ourselves through the images dominant surf culture sells of women and girls, the alternative worlds people actually inhabit, in which they live their lives, open up. The beauty and well-being of a water-life opens, which is at the core of the surfeminist archive. And so too do the places open where women are challenged. Surfeminism brings to light problems of accessing ocean and beach spaces and accessing surf economies. *Access* should be understood broadly, not just as fences that keep out surfers but as legacies of historic exclusions. Lack of access shows racial injustice, blindness to Indigenous sovereignty, homophobia, and inequality in competitive surf purses, sponsorship, surf livelihoods, and the lineup. Access issues toward those who are "different" show when new leadership steps up to change professional organizations, environmental priorities, and oceanside communities.

A historical novelty of surfeminist knowledges is that they originated in and now travel across the world's spaces, by working self-consciously between the publics of university workers and the publics of global surfing. Speaking personally, I didn't start out in 2010, as the author of a book, trying to create any of this. It emerged dynamically, in collaboration, bit by bit. In the panic after Trump's election in 2016, the international forum *Signs: A Journal of Women in Culture and Society* urged feminist scholars to bridge academic and larger feminist publics and create new movements.[23] Surfeminism and the Institute for Women Surfers became attempts at bridging and building new movements. From its inception the institute set political goals related to racial diversity, queer surf subjectivities, equity in women's competitive surfing, and decolonial surfing, all informed by environmental justice perspectives. We could put it this way: that the institute understood "issues of access" to apply also and especially to ourselves. We also set goals for accessibility in how to talk to each other. Fusing university and nonuniversity knowledges in the service of local/global feminist social change means valuing "street knowledge" and grassroots expertise while also valuing the conceptual work and more formal research findings of university people. To communicate these distinct knowledges in language that is nonspecialist and therefore more accessible is often wrapped up in other justice issues. Which is to say that the fusing of knowledges between publics is a beautiful goal if very imperfectly realized.

For a conference like this one at San Diego State, which has many scholars but many others who work elsewhere than universities, the between-publics aspirations of our work together is important to get as right as we can. Collaborations require relational skill and are crucial if the knowledges produced and activities put in play are to remain informed by and, especially, accountable to diverse constituencies. What has helped us with these imperfect exchanges is to reframe fundamentally what the institute "is." The institute is not an "it." The institute is an "us," relational. The "us" cares about across-geography cooperation, linking feminists to one another around the world. We care about each other and care for each other's knowledges.

Coalitional Relations

When our colleague Dina Gilio-Whitaker works to decolonize surfing or talks about settler privilege, reminding us that everywhere one surfs in the US is Indian Country, she's also talking from histories about Indigenous women's leadership in environmental justice across generations. All of this work is available in her new book *As Long as Grass Grows: The Indigenous Fight for Environmental Justice, from Colonization to Standing Rock*. In other words, the overlapping of issues, the mixed-together aspects of feminist

Indigenous environmental justice work, is evident. Moreover, she is making herself available to coalitional friendship as she teaches us about LaDonna Brave Bull Allard, a Standing Rock Sioux tribal historian and the founder of Sacred Stone Camp. In terms of surfing, what Gilio-Whitaker frames is the idea of territoriality as an example of white masculine settler privilege. This kind of decolonial insight is a treasure for us in the institute but also here at this conference. Environmental injustice begins with settler dispossession of Indigenous lands and white superiority and the installation of settler gender hierarchies which deauthorize Indigenous women's revered communal stature. That starting place, detailed in *As Long as Grass Grows*, is a wholly different diagnosis of an environmental problem.

Taking surfeminist briefs in other different directions, there are the singular leaders Rhonda Harper, whom I mentioned at the outset, and the public historian Alison Rose Jefferson. Both have been key figures to urge commemoration of the so-called "Inkwell" historic site on the Santa Monica beachfront, a place famous in African American leisure and recreation circles in the era of Jim Crow. The justice issues here are not simply "inclusion," or more women in the lineup or the pages of surf magazines. They involve Black women, actors of the global majority, taking the leadership stage at every level of surf commerce and culture. The point for feminist environmental visions of the future is to get behind these global-majority leaders, women whose ideas and political visions should direct us.

Returning to the idea noted earlier of women as the "best bet" for a healthy future, I see surfeminism joining with other feminists who support people of global majority as leaders of our justice programs. We need new voices, leaders. As I prepared examples of surfeminist environmentalisms I could share tonight, I realized it's impossible to survey them all with any proper due. Some deal with the meanings of issues of access as I've been describing them. I could detail more the work in the US of Cassie Comley, Jennifer Savage, Olivia Van Damme, Marley Reynosa, and so many activists and researchers who are putting their hearts and minds to this moment. Others, like Apryl Boyle, talk about reconceiving "environment" so we think of sharks, large marine mammals, and climate justice. From Oceania, I'd mention one coral farmer, Risu Kalotiti, a surfer and activist, who heads up a girls-surf initiative called Solwata Sistas near Port Vila, the capital of Vanuatu, an archipelago country of eighty islands in the South Pacific. When Kalotiti talked about coral restoration with us at the Institute Oceania, she talked about warming seas, bleaching, outbreaks of crown of thorn starfish, level-5 hurricanes, plastics pollution, and her own luck to come from a family where the father protects his daughter's right to surf.[24] That is, feminist environmentalism for her conjoins discussions of patriarchal authority, histories of coloniality/postcoloniality and Indigeneity, and rich capitalist states' petrocultures and tourism.

I spoke earlier about "issues of access" as important sites for feminist intervention. Hidden or intangible barriers to access index for us sites of social violence (racism, sexism, homophobia, settler occupation). They are sites for democratic struggle and battles for sovereignty. The ideal of beaches as spaces of democracy expresses an important if complex justice program. Access is a right protected by the California Coastal Act, as Californians here will know very well. That right, which is a civil rights mandate, is also understood to be an environmental justice right, which can put into law protections for sacred Indigenous sites. Of course, these kinds of rights, premised on democratic institutions and representation, are precisely what authoritarianism assaults.

Moving toward a close, I want to renew attention to conceptual points as takeaways about feminist environmentalism. In the institute trainings, we often talk about the power of concepts to help us interpret information. I am trying for that principle here. In Western philosophy—which underwrites official knowledges in universities—the world is separated into realms of culture and nature, mind and body, male and female, civilized and primitive. Those realms are not equally valuable. One is better than the other: culture must rule over nature, as mind must rule over body, and civilization over the primitive. It's important to notice these are gendered orderings, racialized orderings. Culture and mind associate to maleness and whiteness, and they "supervise" female nature and body. Of course, Western thought is not the only system of thought in the world, or in this room. We have many among us who can and are teaching us, as they have today, about Native Hawaiian thought, about Indigenous thought of Turtle

Island (North America), about traditional resource custodianship. Still, Western philosophy is the authoritative order of university knowledges and underwrites colonial, patriarchal, and racial capitalist logics. We who want governments to radically reorient policy are in a high-stakes fight now with these very ideas and hierarchies, and it helps to identify the fight clearly.

Under racial capitalism, nature's bounty or the ability to generate life is assumed to belong to those who can control it. Like nature, women too are subject to battles over control of their reproductive ability. Male domination of courts, families, economies, churches, medicine, religion, knowledge, political organizations, all of it, male domination vies for the upper hand. Women's reproductive labor, the labor of care and of reproduction, meaning of raising children but also reproducing social life—the world's most intensive forms of labor—represents not only a civil rights issue but an environmental justice issue. Women's rights and the rights of nature, so to speak, are tethered to each other. Neither women's bodies nor the body of nature are unlimited in what they can give.

Clearly, we live in urgent times. Misogyny on a new global scale, climate crises, challenges to democracy worldwide and in the US. To deal with any one of these issues, we'll need to deal with them all. New alliances are essential, including of mainstream eco-organizations with feminist environmentalists. Since I know so many of us are very committed environmentalists, consider supporting women's liberation efforts as another way to do your environment work. Not "including women" per se, but fighting for justice, for an end to sexism and male domination. Teach others to notice how assaults on women and planet are part of a continuum of dominating logics. The most reliable way to ensure new authorities in positions of leadership is to not reappoint the same groups of people who have brought us the problems we face. We need the leadership of women and people of color and Indigenous people. The Women's Environment and Development Organization (WEDO) sees itself as doing advocacy work, which includes, importantly, the training of allies and of capacity building among new constituencies about links between gender equity and positive environmental change. Among us here, Dina Gilio-Whitaker in *As Long as Grass Grows* urges productive alliance building between environmental justice projects. She also is doing her own consulting now, in that vein.

The IWS also has been building alliances, feminist alliances, and we have principles for how to help along what often are challenging relational dynamics between women. Do not compete with each other as women, make our relationships as important as our politics and our projects. We need each other for this battle we face; we must care for one another. Our male allies can be thoughtful about these challenges and remind us to not be confused about our priorities when relations are tricky. There is no single answer to complex global problems. There are many right answers. Part of what I hope to have happen by coming to the conference this weekend is to build connections, create new forms of kin, so we have better conversations and thinking and relationships. I would urge anyone to reach out to me to talk more. I would again like to thank Jess, David, and Mike for reaching out to me. I look forward to knowing everyone better and fighting the good fight together. Thank you.

It's a welcome charge to write briefly as we go to press in 2024. Brevity allows one to write a list; a list seems manageable. A global pandemic outbreak, over but continuing. In the US, a massive reckoning with white supremacy following the police murder of George Floyd. Voting rights under siege. All-out war on women's reproductive autonomy and health made legal by the Supreme Court overturning abortion as a constitutional right. Like the January 6 insurrection in Washington, DC, these events signal the continuing slide of the world's most recognized democracy into authoritarianism. The fact former president Trump faces four criminal indictments and is nonetheless the Republican Party's nominee for the 2024 general election is further evidence. Surely it is better that, since this keynote was first delivered in 2018, a US presence now sat the tables of the 2021–23 COP26, COP27, and COP28 Climate Conferences. It is better too that the words *transition away from fossil fuels* were made official. At the same time, the word I continue to read most often is *insufficient*. Some leaders of small island nations at COP28 did not attend for the closing gavel, while some cried openly as the gavel fell.

We live in ever more dangerous political times, including brutal new wars. Surprises, good ones, are out there, including surfeminists who correspond over WhatsApp about the joys of surf life, a new book by Dani Roberston on Dark Skies, a couple new babies, two grad students now PhDs. Still. There's been Brexit chaos, pandemic illnesses, Australian bushfire updates and reports about California rogue fires and atmospheric rivers, so-called "rivers in the sky," dumping huge amounts of rain. Always also whatever latest outrage about sexist images or leadership denied in surf organizations. The smatterings of writing and public discussion about authoritarianism available in 2019 have grown exponentially. *On Tyranny*, by Timothy Snyder, widely considered a primer with lessons for survival and resistance.[25] More recently he is writing about fascism, democracy, and the Ukraine War and lecturing in Ukrainian in Kiev and other Ukrainian cities. *Strongmen*, by Ruth Ben-Ghiat, equips readers with a playbook for authoritarian regime-making.[26]

There is no excuse again for being caught so flat-footed. If one considers the clarity of these thinkers to be a good tiding, perhaps then more good tidings come from two additional *Atlantic* pieces. One by Anne Applebaum, "The Bad Guys Are Winning," and the other, Barton Gellman's "Trump's Next Coup Has Already Begun."[27] Between them, they alert readers to new strategy-making networks between global authoritarians, and they alert us to how much better the GOP is positioned today to undermine the next US elections. That is, they prepare us well for difficulty.

Returning to surfeminism. Recent pandemic times have focused people on local living, staying put. But not on staying quiet. After George Floyd's murder, a series of paddle-outs around the world showed solidarity. The idea for the paddle-outs gesture came from Rhonda Harper. The Institute for Women Surfers, which paused activities and a planned conference in 2020 due to the pandemic, is stirring back to life. A Google search of "surfeminism" shows modest results, though international usage of the term in French, English, Spanish, German, Icelandic, and perhaps others I don't know about, is interesting and hopeful. In fact, we cannot know what comes from efforts that begin in one part of the world and travel. What we can know is to keep at it, in the places we live. Paraphrasing the Zapatistas, to make a world where many worlds fit.

Notes

1 My thinking on coalition is shaped by the ever-relevant "Coalition Politics" by Reagon, the confrontation with her own white racism of Pratt in "Identity: Skin Blood Heart," the tempered sense of being "on the way" to coalition of Ruíz and Dotson in "On the Politics of Coalition," and the affirmation that "the substance of political work is not always about 'getting it right, but about committing to the process,'" which King borrows from Amadahy and Lawrence in "Indigenous Peoples and Black People in Canada: Settler or Allies?" (page 66). King, "Interview with Dr. Tiffany Lethabo King." The practice of a coalitional feminism is at the center of my forthcoming *Living West as Feminists: Conversations about the Where of Us* (2024).

2 Beinart, "The New Authoritarians."

3 Gogoi, "Analysis."

4 McDonald, "Climate Kings."

5 Wu, "Shutting Down US Climate Action."

6 Kamal, "Climate Migrants Might Reach One Billion by 2050."

7 Beinart, "The New Authoritarians."

8 Alter, "Brazilian Politician Tells Congresswoman She's 'Not Worthy' of Sexual Assault."

9 Ellis-Petersen, "Philippines."

10 Ellis-Petersen, "Philippines."

11 Beinart, "The New Authoritarians."

12 Beinart, "The New Authoritarians."

13 I am drawing trajectories of countries' histories from, among other sites, Arruzza, Bhattacharya, and Fraser, *Feminism for the 99%*.

14 For more information about #feministresistance, please see "#FeministResistance," *Signs: Journal of Women in Culture and Society*, http://signsjournal.org/feministresistance. Also please see the ranging conversation found in Enloe et al., "Ask a Feminist."

15 Women's March, "Women's March: Agenda 2019."

16 Arruzza, Bhattacharya, and Fraser, *Feminism for the 99%*, 1–13.

17 Carrasquilla, "Manifiesto 8M"; and Jones, "More Than 5m Join Spain's 'Feminist Strike,' Unions Say."

18 A classic essay on this topic is Cronon, "The Trouble with Wilderness."

19 For the "best bet," see advocacy organization Women Deliver, "Invest in Women to Tackle Climate Change and Conserve the Environment," accessed June 3, 2024, https://womendeliver.org/investment/invest-women-tackle-climate-change-conserve-environment.

20 See Alaimo, *Bodily Natures*; Mies and Shiva, *Ecofeminism*; Gaard, "Ecofeminism Revisited"; Federici, *Re-enchanting the World*; and hooks, *Belonging*. Schumacher, "My Mother Is a Fish"; Rebecca Olive, Moving Oceans, accessed May 6, 2024, https://movingoceans.com (quote drawn from landing page); also listen to podcast by Olive, "Ecofeminism, Sports, and Leisure Culture with Dr. Rebecca Olive." For ecofeminist and nonhuman nature relations, see Rebecca Olive, "Living with Sharks," Moving Oceans, accessed June 3, 2024, https://movingoceans.com/multi-species-communities/living-with-sharks. On blue spaces, see, Olive and Wheaton, "Understanding Blue Spaces"; Humberstone, "Engagements with Nature"; Ruttenberg, "Is Sustainable Tourism Possible?"; also see Ruttenberg's Tarantula Surf platform, accessed June 3, 2024, www.tarantulasurf.com; and Gilio-Whitaker, *As Long as Grass Grows*.

21 For more, see Comer, "What Leisure?."

22 For selections of this work, see "Exposure: Surf Photographer and Filmmaker, Elizabeth Pepin Silva," Surf Channel Television Network, YouTube, accessed June 3, 2024, www.youtube.com/watch?v=xCKaxeLFPoc.

23 See "#FeministResistance."

24 Please see Institute for Women Surfers, "2019 Research Report."

25 Snyder, *On Tyranny*.

26 Ben-Ghiat, *Strongmen*.

27 Applebaum, "The Bad Guys Are Winning"; and Gellman, "Trump's Next Coup Has Already Begun."

Bibliography

Agnew, Megan. "Big Wave Women: Meet the Female Surfers Fighting Sexism on the Beaches." *Times* (UK), April 28, 2019.

Alaimo, Stacy. *Bodily Natures: Science, Environment, and the Material Self*. Bloomington: Indiana University Press, 2010.

Alter, Charlotte. "Brazilian Politician Tells Congresswoman She's 'Not Worthy' of Sexual Assault." *Time*, December 11, 2014. https://time.com/3630922/brazil-politics-congresswoman-rape-comments.

Applebaum, Anne. "The Bad Guys Are Winning." *Atlantic*, November 15, 2021. www.theatlantic.com/magazine/archive/2021/12/the-autocrats-are-winning/620526.

Arruzza, Cinzia, Tithi Bhattacharya, and Nancy Fraser. *Feminism for the 99%: A Manifesto*. London: Verso, 2019.

Beinart, Peter. "The New Authoritarians Are Waging War on Women." *Atlantic*, January/ February 2019.

Ben-Ghiat, Ruth. *Strongmen: How They Rise, Why They Succeed, How They Fall*. London: Profile Books, 2020.

Carrasquilla, Olmedo. "Manifiesto 8M. Hacia la Huelga Feminista 2019." *Radiotemblor*, November 2, 2019. www.radiotemblor.org/manifiesto-8m-hacia-la-huelga-feminista-2019.

Comer, Krista. "Beaches as Spaces of Democracy: Center Hosts Women Surfers Conference." The Bill Lane Center for the American West, December 15, 2017.

———. *Living West as Feminists: Conversations about the Where of Us*. Lincoln: University of Nebraska Press, 2024.

———. "Surfeminism, Critical Regionalism, Public Scholarship." In *The Critical Surf Studies Reader*, edited by Dexter Zavalza Hough-Snee and Alexander Sotelo Eastman, 235–62. Durham, NC: Duke University Press, 2017.

———. *Surfer Girls in the New World Order*. Durham, NC: Duke University Press. 2010.

———. "What Leisure? Surfeminism in an Era of Trump." *Palgrave Communications* 5, no. 42 (2019): 1–6. https://doi.org/10.1057/s41599-019-0250-9.

Cronon, William. "The Trouble with Wilderness; Or, Getting Back to the Wrong Nature." *Environmental History* 1, no. 1 (January 1996): 7–28.

Ellis-Petersen, Hannah. "Philippines: Rodrigo Duterte Orders Soldiers to Shoot Female Rebels 'In the Vagina.'" *Guardian*, February 12, 2018. www.theguardian.com/world/2018/feb/13/philippines-rodrigo-duterte-orders-soldiers-to-shoot-female-rebels-in-the-vagina.

Enloe, Cynthia, Agnieszka Graff, Ratna Kapur, and Suzanna Danuta Walters. "Ask a Feminist: Cynthia Enloe Discusses Gender and the Rise of the Global Right with Agnieszka Graff, Ratna Kapur, and Suzanna Danuta Walters." *Signs: Journal of Women in Culture and Society*, July 5, 2018. http://signsjournal.org/cynthia-enloe.

Federici, Silvia. *Re-enchanting the World: Feminism and the Politics of the Commons*. Oakland, CA: PM Press, 2018.

Gaard, Greta. "Ecofeminism Revisited: Rejecting Essentialism and Re-placing Species in a Material Feminist Environmentalism." *Feminist Formations* 23, no 2 (2011): 26–53.

Gellman, Barton. "Trump's Next Coup Has Already Begun." *Atlantic*, December 6, 2021. www.theatlantic.com/magazine/archive/2022/01/january-6-insurrection-trump-coup-2024-election/620843.

Gilio-Whitaker, Dina. *As Long as Grass Grows: The Indigenous Fight for Environmental Justice, from Colonization to Standing Rock*. Boston: Beacon Press, 2019.

Gogoi, Pallavi. "Analysis: How the Rise of the Far Right Threatens Democracy Worldwide." NPR, January 21, 2019. www.npr.org/2019/01/21/687128474/analysis-how-the-rise-of-the-far-right-threatens-democracy-worldwide.

hooks, bell. *Belonging: A Culture of Place*. New York: Taylor and Francis, 2008.

Humberstone, Barbara. "Engagements with Nature: Ageing and Windsurfing," 158–69. Accessed May 6, 2024. www.semanticscholar.org/paper/Engagements-with-nature%3A-ageing-and-windsurfing-Humberstone/727e05d5be09b50ea321868odb442c3790232164.

Institute for Women Surfers. "2019 Research Report." Accessed May 6, 2024. www.instituteforwomensurfers.org/institute-2019/2019-research-report.

Jones, Sam. "More Than 5m Join Spain's 'Feminist Strike,' Unions Say." *Guardian*, March 8, 2018. www.theguardian.com/world/2018/mar/08/spanish-women-give-up-work-for-a-day-in-first-feminist-strike.

Kamal, Baher. "Climate Migrants Might Reach One Billion by 2050." Inter Press Service News Agency, August 21, 2017. www.ipsnews.net/2017/08/climate-migrants-might-reach-one-billion-by-2050/.

King, Tiffany Lethabo. "Interview with Dr. Tiffany Lethabo King." *feral feminisms: Complicities, Connections, and Struggles: Critical Transnational Feminist Analysis of Settler Colonialism* 4 (Summer 2015): 64–68. https://feralfeminisms.com/lethabo-king.

lisahunter, ed. *Surfing, Sex, Genders, and Sexualities*. New York: Routledge, 2018.

McDonald, Samuel Miller. "Climate Kings: How a New Generation of Authoritarian Leaders Are Using Climate Change to Seize Power." *New Republic*, July 30, 2018. https://newrepublic.com/article/148861/climate-change-authoritarian-leaders.

Mies, Maria, and Vandana Shiva. *Ecofeminism*. London: Zed Books, 2014.

Olive, Rebecca. "Ecofeminism, Sports, and Leisure Culture with Dr. Rebecca

Olive." *Transnational Perspectives* podcast, March 17, 2021. https://www.youtube.com/watch?app=desktop&v=rUmfmOKz88s&t=1490s.

Olive, Rebecca, and Belinda Wheaton. "Understanding Blue Spaces: Sport, Bodies, Wellbeing, and the Sea." *Journal of Sports and Social Issues* 45, no. 1: 3–19. https://doi.org/10.1177/0193723520950549.

Pratt, Minnie Bruce. "Identity: Skin Blood Heart." In *Yours in Struggle: Three Feminist Perspectives on Anti-Semitism and Racism*, by Elly Bulkin, Minnie Bruce Pratt, and Barbara Smith, 1–57. Chicago: Long Haul Press, 1984.

Reagon, Bernice Johnson. "Coalition Politics: Turning the Century." In *Home Girls: A Black Feminist Anthology*, edited by Barbara Smith, 354–68. New York: Kitchen Table, Women of Color Press, 1983.

Ruíz, Elena, and Kristie Dotson. "On the Politics of Coalition." *Feminist Philosophy Quarterly* 3, no. 2 (July 6, 2017). DOI: 10.5206/fpq/2017.2.4.

Ruttenberg, Tara. "Is Sustainable Surf Tourism Possible?" *Second Breakfast* podcast with Emma Roggenkamp, June 11, 2023. https://surfwithamigas.com/is-sustainable-surf-tourism-possible-with-tara-ruttenburg.

Schumacher, Cori. "My Mother Is a Fish: From Stealth Feminism to Surfeminism." In *The Critical Surf Studies Reader*, edited by Dexter Zavalza Hough-Snee and Alexander Sotelo Eastman, 284–302. Durham, NC: Duke University Press, 2017.

Snyder, Timothy. *On Tyranny: Twenty Lessons from the Twentieth Century*. New York: Tim Duggan Books, 2017.

Women's March. "Women's March: Agenda 2019," last modified 2023. https://assets.ctfassets.net/2691xhtiliof/7DCoPyhDZKncrZS1wldcOw/00f4918d3074fb2af94cc4fd9749ad60/2019Women-sAgenda_small.pdf.

Wu, Brandon. "Shutting Down US Climate Action Is about More Than Climate Change Denial." *act!ionaid*, March 28, 2017. www.actionaidusa.org/blog/shutting-down-us-climate-action-is-about-much-more-than-just-climate-denial.

PART II
BO(A)RDERLANDS

5

Apane niwii-nanda-gikendaanan (I Will Always Seek to Learn These Things)

NICHOLAS REO

I have been a beginner surfer for over thirty years and a beginner Anishinaabe language speaker for about twenty-five years.[1] My struggles and successes in both pursuits have been remarkably similar. And I finally sorted out that paying attention to one helps the other. My surfing breakthroughs are helping me with my Indigenous language work, and vice versa. The connections between these learning domains are more than analogous or a helpful intellectual connection. Being a surfer and being an Anishinaabe man who is actively learning my Indigenous language shapes how I carry myself in and out of the water and in and out of Anishinaabemowin (Anishinaabe language) circles. I enact both of these knowledges and energize mind-body-spirit connections when I study, when I practice, when I surf, and when I speak my community's original language.

Noticing these connections has accelerated my learning. I still lack confidence, make loads of mistakes, speak and surf awkwardly, and am constantly having to relearn the basics. But I understand and speak Anishinaabemowin and surf better now than ever before. And after stagnating for decades, I am starting to loosen up and feel more fluid in and out of the water.

I have transformed my relationship with Anishinaabemowin and with the sea through culturally specific heart-mind adjustments that have helped me to enjoy the learning processes immensely, no matter how gradual the learning curves are.

Surfing and Indigenous Language Revitalization as Decolonial Spaces

Language revitalization and surfing can be decolonial spaces for Indigenous peoples and for our non-Indigenous neighbors. As Kanaka scholar Isaiah Helekunihi Walker points out in his 2011 text, *Waves of Resistance: Surfing and History in Twentieth-Century Hawaiʻi*, Kanaka Māoli have consistently and effectively used *ka poʻina nalu* (surf zones) as spaces of resistance to settler colonial structures such as policies intended to disenfranchise Indigenous Hawaiians. *Ka poʻina* are zones where Kanaka Māoli and other Indigenous wave riders figuratively and sometimes literally punch back against space-invading settlers in the lineup and onshore.

One of the many ways settler populations and their governments have systematically attempted to eliminate or neutralize Indigenous populations is by attacking our languages. Language erasure was codified through policies like the Indian Civilization Act of 1819 in the United States, violently punctuated through corporal punishment in the residential schools, and continues today through the ideology of monolingualism.[2] Ojibwe scholar Anton Treuer explains the importance of Indigenous languages in *The Language Warrior's Manifesto: How to Keep Our Languages Alive No Matter the Odds* (2020), stating that "nothing grounds a person or a community more powerfully in indigeneity than carrying the tribal language."[3] Historically, non-Indigenous populations demonstrated a clear understanding of the centrality of our languages to our cultures by focusing so violently on monolingualism. When acts of physical violence and attempted genocide proved ineffective, settler colonial logics of elimination assumed that killing our languages would kill us, culturally. But we have resisted and are resisting this ontological violence by treasuring our remaining speakers, creating Indigenous language nests, building language-immersion schools, and more. Linda Tuhiwai Smith describes Indigenous-language work as one of the primary Indigenous projects of decolonization.[4]

Routes through an Anishinaabek Sea of Islands

I was raised primarily in the suburbs of Detroit, Michigan. My mom is Anishinaabe, and my dad is white, with genealogical ties to Croatia and Italy. So how does a mixed Anishinaabe who grew up a twelve-hour drive from the ocean fall in love with surfing?

My mom moved us to the Detroit suburbs when I was entering middle school in the mid-1980s. My friend Mike Barrett had an early version of a snowboard called the Burton Backhill that we would ride at the sledding spots in our neighborhood. Technically it was a snow surfer or "snurfer." I skated a little in those days too, and between skateboarding and riding Mike's Burton Backhill, I was getting the feel for sliding sideways. Ski areas started allowing snowboards on their lifts around this same time, and I have been an avid snowboarder ever since they "legalized" the activity in the 1980s.

In 1988, when I was fifteen, I moved to Naples, Florida, to live with my dad, who had moved there a few years prior. As a snowboarder and skater, I fit in with the surf crowd and quickly became friends with Chris Soto and Brad Schenevar. These two men became my lifelong friends and surf mentors, and I cherish them both to this day. Most of my surf experiences over the past thirty-plus years have been in the water with Chris. Brad passed away in 2001, and whenever I'm surfing, it feels like he's in the water with me. My connection to surfing started with day trips to the East Coast with Brad and Chris. We would drive three hours or more to surf spots like Spanish House, a local surf break on the Sebastian Inlet. Neither of these friends ever surfed competitively. They are soul surfers who, to me, embody surfing and the fluidity of the ocean, two men who made life decisions that enable/d them to do what they love and be in the ocean as much as possible.

My connection to the sea runs deeper than those East Coast surf trips in 1988 and 1989. All aspects of my genealogy connect me to the sea, including my European and North American roots. I haven't learned enough about my European roots to say with confidence whether my Croatian and Italian relations identify more with the mountains, the coast, or both. I am much more in touch with my Anishinaabe genealogy and will explain how the Anishinaabek are both freshwater and saltwater coastal peoples.

The central portion of Anishinaabewaki (Anishinaabe homelands) is located in the Great Lakes region, known for its vast, unsalted waters. It is a watery place, covered by scores of rivers, inland lakes, ponds, wetlands, and most prominently the five Great Lakes that make up one-fifth of our planet's fresh surface water. Gichigami (Lake Superior) alone covers an area of eighty-two thousand square kilometers, and it has but one outflow, the powerful St. Mary's River at Baawiting. Baawiting (place of the rapids) is the geographical and spiritual epicenter for my particular Anishinaabek tribal nation, the Sault Ste. Marie Tribe of Chippewa Indians.

Since time immemorial, across all of Anishinaabewaki, *gete*-Anishinaabek (Anishinaabek of long ago) traveled extensively along trail systems that followed our rivers and lakeshores, and on water in our *jiimaanan* (canoes). *Wiigwaasi-jiimaanan* (birchbark canoes) are an ancient Anishinaabek technology that, from a performance perspective, rivals any flat-water canoe ever built. But thinking of our *jiimaanan* merely as technology does not do justice to the deep connections these watercrafts facilitate between Anishinaabek and *nibi* (water). Our *wiigwaasi-jiimaanan* and our *mitigo-jiimaanan* (dugout canoes), like the wave-riding vehicles built by other Indigenous peoples around the world, actively facilitate and participate in our intimate relationship with *nibi*. As Vicente Diaz and others have pointed out, Indigenous watercrafts help create important three-way bonds between land, sea, and Indigenous peoples both physically and metaphorically.[5]

For our Anishinaabek, the land connection in this three-way relationship is provided through the gifts of trees. Trees are generous and intelligent beings. They are spiritual entities and our first relations.[6] Anishinaabek build *wiigwaasi-jiimaanan* using birch bark for the skin, ash or other hardwood splints for ribs and gunwales, spruce roots for lashing, and pitch for waterproofing. We honor these gifts from our enrooted relations by actively using our *jiimaanan* on the water. As long as we keep using our *jiimaanan* and honoring these gifts, the spirits from harvested trees carry on with us on our canoe journeys.

Anishinaabek have a deep, loving relationship with water. Like trees, water is also a generous ancestor. The gifts of water are so central to life on Earth that Anishinaabek regard water as life. As Minogiizhgad, an Anishinaabe language warrior from the Walpole Island First Nation, explains, "In our language when we say bi—just that sound alone—it acknowledges life. There's something about that sound that connected with our people, our ancestors, as they understood it. It was so clear. Bi, nibi. In our language when we say 'nibi,' we're referring to water. But it's so much more than that. Nibi is life."[7] In this way, *jiimaanan* are an important part of Anishinaabek coastal relationalities.

Hundreds of millions of years ago, this same region had its own oceanic coastlines. Whenever I see a Petoskey stone, fossilized rugose coral found in the region, I am reminded of my kinship to the sea. *Asiniig* (stones) are ancient relatives to the Anishinaabek. When I stare into the fossilized markings tattooed on the bodies of these ancient, spiritual beings, I see a kaleidoscope of surfable barrels. I imagine our Anishinaabe homelands as a marine coastline rich in hollow waves. I see ancestral fishes showing off their best moves while being cheered onshore by the wind-swept, fringed arms of ferns. Perhaps our most ancient relatives, like *name* (sturgeon) and *giizhik* (northern white cedar) carry memories of Devonian surf.

The Anishinaabek migrated to the Great Lakes in long-ago times. Our oral history and ceremonies remind us that we originated on the East Coast among the Wabanaki.[8] When I lived in Gedakina from 2012 to 2023, I often thought about the *gete*-Anishinaabek who once lived there, and that thought helped me feel connected.[9] I would imagine *gete*-Anishinaabek as wave riders, despite how unlikely or unsupported that idea is. Prophets visited these ancient ones and foretold great suffering. Those compelled by the prophesies made a long journey to find a new homeland in the Great Lakes, during a time when life was peaceful and in balance. What characterized the good life these ancient ones had cultivated back then? Maybe they were living in surf villages near the best waves in Gedakina. Picture the Atlantic aunties doing cheater fives on ironwood logs covered in brightly colored floral patterns. Uncles waiting patiently out back to paddle *jiimaanan* into the biggest set waves. Sounds like *mino-bi-*

maadiziwin to me![10] For those who heeded the warnings of the prophets, were some of the most treasured relationships they left behind with the waves of rocky point breaks? I'm using my imagination to conjure these wave-riding ancestors, but I am certain of our fluidity as Anishinaabek. The Anishinaabek are a dynamic people. Parts of our collective anchor us through place-based relationalities, while others are constantly moving, expanding worlds, building family relations, and responsibly traversing our own Sea of Islands.[11]

These may sound like a surfer's random daydreams, but they have real meaning as reminders of the connection my people have to the sea. I am also connected to the sea as a human born from water. I feel connected because "we sweat and cry saltwater, so we know that the ocean is really in our blood."[12] Agamiing-bemaadizid nindaw wenji-mishiikenh dibendaagoziyaan (I am a coastal person because snapping turtle is the one [clan] I belong to).

Geget niminwendaan nanda-gikendamaan (I Really Like the Pursuit of Knowledge)

Shortly after high school graduation, my friend Chris Soto moved from Florida to California's Central Coast to be near better waves and the West Coast branch of his family. For the next two decades plus, I visited Soto in California about every other year, and surfing was a central focus of our visits. Those trips were the only times I surfed during that long chapter of my life. We would surf intensely, often more than once per day. I was immersed in surf for these brief periods, trips that punctuated months to multiyear spans with no surf. With hindsight, I now recognize that progression in something as challenging as surfing requires regular practice—as in multiple times per week, over an extended period of time. Like Chris did with his move to the West Coast, you have to make adjustments to create space in your life for surfing if you want to learn (table 1).

In the winter of 1992 or 1993, Brad, Chris, and I met up in Los Angeles and worked our way up the coast to Big Sur, California, surfing along the way. At the far northern end of this trip, we camped in Big Sur with Chris's

TABLE 1. Tips that apply in surfing and Indigenous language learning

ADVICE	IN SURFING	IN LANGUAGE LEARNING
Make space in your life for these practices.	Surf as often as you can. Live near a surf break if possible. When you can't surf, focus on conditioning and muscle memory out of the water.	Speak the language as often as you can. Live in communities and/or households with other speakers. When you aren't around speakers, practice verbs and build useful vocabulary.
Reducing chaos and complexity gives you a chance to succeed.	Practice on a big, stable surfboard in swell and crowd conditions that are appropriate for your abilities and aren't intimidating.	Focus on a particular type of verb and/or discourse context (e.g., kitchen talk); initiate conversations focused on what you are practicing.
Train, and then practice.	Surfing offers very little repetition, making it hard to hone skills. Build surf-specific skills, balance, and strength by training out of the water.	Study basic grammar and vocab. Tune your ear by listening for patterns in fluent speech. Then practice what you've studied in conversation with advanced speakers.
Occasionally push beyond your comfort zone.	Surf in bigger swells OR bigger crowds once in a while, taking appropriate safety precautions.†	Join in conversations with advanced speakers in a variety of contexts.
Find spaces to practice where you feel comfortable making mistakes. Relax, and have fun.	Spend time surfing in learner zones, places where surf schools take beginners, even if you aren't a brand-new surfer. Nobody cares how good you are at surfing, especially in these spaces.	Use your language when communicating with first relations in spaces like forests or while surfing. The whales and trees aren't judging how well you speak your language.
Making mistakes is a critical part of learning.	Learn to like falling. Enjoying your falls will make them less scary and help you relax. You surf better, progress faster, and are less likely to get hurt when you relax.	Let go of your insecurities and guilt about not being fluent. It's not your fault, and all that matters is that you try to participate. Don't take yourself too seriously.
Record and observe yourself to identify areas for improvement.	Have someone film your surfing occasionally, even if you hate watching the footage. Compare your movements to other surfers, and use your coach's eye to look for areas for improvement.	Record and listen to yourself speaking regularly. Make recordings of yourself saying sentences that fluent speakers have previously recorded so you can compare your speech to theirs.

TABLE 1. *continued*

Unconditional love is at the core of your relationships.	The ocean is an ancient, living ancestor who loves you deeply. Accept her unconditional love, and relax as a grandchild would when visiting their grandparents.	The spirit of your language knows and loves you and wants you to engage. Your community and ancestors are all rooting for you to learn your language and love you no matter how well or poorly you speak it.

† This tip needs to be approached with significant precautions. If your surfing is tentative in three- to four-foot waves, it is dangerous and foolish to try surfing in seven- to eight-foot conditions. Surf with friends who are strong swimmers and who will keep an eye on you and know your limits. If surfing in crowded lineups makes you nervous, practice in crowded, beginner-friendly surf zones on small days to get used to navigating crowds safely. Soft-top surfboards are safer in crowded surf than traditional fiberglass boards.

uncle Dave and a close family friend named Watson, both Central Coast locals. Our first morning in camp, a storm rolled in with overhead swell and steady rain. We were surfing a point break, and paddling out was relatively easy. But once I was in the surf zone, I sat there afraid to go for a wave. It was raining, the waves were a couple feet overhead, and we were in notoriously sharky waters. My strategy was to stay way outside, beyond where the biggest set waves were breaking, and just watch my friends surf. In self-preservation mode, I confessed that I was scared to even try for a single wave and asked if there was a way back to the beach that was easy, like our paddle-out. Chris and Brad laughed, replying, "Nope. We'll keep an eye on you, but you gotta go take your beating."

I had several things working against me that day in Big Sur. First, the surf conditions were beyond my comfort zone. Second, because I surfed only once in a great while, I was not in good physical condition for surfing. And I was borrowing a surfboard that wasn't ideal (too short) for my skill level. That said, pushing myself a little helped by raising the bar of my comfort zone.

Surfing in challenging conditions reset the bar of my psychological comfort zone, a strategy that works in Indigenous language learning too.[13] In Indigenous language work, your comfort zone may have to do with how much English versus Anishinaabemowin is used in a conversation, how fluent the people are who you are speaking with, or how well you know them. In surfing and language work, pushing myself beyond my comfort zone has helped me learn. But this strategy backfires if you take it too far. I would be a much better surfer and Anishinaabemowin speaker today if I had practiced within my comfort zone more often, punctuating these experiences by occasionally pushing myself in more challenging conditions.

I grew up in a diasporic, urban Indian family with no Anishinaabemowin speakers. I never heard our language as a child, though both my maternal grandparents grew up with the language in their homes to some degree. I had my first introduction to the language as an undergraduate student at the University of Michigan. I benefited greatly from getting to know the instructor, Hap-ba (McCue) of Curve Lake First Nation, but unfortunately these classes did not help me build a foundational understanding of Anishinaabemowin. I learned vocabulary and memorized phrases but gained little understanding of how to create or understand basic sentences.

Several years later, I participated in a yearlong weekend immersion program. Our learning environment was Anishinaabemowin *eta* (100 percent Anishinaabe language) during the two-and-a-half-day sessions, and we were encouraged to practice on our own in between immersion weekends. The fluent instructors did their best to help beginners like me follow what was being shared. They used lots of body language and props and acted out situational sketches. But because I lacked a basic understanding of the structure of our language, I felt completely lost throughout the program. Other than a few words here or there, I had no idea what anyone was saying. I was way out of my comfort zone. This was a very busy time in my life, and I wasn't able to follow my instructors' suggestion to practice the basics between immersion weekends, so I stagnated. I kept my distance, too scared to participate, just like that day surfing at Big Sur.

By 2018, I finally got fed up with being a lifelong beginner and committed to becoming a more fluid Anishinaabemowin speaker and surfer. Given my location, I started with language. I connected with other Anishinaabe people living in Gedakina, and we formed an Ojibwe language circle. We started meeting regularly and supporting one another as language learners, all at different stages in our learning journeys. We gathered all our respective books, tapes, games, and other language resources and began putting more time into learning Anishinaabemowin. About one year in, I realized I still wasn't making much progress, so I called my friends Mike Zimmerman and Meg Noodin to ask for help.

Meg and Mike are second-language speakers who have dedicated their lives to teaching Anishinaabemowin. They offered some basic advice, asking, "Do you have the verb charts?" This simple prompt kicked off the next step in my learning journey: becoming familiar with the four verb types in our language. I focused on one verb type at a time and familiarized myself with the most common prefixes and suffixes involved in conjugations.[14] This work helped train my ear as a listener so I could discern who was being spoken about in each sentence. Mike and Meg shared further, "When you have time to visit with speakers, tell them how you've been focusing your studies, and ask them to speak to you using those verb types or vocabularies." This suggestion helped foster situations where I could participate and experience some successes as a language learner.

Their advice made so much sense. Anishinaabemowin is a verb-heavy language. Around two-thirds of our language is made up of verbs. All these verbs are necessary because our language is action oriented, not object oriented. Roughly twenty-three years after my introduction to the Ojibwe language at the University of Michigan, I finally had a real breakthrough learning our beautiful language.

My friends shared this advice in the lead-up to the 2019 meeting of the Native American and Indigenous Studies Association (NAISA). The timing presented a great opportunity to connect with Anishinaabemowin speakers and try to engage in some basic conversation.

The NAISA conference was held at the University of Waikato in Aotearoa. I traveled to Aotearoa early with plans to conduct a couple interviews for a new film project before the conference started. The interviewees canceled our appointments, leaving me with a week of free time that I decided would be best spent surfing in the Northland region. My first stop was Ahipara, where I linked up with locals Leon and Mike. These guys generously welcomed me into their daily surf routine, loaned me a beginner-friendly board, and guided me into a lot of waves. Leon offered some wise tips. He suggested I get on bigger boards and get to my feet as often as possible. He said I needed more repetition on smaller waves and to start each session riding broken waves all the way to the shore, and then, once I found my balance, to try catching unbroken waves and going down the line. His advice worked. I was standing up and riding waves consistently for three days in "the land of the long white cloud."

Later in the week, I traveled to Ōakura on Northland's east coast. I rented a room from Justin Smith and Ngawhai Kena-Smith, *te reo* Maori specialists. Justin loaned me a cherry red longboard, and I headed to an isolated embayment for a sunset session. The protected bay was stunning—more beautiful than anything I had ever seen. The waves were waist-high and easy to catch on Justin's longboard. I surfed for the last two hours of daylight all by myself and caught countless little backside waves.

For decades I had been surfing in what felt like chaotic conditions, mostly missing waves, falling nine out of ten tries, slipping out, getting sent over the falls, and only rarely standing up for more than a second or two. After decades of falling and failing to progress, the things that every beginner surfer wants to do finally started to click: consistently locking into a trim line, sorting out how to accelerate and connect wave sections, completing rides without falling, turning out at the end of a ride and paddling back for another go. I remember wondering if I was dreaming, or perhaps I was surfing the *manidoo-miikana* (spirit path/Milky Way)?

During that surf session, I thought a lot about Meg and Mike's Anishinaabemowin advice and realized that their wise words were very similar to Leon turning me on to bigger surfboards and smaller waves. Both Meg and Leon were trying to reduce the chaos in my experiences so that I could have a bit of success (see table 1). Experiencing the joys of these activities can motivate you to keep working on them and to not give up. Leon and Justin gifted me with joyful surfing experiences that strengthened my resolve to finally become more fluid on a board.

In the lead-up to the NAISA conference, I worked on animate intransitive verbs regularly for about a week, practicing conjugations using all our different pronouns, past and future tenses, and forming questions. I didn't have the conjugations completely down, but I was making progress. I connected with several Anishinaabemowin speakers at the conference and talked with a few of them about my language-learning process. During our lunch break one day, I crossed paths with a speaker named Miskwaanikwad, and I stuttered a bumbling little impromptu question, "Azhigwa gigii-wiisin ina?" (Did you eat already?) "Eyaa" (yes), he replied with a smile, perhaps knowing that I was taking an important step as a beginner speaker.

Miskwaanikwad may have recognized that I was pushing my comfort zone, but he couldn't have known just how significant this basic interaction was for me. Despite being a beginning speaker for over twenty years, I believe this was the first time I had ever uttered a fully improvised sentence in Anishinaabemowin. For twenty-plus years, when I used Ojibwe greetings or asked people how they were doing, it was all memorized. Weather talk? All scripted questions and replies. Texting in the language? Always composed using reference materials to ensure proper grammar. This moment was different. With a little preparation, the question flowed out of me naturally. For the rest of the conference, whenever I connected with another Anishinaabe, I challenged myself to speak to them about something unscripted in our language. The experience was a personal milestone.

When Anishinaabe people say our language is "alive," we don't just mean figuratively, that people are actively using the language. We also mean literally, that our language is *manidoo* (a spirit being) with agency and abilities. Our language can influence people and outcomes in the world but also requires that people breathe life into the language through active use. After that brief interaction with Miskwaanikwad, a joyful rush of energy pulsed through my body. The energy I felt was the spirit of our language acknowledging an important first act, like when a child takes their first steps.

I have felt the spirit of our language many times before: when hearing the language spoken beautifully by *gichi-aya'aag* (elders) and *abinoojiinyag* (children), hearing old and new songs in our language, listening to our legends in the language. In these moments, I feel a joyful energy pulse through my body, sometimes so strong that my eyes fill with salty tears. Perhaps you have felt this energy before in the presence of your own language. This experience, and the one I had surfing earlier that week, had nothing to do with pride in personal accomplishment. The emotions I experienced in Aotearoa came from connection and kinship. I was overwhelmed with love for the ocean and my language, and the unmistakable feeling that they loved me back.

Toward the end of the mid-1990s California surf trip I described earlier, we spent several days surfing in and around Los Osos, and the waves were consistently overhead. One day we were surfing a beach break coveted by locals for its fast, steep waves capable of producing barrels. The waves rolled in relentlessly one after the other with no lulls in the action. Paddling in to beach breaks can be a lot of work, especially if there is not an obvious rip or channel that can help pull you out past the breaking waves. That day in Los Osos, I couldn't get outside past the breakers. I tried to get through the wall of waves for a solid half hour before tiring out and giving up. I was exhausted, frustrated, and a little jealous of my friends, who by that time had each ridden at least a couple nice waves.

Sitting in the sand and watching my friends surf, I caught my breath, calmed down, and began talking to the ocean. This was the first time I remember talking aloud to the sea, verbally acknowledging her as a powerful, spiritual being. I recall thanking the sea for all her amazing gifts and expressing my intention to connect with her. Instead of running back into the water to try to do whatever I pleased, I respectfully asked permission to reenter. Tired and perfectly willing to take no for an answer, I sat and paid attention to my feelings and my surroundings, as this is often how we receive answers from *manidoog*. Feeling welcomed back into the water, I grabbed my board and started paddling. This time, after a few duck dives, I quickly got past the breaking waves.

Despite some good attempts, my skills were not up to the task of riding those fast, hollow waves. The session helped my skill development a little by pushing my comfort zone. More importantly, I learned a life lesson about acknowledging the sea as a living ancestor and taking a more spiritual approach to surfing. This experience was the beginning of a shift in my surfing mentality and my relationship to water. I began to recognize that the purpose of surfing and other fresh- and saltwater activities for me is not just recreational but relational.

Indinawemaaganag endanakiiwaad iwidi nibiikaang (My Relatives Who Live There in the Water)

Waves travel thousands of miles before reaching their coastal destinations. Land and sea embrace as each wave reaches shore. Many parts of creation gather to celebrate the culmination of a wave's journey, including *giizisoog* (sun and moon), *nibi* (water), *asiniig* (stones), *noodinan* (winds), *zaakiiyig* (plants), *giigoonyag* (fishes), *bineshiinyag* (birds), *manidoog* (spirits), and *bemaadizijig* (people). Surfing allows me to participate in these sacred gatherings. As an Indigenous surfer, I'm inspired by Waiti and Awatere, who point out that Māori people *whakapapa* (connect through genealogy) to all these parts of creation, including Ātua (gods or ancestors with influence over particular domains), and show how Māori surfers embody coastal relationalities through their intimate engagements with the sea.[15]

I spend a lot of my surf sessions paying attention to more-than-human relatives, greeting them, thanking them, and asking them how they are doing. I ask waves that pass under my board about their journeys and whether approaching waves will take me to shore. I ask birds what weather is headed our way (table 2). I also take time to acknowledge other surfers in the lineup, greeting them with a smile and willingness to chat.

Many of the Indigenous surfers I know will greet the ocean, say a prayer, or make an offering before paddling out. I've learned about these and other Indigenous surfing practices from many different individuals, including Jason Whaturia, an Auckland-based surfer who taught me that surf breaks are critical zones for Indigenous language use.

Jason taught me to always speak my Indigenous language while surfing. This learning aligns with something my elders often say, that our first relations understand us best when we speak Anishinaabemowin. He was also talking about the politics of surf zones. Using our original languages in the surf communicates that Indigenous individuals are in the lineup. Local, non-Indigenous surfers can sometimes get territorial over surf spots, treating people they don't recognize harshly. When local Indigenous surfers speak their languages in the lineup, it is a reminder of who is really

TABLE 2. Anishinaabe surf language

boozibiiyaashk; boozibiiditibaashkaa	s/he gets on or boards a wave, surfs
digow(an)	wave(s)
gichi-zhiiwitaagami	great salty lake, ocean
giiyaashkaa	there are waves
mamaangaashkaa	there are big waves
dabasaashkaa	the waves are low, small
minoshkaakaaning	a place with good waves
noojitoodaa minoshkaang!	let's go find a place with good waves!
aaniindi waa-niminaawe'oyaan?	where should I paddle out?
giwaa-wiijiiwin ina?	could I go with you?
giinitam / niinitam / wiinitam boozibiiditibaashkaan	your turn / my turn / her/his turn to surf
minogwekigaabawi	s/he turns well while standing, makes nice turns
niigaanigaabawi	s/he stands in front, "nose rides"
oniigaanagoodoon wanakozidan	s/he hangs them in front, just the tips of her/his toes / hangs ten

local. And when Indigenous surfers are friendly in the lineup, in spite of legacies of being dispossessed from our own homelands, it demonstrates genuine love and generosity.

I have had the honor of visiting Hawaiʻi and during these visits I often hear surfers *ʻōlelo* Hawaiʻi (speak Hawaiian) together in the water. By using Hawaiian language in the *ka poʻina nalu*, Kanaka Māoli surfers make an important political statement in the context of the settler colonial state. The Kingdom of Hawaiʻi is continually impacted by extractive economics in the form of tourism, agriculture, and military occupation. Nonlocals and tourists crowd *ka poʻina nalu* throughout the archipelago, often to the dismay and frustration of the people whose ancestors invented and taught the world about surfing.[16] When Indigenous people from Hawaiʻi and elsewhere surf their local breaks, their presence communicates to other surfers that they never left and that surf zones are part of their homelands, inherently Indigenous spaces.[17]

My family and I spent July–December of 2021 living on Oʻahu. I am eternally grateful for the experiences we had and relationships we built that half year in Hawaiʻi. We experienced south swell season and north swell season, and I surfed all but maybe three to four days over the span of five months. I often spoke Anishinaabemowin while surfing in Hawaiʻi as a way to connect with more-than-human beings and practice my language. And when other Indigenous surfers heard me speaking my language, it created openings for discussion. As an Anishinaabe visitor in the Hawaiian Kingdom, I wanted to make connections with Kanaka Māoli and other locals. I wanted to build new friendships and expand my network of Indigenous relations. Speaking my language in and out of the water helped facilitate those connections.

Niminwendaan gawiseyaan azhigwa (Now I Enjoy Falling)

Surf zones are ideal spaces to practice speaking Anishinaabemowin because I feel more relaxed and willing to make mistakes. The sea turtles and gulls don't care if I bumble my words or conjugate a verb wrong. When I speak Anishinaabemowin with other Anishinaabek, I worry too much about saying things correctly. I'm afraid of making mistakes, and this stifles my learning. What am I so worried about, that people will know I've been a beginner for decades? Or that someone will chastise me for my mistakes? That's nonsense, of course, and is all in my head. Our people treasure fluent speakers, but nobody is going to think less of you because you make mistakes as a learner. The most important thing is that we show up and participate—that we contribute to the resurgence and vitality of our languages. Practicing Anishinaabemowin while surfing helps me unlearn my insecurities so that I can be braver and more talkative when speaking the language with other Anishinaabek.

Learning anything difficult requires making lots of mistakes. You will fall off your board a thousand times while learning to surf, and you'll make a thousand mistakes learning your language. After all these years, I finally learned to embrace falling and fumbling words as positive and necessary parts of learning. These stumbles will persist for years, and so I'm learning to embrace and enjoy them. I can't just aim to make fluid turns on a surfboard; I also need to strive for more fluid falls. I'm learning to laugh at my surfing mistakes and my broken Anishinaabemowin and let go of my ego. Worrying about mistakes makes you tense and hesitant and creates unnecessary obstacles.

This particular learning hit me hard in 2021 during a surf session at Laniakea on the North Shore of O'ahu. The wave and crowd conditions were at the upper edge of my comfort zone. I was nervous and hesitant to go for waves. Looking out toward the horizon, I saw three large set waves coming our way. A local uncle to my left saw the sets coming at the same moment as I did, and we started paddling side by side toward the waves, hoping to get past them before they broke. I was struck by how excited this other surfer looked. To me, the three-wave set was like a menacing thunderstorm darkening our horizon. We glided easily over the first wave and narrowly made it over the second. These were easily the most powerful waves I had ever encountered in my thirty-plus years of surfing. The third and final wave was the biggest yet. It started to break while this local uncle and I were still climbing up the face. I put everything I had into one final stroke, then grabbed rail and pushed my board through the lip of the cresting wave. We barely squeaked past the wave on our large, buoyant boards, but we safely got through to the other side. I looked wide-eyed over at the other surfer, and we both laughed. Mine was nervous laughter, but his telegraphed elation.

Once I was safely past those breaking waves, I sat for a few minutes and wondered how he stayed so calm in that tense situation. I listened to my heart, and an answer came quickly. *Zaagi'idiwin* (love). In that moment, I was reminded of our Anishinaabe-*izhitwaawin* (original beliefs) about *zaagi'idiwin*. We are taught that Shkaakaamikwe/Mother Earth gives and gives and gives to us because she loves us unconditionally. *Giizis* rises every day without fail, offering warmth and unconditional love. *Zaakiiyig* (plants) give us medicine, food, oxygen, shelter, and heat, and their love for the Anishinaabek is endless and unconditional. All of creation offers up their individual gifts with unconditional love, including *gichi-zhiiwitaagami* (the sea). *Gichi-zhiiwitaagami* gives surfers wave after wave after wave. No matter how much we surf, the waves just keep coming.[18] And waves are just one small gift the sea gives to humans and the rest of creation.

The love I feel from and for the ocean reminds me of the love between a grandparent and grandchild. The love a mother has for her child is unconditional and perhaps the strongest love of all. With that motherly love comes a certain fear of loss and ferocious protection of the child. The love a grandparent has for their grandchild, in comparison, is lighter—a joyful love with less worry. That day surfing Laniakea, I thought about *zaagi'idiwin*, and I started to feel like I was at my grandparents' house. I became perfectly relaxed. I felt embraced. I was a visitor in the Hawaiian Kingdom but at home in the sea, like a grandchild in their grandparents' home.[19] I thought about those big set waves, and I pictured a grandparent picking up their grandchild and tossing them playfully into the air. The grandchild has no control over the situation other than their own reaction. They don't panic. They aren't scared. They are relaxed and screech joyfully as they become weightless in the air before gravity pulls them back down for a soft landing in their grandparent's powerful hands. When I get nervous while surfing or speaking Anishinaabemowin, I visualize this scene. My heart fills with *zaagi'idiwin*, and I relax and enjoy the ride.

Notes

1 I want to start by acknowledging all the Indigenous language teachers and language revitalization advocates around the world, including those who have walked on, those still working and retired, and those young ones who are just beginning their language journeys. I offer my sincere thanks to all my patient language teachers over the years, including those mentioned directly in this essay as well as Mino Giizhgad, Migizi Sullivan, Amy McCoy, and Helen Roy.

2 S. Dowling, "Elimination, Dispossession, Transcendence: Settler Monolingualism and Racialization in the United States," *American Quarterly* 73, no. 3 (2021), 439–60.

3 Anton Treuer, *Language Warrior's Manifesto: How to Keep Our Languages Alive No Matter the Odds* (St. Paul: Minnesota Historical Society Press, 2020), 13.

4 L. T. Smith, *Decolonizing Methodologies: Research and Indigenous Peoples*, 2nd ed. (London: Zed Books, 2012), 148–49.

5 For discussion of the importance of canoes in Indigenous ways of knowing and being and in context of decolonization, see, for example, V. M. Diaz, "Voyaging for Anti-colonial Recovery: Austronesian Seafaring, Archipelagic Rethinking, and the Re-mapping of Indigeneity," *Pacific Asia Inquiry* 2, no. 1(2011): 21–32; K. Mikraszewicz and C. Richmond, "Paddling the Biigtig: Mino Biimadisiwin Practiced through Canoeing," *Social Science and Medicine*, 240 (2019): 112548; C. S. Perez, *Navigating CHamoru Poetry: Indigeneity, Aesthetics, and Decolonization* (Tucson: University of Arizona Press, 2022).

6 I picked up on this term from Robin Michigiizhigookwe Clark and now use it in place of "natural resources" because it emphasizes relatedness rather than use or ownership and acknowledges that all other parts of creation came "first," before humans.

7 As quoted in C. A. Fox et al., "The River Is Us; The River Is in Our Veins": Re-defining River Restoration in Three Indigenous Communities," *Sustainability Science* 12 (2017), 521–33.

8 E. Benton-Banai, *The Mishomis Book: The Voice of the Ojibway*, Red School House, 1988. www.pbs.org/video/wpt-documentaries-ojibwe-history.

9 Gedakina is what the Wabanaki peoples call their homelands. Since we were formerly a singular East Coast group, Wabanaki and Anishinaabe languages are related. As an Anishinaabe language learner looking at the word *Gedakina*, I recognize *aki*, meaning land, earth, or country, and the *ge* prefix, indicating that it is all of ours (inclusive), meaning the land is a part of us and collectively we have responsibility to care for her. I relate more to this place name than the lazy and violent colonial moniker of "New England," which simply rubber-stamps a European place name in an attempt to erase Indigeneity from the landscape.

10 *Mino-bimaadiziwin* is an Anishinaabemowin term that translates roughly to "the good life." It refers to living well, healthy, and in balance. These original teachings are the foundation of Anishinaabek morality. "Niizhwaaswi G'mishomisinaanig (Our 7 Grandfathers)," Ojibwe.net, accessed July 7, 2024, https://ojibwe.net/projects/the-seven-grandfather-words-by-helen-roy-fuhst.

11 E. Hau'ofa, "Our Sea of Islands," in *Asia/Pacific as Space of Cultural Produc-*

tion, edited by Rob Wilson and Arif Dirlik, 86–98 (Durham, NC: Duke University Press, 1995).

12 Teaiwa quoted in Hau'ofa, *Dreadlocks in Oceania* (Suva Fiji: Department of Literature and Language, University of the South Pacific, 1997), 124. This widely cited and poetic quote is also contextualized in the introduction to *Sweat and Salt Water*, compiled and edited by Katerina Teaiwa, April K. Henderson, and Terence Wesley-Smith (Honolulu: University of Hawai'i Press, 2021).

13 Surfing in conditions beyond your comfort zone should be done only within reason and safely. I had a fair bit of Pacific Ocean surf experience before trying solid waves at Big Sur. I had surfed many times in the shoulder- to head-high range before challenging myself to paddle out into slightly larger conditions. I also had four advanced surfers, including three locals, all keeping a close eye on me that day, and we had the spot to ourselves, so I wasn't endangering other surfers outside of our group. Be smart, and stay safe!

14 To improve your ability to participate in conversational Anishinaabemowin as both a listener and a speaker, an important step is mastery of animate intransitive verbs. For an excellent introduction, see A. Treuer, "Animate Intransitive Verbs in Minnesota Ojibwe," *Oshkaabewis Native Journal* 6, nos. 1–2 (2003): 137–74.

15 J. T. A. Waiti and S. Awatere, "Kaihekengaru: Māori Surfers and a Sense of Place," *Surf Break Management in Aotearoa New Zealand. Journal of Coastal Research*, edited by K. R. Bryan and E. A. Atkin, special issue no. 87 (2019): 35–43.

16 Hawai'i has its own unique categories of ethnic identity, which include "locals" who are non-Indigenous but were raised in the archipelago and have been acculturated to Hawaiian social norms. For a discussion of Indigenous, local, and haole identity in Hawai'i, see J. Y. Okamura, *Ethnicity and Inequality in Hawaii* (Philadelphia: Temple University Press, 2008).

17 Much has been written about the cultures, history, and politics of surfing in Hawai'i, perhaps the most in-depth treatment in I. H. Walker, *Waves of Resistance: Surfing and History in Twentieth-Century Hawai'i* (Honolulu: University of Hawai'i Press, 2011). Also see Walker's other works, including his contribution to this volume. Regarding the politics, histories, and cultures of Indigenous surfing in other regions, see, for example, works by Jordan Waiti (Aotearoa New Zealand), Colleen McGloin (Australia), and Page West (Papua New Guinea), among others.

18 For a beautiful expression of this same sentiment, see Albert Falzon's interview in the 2019 film *Thank You Mother* by Ishka Folkwell, https://needessentialseu.com/pages/films.

19 I recognize the slippery slope that I am walking with this statement as a non-Hawaiian person. There is a long and problematic history of non-Hawaiians trying to stake claims to parts or all of the Hawaiian Kingdom and making themselves feel "at home" without any genealogical ties or taking any responsibility to support the islands, ocean, or kingdom. The spirit of what I am sharing here is that the sea is a living ancestor who loves us and who enjoys our engagement the way a grandparent enjoys spending time with their grandchildren. I recognize the need to always be a responsible visitor when traveling and don't take lightly my positionality in those spaces.

6

Reflection on *Boarder X*, a Traveling Exhibition

Carving Out Paths to Decolonize Galleries and Laying Claim for Space to Thrive

JAIMIE ISAAC

On national tour from 2016 to 2022, the *Boarder X* exhibition toured across Turtle Island (Canada) from coast to coast, taking over seven different galleries and museums to change and nourish those spaces with the energy and inclusion of a growing decolonized skate community. I curated this exhibition and organized with the Winnipeg Art Gallery, with the intent to gather and invite artists representing Indigenous nations of mixed ancestry from across Turtle Island, who practice(d) skateboarding, surfing, and snowboarding. These artists included Jordan Bennett (Mi'kmaq), Bracken Hanuse Corlett (Wuikinuxv/Klahoose), Roger Crait (Cree), Steven Davies (Snuneymuxw), Mark Igloliorte (Nunatsiavut Inuit), Micheal Langan (Saulteaux) of Colonialism Skateboards in collaboration with Kent Monkman (Cree), Mason Mashon (Cree), Meagan Musseau (Mi'kmaq), Meghann O'Brien (Kwakwa̱ka̱'wakw/Haida), Les Ramsay (Métis), and Amanda Strong (Métis), as well as many additional amazing local artists from each exhibition venue region involved in the programming and ramp build. In 2021 *Boarder X* won the Canadian Museum Association Outstanding Achievement Award, meant to help set community benchmarks of excellence, for its achievement for bringing life to the museum by demonstrating and celebrating how art can be transformative.

Boarder X was designed to celebrate intersections of cultures, art, and boarding. Its title derives from the boardercross competition, which involves multiple riders on a downhill obstacle course. The *X* in *Boarder X* also represents the intersecting themes, cultures, identities, and narratives in the exhibition. The title's use of *boarder* also evokes its homophonic relative, *border*, and the act of crossing borders literally and figuratively to reconnect and reengage with land and seascapes that have been divided and appropriated into colonized, bordered lands. This exhibition highlights artists and communities mobilizing their histories, enacting a cultural continuum of active presence through contemporary ways of being on the land and waters in order to decolonize, reclaim, and challenge conformity, stereotypes, and status quos. It allowed for an observation of how board culture examines contested spaces and places; political, cultural, and social borders; hybrid identities; and traditional territories. Surfing, skateboarding, and snowboarding demonstrate a knowledge, connection, respect, and understanding of the land and water. *Boarder X* brought together narratives of Indigeneity, decolonizing, sovereignty, resistance, gender equality, environmental concerns, colonization, and political and cultural clashes through interdisciplinary art and activated programming. The ways in which Indigenous and mixed-ancestry riders and artists navigate and understand environmental, political, cultural, and social climates are transformational and transcendental. Skateboarding and snowboarding relate to Indigenous ways of being with deep tides and histories through the history of Indigenous surfing.

Binding Ties

Boarder X tested boundaries and found synergies between the concepts of "countercultures," "boarding," and "Indigeneity." The heart of this project is dedicated to youth and finding kin of all ages across Turtle Island who understand what it means to live these intersections. My own connections to board practices inform this exhibition. I am of mixed heritage: Anishinaabe, member of Sagkeeng First Nation, and an intergenerational survivor on my mother's side, and of British heritage, second-generation Canadian on my dad's side. When I started snowboarding at eleven, snowboarding and skateboarding weren't as mainstream as they are now. Looking back, challenging mainstream normative behaviors in ways that were significant to growing up, going against the grain as a resistant youth, I exercised a refusal that I think paved the way for my career as a curator working to change institutional norms.

Before the bounty of parks we enjoy now, we navigated the city to find parking lots, parkades, and old bowls, dodging intolerant security guards. Until the mid-1990s, snowboarding was considered dangerous and was prohibited from many ski resorts in Canada, but in 1998, the Olympics finally made it "socially acceptable" as an official sport, which interestingly influenced new skiing styles today. I was never any good at skiing, so I tried snowboarding, and something clicked. I belonged to a small, supportive community of friends on the hill and on the streets. I rode almost every day and became comfortable—confident even—in my skin and on my board(s). My mum and a good friend signed me up for my first competition when I was thirteen years old. I won a few provincial competitions, which led to me competing in the nationals, being a snowboarding instructor, getting a judging certification, attending summer camps at Camp of Champions in the giants of Blackcomb, British Columbia. I was by no means a professional, but it was my life and was an interesting exercise in gender and race politics. I was often told, "You're good . . . for a girl," a backhanded compliment paralleled by, "Oh, you're *Native*?! Well, you're one of the good ones." These intolerant measures of worth only strengthened my resolve to defy them. I broke and rebroke my arms skateboarding and stage diving, raked and cut my skin on the concrete too many times to remember, broke ribs, and sustained blackened bruises. In my journey of learning to surf, I am continuously humbled, as it offers incredible teachings of humility and respect. The ocean, land, and mountains are powerful forces, a reminder of how small and temporal you are in their great perpetual vastness. Being on the land and on the water attune people to humanly and earthly fragility, to the fact that nature and time are precious. Surfing, skateboarding, and snowboarding have provided me with a lens that informs how I occupy and experience the world. Many elders and knowledge keepers teach us about the respect for the land and waters that sustain the world. The land is not to be conquered, contrary to so many extreme-sport advertising messages, so *Boarder X* stood in tension to commercialization and the "conquering" vernacular. It is a skill to see, learn, analyze, and understand the landscape, whether by trying to read the waves and wind, to understand the ocean floor, to anticipate the swells, or by moving though many various mountainous terrains. These movements attune the body to the land and are respectful responses to the land—based not on controlling the land and water, contrary to the man-versus-nature discourse but rather on recognizing human existence in relation to the vast geographies, ecosystems, and organisms. This is especially true in the Anthropocene, as we are increasingly forced to acknowledge how human actions have altered the natural processes on Earth and in turn changed how we survive, play, and act in relation to and on the land.

Global Context

So how do skateboarding, snowboarding, and surfing relate to Indigenous ways of being? The concept of Indigeneity ties the environmental to the familial: relating to "Indigeneity as a collective community built upon the interconnections, interrelationships of a group, not just through human relationships but on the basis of our relationships to the land."[1] Being involved in these ways of life and spending time on the land can be at once transformative, peaceful, and thrillingly terrifying, providing a heightened sense of self and vitality. Indigenous botanist Robin Wall Kimmerer explains that the awakening of a wider ecological consciousness requires the acknowledgment and celebration of our reciprocal relationship with the rest of the living world: "Old stories and new ones can be medicine for our broken relationship with earth, a pharmacopoeia of healing stories that allow us to imagine a different relationship, in which people and land are good medicine for each other."[2] There are Indigenous roots that are effaced in mainstream histories. Surfing has been a sport and cultural practice for Pacific Indigenous relatives for millennia, existing before European contact. In his book *Waves of Resistance*, Kanaka Māoli historian Isaiah Helekunihi Walker argues that, despite facing oppression on the land, many Native Hawaiians have found refuge, autonomy, resistance, and identity on the waves as a Native Hawaiian realm by resisting colonial encroachment in the *poʻina nalu* (surf zone):

> While surfing was a thriving aspect of Hawaiian culture in ancient days, in the twentieth century it served as both a refuge and a contested borderland for many Native Hawaiians. In other words, it was a place where Hawaiians felt free, developed Native identities, and thwarted foreign domination. As Hawaiian surfers secured control over ka poʻina nalu, haole colonial authority was less influential there. On land, many Hawaiians were marginalized from political, social and economic spheres during much of the twentieth century. Yet in the ocean Native surfers secured a position atop a social hierarchy.[3]

Walker draws from a deep history to describe the precontact connections to surfing, the historical struggle of Hawaiʻi's political territory with white settlers, and the legacy of Duke Kahanamoku and Eddie Aikau in establishing Hawaiian authority and presence, while also underlining gender politics with respect and acknowledgment to Hawaiian women in the sport as equal or sometimes dominant. He describes the strength in performing relationship with the land by practicing a long-established way of being woven deeply into Hawaiian epistemologies, surfing on their lands of origin, carving out zones of refuge, of authority, and sovereignty. Turtle Island Indigenous scholars Alfred and Corntassel refer to the idea of "zones of refuge, from colonial powers that are spaces of freedom, strength and authenticity, where true power as Indigenous people ultimately lies in our relationships with our land, relatives, languages, and ceremonial life."[4] Likewise, in Australia, "in its contemporary state, Indigenous surfing in Australia constitutes a pedagogical practice as well as a form of pleasure: surfing is both a reclamation of cultural pride and an affirmation of precolonial sovereignty."[5] Based on nationhood and region, relationships with the land and water are diverse. Though a statue of Duke Kahanamoku faces the ocean from the boardwalk in Waikiki, the mainstream or commercialized surf culture maintains an erasure of complex Indigenous origins and continuity. In "How American Surf Culture Was Built on a History of Indigenous Erasure," Colville scholar and activist Dina Gilio-Whitaker describes how tensions about localism and territorialism in surf culture have roots in the history of American imperialism against the independent nation of Hawaiʻi. She further notes that common surf histories efface the Indigenous Hawaiian ancestry of George Freeth, who brought surf culture and beach culture to California, while simultaneously mirroring the erasure and genocidal policies of the Indigenous peoples in California and throughout the United States and Canada.[6] The land and resources were being stolen, exploited, and appropriated from Indigenous resources for the interest of settler ones. Delving further, Gilio-Whitaker explains, "In the context of settler colonialism, appropriation is always about the continual remaking of indigenous space into settler space, at both material and discursive levels of culture and politics. American surf culture is thus reflective of and complicit in larger, ongoing colonial projects to dispossess indigenous peoples—in this case, Kanaka Māoli —of their ancestral places and culture."[7]

In thinking about these histories and the birthplace of surfing, I was drawn to Dr. Maulani Aluli Meyer's thoughts on Hawaiian epistemologies. She writes, "Think on these things and you will come to the inevitable conclusion that as we lived scores of generations upon this beloved and breathtaking landscape, we had views on this matter because we thrived here. And from that thriving came the highest expression of a people: Art. We lived artistic lives. In our speech, in our countenance, in our health, in our spirit, in our leisure, in our work, in our art."[8]

THRIVANCE

As an Anishinaabe *ikwe*/woman who enjoys snowboarding, skateboarding, and surfing and is now introducing my son to these ways of life, I think about what my mother and grandmother taught me about the Anishinaabe concept of *mino-pimatisiwin*, meaning "walking in a good way," living life in a good and healthy way. The concepts and actions of resistance and survivance are rooted in self-determination and have provided an agency for Indigenous ways of being that both resist colonial repression and survive colonial oppression. *Thrivance* is a term that celebrates a resurgence of

Indigenous people creating and thriving in self-determined and sovereigned environments. Resistance and survival actions of Indigenous ancestors gifted the next generation's resiliency and courage. Greg Hill furthers Gerald Vizenor's concept of "survivance," explaining it as the precondition to "thrivance."[9] I think we are not yet at a moment of transcendence, from survivance to thrivance, as there are uphill battles for Indigenous people and so many challenges persist systemically in society, but with *Boarder X*, thrivance is illuminated by artists' work and the Indigenous youth mobilizing and living the *mino-pimatisiwin* way through the connections to board culture and Indigenous self-determination and self-representation, working simultaneously for generations to persist, survive, and thrive on the land. Scholar of Michi Saagiig Nishnaabeg ancestry Leanne Betasamosake Simpson wrote that "we need intellectuals," and I would add Indigenous athletes, artists, and knowledge keepers of the land in this context of the exhibition and essay, "who can think within the conceptual meanings of the language, who are intrinsically connected to place and territory, who exist in the world as an embodiment of contemporary expressions of our ancient stories and traditions, and that illuminate mino bimaadiziyin in all aspect of their lives."[10] Embracing the land through adaptation of ways we move on the land is a resurgence of cultural connection and knowledge of the land.

Boarder X presented a cultural thrivance of active Indigenous presence, despite the media's focus on deficiencies and daunting statistics of addictions, suicides, and homicides of Indigenous youth across occupied Canada. Access to opportunity is important to acknowledge and take responsibility and action toward. Skateboarding, snowboarding, and surfing should be for everyone. Many grassroots initiatives by organizations, companies, and individuals have crossed that barrier to assist in inclusion. One of the most revolutionary of these is Skate Nation Youth, a self-determined Indigenous-led organization founded January 2021. The founding members are Rose Archie, Joe Buffalo, and Dustin and Tristan Henry, all professional skateboarders who came together with a mission centered on "empowering Indigenous youth to embrace their right to self-determination through the positive impact of skateboarding and a vision to empower youth, create leadership and togetherness within the community and inspire the youth through their skateboarding workshops."[11] As a group they are inspiring for the work they do with youth and community, leading life-changing legacies. Beyond providing the equipment to make boarding sports accessible, they teach skateboarding, build self-esteem, and promote mental, emotional, and physical health as well as cultural pride in communities across borders.

Surfing and skateboarding didn't start as a way of life for middle-class people. It has Indigenous and counterculture roots that were born from ingenuity, adaptation, and imagination. This exhibition celebrated adaptation for survival, activism, perseverance, and mobilization in connecting to the land, ancestors, culture, spirit, personhood, and nationhood. It reflected on cultural, political, environmental, and social perspectives in relation to the landscapes and territories we occupy. The actions of cultural and physical transformation are the manifestations of embodied energies that are creative expressions.

Instilling Radicalness in the Curatorial Field

Boarder X exercised strategies that center Indigenous epistemologies, protocols, and ways of being that confronted and dismantled systemic institutional behavior. My experiences in the curatorial field required taking risks, trying different methods as a curatorial process, trials and errors, and putting theories into actions, and they have had long-lasting impacts. The heart of this exhibition is dedicated to youth. I wanted to carve out a space in the institution with this exhibition where Indigenous youth and skateboarders would feel central, welcome, and empowered. When youth saw themselves reflected in these spaces, I believe they saw themselves being honored.

When I shared my desire to build a skate ramp inside the Winnipeg Art Gallery, as part of changing institutional space, there was some pushback and hesitancy. I insisted, as it was integral to the premise of critiquing social spaces and the insistence of Indigenous inclusion, so I reached out to Vans Canada about a sponsorship for this exhibition, and they were supportive beyond my expectations to fund the ramp and an ambitious program of community engagements that would enact inclusive radical spaces for engagement. For *Boarder X*'s opening night at the Winnipeg Art Gallery, we worked with Vans and the amazing local skate community to build a massive vert (vertical) ramp that transformed the gallery's soaring atrium into a skateboard park. The park was complete with a floor mural skate deck painted by local Indigenous Winnipeg mural artists Kenneth Lavallee, Peatr Thomas, and Mike Valcourt with help from Graffiti Gallery's curator and artist, Pat Lazo. A mini model of the Winnipeg Art Gallery was constructed as a grind box to skate, designed by Luke Palka to have my desired idea of a Godzilla-like effect when skated on. I worked with Hanwakan Whitecloud and Graham Constant, members of the now disbanded Red Riding Media—an all-Indigenous skateboarding crew that I began working with in 2009 for the Truth and Reconciliation national event skateboarding demonstration on survivance. I invited them into the space to skate opening night, spotlighting a time for them to skate and paying them CARFAC (Canadian Artists Representation recommendation for fees) performance art rates. We ran a film festival showing skate, snowboarding, and surfing international films that spoke to the themes in the exhibition. One of the films we showed, featuring artist, Indigenous haute couture fashion artist/weaver, and ex-professional snowboarder Meghann O'Brien, was *The Little Things*, a short film about inspirational, environmentally conscious riders considering the importance of protecting and living in balance with the environment. Indigenous artist and skateboarder Peatr Thomas and I received training from Roararockit Skateboard Company to make skateboard decks from scratch, a train-the-trainers program. We held a free three-week workshop to teach youth how to make and design their own boards.

The Winnipeg Art Gallery and the Art Gallery of Alberta concurrently hosted *Boarder X* and *Vernon Ah Kee: cantchant*, an installation composed of a three-channel video, text, portraiture, and suspended surfboards by Australian contemporary artist Vernon Ah Kee (Kuku Yalandji, Waanji, Yidinji, and Gugu Yimithirr) from the collection of the National Gallery of Canada. Referencing the 2005 Cronulla race riots that took place near Sydney, Australia, *cantchant* provides a compelling statement on the racially motivated conflicts between white Australians and more recent, non-Western immigrants to the country. Vernon Ah Kee transforms the irony of the riot chant "we grew here; you flew here" into the proclamation "we grew here," which is reinforced by the suspended shields displaying Yidinji patterns and the colors of the Australian Aboriginal flag. One must pass through the suspended shields/boards to view a video of professional Aboriginal surfer Dale Richards riding one of the boards. In the video, the surfboard becomes a metaphor for the Aboriginal body and the violence enacted upon Aboriginal peoples. At the exit, portraits of the artist and members of his extended family are revealed on the bottoms of the shields/boards, signifying continuing Aboriginal presence. Presented alongside *Boarder X*, Vernon Ah Kee's *cantchant* explores similar notions of cultural identity, ownership, and land claims in response to political conflict and disputed territories in Australia.

The *Boarder X* exhibition tour traveled coast to coast from 2017 to 2022, and I worked closely with Vans and each curator at every institution to design programming and connect with community. This was an integral part of the exhibition legacy, to go beyond the exhibition and involve programming and education in the experience of *Boarder X*. *Boarder X* left Winnipeg for the Mackenzie Art Gallery in Regina, Saskatchewan, in 2017, where, like Winnipeg, skate ramps and features were built into and skated within the gallery space, in partnership with Vans and a local skate shop, Tiki Room. It was kept in the gallery as programming space for the duration of the exhibition, and for film screenings and invitations to the local Indigenous skate community. We hosted free skate clinics for audiences during the opening weekend. The director at the time, Anthony Kiendl, was a former skateboarder and overall supporter of the exhibition.

With the Art Gallery of Alberta, Edmonton (AGA), in 2018, *Boarder X* was reunited with the National Gallery of Canada's installation *Vernon Ah Kee: cantchant* and took up the whole top floor of the gallery and front entrance of the architecturally robust gallery with a large vert (vertical) ramp and a stunning mural by Mobilize, a youth organization and Cree fashion company. The opening night at the AGA usually requires an entrance fee, but it was waived as part of the agreement for the opening. Many invites went out to the local Indigenous community and the general public, and in particular the local youth were invited to take part in all-weekend skate clinics for free. This was intentionally structured into the programming as a way of removing socioeconomic barriers to attend.

The Rooms gallery in St. John's, Newfoundland, opened in 2019 with a vert ramp and weekend clinics, featured on a national show called *The Exhibitionists* on CBC (Canadian Broadcasting Corporation). In 2020 the Nanaimo Art Gallery in British Columbia hosted a mini ramp for the entire duration of the exhibition and invited local Indigenous knowledge keepers and artists to present tours. (It certainly helped working with skateboarder curator Jesse Birch for the programming and ongoing skate actions). We had a Vans-sponsored event to surf and clean up the beach in Tofino, British Columbia, and a plan to shut down a main street in downtown Nanaimo for skate features and bring in the Skate Nations Youth to present, demonstrate, and teach. However, the COVID-19 pandemic made this programming impossible.

In 2020–21 the Squamish Lil'wat Cultural Centre in Whistler, British Columbia, hosted *Boarder X* and worked with the Indigenous Lifesport Academy, formerly the First Nations Snowboard Team, to support the representation of local artists' work and skateboard auction. The auction of artwork went to supporting the Indigenous Lifesport Academy, which was led by Court Larabee. The ILSA creates social change and development within Indigenous communities and for decolonizing sport. ILSA provided Indigenous youth with opportunities to play, express themselves, improve both their mental and physical health, as well as learn skills such as snowboarding, skateboarding, biking, climbing, hiking, and golf that can benefit them long into their adult years. These healthy sport-based outlets assist in the relief of conscious and subconscious stresses induced by intergenerational trauma within Indigenous communities. The pandemic was also a hindrance in providing the intended plans for programming and engagement, unfortunately, with the potential we had in Whistler and with this amazing crew.

In 2021 and 2022 *Boarder X* arrived at its last stop, at the Museum of

Vancouver (MOV), where I worked with curator Sharon Fortnay to delve into the collection and pair the work from the touring show with historical items from the MOV's collection, as well as contemporary items from coastal Indigenous producers of snowboard and skateboard activities. To activate the mini ramp in the space for duration of the exhibition, Skate Nations Youth held clinics to teach groups that signed up or groups that they made space for and held existing relationships. These were an integral part of building the ramp for use and programming. There was a sister community exhibition that was born from *Boarder X* with the Museum of Vancouver to engage Takeover Skateboard group and host the Skate for Change with I DREAM LIBRARY's *Our Stories Live Here* exhibition. This provided local context and photos of folks/youth from the skate community, two of whom are amazing photographers, Norma Ibara and Tristan Henry of Skate Nations Youth.

All of the programming and partnerships are essential in contemporary curating. The opening night at the WAG brought in well over nine hundred people, some who skateboarded right into the gallery and many who had never been to the art gallery before. As the exhibition toured, I was stoked to witness how opening nights at galleries and museums transformed the spaces and invited communities into galleries by infusing unique programming. I think of further ways to enact reciprocity and responsibility beyond empowerment. Exhibitions like *Boarder X* instill a radicalness within institutions to support Indigenous inclusion and engagement.

In 2014–15, when *Boarder X* was conceived, it was the first exhibit to connect Indigenous culture to the trifecta of skateboarding, snowboarding, and surfing. While the exhibition *Ramp It Up* opened at the National Museum of the American Indian in 2009 and focused on Indigenous skateboard culture, there has not been a specific exhibition dedicated to purely Indigenous culture, boarding, and the relationship to land reclamation. There have been a few exhibitions that focus primarily on skate culture as a whole, with many having an abundance of designed decks, but *Boarder X* was positioned apart from these "deck shows."

Working with *Boarder X* Artists

Researching Indigenous artists that skate or snowboard or surf or do them all, as a way of demonstrating the relationship to the land, water, and their cultures, was fun. It was an organic and layered process in building relationships with artists and gauging their interest in becoming involved in the project. Developing meaningful relationships requires time, and on some level wished I had more time with everyone to go snowboarding, skating, or surfing. Each artist speaks to their own work, so I am careful to speak not on their practices but only on the work in the context of the show. I respect all of the artists in this exhibition and praise them for their artistic practices and experiences. The artists represent nations from the West to East Coasts of Turtle Island. As I continue to do research in this area, I see more artists and am chuffed this show contributes to that growing dialogue.

I used to work for the Aboriginal Peoples Television Network and appreciated the way Indigenous stories were told through Indigenous perspectives, through a self-determined lens. While I was enjoying watching APTN's *UnderExposed* series, which was about sport journalists documenting adrenaline-based sports, I was introduced to Saddle Lake Cree artist Mason Mashon and his exciting work as a photographer living in Whistler, British Columbia, for the Sea to Sky Corridor (a region that stretches from the shores of Horseshoe Bay in western British Columbia to the mountains of Whistler in the North Cascades mountain range). Mason surfs, snowboards backcountry, and mountain bikes, and lived part-time in a tipi on top of a mountain in the winter. He travels the world to photograph professional athletes in beautiful places, and the images he captures go beyond just documentation, having meaning and sight lines that make the viewer feel like they are there in that moment. The images in the exhibition present his creative approach to studying perspective. His experience as an athlete and ultimate respect for the land is felt with his images; Mason understands the landscapes, and it shows. The wall mural in the exhibition is printed large scale to make the viewer feel as if they are the one perched on the sweeping mountain of pristine snow.

Mason also crafted and shaped a binding-less powder board for the exhibition from a yellow cedar driftwood he found on the beach. It is a rich golden brown, lacquered shiny with inset seashells and sand nestled in a knot on the backside, while the front has a cedar mat woven together by Meghann O'Brien, whom Mason has often photographed snowboarding.

Also from the West Coast, Haida Kwakwaka̱'wakw Irish artist Meghann O'Brien forms contemporary connections to the world that her ancestors knew, locating her teachings from the land and natural materials she used to weave. In her words, "The origins of my practice are rooted in spending time on the land: vast stretches of forest and sea along the inside passage," and her textile work "connects to the rhythms and patterns of the natural world and creates a continuity between herself and her ancestors."[12] As a professional snowboarder, O'Brien has been featured in various films and *TransWorld* magazine. She still rides but differently now. Her weaving practice has transformed her worldview and renewed her relationship with snowboarding, a relationship that perceives the mountains and the mountain materials with a deep reverence and respect. Considering notions of time, Meghann wove together the Chilkat robe *Sky Blanket* from mountain goat hair; she brings together references to the past, present, and future, and the dualities that balance of the world. Knowing Meghann has given me a higher regard for the practice of weaving and an understanding how long and involved it is to apprentice, research, design, and then patiently weave a beautiful, storied artwork that translates cultural cosmos and continuums. In 2017, O'Brien let me know that *Sky Blanket* could not be part of the touring exhibition because it needed to be in her community and in ceremony. I couldn't stand the thought of losing this invaluable work from the exhibition, so I asked her what she thought about making a 3D twin, a clone surrogate, or digital version of it to maintain a significance with the touring exhibition so the original could live with community active in cultural continuity. O'Brien was interested and found a way to digitize *Sky Blanket* into what became *Wrapped in the Cloud*. O'Brien worked with Kate Hennessay, Hannah Turner, Conrad Sly, and Reese Muntean to take three hundred photographs stitched together to create a high-resolution digital model and animation of the original *Sky Blanket*, which really became its own living object, critically reframing museum practice and gallery ethics and centering Indigenous values in the sacred. Thinking through how digital strategies can change museum practice and repatriation models is vital for cultural continuity and adaptations, reclamations, and decolonized practices.

From the other side of Turtle Island, on the East Coast, Mi'kmaq/Ktaqmkuk artist Jordan Bennett has joked that our studio visit for this show happened while sitting on surfboards in the crystal-blue water of Hawai'i chatting between lulling waves in Waikiki during NAISA 2016. I had worked with Jordan Bennett beforehand and have followed his work closely for a while. His film, *Basket Ladies*, is an affectionate tribute to the knowledge of basketmaking, weaving, and the epistemologies of the Mi'kmaq people. The film is of Jordan visiting his auntie and uncle and conversing about the basket ladies—women who weave baskets in the community—and about his family lineage. The video is interspersed with Jordan in his studio working to visually transcribe and pyrograph teachings onto an extended longboard as a visual vocabulary, coded for him and his nation and family to learn cultural knowledge and history, etched on a board he mobilizes as he rides down the hill to indicate cultural continuance through contemporary means. The large carved disks are a marriage of the knowledge bases from the West and East Coasts. He works on yellow cedar disks he was gifted from the family with whom he apprenticed in British Columbia.

Also Mi'kmaq/Ktaqmkuk, artist Meagan Musseau made *L'nu Jacket* as a snowboarding jacket with the help of some of her matriarchal family members. *L'nu Jacket* is a cultural statement of fashion, with parts of it woven together from satin strips like those of the colorful vinyl splits she uses to mimic ash wood baskets made by Mi'kmaq women for centuries. Meagan calls upon the matriarchal memories, ancestral guidance, and mentorship of her ancestors within her work. Her *L'nu Jacket* is black with a fur collar, shiny neon tailoring in satin, and a bold beadwork pendant. This garment looks like a new luxe snowboarding jacket but shows ties to an older Ktaqmkuk history through the colors of quillwork and beading. Meagan relates to her snowboarding practice as living with a "healthy mind, body, and spirit as a way to navigate terrain," and I have come to see how this idea extends to the cultural and social terrains she exists within. The material and colors in the jacket reflect the beauty from the land.

In a celebration of materiality, going to Les Ramsay's studio in Vancouver was an experience in material appreciation, taking in his mass collection of textiles for his assemblages. He showed me completed works and work in progress. Ramsay produces assemblages with textiles, domestic craft, and painting mediums to construct large abstractions stretched on rectangle compositions. Embedded humor and kitschy themes lie within his work, coupled with layers of balanced irregularities that are aesthetically playful and allow the eye to wander over the planes of materials placed together with artistic intention. Unlike his other works in the show, *Series of Pleasant Thoughts* sits on fake citrus (very real-looking oranges) on the gallery floor. Its placement works to question value systems between mediums of painting and craft. Les showed me some videos of skateboarding too, and although he assured me his work does not cross the boundaries to include skateboarding or cultural connection within his art practice, as a curator with a specific point of view, I could identify a quality of design and sense of balance in his assemblages that contain a slight architectural lens of spatial placement and reading from a skateboarder's point of view. Or, maybe, Les is a skateboarder, an artist, and Métis. Without the intersection, period.

Métis artist and celebrated filmmaker Amanda Strong snowboards and skates. Her practice in stop-motion animation and photography evokes, as she puts it, "the iconic photo sequence in skateboard/snowboard photography," as it aligns with the process of capturing movement in the single frames of stop-motion. One of the many qualities I appreciate about Amanda's work is her attention to detail; the puppet's fashion is based on a pair of her old pants, the emblem on the hat and skateboard, the weather-worn building and windows. The diorama of her "self-puppet" shows an Indigenous woman mastering a kickflip; every frame is documented, from the pop-up to the board rotation under the body to the transitional landing, so precise it could be a manual of how it's done. Amanda and I spoke about gender fluidity and gender expectations, since we had similar experiences of growing up defying stereotypical expectations of what a girl was supposed to be and how she was supposed to act. Amanda referred to the board as a vehicle to break free of those constraints and "move"—which I feel is indicative in the way of *mino-pimatisiwin*.

I met Inuk artist Mark Igloliorte in 2011 at the Indigenous Curatorial Collective's conference and saw his solo show in a small now-closed gallery in Toronto. I told him about this show I was curating soon and that he would have to be involved based on his work and experience. Instead of a conventional studio visit, we visited at one of his favorite bowls in East Vancouver. Mark created new work for the exhibition, building on a body of work using the kayak and skateboarding as self-propelled vehicles to explore cultures in the precolonial North and modern urban South. On English Bay in November, he had artist Navarana Igloliorte film him conducting an "Eskimo roll" in his sea kayak; after many attempts, he achieved a full rotation.[13] That summer, Navarana filmed him kickflipping a set of stairs at the University of British Columbia. Both videos flank Mark's skateboard with an image of a yellow sea kayak. The rotational gesture shared by the kickflip and roll is a metaphor for cultural resurgence, a cultural continuum that mobilizes cultural knowledge physically forward. A large part of the boarding industry is about producing videos either to motivate people to push harder as practitioners or to be awe-inspiring to spectators; either results in a "transfer of energy," as Mark has pointed out. Mark's *Kayait* series further calls forth knowledge of the land and transitions of being.

Meeting Wuikinuxv, Klahoose, Kwakwa̱ka̱'wakw artist Bracken Hanuse Corlett and working with him on a couple projects opened up my knowledge of just how diversely his art practice extends: from music to painting and covering buildings with his designs. He works in a big way; I think his motto should be "Go big or go home." His work he made for the exhibition is unreal. He made a ramp sculpture that people want to use but can't. His skate-or-die ramp launches into a colonial history of the potlatch ceremony banned in Canada for sixty-six years, over three generations of people displaced from their ways of life, governance, and cultural identities. Bracken describes the potlatch as keeping his people moving forward in a good way: if it ceases, they will die. In transforming the '80s skate mantra of "skate or die" into "potlatch or die" Bracken stimulates the compulsion to survive and live. He adorned the ramp with copper figures and skulls to signify the Big House where the potlatch ceremonies are held. To keep moving forward in mobility and movement is to live in a good way for the future.

Addressing colonialism in the show is continued with Colonialism Skateboards owner, Saulteaux from Cote First Nation, Micheal Langan's collaboration with Kent Monkman (Cree artist), which dynamically unites Indigenous self-determination, art, history, and education. Through Colonialism Skateboards, Micheal educates people about Indigenous Canada's history and culture. Using the deck as canvas, he uses skateboard graphics to speak to history in Canada. By collaborating with scholars, writers, and artists, Colonialism boards have dealt with the buffalo genocide, the Indian hospitals, and the residential school legacy, as well as celebrating Indigenous culture and the complexities that exist within Indigenous cultures. The work in the exhibition is a collaboration with Kent Monkman that reproduces two paintings dealing with colonialism, *The Scream* and *The Four Continents*. *The Scream* represents a horrific scene of children being torn away from their parents by Royal Canadian Mounted Police, nuns, and priests as mandated by the government under the residential school policy. What is so powerful is that as the skateboards are skated on, the images become transformed; with active mobilization, the history of colonial violence is "skated off," as a method of transcendence.

I learned about Coast Salish Snuneymuxw artist Steven Thomas Davies's film and surfing practice. I was curious whether his films on Indigenous cultural and political matters ever crossed into or engaged with his practices as surfing, snowboarding, and skateboarding. For the exhibition, Davies created the film *driftin*, repurposing footage of him skateboarding, snowboarding, and surfing with friends on Vancouver Island. Without sound, the film is nostalgically beautiful, out of focus, and grainy. The salvaged material silently speaks of settler colonial occupation and pays homage to unceded land and the original people of British Columbia. The mash-up quality of the film also echoes the DIY boarding videos kids have long made, watched, and shared together—referencing film as a highly influential tool to inform. The installation in the exhibition is set up to look like you're in someone's home recreation room with old magazines to read.

Mixed Cree artist Roger Crait used to skate for over a decade on the "gritty" streets of Winnipeg, a city that has a population of more than seventy-eight thousand Indigenous people. Roger's work is powerful, as it relates the uphill battle Indigenous people face intergenerationally from the impacts of ongoing colonial violence. *Me Terminated* deals with personal struggles, mental health, and the suicide epidemic among Indigenous youth in Canada. *Constitutional Rites* recalls the 2005 case of an Indigenous youth, Matthew Dumas, who was shot and killed by a Winnipeg police officer in the city's North End. The "weapon" Dumas was holding was a screwdriver, and the police officers received paid leave without repercussions. This represents one of many cases of wrongful deaths and failure to protect children in the child welfare and justice system in Canada. *The Death Painting* represents the owl, and in many nations the owl is a symbol for death. Here, the owl is facing the viewer and flies over a dystopian cityscape. The sun is either rising or setting, and the feeling is frantic. On the other hand, what balances the painting is the green horizon where flowers bloom, and that is where the eyes rest, and there is peace.

To end this chapter in reflection on the project *Boarder X*, working with the artists, community, the sponsor Vans, and galleries has been one of the most significant areas of personal and professional vibrancy, growth, and pride. I take pride and comfort knowing that there are skate/snowboard communities globally affirming sovereignty and claiming space, resisting white supremacy and fragility, empowering community, decolonizing corporate interests, correcting and educating the public about Indigenous culture by means of mobilizing antiracist and solidarity movements, surviving and thriving, cultural transmissions, building resilience, leadership with environmental defending and protection—and in conversation and context with Indigenous skateboarding, snowboarding, and surfing.

Notes

1 Shawn Wilson, *Research Is Ceremony: Indigenous Research Methods* (Halifax: Fernwood, 2008), 80.

2 Robin Wall Kimmerer, *Braiding Sweetgrass: Indigenous Wisdom, Scientific Knowledge, and the Teachings of Plants* (Minneapolis, MN: Milkweed Editions, 2013), x.

3 Isaiah Helekunihi Walker, *Waves of Resistance: Surfing and History in Twentieth-Century Hawaiʻi* (Honolulu: University of Hawaiʻi, 2011), 2.

4 Taiaiake Alfred and Jeff Corntassel, "Being Indigenous: Resurgences against Contemporary Colonialism," in *Racism, Colonialism and Indigeneity in Canada*, edited by Martin J. Cannon and Lina Sunseri (Oxford: Oxford University Press, 2011), 142.

5 Colleen McGloin, "Indigenous Surfing: Pedagogy, Pleasure, and Decolonial Practice," in *The Critical Surf Studies Reader*, edited by Dexter Zavalza Hough-Snee and Alexander Sotelo Eastman (Durham, NC: Duke University Press, 2017), 197.

6 Dina Gilio-Whitaker, "How American Surf Culture Was Built on a History of Indigenous Erasure," *The Inertia*, December 1, 2015, www.theinertia.com/surf/how-american-surf-culture-was-built-on-a-history-of-indigenous-erasure.

7 Gilio-Whitaker, "Appropriating Surfing and the Politics of Indigenous Authenticity," in *The Critical Surf Studies Reader*, edited by Dexter Zavalza Hough-Snee and Alexander Sotelo Eastman (Durham, NC: Duke University Press, 2017): 228.

8 Maulani Aluli Meyer, *Hoʻolu: Our Time of Becoming* (Honolulu: Ai Pohku, 2003), iiiv.

9 Greg A. Hill, "Afterward: Looking Back to Sakahan," *Art Monthly Australia* 262 (August 2013): 13–17. Vizenor's concept of survivance defined: "Survivance in the sense of native survivance is more than survival, more than endurance or mere response; the stories of survivance are an active presence . . . the native stories of survivance are successive and natural estates; survivance is an active repudiation of dominance, tragedy, and victimry." He says, "Native transmotion is survivance, a reciprocal use of nature, not a monotheistic, territorial sovereignty. Native stories of survivance are the creases of transmotion and sovereignty." Gerald Vizenor, *Fugitive Poses: Native American Indian Scenes of Absence and Presence* (Lincoln: University of Nebraska Press, 1998), 15.

10 Leanne Betasamosake Simpson, *Dancing on Our Turtle's Back: Stories of*

Nishaabeg Re-creation, Resurgence and a New Emergence (Winnipeg: ARP Books, 2011), 31.

11 *Nations Skate Youth Book* (Vancouver, BC: Nations Skate Youth, 2022), nationskateyouth.com.

12 Meghann O'Brien, artist statement.

13 *Eskimo roll* is a racially charged term for a kayak roll, the act of righting a capsized kayak by use of body motion and paddle together.

7

Origin Stories of "Radical"

The Dogtown Imaginary and Inheritors of the Z-Boy Revolution

CHASE BUCKLEW AND DAVID KAMPER

> There is a place where America's Manifest Destiny collides into the Pacific Ocean. A place where the fabled Route 66, the roadway of American Dreams, terminates. This is Dogtown.
>
> *DOGTOWN AND Z-BOYS* (2001)

What was once "Dogtown" is now known to many as "Silicon Beach." Technology workers, whose corporations have arrived in droves, intermingle with people currently experiencing homelessness and drug addiction. These tech firms have vastly changed the landscape of modern skateboarding's birthplace. New media titans (like Google, Snapchat, and YouTube) have attracted "tech bros" to Silicon Beach from far and wide by promoting a lifestyle of the fabled utopia of urban grit and radical cool. One can skateboard to work in an office with expansive ocean views. As the Google Venice headquarters puts it: "More boardshorts than boardroom, high tech meets high tide at Google L.A."[1]

This chapter critically examines the seeds of white (hyper)masculinity in the Dogtown "revolution" and almost all modern skateboarding in its wake. The mythmaking of radical skate and surf culture found in the Dogtown and Z-Boy story has a potent legacy that transformed skateboarding from midcentury consumer culture fad to a counterculture rebellion (Yochim 2010, Butz 2012). *Dogtown and Z-Boys* has indelibly become the origin story of modern skateboarding. This narrative begins in the mid-1970s, when Craig Stecyk's gonzo journalism crafts the lore around a youthful group of innovative skaters in coastal Los Angeles—but it is not until original Z-Boy Stacy Peralta's 2001 film, *Dogtown and Z-Boys*, that this myth becomes fully codified as the origin story and dominant narrative of modern skating.[2] This groundbreaking film received much critical acclaim and captured the imagination of many (including the authors of this chapter), particularly for its revelatory depiction of a revolutionary counterculture aesthetic. However, like all origin stories and master narratives, much is to be found in their aporias.

Scholars of skateboarding have pointed out the discrepancies in the radicalness of the Dogtown story, particularly in how it reifies white male exaltation. We contribute to this analysis by focusing on "Dogtown" as a strategically imagined locale that selectively highlights parts of south Santa Monica and north Venice, California. This area has a far richer and more diverse social geography than what is found in the conventional Dogtown story, which, instead, obfuscates some key aspects of the area's radical history and centers on white teenage, male rebellion. Reexamining these places made invisible captures the more diverse influences implicit in modern skateboarding. We attend to alternative histories of the area to recenter the BIPOC skaters and surfers who have taken up the mantle of the Dogtown revolution in what, we argue, is a far more progressive fashion.

Critiques of authenticity and radicalness of any counterculture movement ought to be expected. Authenticity requires gatekeeping whereby a limited few get to define what amounts to a real countercultural gesture. As Dick Hebdige (1979) teaches, cultural forms that begin as "resistant" to the mainstream almost always get commodified by mass culture, thereby undoing their countercultural "authenticity" (see also Gelder 2005). Ultimately, under late capitalism, the quest for something that is "authentically" countercultural becomes a recursivity of never-ending regressions to increasingly narrow the features of a style that counts as authentic. In other words, the "authentically radical" is always a moving target, as the line of what's more radical is continuously pushed outside the limits of the mainstream.[3] Silicon Beach is an excellent example of this phenomenon:

the appeal for Dogtown becomes attractive to the masses and is included in corporate agendas, thus rendering an inauthenticity to would-be transgressives. The legacy of Dogtown illustrates this phenomenon, while subsequently reinforcing dominant narratives of white masculinity.

The Dogtown origin story simultaneously heralds the socially outcasted underdog skaters *while* centering and reifying their white normative masculinity (Kusz 2007, Yochim 2010). Consequently, the legacy of Dogtown continues to center white male skaters irrespective of the diversity that, to some extent, did exist in the original Z-Boy crew.[4] This chapter interrogates this privileging of masculinity and whiteness to see what is left out of the Dogtown story, to better understand the consequences of locating modern skating at this moment, this place, and among this cast of heroic delinquents. We are not the first to question the Dogtown origin myth: Kusz (2007) points out that the film explicitly avoids any discussion of race and that therefore whiteness becomes the unmarked dominant frame of this period of skateboarding; Louison (2011) focuses on Stecyk's journalistic integrity, noting his factual liberties and strategic omissions, which make it seem as if the Dogtown skaters were the only figures participating in the revolution of skateboarding in the 1970s; Sueyoshi (2019) analyzes the film's portrayal of the three Asian Americans in the Zephyr crew (Shogo Kubo, Peggy Oki, and Jeff Ho), arguing that not enough is made of their contributions to this radical age of skating, especially given the ways Asian Americans were marginalized and emasculated in other contemporaneous arenas of popular culture.[5] Our intervention builds on these critiques with a particular focus on recuperating the rich racial diversity of the place that Stecyk and Peralta roughly delineate as "Dogtown." We seek to rewrite the racial geography of this space as a way to better understand both the radical genesis of the Z-Boy crews and why BIPOC today would be drawn to the countercultural narrative of skateboarding in general and Dogtown in specific.

This chapter starts with the origin story of Dogtown and its imagined geographies. Here, we consider what is left out of the narrative and its relationship to larger discourses of Manifest Destiny and settler colonialism. Next, we examine how the Dogtown origin story creates a myth of "authenticity" and the "radical" and how this has become the dominant discourse of modern skateboarding. Lastly, we locate what is missing in this narrative of authenticity in terms of BIPOC and other marginalized groups whom we propose are drawn to the countercultural narratives of skateboarding and surfing. We argue that these skaters, surfers, and artists are better positioned to employ skateboarding's radicalness toward transformative and progressive ends, and perhaps are even more "radical" than the Z-Boys ever were themselves.

Of Dogtown and Origin Stories

Peralta's cinematic narration begins in 1905 with Abbot Kinney, a wealthy real estate developer from New Jersey, who sought to replicate the famed Italian city in LA by building a network of canals. However, habitation in Venice did not start there. There are several reported Tongva place names for the Santa Monica and Venice area—while there is thin archaeological evidence, the place names illustrate that this area was (and still is) significant to the Tongva, the Indigenous people originally caring for this land. For example, just a few miles south of Kinney's Venice canals were two important Tongva villages: Saa'anga and Waachanga (McCawly 1996). Today, the Ballona Wetlands are known by this non-Indigenous name, but before colonization, this land provided fertile grounds to sustain the Tongva people for centuries. In the eighteenth and nineteenth centuries, the Tongva and other local tribes suffered forced missionization, relocation, and assimilation such that by the time of Kinney's construction, anthropologists erroneously (and racistly) declared the Tongva to be "extinct" (Valdez Singleton 2004; Tourres-Rouff 2013; Akins and Bauer 2022).

Beginning the story with these bastardized canals is a curious place to start, given most of the other points of demarcation for Dogtown are at least a mile away. We first see our heroes surfing among the wreckage of the legendary Pacific Ocean Park (POP). This surf spot, located between Navy Court and Pier Street, on the north end of the Venice township and the south border of Santa Monica, is a full two miles from Kinney's scenic waterways.[6] Not that accuracy is critical here, but this points to the ambiguity of the Dogtown legend in the first place: where exactly is Dogtown?

According to Stecyk, the name comes from gang lingo designating several spots in this area as something "-town" (e.g., "DogTown, Ghost-Town, SmogTown . . . FrogTown [*sic*]") (Stecyk and Friedman 2000, 11). These "street gang logistics" (Stecyk and Friedman 2000, 11) imply both an amorphous shifting of turf and an insider's knowledge of locale, a sort of "if you know, you know." Stecyk employs the connotation of dangerous gang mentality and solidarity for his description of gritty "bad boy" skaters, none of whom he claims are actual gang members—nevertheless, locating them in Dogtown gives them a street gang–adjacent toughness. Of course, revealing any of the Z-Boys as actual gang members would violate one of the first tenets of any gang culture: don't snitch. Walking this fine line allows Stecyk to put the heroes of his story in gang culture but not of gang culture. Indeed, one of the early Dogtown articles Stecyk wrote for *Skateboarder Magazine*, "The Westside Style or Under the Skatetown Influence" includes images of Nathan Pratt and Jose Gallan skating in street gang clothing (Stycek and Friedman 2000).[7] Pratt's outfit references "cholo" culture: sunglasses, bandana, white T-shirt, and firmly creased khaki pants.[8] Behind him, graffiti marks a concrete wall with the now-famous Dogtown logo: the words *dog* and *town* are framed in a religious cross where *dog* is oriented horizontally and *town* vertically, sharing the *o* to complete the cross. Gallan is in front of three Chicano men leaning against their lowrider, parked in front of a cinder block wall covered in gang-style graffiti tags.[9] Using this street gang imagery and implied association allows Stecyk to construct an authenticity that is both appealing and gatekeeping in that it limits the crew to a discrete but, also, ultimately undefinable geographic location.

Here, community defined by participation gets conflated with community defined by geographic locale. Stecyk's geographic ambiguity and narrative imaginary blur this distinction, allowing "Dogtown" to represent a mythologized urban, counterculture, bad boy, radical ethos. However, the aporia in this myth reveals the cracks in its gritty hypermasculinity. In terms of geography, the articles and the film also mention other Z-Boys' skate spots: Kenter Canyon and Bellagio and Paul Revere Middle Schools, none of which are in Dogtown. The myth also tells of backyard pool skating all over LA suburbs. These are not the places of Chicano and Black street gangs but rather upper-middle-class white flight neighborhoods: Brentwood, Pacific Palisades, and Encino.

Another selective choice is the narration of founding team member Peggy Oki. Her role is not hidden but told in a limited, one-dimensional way. The film never mentions the fact that she was the only college student on the team, a clear departure from the "bad boy" narrative. We, however, argue that this makes her participation in the Z-Boy crew all the more interesting and radical. Greater explanation of her relationship with this ragtag crew of boys in or (barely) out of their teens could radically critique the "model minority" mythos so readily applied to Asian Americans (Sueyoshi 2019). Or take Marty Grimes, a Black skater who was given a very small amount of screen time in the film. His participation and relationship with the rest of the skaters, as the only African American skater, is fascinating to us but glossed over by Stecyk and Peralta (see Williams's [2022] excellent work on Grimes and other skaters of color).

This close reading of the film is not to bury the Dogtown heroes or even Stecyk and Peralta for that matter, but to say that like all storytelling, what gets defined as/included in "Dogtown" depends on what aspects of the narrative Stecyk and Peralta want to tell. However, their choices, of course, have consequences. The blurring of geographic location and the composition of the crew creates a legacy of beautifully creative style, envelope-pushing, risk-taking, and alluring countercultural rebellion. But it also can reify toxic normative white masculinity and cultural appropriation. Important to note here is the relationship between Venice Beach and Santa Monica, during both the mid-1970s and the early 2000s, when the film was released. During these eras, Santa Monica was considered elite and wealthy, whereas Venice Beach was considered rougher and "bohemian."[10] Stecyk and Peralta maintain this dichotomy to tell an underdog story and therefore often index parts of Venice that do not squarely fit into their geographic framing of Dogtown but do the geopolitical work of distinguishing class by contrasting Venice to Santa Monica. Perhaps this distinction is more important for early-2000s viewers of the film than those living in LA in the 1970s, but what this vagueness points to is the mythmaking of the Dogtown story—it is a move of geopolitical discourse, not of straight geographic mapping. We assert that other important historical moments, neighborhoods, and events can be conceptualized as relevant to the "Dogtown" neighborhood and are not included in this version of the story—instances critical to the nonwhite history of LA and the Santa Monica/Venice area.

The producers of "Dogtown" skip quite a lot in their brief history of the area. They fail to acknowledge that the land had long been settled by Indigenous Tongva peoples and the later heavy influence and prevalence of Black and Latinx populations. The area of Oakwood, which includes parts of the "Dogtown" area, was one of the only neighborhoods where Blacks and Latinx people were allowed to purchase property on the west side of LA after redlining made it impossible for most BIPOC.[11] By the 1950s, the area became known as the "Slum by the Sea."[12] Mainstream media helped construct this image of Venice as "slum" by highlighting and exaggerating coverage of gang violence in Venice, essentializing and indicting the BIPOC residents as gang members (Tatum 2011, 11). Stecyk capitalizes on this image of Venice to create the dangerous mystique of Dogtown—indeed, Stycek claims the term *Dogtown* as the gang term for the area in question. This appropriation is also visual, as Stecyk's photo essays and the later film reference gang imagery to index gritty toughness, without fully contextualizing within the racial history of West LA. When we sift through erased histories, for example, Latinx Venice pro surfer Ricky Massie emerges as a former gang member and pro surfer who competed for a spot on the 1996 World Tour. Massie can be read about only in backlog issues of the *LA Times*, and he is certainly not mentioned in the film.[13] In total, the "grittiness" just becomes a signifier of rebellion against society, completely divorced from the actual people of color who had complex relationships to these "gangs" (Kusz 2007).

Delving further into the marginalized history of the area, we find the Aragon Ballroom, a club frequented by Chicanx youth in the 1940s. Many of these youth were known as the zoot-suiters by their characteristic style of dress that was, in large part, a political statement. Zoot suits featured billowing trousers, high-waisted and pegged at the ankles, and padded wide-shouldered jackets. This excess fabric was a protest of the rationing mandated for a war effort that they believed had little benefit for people of color stateside. (Mazón 1984; Pagan 2003). The Aragon Ballroom was on Lick Pier, the precursor to Pacific Ocean Park, among the ruins of which the Z-Boys famously surfed and pushed off concrete chunks to scare nonlocals from surfing the spot. Generally, zoot-suiters were welcome at this dance hall. The Lick Pier was a place where they were free to express their rebellion against the stifling white culture in LA previous to and during World War II. However, the freedom of expression of their cruising in packs up and down the pier in their zoot suits also made them the ire of servicemen temporarily stationed in LA. The Aragon Ballroom became a flashpoint for the infamous Zoot Suit Riots. Pagan (2003) details the events of May 1943, when a gang of Navy sailors savagely attacked a group of Chicanx youth simply for wearing zoot suits. All of this took place in the area that Stycek would later call Dogtown. In terms of the African American history of the area, just a few blocks from the POP and the Zephyr surf shop is a beach known as the "Inkwell." Discussed in more depth below, the Inkwell was the only beach in the area that Blacks were allowed to frequent without getting harassed, as early as the 1920s up until the 1960s, when the Santa Monica beaches became segregated (Jefferson 2009). Unmarked and unscathed, our Z-Boys emerge amid this cultural backdrop and influence as the pioneering trailblazers (as opposed to the Indigenous, Black, and Chicanx that came before them) of the geographic space, blending easily into the manufactured narrative of the film and its surrounding mythology.

At times, the rhetoric of *Dogtown and Z-Boys* parallels that of Manifest Destiny. The Z-Boys are often referred to as "pioneers" and "outlaws," hearkening back to a Wild West fantasy and overlaying white exceptionalism onto the emergence of modern skateboarding. The film begins with narrator Sean Penn's dramatic declaration of this chapter's epigraph, which frames Dogtown as the place where Manifest Destiny terminates. This seems less a celebration of the end of settler colonialism than an acquiescence that Venice is the place where the "American Dream" goes to die. Indeed, it is a tribute to the gritty remnants of American settler and consumer culture, setting up Dogtown as the ultimate countercultural mecca, an antithesis to midcentury American excess. The film's highlighting of the POP, and its ultimate ruin, represents this tension. Originally built by the CBS broadcasting network as a seaside version of Disneyland, with similar aesthetics and escapes to "other" worlds, the POP was a carnivalesque wonderland of entertainment for tourists and suburban Californians. The film portrays the Z-Boys as reveling in its destruction and dangerous dilapidation as antiheroes mocking the lost innocence of the POP.

However, Penn's narration is not a critique of Manifest Destiny but an assertion of a debased fact, apropos of what is missing from the entire Dogtown mythos: a mindful consideration of settler heteropatriarchy. Patrick Wolfe (1999) teaches that settler colonialism erases Indigeneity as a means to legitimize control of land. Iain Borden (2001) teaches that, at its most innovative and transgressive, skateboarding reclaims and repurposes landscapes. To be sure, we admire this gesture of skateboarders most and are not suggesting that skateboarding is an act of settler colonialism, but what good is the film's reference of Manifest Destiny without actually critiquing it? The Z-Boy reimagination of space and built environment is beautifully subversive, but this radicalness is limited by obscuring nonwhite actors who were physically (and cinematically) removed from that same landscape. Moreover, there are political implications of young white men assuming roles of racial otherness as part of their countercultural ethos.

Much of the subversive subtext of the film is pushed through the audio and visuals, setting the scene for the would-be progressive progenitors. For example, a Black Sabbath track ushers in the bad boy image of Skip Engblom. He waxes poetic on how in the Dogtown days they preferred "Latina women with big hair" to white women. This purported valuing of Chicanx culture over whiteness merely reifies the exoticization of women of color, objectifying Chicanas as accessories to reaffirm a countercultural narrative. In other scenes, V-13 and MS-13 graffiti splash across the screen along with footage of guys surfing the wreckage of POP. Gang members and those behind this Chicanx aesthetic are ominously absent. "Cholo" and lowrider culture is highlighted only to signify otherness without the actual artistic individuals and rebellious characters who created it. Of course, the gang and street art was not even considered "outsider art" until folks like the Dogtown crew started to use it for their purposes, reconfiguring and appropriating the style for their ends.

This critique of the origin story of modern skateboarding may seem as if we wish to condemn the Z-Boys and its progenitors. But it is the mythmaking of Dogtown, not the skaters per se that we find troubling. Analyzing the Z-Boy crew in this regard is a bit trickier for two reasons: the only real access we have to their thinking is curated by Stycek and Peralta as nostalgic reminiscence of the Dogtown revolution, and the origin story codes them as (unmarked) white, but given the demographics of Venice/Santa Monica, their racial identities were probably far more complex. Neftalie Williams (2022) insightfully points this out about Marty Grimes. The Z-Boys' willingness to include Peggy Oki and Shobo Kogu and later Grimes alludes to their willingness to let the skating speak for itself irrespective of race. In the racially charged Los Angeles of the 1970s, this kind of integration was uncommon, making it extremely brave for Grimes to trust these mostly white skaters, especially given the race riots witnessed in his high school (Williams 2022). According to legend, it was Jay Adams of all people who invited both Oki and Grimes to join the crew (Sueyoshi 2019; Williams 2022). Adams has arguably the most problematic record on race and gender—drawing swastikas on his decks, making racist jokes, and even being convicted for gay bashing—yet he admired their skating. Another original Z-Boy, Tony Alva, does not easily code as white and has since claimed both Chicanx and Native American heritage, but the Dogtown story does not make clear if this was an important part of his identity back then. Lastly, we should not overlook Stacy Peralta's Latinx surname, yet it, too, is unremarked upon. This is all to reinforce Williams's point that the Z-Boys were perhaps more inclusive than most contemporaneous LA youth and that we should not underestimate the agency and comfort level these skaters of color must have had with their white counterparts in order to identify collectively with them. While the Z-Boys were not necessarily progressive activists, they certainly seemed OK with racial ambiguity and intermixing.

This inclusivity was most likely the product of the long, racially diverse history of south Santa Monica and north Venice. The Z-Boys grew up in a relatively desegregated area that was a fertile ground for racial tolerance, hence we are arguing for centering the real locale over Stecyk's imaginary one. As two scholars who skate (albeit poorly), surf (much more adeptly), and have (at one time) been residents of "Dogtown," we chose to reconsider the Dogtown mythology because we cherish it. Yet as scholars of critical theory, we feel it is imperative to celebrate *Dogtown and Z-Boys* for what it is *and* hold it responsible for what it is not and to promote the people and histories it obscures. What we adore about the Dogtown legend is the rebellious ethos and its transformative potential. But today we see this counterculture spirit best exemplified in BIPOC and female/trans/nonbinary skaters and surfers, who have inherited the countercultural revolution of the Dogtown legend. These marginalized folks have been drawn toward the liberatory aspects of skateboarding and surfing and have made it more inclusive and arguably more radical. The balance of this chapter considers this newer generation of skaters and surfers.

Gendered Mythologies of Skateboarding

Despite the "freedom-from-rules" and "antiestablishment" attitudes that draw many to skateboarding, like any subculture, it has informal codes of behavior and practices. Stylistic concerns and discrete rituals are frequently used to regiment skater identity and regulate interpersonal and spatial relations. Most habits and behaviors are based on the practicality of not getting in the way of someone trying a trick or avoiding high-speed collisions between people wearing very little in the way of protective gear (if any at all). Nonetheless, there are unwritten rules of style and attitude that both mark the "cool" skaters and can be intimidating for outsiders. Much of this intimidation is based on relative skill. That is, the skateboarders pulling off the most difficult tricks are often awarded the most respect, and novices tend to be hesitant to compete for space/time at a skate spot when relative experts are present. However, the demarcation of "cool" or "punk" is rarely based on merit/skill alone.

Like many kinds of antiestablishment "cool," semicovert codes often reproduce a heteropatriarchy where men define the terms of who is an authentic skater and who is not. Not surprisingly, women or gender non-conforming people are often left out. Atencio, Beal, and Wilson (2009) document the way male skaters often mark female skaters as "posers" based largely on gendered norms. Male skaters tend to connect notions of "risk" (how much a skater is willing to do a trick that will put their body in harm's way) with "authentic" skateboarding: those not taking real risks are not real skaters (Atencio, Beal, and Wilson 2009). This notion of bodily risk is highly gendered, such that the physical risks male skaters take at their bodily expense is valued over the risk of humiliation and emotional stress that female skaters open themselves to by entering a male-dominated sport. Moreover, given the chauvinist past of skateboarding, girls and women are potentially putting themselves at greater risk to bodily harm in terms of physical, emotional, or sexual assault when engaging in skater scenes (Porter 2003). As legendary pro Cara-Beth Burnside succinctly puts it, "Who wants to go skateboarding at age 13 and get made fun of by guys" (in Porter 2003, 25). Moreover, since the late 1970s, a prominent slice of skate culture has valorized hard partying, sexual promiscuity, and explicit, semipornographic, and objectifying imagery of women. This is not to suggest that skate culture has more chauvinism than mainstream American culture, per se, but that it certainly is not void of it, and that perhaps woman skaters who spend time in certain skate subcultures are taking as much bodily risk as any male skater trying to pull off an extreme trick.

Promoting a devil-may-care attitude as "real" skateboarding can be traced back to the Dogtown skaters who were valorized for more and more extreme skating in pools. This romanticization of risk was further intensified by the popularity of ramp skating in the 1980s and every increasing effort to get bigger and bigger airs, culminating in the 2000s with the X Games and skater-influenced antics of MTV's *Jackass* franchise, a one-upmanship of who was willing to do the most extremely dangerous stunt. *Jackass* was cocreated by Jefferey Tremaine, editor of the skateboarding magazine *Big Brother* (notably a Larry Flint publication), and featured professional skaters such as Bam Margera, Rob Drydek, and Jason Acuña.[14] This kind of skateboarding is not only overwhelmingly male, it is overwhelming hetero-masculinist and obscures the women's roles in the history of skateboarding, making it even more intimidating for girl/woman-, nonbinary-, and noncisgender-identified people to fully participate as skaters (Beal and Wilson 2004). Despite this frequently unwelcome attitude, women have still skated and will continue to — indeed, the future of the growth of skateboarding will likely depend on women, nonbinary, and noncisgendered people. This hetero- and hypermasculinist spirit has been changing over the last quarter of a century due in large part to more women, nonbinary, and noncisgendered skaters claiming a place for themselves within skateboarding by creating their own crews, zines, videos, and social media accounts for and of female skaters; establishing skate schools/camps for girls; and advocating for all-woman skate events and female-only jams within larger skate contests. All of this has created more accessible avenues for girls and women to start skating without having to deal with much of the chauvinism in skating (see Beal 1996; Porter 2003; Beal and Wilson 2004; Kelly, Pomerantz, and Currie 2005; MacKay and Dallaire 2012; Atencio et al. 2018; Borden 2019).

This increased participation is crucial because women have always been a part of skating from its hobby beginnings and through the late 1970s and into the '80s, as skateboarding entered its first financial boom and skateboarding became a "profession" (Beal 2013; Borden 2019). Beginning at the end of the 1980s, select female skaters were included and occasionally featured in skate videos. Cara-Beth Burnside was the first woman on the cover of *Thrasher* magazine (1989) and the first to have a signature Vans shoe (1999). Later Toy Machine heavily promoted team rider Elisa Steamer as she also made the *Thrasher* cover. However, despite this uptick in female recognition, most mainstream skateboard media were still portraying women as bikini-clad fans of male skaters and not as active, equally ass-kicking participants. Feminist-identified skaters created underground zines in direct response to this mainstream skating misogyny (Porter 2003, 2007). These zines built connections leading to female skate crews that regularly skate together, claiming the space in a skate spot to counter sexist (and sometimes even violent) male skaters (see Porter 2003; Kelly, Pomerantz, and Currie 2005; MacKay and Dallaire

2012; Atencio et al. 2018; Borden 2019).[15] In many ways this expansion of women into skateboarding reached a relative zenith with the advent of the All Girl Skate Jam, founded by Patty Segovia in 1997 (Borden 2019). This female-skater-only event has been tremendously empowering to women skaters worldwide and was so successful that Vans bought the rights and included it as part of their annual Warped Tour (Atencio, Beal, and Wilson 2009; Borden 2019). Feminist successors to the All Girl Skate Jam include skate organizations Girls Riders Organization, Skate Like a Girl, and MAHFIA.TV, and many more.

However, despite some larger embracing of women and nonbinary skaters, feminism in skateboarding still resides as a grassroots subculture, for the most part on social media and in planned meetups to skate together. This dichotomy of grassroots social media versus mainstream exposure can also be found for skaters and surfers of color. The balance of this chapter examines two examples within subcultures of surfing and skating that embody a countercultural, resistive ethos that is not as commercialized as the Z-Boys' "rebellion." In the last section, we discuss the way that BIPOC, women, and nonbinary folks are drawn to the radicalism of skateboarding and surfing mythologized in the Dogtown origin story and make it their own without reinscribing heteropatriarchy.

Skidskunx

Like many other major urban centers in the greater Southwest, Salt Lake City is a part of the Navajo diaspora.[16] It is currently home to Selina Mullen, a Diné who identifies as nonbinary (with she/her and they/their pronouns) *and* a skateboarder (Mullen interview with author 2020).[17] Selina makes fantastic pop art by drawing on the counterculture ethos of skateboarding to comment on oppressive gender normativity, white supremacy, and settler colonialism. Her/their main form of expression are stickers and wearables, with representations of Navajo skate punks, sold under the shop name "Skidskunx Art: Indigenous Resistance."[18] Hardcore, heavy metal, punk, and goth music have always been very popular in the Navajo Nation (see Soltani Stone and Zappia 2020), and Selina acknowledges this history with animation-style drawings of Diné women, men, and nonbinary folks. These figures wear elaborate combinations of "traditional" velvet skirts;[19] German silver belts; squash blossoms; turquoise rings and bracelets; *kél-chí′* (historical Diné footwear/leg wraps); *tsiiyéél* (sacred Diné hair buns); punk or heavy metal band T-shirts (e.g., The Addicts, Circle Jerks, Megadeth, Black Flag); mohawks; leather jackets; leather studded bracelets and chokers; tattoos; piercings; anarchy symbols; rainbow Pride insignias; or upside-down American flags. Many drawings also feature skateboarding and skate brands (e.g., Vans, Thrasher, Spitfire, Independent, Santa Cruz, or Skate and Destroy). The conjoining of these symbols establishes a distinctly contemporary vision of Indigeneity asserting that Navajo youth can be both skaters and Navajo. Selina claims the countercultural movement of skateboarding and its musical adjacencies (punk, heavy metal, goth) to be as much a part of Navajo culture as they are a part of Dogtown and its progeny. Even further, Skidskunx's art contends that certain skate/punk countercultural elements may be as "Navajo" as *tsiiyéél* hair buns, velvet skirts, and turquoise and silver jewelry are. Many styles now synonymous with Diné cultures, like velvet skirts and silver jewelry, originated outside of the Navajo Nation but became indigenized (even "traditionalized") by the Diné people, and skateboarding and punk rock are no different. What counts as "counterculture" about skateboarding does not belong to the origin myth of Dogtown any less than silver jewelry making belongs to German and Mexican blacksmiths, from whom the Navajos adopted the art form. Counterculture is transhistoric and manifested in many communities in almost infinite forms of articulation.

Most apparent, Skidskunx's art is decidedly anti white supremacy and decolonial. Many of her/their works feature figures standing up to police brutality, donning "ACAB" slogans—clear references to Black Lives Matter and antipolice movements. Another is a T-shirt design consisting of a Navajo skater doing a kickflip encircled by the phrase "You're Skating on Native Land." Perhaps the most politically powerful aspects of Skidskunx's art are the words emblazoned across the bottom of the animated figures' skateboard decks, on their leather jackets, or in their earrings: the decolonial battle cry "Land Back," meant to provoke awareness to the theft of settler colonialism. "Land Back" has become a contemporary movement of Indigenous activism. It is a radical, deeply countercultural call for proactive solutions and restitution. "Land Back" is the notion that being serious about decolonizing means imaging ways to return some (if not all) of Indigenous land to its historical, precolonial caretakers.[20] Equally significant, her/their art promotes progressive and tolerant understandings of gender and sexuality through images questioning heteronormativity and displaying various gender and sexual identities. For example, one drawing is of two Navajo women in a romantic embrace, and another, labeled "Decolonial Drag," proudly promotes Indigenous nonbinary identity, featuring a gender-fluid person queering "traditional" Navajo grandma attire.

Perhaps the most radical (and amusing) image is a young woman, adorned with several conventional Navajo clothing and items, acting as a dominatrix, holding a leash around the neck of an S&M, black-latex-clad figure, on all fours and wearing a "Make America Great Again" hat. This image radically combines a tolerance for an expansive notion of "normal" sexuality with a rebuke of the most recent expressions of white supremacy. This image inverts the power dynamic of white supremacy by displaying the Navajo woman making the "Trumper" heel to the height of her Indigenous pride, belittling him and leashing his violence. Moreover, the red cap is not just an easily recognized symbol of Trump supporters but also an important symbol of the settler colonial aspects of Trumpers' white supremacy. Skidskunx mocks Trump's promise to restore America's greatness by illustrating how it erases the fact that the "America" to be saved is on stolen land. The power in her/their art lies in the way it forcefully subverts how white supremacy and settler colonialism have sexualized Indigenous female bodies to serve the rapacious appetites of white men (see Murdock 2020).[21]

The transgressive ethos Skidskunx directs toward settler colonialism and white power does parallel the Z-Boys' antiestablishment attitude. However, combining skateboarding semiotics with her/their own radical ethos of Indigeneity, feminism, and embodied notions of gender and sexuality, Selina is able to "rebel" against dominant culture with transcendent possibilities not commonly seen from the prototypical disaffected, rebellious white boy skater. Selina takes the radical spirit of the Dogtown origin story and uses it to critique the institutions with the most power in the United States: the police and the presidency. What distinguishes Selina's rebellion, as an Indigenous nonbinary skater, from the Dogtown predecessors is that she/they explicitly point to the political nature of her/their radicalism. This is a kind of political and racial radicalism the Dogtown myth alludes to but fails to fulfill. Instead it is a nihilistic and amorphous rebellion, never clear what they were rebelling against and why.

Color the Water

A revolutionary politics of race similar to Skidskunx's has resurfaced in the same area that Stecyk indeterminately labeled Dogtown, in the wake of the overwhelming volume of police violence across the United States. Color the Water, a grassroots collective of BIPOC surfers, formed to participate in the Black Lives Matter movement's unforgettable uprising of summer 2020. The grassroots group began in June 2020, when the historically Black beach in Santa Monica, often called the "Inkwell," hosted one of the largest paddle-outs ever to honor George Floyd and Breonna Taylor.[22] This spawned multiple others across the California coast and beyond. In the Hawaiian tradition of collective mourning in the ocean, these events honored the lives of Floyd and Taylor and other Black lives lost at the hands of police violence.[23] At the "Inkwell's" paddle-out, Black surfer Lizelle Jackson met Asian American surfer David Malana. Noticing a need for organization and sustained action across multiethnic BIPOC surfers, they formed an antiracist collective and surf school. Color the Water (CTW)'s founding principles are based on offering "free anti-racist surf support and media for all BIPOC." As described by their website, CTW is "a community for anti-racist BIPOC to reclaim space in the ocean through joyful, defiant liberation seeking surf guidance, protection, celebration, education and media."[24] Today, it is a multipronged organization, with the primary purpose of encouraging BIPOC people to surf by pushing for representation and the recentering of coastal BIPOC and water leisure histories. Their online mission continues as follows: "We believe that by offering a surf space that embodies principles of anti-racism that include internal and external decolonization [and a] rejection of dominant surf narratives steeped in white supremacist legacies . . . we can be a part of genuinely dismantling the interlocking systems of oppression that continue to insidiously and overtly destroy us."[25] CTW's power is resplendent in their media portrayal of the joy of BIPOC surfers like Jameelah Booker, who in one social media post dances exuberantly in the parking lot and then with grace and agility in the water on her board. Booker recently picked up the sport but is already a talented surfer, a clear manifestation to the work of the CTW instructors. In no time she was taking waves left and right, anywhere from one to five feet, trimming and staying ahead of the breaking wave like someone with many years of wave-riding experience.

CTW models the transformative potential of surfing's radical antiestablishment spirit, allowing avenues of interracial collaborations while highlighting the importance of telling the stories and preserving the preexisting coastal nonwhite history of the area. In fact, the birth of Color the Water occurs not far from the Inkwell, a beach just a few hundred yards from the original Zephyr surf shop. As mentioned above, the Inkwell plays a significant role in the Black history of Los Angeles, particularly in the "Dogtown" area. Established as one of the only beaches African American Angelenos were allowed to frequent, the Inkwell served as a rare coastal site of leisure from 1905 to the 1960s (Jefferson 2009). Due to the particular Southern California version of Jim Crow, beach access for Black folks was restricted to only a few spots. The Santa Monica beach spot that Black folks were able to frequent without too much hassling was between Bicknell and Bay Streets (Jefferson 2009). The original Zephyr surf shop was on Bay and Main, just two short blocks from the Inkwell. Moreover, the Inkwell is at the bottom of Bicknell Hill, the spot the Z-Boys would famously bomb down on their skateboards in between surf sessions. The coastal segregation in Southern California severely limited opportunities for Black folks to participate in ocean sports. A rare exception were 1940s surfers like Nick Gabaldón, an African and Mexican American surfer, who is thought to be one of the first Black and Mexican American surfers in the United States (Jefferson 2009). While Stycek and Peralta may not have known this history when writing the articles and making the film, it is hard to believe that growing up and skating in "Dogtown," one did not have a sense of the extent to which Ocean Park was a historically Black neighborhood. Indeed, Black skateboarder Marty Grimes was a key part of the second iteration of the Dogtown crew that focused more on pool skating when the Zephyr Team disbanded.

CTW are the inheritors of both Nick Gabaldón's legacy (and that of countless African Americans who frequented the Inkwell) *and* the countercultural ethos at the heart of the Dogtown myth. As we assert in our discussion of Skidskunx, centering this countercultural legend on BIPOC surfers and skaters instead of white skaters might lead to more transformative narratives than the *Dogtown and Z-Boys* story. CTW use their radical and revolutionary positioning to enact positive change and engage the diverse community surrounding the geographic area while allowing access to the sport and culture of surfing and skating to BIPOC folks. The ambiguous geographic space that has become labeled "Dogtown" holds a long history of racial and athletic radicalism which includes, but is not limited to, the account of the Zephyr Skate Team and the Z-Boys. The point of this chapter is to explore what is obscured by the Dogtown origin story and its insistence on mainly reproducing a white patriarchal narrative. This narrative has stayed with skating and surfing for a long time and is only recently being challenged in the water, on the streets, and in the media. If we seek to fulfill the radically transformative potential of surfing and skating, we must include BIPOC, queer, and nonbinary voices in the sport's origin story.

Conclusion

The Dogtown origin story portrays the Z-Boys as both innovators and outcasts. They channeled their (perceived) marginality toward an anti-establishment and DIY sensibility to create a new kind of skateboarding. Although this ragtag countercultural crew in some form merely reinforced certain dominant categories like masculinity and whiteness, the legend surrounding the Z-Boys is a powerful story of rebellion that has coded skateboarding as such ever since. This rebellion easily maps onto BIPOC skaters and surfers' marginal position in American society and certain cultures of skateboarding and surfing and provides an avenue for BIPOC skaters and surfers to use this rebellious energy against settler colonialism and anti-Black racism. While Stecyk's countercultural imaginary leaves out some key radical influences with a long history in the Venice/Santa Monica area, the narrative also provides enough space for BIPOC to pick up the mantle, marshaling skateboarding toward their own radical causes.

Today, a vastly changed iteration of the imagined space of "Dogtown" exists in the heart of Venice with the influx of tech company transplants and others attracted to the area for various reasons, such as the proximity to the beach, the surfing spots, the culture and history. Yet ravaged by the pandemic, the area still holds a large population of unhoused people next to media and tech conglomerates recruiting recent college graduates, so much so that the greater Venice and south Santa Monica area has become known as "Silicon Beach." In the wake of this seismic economic shift, we believe it is imperative to tell a broader story of the area, one that attends to the rich and radical histories ignored, buried, or sidelined by the narrative of the Dogtown and Z-Boys franchise.

Allow us then to end with one more example of BIPOC reinvigoration of the Dogtown legacy and its mythological geography. Today, just off of the world-famous Muscle Beach on the Venice Boardwalk site is an extensive skate park that includes two bowls, a large transition/pump track, and an even larger flat street skate area with several ledges and rails. On any given day, you can find Diné skater Di'Orr Greenwood there, either working on her tricks or teaching a skate lesson to any young kid who wants to learn to skate (Greenwood interview with author 2020). While this land is far from Di'Orr's people's homeland, by skating here, she still claims the space for Indigenous people and Indigenous skaters. Hence, this skate park on the edge of the Pacific Ocean is decidedly not the place where Manifest Destiny and the American Dream terminate, but rather where skaters of color like Di'Orr are reclaiming and repurposing a radical tradition found in modern skateboarding's birthplace.

Notes

1 Google Careers, "Los Angeles," accessed June 1, 2022, https://careers.google.com/locations/los-angeles.

2 Greg Beato's 1999 article "The Lords of Dogtown" in *SPIN* magazine also greatly contributed to the mythologizing of the Z-Boys as well (reprinted in *Youth Subcultures* 2007).

3 Arguably, that is exactly what we are doing with this essay by asserting that women, nonbinary, and BIPOC skaters are actually more (authentically) countercultural than the Dogtown legends. Perhaps someone else will come along after and trump us with an even more punk version of skateboarding narratives.

4 This diversity extended to a few Asian American skaters, one Mexican American skater, one Black skater, and one woman. As Kusz (2007) argues, the more recent mythmaking of these skateboarding progenitors (as presented in Peralta's film) simultaneously codes the Dogtown skaters of color as white through a "color-blind" narrative of the team and uses the marginal amount of ethnic diversity to disavow a critique the skaters' white privilege.

5 In particular, Sueyoshi notes that Jeff Ho has publicly declared his unhappiness that the film portrays the Zephyr surf shop as anything other than his sole creation and enterprise, not a partnership with Engblom and Stecyk as the film suggests (2019; see also Borden 2019 and Butz 2012 for their excellent distillations of these critiques).

6 Today, most of the homes lining the canals are multimillion-dollar vacation homes and Airbnbs, many of which remain uninhabited much of the year.

7 In the original August 1976 issue of *Skateboarder Magazine*, the author is listed as John Smythe. Smythe is one of Stecyk's nom-de-plumes (Stecyk and Friedman 2000, 7).

8 The terms *cholo/a* has had a long history in the Southwest, dating back to the nineteenth century, and has had evolving meaning and connotation ever since (Tatum 2011). Tatum (2011) notes that for most of the term's history it was derogatory; however, in the last forty to fifty years, in Southern California, it has come to describe a certain kind of street aesthetic that connotes Chicanx pride and in many ways strength/power in ways not that dissimilar to the zoot suit or pachucos/as aesthetic. Tatum (2011) and Vigil (1988) also note that outsiders to Chicanx communities often mistake the "cholo/a" aesthetic for explicitly gang culture. While some who don the cholo/a aesthetic may participate in Chicanx gang life, many do not. It seems to us that Z-Boys

were drawing on this aesthetic for its gang proximity if not at the very least its countercultural power. While it could also have been an act of Chicano pride, neither the film nor Stycek's articles ever state this, and it is unclear the extent to which any of the Z-Boys actively identified as Chicano, including Pratt, whose photograph we referenced. We interpret this as more appropriative than participatory.

9 We note that it is racist and essentializing to suggest that all urban Chicano men or those driving lowrider or urban graffiti is inherently gang related or even nefarious at all; however, we contend that the makers of the Dogtown mythos are absolutely trying to signify street gang imagery.

10 It should be acknowledged here that the term *bohemian* itself is a misnomer based on racial otherness and appropriated by mostly white artists and writers to signal an "outsider" status. The term *bohemian* has been haphazardly used to describe the culture and life of the Romani people, a racial minority who, having traveled to Western Europe, were assumed to have traveled from the area of Bohemia, located in the current-day Czech Republic. Indeed, many Romani may have traveled from or through the area, but it is now generally agreed upon that they most likely were pushed westward from northern India. Nevertheless, in turn-of-the-century Paris, artists and writers popularized the term *bohemian* to describe their own counterculture by referencing the Romani people (who were by no means included or invited to participate, nor were they to reap any benefits whatsoever from the movement). The term has been co-opted and appropriated by various aesthetic movements, here, notably, by the artists and writers in Dogtown.

11 J. Divinity, "A Tale of Two Venices: Before There Was Dogtown, There Was Oakwood," Knock-la.com, 2020, https://knock-la.com/venice-oakwood-black-neighborhood-history-a270785f0a04. Redlining is a process in which banks and institutions were allowed to deny affordable mortgage rates to people based on their racial identification. Housing in particular areas was routinely denied to nonwhites by gouging mortgages and other expenses for some and not for others. As a result, certain areas in American cities, especially LA, have become racially segregated based on historically institutionalized practices. See also Widener 2024.

12 Ruth Fowler, "Venice Beach: From Nasty to Nice," *Guardian*, January 30, 2010, www.theguardian.com/travel/2010/jan/31/losangeles-california.

13 Dennis Romero, "The Outsider," *LA Times*, July 15, 1996, www.latimes.com/archives/la-xpm-1996-07-15-ls-24256-story.html.

14 Due to the success of *Jackass*, Margera and Drydek both were given MTV spinoff shows with a similar ethos.

15 For example, in 1991 Mark "Gator" Rogowski pleaded guilty to assaulting, raping, and murdering a woman; Jay Adams went to prison in 1982 for a gay-bashing incident; and Sal Rocco committed what we would consider to be a grave act of symbolic violence by creating Bitch Skateboards whose (sadly popular) logo was a man holding a gun to a woman's head.

16 See Ramirez (2007) for a broader discussion of the American Indian diasporas and migrations back and forth between reservations and urban centers.

17 *Diné* is the Indigenous term for what settlers have labeled *Navajo*.

18 The Skidskunx Art shop is mainly through redbubble.com, an online marketplace for independent artists to promote their work. It is generally consistent with the DIY ethos of skateboarding and used by many skateboard artists, especially Indigenous ones.

19 We use the term *tradition* in quotes because is it so fraught with settler notions of time (see Rifkin 2017). As Laguna Pueblo author Leslie Marmon Silko asserts, tradition has always adapted to the needs of the present, never static. Here, we are using it as shorthand for styles and symbols that index historically accepted Navajo semiosis (cited in King 2008).

20 An important thing to note about the Land Back movement is that, like the prison abolitionist movement, it is grounded in pragmatism, not merely ideology. It is not calling for an immediate reversal of 150-plus years of practice and policy that would produce an inordinate amount of chaos. Instead, it promotes several critical small steps that would have a huge impact on current Indigenous relationships to land—such as working out leasing agreements, joint jurisdiction, or comanagement. The idea is not that all non-Indigenous people and entities should forfeit any land that they occupy (just as prison abolition does not mean immediate release of all prisoners or no consequences for crime), but rather that America is way out of balance in terms the lack of Indigenous control of land and that Indigenous people should have far greater access to land lost to settler colonialism.

21 One last beautiful irony here is that, as mentioned, Selina sells her/their art on redbubble.com, which is very convenient in that it takes images created by artists and offers consumers the options of putting this art on stickers, book bags, T-shirts, sweatshirts, and mugs. The website provides stock models displaying the various items available. There are a handful of multicultural, multiethnic models, but there are also some distinctly white models. Seeing

these white folks model the transgressive imagery of Skidskunx/Selina adds a whole new (unintended, but nevertheless powerful) rebuke of whiteness.

22 The term *Inkwell* has been used in a derogatory fashion by early-twentieth-century white folks, marking and mocking the specific beach that Black folks frequented—with the obvious metaphor of Black bathers turning the ocean water black. This term has been used not only for the Ocean Park beach location we are describing but also for many segregated beach spots up and down the California coastline (Jefferson 2009). Alison Rose Jefferson (2009) has noted that for some the term is still offensive, but other Black beachgoers and surfers have reclaimed the term with pride. The latter is certainly the case for Color the Water.

23 Paddle-outs are ceremonies in which surfers will paddle out into the ocean on their surfboards, form a circle, and pay tribute to a life that has been lost. The tradition is believed to have come from the surf revival of the late 1800s/early 1900s, in which Native Hawaiians practiced surfing as a way to rebel against colonial powers. The most globally noted large-scale paddle-outs were in honor of Hawaiian surfers Duke Kahanamoku in 1968, at Waikiki, and Eddie Aikau, in 1978 which took place in Waimea Bay. Paddle-outs continue to be a way to pay tribute and honor lives among the surfing community around the world.

24 "Joyful Anti-racist Surf Lessons for BIPOC," Color the Water, accessed June 17, 2024, www.colorthewater.org.

25 "About Us," Color the Water, accessed June 17, 2024, www.colorthewater.org/aboutus.

References

Akins, A. B., and W. J Bauer. 2022. *We Are the Land: A History of Native California*. Berkeley: University of California Press.

Atencio, M., B. Beal, and C. Wilson. 2009. "The Distinction of Risk: Urban Skateboarding, Street Habitus and the Construction of Hierarchical Gender Relations." *Qualitative Research in Sport and Exercise* 1, no. 1: 3–20.

Atencio, M., B. Beal, Z. Wright, and E. McClain. 2018. *Moving Boarders: Skateboarding and the Changing Landscape of Urban Youth Sports*. Fayetteville: University of Arkansas Press.

Beal, B. 1996. "Alternative Masculinity and Its Effect on Gender Relations in the Subculture of Skateboarding." *Journal of Sport Behavior* 19, no. 3: 204–20.

———. 2013. *Skateboarding: The Ultimate Guide*. Westport, CT: Greenwood.

Beal, B., and C. Wilson. 2004. "'Chicks Dig Scars': Commercialisation and the Transformation of Skateboarders' Identities." In *Understanding Lifestyle Sports: Consumption Identity, and Difference*, edited by Belinda Wheaton, 31–54. London: Routledge.

Beato, G. 2007. "Lords of Dogtown." In *Youth Subcultures: Exploring Underground America*, edited by Arielle Greenberg, 21–35. New York: Pearson Longman.

Borden, I. 2001. *Skateboarding, Space and the City: Architecture and the Body*. Oxford, England: Berg.

———. 2019. *Skateboarding and the City: A Complete History*. London: Bloomsbury Academic.

Butz, K. 2012. *Grinding California: Culture and Corporeality in American Skate Punk*. Bielefeld, DE: Transcript-Verlag.

Gelder, K., ed. 2005. *The Subcultures Reader*. New York: Routledge.

Hebdige, D. 1979. *Subculture, the Meaning of Style*. London, Methuen.

Jefferson, A. R. 2009. "African American Leisure Space in Santa Monica: The Beach Sometimes Known as the 'Inkwell,' 1900s–1960s." *Southern California Quarterly* 91, no. 2: 155–89.

Kelly, D. M., S. Pomerantz, and D. Currie. 2005. "Skater Girlhood and Emphasized Femininity: 'You Can't Land an Ollie Properly in Heels.'" *Gender and Education* 17, no. 3: 229–48.

King, T. 2008. *The Truth about Stories: A Native Narrative*. Minneapolis: University of Minnesota Press.

Kusz, K. 2007. *Revolt of the White Athlete: Race, Media, and the Emergence of the Extreme Athletes in America*. New York: Peter Lang.

Louison, C. 2011. *Impossible: Rodney Mullen, Ryan Sheckler, and the Fantastic History of Skateboarding*. Guilford, CT: Lyons Press.

MacKay, S., and C. Dallaire. 2012. "Skirtboarder Net-A-Narratives: Young Women Creating Their Own Skateboarding (Re)Presentations." *International Review for the Sociology of Sport* 48, no. 2: 171–95.

Mazón, M. 1984. *The Zoot-Suit Riots: The Psychology of Symbolic Annihilation*. Austin: University of Texas Press.

McCawley, M. 1996. *The First Angelinos: The Gabrielino Indians of Los Angeles*. Banning, CA: Malki Ballena Press.

Murdock, E. G. 2020. "This Land Was Made for . . . : (Re)Appearing Black/Brown Female Corporeality, Life, and Death." *Hypatia* 35, no. 1: 190–203.

Pagan, E. O. 2003. *Murder at the Sleepy Lagoon: Zoot Suits, Race, and Riot in Wartime L.A.* Chapel Hill: University of North Carolina Press.

Peralta, S., dir. 2001. *Dogtown and Z-Boys*. Sony Pictures Classics.

Porter, N. L. 2003. "Female Skateboarders and Their Negotiation of Space and Identity." Master's thesis, Concordia University.

———. 2007. "She Rips When She Skates: Female Skateboarders as Active Subcultural Participants." In *Youth Subcultures: Exploring Underground America*, edited by Arielle Greenberg, 121–35. New York: Pearson Longman.

Ramirez, R. K. 2007. *Native Hubs: Culture, Community, and Belonging in Silicon Valley and Beyond*. Durham, NC: Duke University Press.

Rifkin, M. 2017. *Beyond Settler Time: Temporal Sovereignty and Indigenous Self-Determination*. Durham, NC: Duke University Press.

Soltani Stone, A., and N. A. Zappia. 2020. *Rez Metal: Inside the Navajo Nation Heavy Metal Scene*. Lincoln: University of Nebraska Press.

Stecyk, C. R., and Glen E. Friedman. 2000. *Dogtown: The Legend of the Z-Boys*. Brooklyn: Akashic Books

Sueyoshi, A. 2019. "Skate and Create: Skateboarding, Asian Pacific America, and Masculinity," *Amerasia Journal, Special Issue on Sport in America* 41, no. 2: 2–24.

Tatum, C. M. 2011. *Lowriders in Chicano Culture: From Low to Slow to Show*. Santa Barbara: Greenwood.

Tourres-Rouff, D. S. 2013. *Before L.A.: Race, Space, and Municipal Power in Los Angeles, 1781–1894*. New Haven, CT: Yale University Press.

Valdez Singleton, H. 2004. "Urbanization: The Gabrieleno, 1850–1928." *Wicazo Sa Review* 19, no. 2: 49–59.

Vigil, D. 1988. *Barrio Gangs: Street Life and Identity in Southern California*. Austin: University of Texas Press.

Widener, D. 2024. *Third Worlds Within: Multiethnic Movements and Transnational Solidarity*. Durham, NC: Duke University Press.

Williams, N. 2022. "Before the Gold: Connecting Aspirations, Activism, and BIPOC Excellence through Olympic Skateboarding." *Journal of Olympic Studies* 3, no. 1: 4–27.

Wolfe, P. 1999. *Settler Colonialism and the Transformation of Anthropology*. London: Bloomsbury Publishing.

Yochim, E. C. 2010. *Skate Life: Re-imagining White Masculinity*. Ann Arbor: University of Michigan Press.

8

The Code of the Sea

Race, Gender, and Belonging in Southern California Surf Culture

CASSIE COMLEY

In recent years, sport scholars have turned a critical lens toward lifestyle sport culture to analyze how dominant ideologies are reproduced, resisted, and challenged. It has been argued that sports like surfing and snowboarding offer a greater potential to disrupt power relations and confront dominant cultural norms due to their lesser ties to traditional sporting cultures (Wheaton 2017; Thorpe 2008). At first, a majority of the research focused on women's experiences of marginalization and exclusion, but scholars are beginning to examine the relationship between whiteness and lifestyle sports (Thompson 2017; Stoddart 2011; Comer 2016; Yochim 2010; Kusz 2007; Gilchrist and Wheaton 2011) to better understand why lifestyle sports are often constituted as an overwhelmingly white cultural space. More specifically, scholars are increasingly documenting the ways in which marginalized groups of people navigate predominantly white, heterosexual, male recreational activities, in an effort to unpack how BIPOC (Black, Indigenous, People of Color) experience exclusionary practices and the tools they develop to challenge power relations (Nemani and Thorpe 2016; Mizuno 2018). Building on this body of research, I offer insight into how Mexican American surfers construct a racialized and gendered sense of belonging and analyze why surf spaces in Southern California tend to be exclusionary toward nonwhite male participants. Findings from this study suggest Mexican American surfers' sense of belonging is largely informed by surf relations in the water, such as feeling hypervisible or overly scrutinized when they allegedly violate informal cultural norms and battling against inherently exclusive and discriminatory surf hierarchies.

Scholars interested in exploring, challenging, and transforming power relations embedded within the sport context have recently turned to adopt a critical race theory framework for deconstructing dominant ideologies of gender, race, class, and sexuality, among others. Critical race theory (CRT) can be utilized as both a methodological tool and a framework for exploring and examining acts of racism in a society that "privileges whiteness as it disadvantages others because of their 'blackness'" (Hylton 2010, 3). Before CRT became a comprehensive framework for understanding how racism operates across a multitude of social institutions, it was a legal theory of race and racism with the intention of uncovering how race and racism operate in the law and society (Hylton 2009; Parker and Lynn 2002). The theory was initially used as a tool for scholars to define, expose, and address legal and educational problems in North America, but it is now utilized across multiple disciplines. CRT derives from the central standpoint that we live in a fundamentally racist and unequal society in which resources and power are unevenly distributed (Hylton 2009). By using CRT as a conceptual framework, scholars will be able to explore racism in society by taking into consideration the role of institutions and centering the voices and experiences of those affected by racism at all levels of society, including sports (Hylton 2009, 2010).

Sport continues to be a powerful social institution where cultural meanings about people's interlocking and intersecting identities are created and contested. Therefore, it is imperative for scholars to examine a variety of people's experiences across multiple sporting spaces to further understand issues of identity-based inequalities and relations. CRT studies of sport can directly challenge the prevailing popular belief that sport is a space that is free from societal influence and produce scholarly work with a clear commitment to forms of social justice that encapsulate elements of liberation and transformation (Hylton 2009; see also Solórzano and Yosso 2001, 2005). In the spirit of moving sport sociology research in a direction that centers marginalized voices and challenges researchers to make their investigation political rather than neutral, analyses from this data will be employing a CRT framework to explain how Mexican American surfers experience and perceive identity-based exclusionary practices and discrimination.

As a woman of color and avid surfer, the researcher utilized their "cultural insider" (Olive and Thorpe 2011) status to gain access or "get in" (Berg 2004) to the field. Practitioners of the sport can use their "cultural insider" status, physical ability, and preexisting cultural knowledge to gain access to the desired sporting field (Olive and Thorpe 2011). Gaining access to the field or "getting in" consists of the "various techniques and procedures intended to secure access to a setting, its participants and knowledge about phenomena and activities being observed" (Berg 2004, 67). The researcher spent a year in Southern California collecting data from self-identified Mexican American and white non-Hispanic surfers. A total of seventy surfers were interviewed over the course of a year. The study focused on Southern California due to its high concentration of Mexican Americans that reside in the area (Vasquez 2011; Pulido and Pastor 2013) and its vibrant coastal communities. In addition to this, Southern California is arguably the birthplace of modern surfing (Booth 2001; Ford and Brown 2005; Wheaton 2017). These two factors led the researcher to believe they would have an ample data source to operate with.

In-depth interviews, observations, and participant observations were all used to gather the necessary data for uncovering the everyday experiences of Mexican American surfers. Interviews averaged forty-five minutes in length and occurred in a variety of settings. All participants provided verbal consent, and interviews were audio recorded with a recording device. The researcher transcribed the interviews by hand, and the transcriptions were line-by-line coded for major themes and insights. The findings presented here are a part of a larger study examining how Mexican American surfers experience structural and interactional forms of racism and sexism in public sporting spaces across the beaches of Southern California. Data from this study exposes the subtle and overt ways Mexican American surfers are subjected to discrimination, sexism, and racism inside and outside the lineup to illuminate the structural forces creating unequal opportunities and access in the surf.

In this chapter, the researcher details how Mexican American surfers' gendered and racialized sense of not belonging is inscribed by surf relations in the water, driven largely by localism, locals, and surf hierarchies. Inside the water, all surfers brush up against localism, but Mexican American surfers' racialized and gendered feelings of acceptance extend beyond a few surfers treating them differently. Their experiences are exacerbated by surf relations, which the researcher argues is the configuration of factors framing Mexican American surfers' experiences of discrimination, marginalization, and exclusion. Data suggests racial structural inequality drives the cultural concept of localism, a concept claimed by white surfers to mark the space as white and conceptualize nonwhite surfers as intruders. In turn, surf relations are shaped and reinforced by white surfers' "color-blind racism" perspective, operating as a system of exclusion that disproportionately affects women and Mexican American surfers. These racialized and gendered notions of not belonging reinforce dominant cultural ideologies about surf culture's inherent and embodied whiteness. White surfers' adoption of a "color-blind racism" viewpoint obstructs them from understanding surf cultures' problematic surf relations and history, equipping them with a platform for denying or dismissing BIPOCs' experiences of exclusion. These findings illustrate the ways in which sporting spaces are important sites where racial ideologies and existing patterns of racial and ethnic relations are reproduced (Coakley 2016; Burdsey 2017; Carrington 2015).

The first part of the chapter addresses how the construction of American localism is tied to the legacy of residential segregation: specifically, the ways in which coastal communities have been racialized or shaped by structural racism, creating a context for white upper-class heterosexual males to occupy the top of the surf hierarchy with ease. With that being said, the mechanics of localism also support a settler colonial mindset used to justify locals' perceived ownership of public lands (Gilio-Whitaker 2017). By believing they are entitled to uncontested access to surf-related resources, locals are immortalizing a code rife with contradictions. The second part focuses on how localism drives a "color-blind racism" perspective or mindset. By adhering to this lens, locals are simultaneously defending their actions and condoning discrimination. This section will be interwoven with narrative from participants, in particular Mexican American surfers' experiences with subtle and overt forms of racism and sexism in the surf zone.

Residential Segregation and the Construction of Localism

As previously mentioned, notable scholars have started to examine the relationship between whiteness and lifestyle sports in an effort to understand why lifestyle sports are often constituted as a "white space" or represented as a "cultural space that is overwhelming white" (Kusz 2004, 207). Unpacking the whiteness of surfing spaces unmasks which factors influence why a person of color may not perceive the beach or the sport as a recreational activity for them. For example, findings from Wheaton's (2017) study called attention to perceptions Black surfers had prior to entering the sport. A majority of participants said they perceived the beach as white space and not a very welcoming place for a person of color. Even after learning to surf, requiring frequent trips to the beach, participants still reported feelings of "otherness" in and outside of the water. Assimilating to beach culture was perceived as a challenge for some and others; it was a smoother transition if they had prior exposure to predominantly white spaces within Southern California beach culture. There are significant overlaps between Wheaton's study of Black surfers and this project. Mexican American participants additionally perceived the beach as a white space and reported difficulty assimilating to the residual effects of the Jim Crow era, such as redlining and residential segregation (Jefferson 2009).

Racial segregation has been a defining characteristic of United States cities for nearly a century and has played a significant role in driving as well as maintaining racial and ethnic inequality (Massey and Denton 1987; Hall, Crowder, and Spring 2015). During the Civil Rights era, nonwhite residents could not legally purchase houses or land near the ocean in Southern California (Jefferson 2009). Specifically in California during the 1920s, the city beaches around Los Angeles were typically limited to whites only. Economic factors existed besides legal ones, as the rising price of beach real estate contributed to beach communities becoming increasingly white (Jefferson 2009). Residential segregation in Southern California limited nonwhite people from accessing the coast and inhibited their exposure to beach culture. Despite limited and restricted access to public beaches, segregated recreational spaces became important spaces for nonwhite residents to engage in leisure and pleasure along the beautiful Southern California coastline (Jefferson 2009). Segregated beaches, like the Inkwell in Santa Monica, were and are important recreational spaces for African American beachgoers (Jefferson 2009; Comer 2016). The Inkwell was recently recognized as a historical landmark by the city of Santa Monica (Comer 2016) and is often a site for special events, celebrations, and ceremonies to commemorate the history of African American leisure and pain.

In the United States, racialized structural factors shape and determine what spaces people of color occupy. By examining the "racial demography" (Lipsitz 2011, 12) of the places where people live, work, and play, scholars can begin the process of understanding how exclusion and inclusion operate deeply throughout society. Cultural geographer George Lipsitz (2011) argues a "white spatial imaginary" operates as a central mechanism for obstructing opportunities and life chances in the United States. The belief in a racially specific spatial imaginary is not a theory but a "metaphorical construct that reveals actual social relations" (Lipsitz 2011, 11). Therefore, "whiteness, as an analytical category, refers not only to the ways in which all whites benefit from the association of whiteness with privilege but to the ways in which public spaces are defined by racial demography" (Lipsitz 2011, 12). In other words, public places and social institutions are often informally marked or assumed to be white (Flores-González 2017; Lipsitz 2011; Bonilla- Silva 2010), including public beaches in Southern California (Wheaton 2017). Residual effects of residential segregation coupled with surf culture's white spatial imaginary create a context for the cultural notion of localism to thrive.

Residential segregation is the structure driving localism because small but powerful groups of privileged surfers are hoarding waves and engaging in exclusionary practices to keep outsiders out of the surfing space that they feel entitled to as property owners. Structurally, white upper-class heterosexual males are in the prime position to progress to the status of local and enforce localism because nonwhite surfers historically had limited and restricted access to the coast. Localism can best be understood as a "complicated set of informal rules and hierarchies" meant to impose order on other surfers (Westwick and Neushul 2013, 195) and a "practice through which surfers claim authority to protect their surf breaks and access to waves from newcomers and outsiders" (Olive 2019, 39). Surfers adopting and operating through a lens of localism have a certain "sense of belonging at particular surf breaks" (Olive 2019, 42) and refer to themselves as "a local" or "being local" (Garbutt 2011). This is the definition I will be using when discussing "local" throughout the essay. Despite women and minorities' accelerating presence in the sport (Olive, Roy, and Wheaton 2018; Comer 2010), lineups continue to be dominated by elite white men sitting at the top of the pecking order (Evers 2009). A "pecking order" (Evers 2009), also known as a surfing hierarchy, is an established ranking in the surfing space, with female, nonwhite, homosexual, and other marginalized categories of surfers sitting below white, upper-class, able-bodied heterosexual men (lisahunter 2017; Hough-Snee and Eastman 2017). This ordering can be fluid and flexible depending on the geographical location, but this is typically the norm in surf literature. For American surfers, localism is a mechanism for small but powerful groups of white, upper-class, heterosexual males to establish power in surfing spaces.

Spatial segregation has indoctrinated wealthy communities to hoard amenities and resources, and to exclude "undesirable populations" (Lipsitz 2011, 28). Through this process of exclusion and marginalization, surfing spaces have become racialized, marked as white, and highly localized. The cultural consequences of the white spatial imaginary "naturalizes" and hides residual effects of residential segregation. Oftentimes, the inherent whiteness of surf culture goes unquestioned. Locals, who are overwhelmingly white, fail to recognize the ways in which their actions, behaviors, and unearned privileges extend from structural inequalities that benefit them. Localism and the actions enacted by locals work to exclude Mexican American surfers from the space and make them feel as if they inherently do not belong in the lineup.

Additionally, locals also fail to recognize how structural advantages position them socially and economically above nonwhite surfers. Therefore, racialized structural disadvantages seep into American surf culture, enabling white surfers to remain at the top of the pecking order without being overtly racist. White surfers use the cultural notion of localism to defend their actions and the actions of others. Thus, localism and the maintenance of surfing hierarchies become major tools for white people to mark surf territories as white, and by proxy exclude nonwhite bodies by making them feel unwelcomed. Localism in the American context is also a complex belief system claimed by white surfers to mark spaces as white, preventing nonwhite surfers from accessing public recreational spaces and marking their bodies as "other." For the most part, locals' beliefs and actions stem from a "color-blind" perspective.

Color-Blind Racism and Surfing

Surfers adopting a "color-blind racism" perspective argue that surf-related issues in the water, specifically cases of exclusion, have more to do with the informal rules that regulate the space than race or gender. Most white male surfers and approximately half of white female surfers dismissed any instances of race-related issues in the water and argued instead that surfing is a sport for anyone with access to a surfboard. Most white male surfers agreed that female surfers experience some degree of sexism in the lineup but became visibly uncomfortable when discussing issues related to race. Overall, color-blind racism was the dominant ideology used by white surfers and a small handful of Mexican American surfers to explain racial matters in surfing. The following section will analyze responses to surf-related issues and highlight the ways in which the naturalization and minimization of race frames are applied to understanding how color-blind racism operates within surfing spaces across Southern California beaches.

Eduardo Bonilla-Silva's book *Racism without Racists: Color-Blind Racism and the Persistence of Racial Inequality in America*, exposed the ways in which white people utilize a myriad of frames to explain a host of racial issues in the United States. As he argued, presently most white people allege that they "don't see any color, just people," that people need to stop playing the "race card," and that everyone needs to just get over whatever "race problem" we have in this country (Bonilla-Silva 2010, 1). Most white people believe race is no longer a central factor determining minorities' life chances, but as he argued, these explanations stem from a new racial ideology that he labeled "color-blind racism." A person adopting a "color-blind racism" perspective views racial inequality as the outcome of "nonracial dynamics" and rationalizes minorities' current status as a product of a "naturally occurring phenomena" (Bonilla-Silva 2010, 2). Contemporary racial inequality is reproduced through "New Racism" practices operating in more subtle, discreet, and institutional forms (Bonilla-Silva 2010). New forms of racism are not overt or as "obvious" as racist practices in the past. In general, white people use four frames of color-blind racism to explain a host of racial realities. All the frames can be used simultaneously and interchangeably throughout their explanations of racial realities. In this study, white surfers mainly used two out of the four frames to explain the racial realities of surfers in the Southern California context.

The *naturalization frame* is simply the ways in which white people "naturalize" race- related matters. Adopting this frame allows white people to "explain away any racial phenomena by suggesting they are natural occurrences" (Bonilla-Silva 2010, 28). Common phrases such as *that's the way it is* or the word *natural* are often interjected to normalize events or actions that could otherwise be interpreted as racially motivated or racist. The *minimization of racism* framework suggests that discrimination or racism is no longer a central factor affecting minorities' life chances or opportunities. Specifically, in the case of surfing, people using this framework believe that racism does not affect minorities' opportunities or experiences in the water. Utilizing these frameworks reinforces the color-blind logic, bolstering the myth of nonracialism (Bonilla-Silva 2010). Subscribing to a perspective that ignores how societal forces shape cultural norms blinds white surfers from seeing how the cultural notion of localism is largely influenced by structural racism. Failing to recognize the role residential segregation has played in shaping the racial demography of the sport not only positions white people to normalize whiteness in surf culture, but it also prevents them from seeing how the sport has evolved to be inherently exclusive. The importance and significance of the naturalization frame can best be illustrated by Jerry, a young, white, male surfer who used this frame a few times throughout the interview. For example, Jerry used this perspective to answer the question about why surfing is generally an exclusive recreational activity, regardless of race: "That's just the way it is. That's localism for you. It's not your home. You have to be mindful of that. It's their waves, so you have to be low-key in the water. Don't act aggressive. Mutual respect." Jerry also used this frame to answer the question about facing any race-related barriers when he surfs internationally: "I don't think I get treated differently for the color of my skin or because I'm a white boy. I think I get treated differently because I'm not from around there, like any sort of localism; that's just how it works in every part of the world. That's not your home, so don't expect people to see you and be like, 'What's up, dude,' you know? That's not your spot. You can't expect people to react positively, and I was always really aware of that when I paddled out." In both explanations, Jerry dismisses the probability of other factors creating exclusionary practices by defaulting to localism for any race-related issues of exclusion or marginalization. Even when he traveled to other countries, where arguably the racial makeup of the lineup may be different, he doesn't believe race plays a role in exclusionary practices. Since postracial racial norms don't allow for the open expression of racial views, white people have constructed creative and concealed ways of voicing racial views (Bonilla-Silva 2010). For example, Jerry is utilizing the "rhetorical tool" or "semantic move" of the "anything but race" response (Bonilla-Silva 2010) to naturalize any race-related issues in the sport and reinforce the logic of nonracialism. By stating he does not believe he gets treated differently based on his whiteness, he dismisses the notion that race may affect his or other surfers' experiences in the water.

A handful of Mexican American surfers also believed localism was the main motive of exclusion and marginalization in the lineup. Mexican American surfers gave answers that were more contradictory than those of whites, oftentimes claiming race is not a factor but later in the interview recalling stories where race "may have been a factor." To this effect, Mexican American surfers' consciousness was slightly impacted by color-blind racism but was not the main foundation upon which they articulate their views on racial matters in the lineup. Some Mexican American surfers ascribe to a "slightly color-blind" (Bonilla-Silva 2010) lens to explain their experiences of exclusion and racialized feelings of not belonging. Frank, an older, working-class, first-generation Mexican American surfer illustrates adopting a slightly color-blind racism frame in the following conversation about exclusionary practices: "It would be localism, doesn't matter where it's coming from. It would be localism. Localism drives exclusionary acts. Guys that are locals, they don't want "outsiders" surfing their waves because they see them as their waves, but they are not their waves. They are public waves. Localism overrides everything." At first, he argued localism drives exclusionary acts, but when I asked him if it was different when he started surfing in the 1970s, this is the mixed response he provided: "Localism, it doesn't matter if you're black, yellow, brown, they don't want you at their beach. But if they see some black guy coming down to the beach with a surfboard, they're going to say or think 'who's that [racial epithet]?' 'What's he doing here?' Absolutely." At another part of the interview, Frank also acknowledged that surfers experience discrimination in covert forms: "There is subtle discrimination out there in the lineup, and if anyone tells you it's not there, they're bullshitting. It's out there. There's no doubt about it."

At first Frank used the naturalization lens to explain racial matters in the lineup, by arguing localism is the reason surfers feel excluded and marginalized. In the second quote, he used the minimization of racism frame to claim it doesn't matter if you're "black, yellow or brown," when it comes to localism; locals do not like outsiders regardless of someone's social category. However, he contradicted himself when he commented on what he believed locals would say if they saw a nonwhite surfer on the beach. In the final quote, he completely altered his position on racial matters, by revealing racial discrimination is an issue in surfing and localism is being driven by exclusionary acts toward nonwhite surfers. By the end of the conversation, Frank underscored how discrimination exists in surf culture, but he still relied on the naturalization frame to explain exclusionary practices and marginalization.

White surfers' use of the frames of color-blind racism can be explained in part by their very limited exposure to nonwhites in school, work, and leisure settings. Most white surfers grew up in predominantly white, middle- to upper-class neighborhoods, which increased their levels of social and spatial segregation from minorities. Since segregation and racial preference for friends are due to social preference (Bonilla-Silva 2011), surfers adopting this frame are under an illusion, or delusion, as to how social processes shape surf relations. High levels of social and spatial segregation and isolation from minorities create what Bonilla-Silva (2010) terms "white habitus." A white habitus is a "racialized, uninterrupted socialization process that conditions and creates whites' racial tastes, perceptions, feelings, and emotions and their views on racial matters" (Bonilla-Silva 2010, 104). Because of this, coupled with the fact that most surfing spots are predominantly white, furthering their limited interactions with nonwhites, white surfers' consciousness of racial matters in surfing is largely absent. This is not the case for many Mexican American surfers.

Fall in Line: Experiencing and Untangling Racial Microaggressions in the Lineup

New Racism practices are typically covert and institutionalized and appear to be nonracial. Subtle and often hidden forms of racism have commonly been referred to as racial microaggressions (Solórzano 1998; Smith, Hung, and Franklin 2011), which are the "brief, everyday exchanges that send denigrating messages to people of color because they belong to a racial minority group" (Sue et al. 2007, 273). Microaggressions are insidious and subconscious and can appear in gestures, looks, or tones (Burdsey 2011). Repeat exposure to racial microaggressions can have powerful consequences (Burdsey 2011) and impact groups' opportunities within a given social context (Sue 2010). In the surfing context, racial microaggressions are mostly reflected in nonverbal cues, like stares in the parking lot or lingering glances, or verbal allegations. In rare cases, Mexican American surfers reported experiencing specific forms of microaggressions, commonly referred to as "microassaults" (Burdsey 2011). Microassaults are "explicit racial derogation characterized primarily by a verbal or nonverbal attack meant to hurt the intended victim through name calling, avoidant behavior, or purposeful discriminatory actions" (Sue et al. 2007, 274). Due to the subtle nature of racial microaggressions, Mexican American surfers expressed complications untangling the precise ways in which they experienced them, but instances were illuminated when they compared their encounters to other surfers' experiences. Victoria is a younger working-class third-generation woman of Mexican descent whose narrative provides a glimpse at Mexican American surfer's experiences of racial microaggressions in California surfing spaces:

> But, this one time, I was surfing and there was this older white lady, she is always giving me crap. And she'll tell me things like, "Let other people catch waves." And I'm definitely not the one catching all of the waves. It's like her friends. So I don't know why she has to give me crap, when it's her people catching all of the waves. She is the most noticeable example of someone that thinks I don't belong there, and she carries so much white privilege and entitlement. I don't see her behaving this way towards other white people, that's how I know it's an extension of white privilege. I don't see her doing it to other white girls, especially the ones just learning. She's just always only talking crap to me. It happens regularly, so I don't feel like I am being like hypersensitive. I definitely get a weird vibe [energy] from her, and I'm not exactly sure if it's about race; I could pass for a lot of different ethnicities or races. Definitely more of a localism thing because I'm not from Malibu; I've only been there the last few years. But I see localism, the entitlement of or ownership of space, as an extension of white supremacy because who the hell owns property down in beach communities? I mean, come on, look at the racism and race effects surrounding swimming pools and swimming. Our people were limited or their access was rather limited. Black and brown people didn't have access to water; it was historically restricted.

Victoria was repeatedly subjected to unfair treatment in the water and was singled out for catching "too many waves." She believed this woman intentionally targeted her and made her feel unwelcomed because she was a person of color. Generally, younger Latina/os often believe their racial experiences make them feel "both hyper-visible and invisible, often both simultaneously" (Flores-González 2017, 33). Victoria recognizes her actions and presence in the water is overly analyzed, marking her as distinct. Additionally, from her perspective, she equates the differential treatment as the most recognizable example of white privilege in the surfing space. White privilege is a commonly utilized concept to explain the ways in which "white people simply benefit(ed) from being white" (Pulido 2015, 2; see also McIntosh 1989; Lipsitz 1998). Unearned advantages for white surfers manifest in meaningful forms in the surfing space, as illustrated in this narrative. That is, the other white women surfers are treated with more respect and are afforded more opportunities simply because they are white, despite their lower status as beginner surfers.

From the perspective of a woman of color, who is a minority and an anomaly in the water, it appears that white women surfers receive more opportunities and benefits (waves, respect, and peace of mind) simply for being white. As Pulido (2015) argues, "White privilege highlighted how the individual decisions of whites were not necessarily driven by racial animus, but often were simply a desire to create the best opportunities for themselves and their families, which, in a highly racialized society, reproduced racial inequality" (2). Nevertheless, a dangerous caveat of white privilege is a lack of awareness when it comes to differential treatment toward other nonwhite people. By rarely "unpacking" their privilege, white people do not recognize how their actions may be reinforcing existing racial inequalities and biases. White privilege also does not alarm or cause high levels of uneasiness among white people (Leonardo 2004) nor is racial hostility assumed (Pulido 2015). Victoria recognizes she may not hold a powerful position in the lineup, but as a skilled surfer and respectful participant, she believed the actions of the local woman surfer are interlocked with racial bias and white privilege. The woman may have believed she was simply upholding the informal rules of the sea, but she failed to recognize the ways in which her actions reinscribed power relations in the water. For the most part, white surfers' actions and bodies go unquestioned, and they receive unearned advantages, such as uncontested access to more waves.

Some male surfers interviewed can attest to the ways in which women surfers are differentiated in the lineup, based on their own observations and actions. Specifically, Mexican American men were highly conscious of the ways in which women surfers are treated in the lineup, perhaps due in part to the recognition of their own marginalization. Latinas experienced the most reported cases of marginalization and exclusionary practices. Most notably, Latina beginner surfers reported they felt differentiated because of their ascribed subordinate statuses. Female surfers revealed an implied understanding of the inequitable power relations out in the water.

When asked to comment on female surfers' experiences in surf culture, Alex, a younger, working-class, second-generation Mexican American male, commented: "I think as hard as it is to be a female surfer, I think it's also hard to be a Mexican surfer or nonwhite surfer, you know, to feel like you don't belong, so I can only imagine how a Latina surfer must feel. All I know, is I'm happy to not be in her position!" His comment reveals how female participants, specifically nonwhite female participants, have the least amount of status out in the lineup and are "doubly marginalised" (Nemani and Thorpe 2016, 219) based on their ascribed sex and race. Ascension, a younger, working-class, second-generation Mexican American male surfer, explains how women of color experience exclusion in the water: "People of color and women, people are going to cut them off until the woman says something. For women of color, it's a different scale, not to mention you don't get to experience the pleasure of surfing in peace because you're thinking about gender, race, class, et cetera out in the water. You know people are cutting you off, treating you differently." Ascension's narrative echoes much of what has been said about Mexican American surfers' experiences of racialized exclusion: the feelings of not belonging, reinforced by dominant ideologies inscribed in the sportscape and the lack of joy and peace felt by Mexican American participants. Marginalized groups of people are engulfed by power relations in the water, to the point of their experiences significantly being altered. Following the current trend of scholars examining "multiple marginalizations" (Mizuno 2018;

Nemani and Thorpe 2016; Olive, Roy, and Wheaton 2018) in the lineup, this work also seeks to complicate the ways in which women surfers are differentiated in the water.

Female surfers are acutely aware of gender disparities in the water, but at times they had difficulty deciphering and describing why they believed they were being treated differently. With a variety of factors potentially at play, like gender, race, ability, age, and surf spot, female surfers were left trying to disentangle and second-guess every possible motive behind a male surfer's mistreatment. Sport scholars argue that the source of unequal treatment of athletes stems from "stereotypes about the inherent abilities of female athletes" (Merritt et al. 2019, 485), which can burden their athletic performance. For female surfers, especially women of color, negative stereotypes did affect their athletic performances (and in some cases prevented them from surfing when they were younger). Gendered stereotypes are potent barriers for entry in the sport, often cultivating an "internalized sense that the world sees them as physically incapable," in many cases leading to diminished performances for many women and girls (Merritt et al. 2019, 486). Mexican American surfers are keenly aware of the ways in which they are marginalized and excluded in the surfing space, at times conflicted by the layers of their oppression which can be difficult to untangle and articulate. This significant theme is best summarized by Carolina, a young, working-class, first-generation Mexican American female surfer:

> And I know I've told you this already, but at times I don't know if I am being treated differently by white men because I am a woman, a beginner, a nonlocal, a longboarder, or Mexican American. I just don't know; it's hard to tell, but I definitely feel like an outsider, like I don't belong out here and like I have to ask for permission. Which is so weird because when I surfed recently in Mexico, the birthplace of my parents, the whole lineup was full of brown surfers, you know, like local Mexican surfers. And for the first time, I didn't feel the way I feel when I surf here in Southern California. For the first time, I looked out and I saw other brown people like me. For the first time, I felt accepted, you know, like I belonged in the water. It was a really

beautiful moment for my sister and I, like this was the validation we needed or something to feel like surfers, to see our people doing this sport in our homeland. It felt peaceful, like the way surfing is meant to be.

Concluding Remarks

Mexican American surfers showed a tacit understanding of racial matters in the lineup. At times, it was difficult for Mexican Americans to untangle racism from localism and surf hierarchies, but for the most part, they recognized how these factors were intertwined.

Interpretation of racial matters depended on the surfers' level of consciousness, with some surfers being more aware of how racial dynamics enter and play out in surfing spaces. Approximately one-quarter of Mexican American surfers from this study enrolled in a Chicana/o studies or ethnic studies course in college, providing them with the tools to deconstruct their racialized experiences. For the most part, regardless of a formal background in critical theories of race, Mexican Americans understand their experiences as racialized, recognize how these experiences erode their sense of belonging, and can astutely detect unfair advantages white surfers receive because of white privilege.

Utilizing a critical race theory framework, this essay has highlighted the ways in which color-blind ideology is deeply embedded in Western sport cultures (Leonardo 2004; Burdsey 2011), including lifestyle sports. In this chapter, I highlighted the sticky layers of oppression Mexican American surfers experience in Southern California beaches. First, I underscored how the cultural notion of localism is produced by residential segregation, disadvantaging nonwhite surfers from occupying a higher position in the surf hierarchy. I also argued how residential segregation constructs surfing spaces as "imagined spaces of whiteness" (Wheaton 2017) and discussed the cultural consequences of the white spatial imaginary. Then I described how this phenomenon "naturalizes" as well as hides residual effects of residential segregation. Following this, I demonstrated that most white surfers adopt a color-blind mentality to argue that there are no diversity issues in surfing.

Last, I described how Mexican Americans and women surfers develop racialized and gendered feelings of not belonging, arguing that Mexican American women are subject to multiple marginalizations in the lineup.

References

Berg, B. L. 2004. *Qualitative Research Methods for the Social Sciences*. 5th ed. Boston: Pearson Education.

Bonilla-Silva, E. 2010. *Racism without Racists: Color-Blind Racism and the Persistence of Racial Inequality in America*. Lanham, MD: Rowman and Littlefield.

Booth, Douglas. 2001. "From Bikinis to Boardshorts: 'Wahines' and the Paradoxes of Surfing Culture." *Journal of Sport History* 28, no. 1: 3–22.

Burdsey, Douglas. 2011. "That Joke Isn't Funny Anymore: Racial Microaggressions, Color-Blind Ideology and the Mitigation of Racism in English Men's First-Class Cricket." *Sociology of Sport Journal* 28, no. 3: 261–83.

———. 2017. "Leisure and Diaspora." *The Palgrave Handbook of Leisure Theory*, edited by Karl Spracklen, Brett Lashua, Erin Sharpe, and Spencer Swain, 765–81. London: Palgrave Macmillan.

Carrington, Ben. 2015. "Assessing the Sociology of Sport: On Race and Diaspora." *International Review for the Sociology of Sport* 50, nos. 4–5: 391–96.

Coakley, Jay. 2016. *Sports in Society: Issues and Controversies*. New York: McGraw-Hill Higher Education.

Comer, Krista. 2010. *Surfer Girls in the New World Order*. Durham, NC: Duke University Press.

———. 2016. "'We're Blacksurfing': Public History and Liberation Politics in *White Wash*. *Journal of American Ethnic History* 35, no. 2: 68–78.

Evers, Clifton. 2009. "'The Point': Surfing, Geography and a Sensual Life of Men and Masculinity on the Gold Coast, Australia." *Social and Cultural Geography* 10, no. 8: 893–908.

Flores-González, Nilda. 2017. *Citizens but Not Americans: Race and Belonging among Latino Millennials*. New York: New York University Press.

Ford, Nicholas J., and Douglas Brown. 2005. *Surfing and Social Theory: Experience, Embodiment and Narrative of the Dream Glide*. London: Routledge.

Garbutt, Rob. *The Locals: Identity, Place and Belonging in Australia and Beyond*. Oxford: Peter Lang, 2011.

Gilchrist, Paul, and Belinda Wheaton. 2011. "Lifestyle Sport, Public Policy, and

Youth Engagement: Examining the Emergence of Parkour." *International Journal of Sport Policy and Politics*, no. 3: 109–31.

Gilio-Whitaker, Dina. 2017. "Appropriating Surfing and the Politics of Indigenous Authenticity." In Hough-Snee and Eastman, *The Critical Surf Studies Reader*, 214–35.

Hall, Matthew, Kyle Crowder, and Amy Spring. 2015. "Neighborhood Foreclosures, Racial/Ethnic Transitions, and Residential Segregation." *American Sociological Review* 80, no. 3: 526–49.

Hough-Snee, Dexter Zavalza, and Alexander Sotelo Eastman, eds. 2017. *The Critical Surf Studies Reader*. Durham, NC: Duke University Press.

Hylton, Kevin. 2009. *"Race" and Sport: Critical Race Theory*. London: Routledge.

———. 2010. "How a Turn to Critical Race Theory Can Contribute to Our Understanding of Race, Racism and Anti-racism in Sport." *International Review for the Sociology of Sport* 45, no. 3: 335–54.

Jefferson, Alison R. 2009. "African American Leisure Space in Santa Monica: The Beach Sometimes Known As the 'Inkwell,' 1900s–1960s." *South California Quarterly* 91, no. 2: 155–89.

Kusz, Kyle W. 2004. "Extreme America: The Cultural Politics of Extreme Sports in 1990s America." In *Understanding Lifestyle Sports: Consumption, Identity, and Difference*, edited by Belinda Wheaton, 197–214. London: Routledge.

Leonardo, Zeus. 2004. "The Color of Supremacy: Beyond the Discourse of 'White Privilege.'" *Educational Philosophy and Theory* 36, no. 2: 137–52.

Lipsitz, George. 1998. *The Possessive Investment in Whiteness: How White People Profit from Identity Politics*. Philadelphia: Temple University Press.

———. 2011. *How Racism Takes Place*. Philadelphia: Temple University Press.

lisahunter. 2017. "Desexing Surfing?: (Queer) Pedagogies of Possibility." In Hough-Snee and Eastman, *The Critical Surf Studies Reader*, 263–83.

———, ed. 2018. *Surfing, Sex, Genders and Sexualities*. London: Routledge.

McIntosh, Peggy. 1989. "White Privilege: Unpacking the Invisible Knapsack." *Peace and Freedom* (July/August): 10–12.

Merritt, M., A. Yap, C. Comley, and C. Diehl. 2019. "Stereotype Threat and the Female Athlete: Swimming, Surfing, and Sport Martial Arts." *Handbook of Embodied Cognition and Sport Psychology*, edited by Massimiliano Lorenzo Cappuccio, 485–510. Cambridge: MIT Press.

Mizuno, Eri. 2018. "Multiple Marginalization?: Representation and Experience of Bodyboarding in Japan." In *Surfing, Sex, Genders and Sexualities*, edited by lisahunter, 89–108. London: Routledge.

Nemani, Mihi, and Holly Thorpe. 2016. "The Experiences of 'Brown' Female Bodyboarders: Negotiating Multiple Axes of Marginality." In *Women in Action Sport Cultures:* Identity, Politics and Experience, edited by Holly Thorpe and Rebecca Olive, 213–33. London: Palgrave Macmillan.

Olive, Rebecca. 2019. "The Trouble with Newcomers: Women, Localism and the Politics of Surfing." *Journal of Australian Studies* 43, no. 1: 39–54.

Olive, Rebecca, Georgina Roy, and Belinda Wheaton. 2018. "Stories of Surfing: Surfing, Space and Subjectivity/Intersectionality." In lisahunter, *Surfing, Sex, Genders and Sexualities*, 166–85.

Olive, Rebecca, and Holly Thorpe. 2011. "Negotiating the 'F-Word' in the Field: Doing Feminist Ethnography in Action Sport Cultures." *Sociology of Sport Journal* 28, no. 4: 421–40.

Parker, Lawrence, and Marvin Lynn. 2002. "What's Race Got to Do with It? Critical Race Theory's Conflicts with and Connections to Qualitative Research Methodology and Epistemology." *Qualitative Inquiry* 8, no. 3: 7–22.

Pulido, Laura. 2015. "Geographies of Race and Ethnicity 1: White Supremacy vs White Privilege in Environmental Racism Research." *Progress in Human Geography* 39, no. 6: 809–17.

Pulido, Laura, and Manuel Pastor. 2013. "Where in the World Is Juan—and What Color Is He?: The Geography of Latina/o Racial Identity in Southern California." *American Quarterly* 65, no. 2: 309–41.

Smith, William, Man Hung, and Jeremy D. Franklin. 2011. "Racial Battle Fatigue and the *Mis*Education of Black Men: Racial Microaggressions, Societal Problems, and Environmental Stress." *Journal of Negro Education* 80, no. 1: 63–82.

Solórzano, Daniel G. 1998. "Critical Race Theory, Race and Gender Microaggressions, and the Experience of Chicana and Chicano Scholars." *International Journal of Qualitative Studies in Education* 11, no. 1: 121–36.

Solórzano, Daniel G., and Tara J. Yosso. 2001. "Critical Race and Latcrit Theory and Method: Counterstorytelling." *Qualitative Studies in Education* 14, no. 4: 471–95.

———. 2005. "Maintaining Social Justice Hopes within Academic Realities: A Freirean Approach to Critical Race/LatCrit Pedagogy." In *Critical Pedagogy and Race*, edited by Zeus Leonardo, 69–91. Oxford: Blackwell.

Stoddart, Mark C. J. 2011. "Constructing Masculinized Sportscapes: Skiing, Gender, and Nature in British Columbia, Canada." *International Review for the Sociology of Sport* 46, no. 1: 108–24.

Sue, D. W. 2010. *Microaggressions in Everyday Life: Race, Gender, and Sexual Orientation.* Hoboken, NJ: Wiley.

Sue, Derald Wing, Christina M. Capodilupo, Gina C. Torino, Jennifer M. Bucceri, Aisha Holder, Kevin L. Nadal, and Marta Esquilin. 2007. "Racial Microaggressions in Everyday Life: Implications for Clinical Practice." *American Psychologist* 62, no. 4: 271.

Thompson, G. 2017. "Pushing under the Whitewash: Revisiting the Making of South Africa's Surfing Sixties." In Hough-Snee and Eastman, *The Critical Surf Studies Reader*, 155–76.

Thorpe, Holly. 2008. "Foucault, Technologies of Self, and the Media: Discourses of Femininity in Snowboarding Culture." *Journal of Sport and Social Issues* 32, no. 2: 199–229.

Vasquez, Jessica M. 2011. *Mexican Americans across Generations: Immigrant Families, Racial Realities*. New York: New York University Press.

Westwick, Peter, and Peter Neushul. 2013. *The World in the Curl: An Unconventional History of Surfing*. New York: Crown.

Wheaton, Belinda. 2017. "Space Invaders in Surfing's White Tribe: Exploring Surfing, Race and Identity." In Hough-Snee and Eastman, *The Critical Surf Studies Reader*, 177–95.

Yochim, Emily C. 2010. *Skate Life: Re-imagining White Masculinity*. Ann Arbor: University of Michigan Press.

9

Surfing Queer Lines in Public Spaces

Unlearning Cishetnormativity as Radical Pedagogy

LISAHUNTER

This chapter is written in the lands of the traditional custodians, the First Nations peoples, the Boonwurrung/Bunurong people of the Kulin Nation. It was stolen from them by British colonization in the late 1800s and remains unceded, but with significant and lasting effects to today: where invader colonials, displaced convicts, immigrant settlers, and refugees created a nation "girt by sea," now called Australia, a nation built on violence toward First Nations peoples who nevertheless remain, continuing to share knowledge and work toward a better present and future. The recent Australian nation is built on fabricated absence where British colonizers decided there was a lack of land sovereignty, that humans were absent and so they could claim the land *terra nullius*, meaning nobody's land. These lands, skies, and waters have never been ceded by the First Nations peoples. I pay my deep respects to Boonwurrung/Bunurong Elders past and present, to their custodianship and the creator Bunjil (Briggs 2014), and I extend that respect to all Aboriginal and Torres Strait Islander peoples, and to all First Nations peoples around the world, where disposition, cultural genocide, and a long list of many violences have been suffered. This chapter talks to violences located with the land and sea, in particular of/to/from/by/in the culture of surfing. As we actively learn to understand the historical, intergenerational, and contemporary violences in practices such as surfing, it is valuable to also locate these within larger societal and cultural contexts where differences and solutions may be instructive. In my current location, I work for a future that is more just, reparative, and respectful, recognizing important cultures, histories, knowledges, and contributions that First Nations people have made as the oldest sustained living culture, just as much as in smaller microcultures or fields and subfields such as surfing, locally, globally, and as intersecting with Indigeneity, sex, gender, and sexuality but not limited to such markers. As such, I also acknowledge that colonialization and appropriation of surfing as a "modern" form has strong ties to violences against First Nations peoples, here and beyond our shores (see, for example, Gilio-Whitaker 2015; Gilio-Whitaker and Comer, this volume; Heberling, this volume; Ruttenberg and Brosius, this volume; Walker 2011; Walker, this volume). While these violences are different from the identity category focus of this chapter, abbreviated to "queer," there are also inflections, intersections, and similarities from which to learn, to unite as allies for strategies and support for change, ultimately to engage for healing, respect, learning, and sharing the joys of surf and surfing without negative impact on humans and nonhumans. It is some of these queer lines in public spaces that are illustrated in this chapter. Before locating evidence of surfing queer lines in public spaces, however, it is important to clarify terminology, perceptual categories, and the theoretical lens through which this chapter is presented.

Perceptual Categories, Language, Theory, and *Queer*

Perceptual categories, language, and the ethic-onto-epistemological frame individuals and society make meaning through create shared or different understandings of what is going on. The nature of reality (ontology), how we know about that reality (epistemology), and the values we place on people, places, things, and processes constitute culture individually and collectively. "Surfers' gaze" is a particular way of looking at the ocean to understand where a rideable wave might be, where a line of waves rolling through might best be accessed, how you might approach and ride the wave, and the implications of riding the wave. "Knowing" these things comes from a mix of knowledge: from perhaps experience in the water and in surfing; perhaps understanding tides, winds, and currents and their effects on the changing nature of the wave; beliefs about one's own competence; and an attitude that could be social and environmental entitlement to ride and dominate in and out of the water, in contrast to a cooperative and spiritual relationship with the elements, for example. Being able to perceive the wave and make conscious and nonconscious decisions to "go surfing" and then the success of the session, a period of time spent surfing, will be dependent upon perception and what is perceivable. Likewise, perceptual categories, socialized categories constructed by and learned by humans, have created different groups or categories of people, enabled by the power of the namer, the target person/group's bodies, clothing, ways of moving and speaking, relationship to others, identity, equipment used, et cetera. To use a simplistic example just to make the point, at least in Western English-language cultures, a category "female," as distinguished from "male" (the other half of an assumed sex binary) in modern surfing has been often constituted by stereotypes of long blond hair; more recently, pink boards and clothing; bikinis or a wetsuit that protects only the upper body and torso with neither item being about performance or protection (lisahunter 2017a); and a form of femininity as category woman, their gender, that aligns with their sex (see numerous papers and books listed in lisahunter 2015 and authors' lists in lisahunter 2018a). Their normative sexuality would be assumed to be male-female binary and heterosexual (see previously mentioned lists), within a Western-patriarchy ontology that has been the foundation of modern surfing (see, for example, Comer 2010; Stedman 1997). They would be deemed *cisgendered* and *heteronormative*, both terms often assumed "normal" and entangled as what I refer to as *cishetnormativity* (for further discussion of this language, see lisahunter 2017b, 2018b).

As acts in our everyday practices and in our systems, language plays a part in constituting, and being constituted by, particular bodies, their subjective positions within social spaces, their identities and ways of being (see lisahunter 2015 and 2017c for a theoretical exploration of social spaces and patriocolonial logics in surfing). Where bodies/subject positions/identities are nameable and named, intelligible, there are opportunities for them to be valued or not, and therefore positioned powerfully or not (see lisahunter 2013 and 2017b re visibility and positioning). If particular bodies are not or cannot be named, they may be absented or rendered unintelligible. While this chapter is too brief to unpack the politics and power of naming, clearly the dominant practices and systems that do not need to be named, for example, race, cishetnormativity, and patriarchy, hold power by being assumed as normal, while other categories and names are used in derogatory ways to position people as deficient, deviant, and not normal, such as historical uses of the term *queer*.

The etymology of *queer* in relation to sexuality and gender was initially used in the late nineteenth and early twentieth centuries to constitute perceived/positioned/identifying sexuality as a binary that contrasted with the heterosexual norm, that is, the homosexual gay (male) and lesbian (female). A person "at odds with the normal, the legitimate, the dominant . . . an identity without an essence" (Halperin 1995, 62), "the open mesh of possibilities, gaps, overlaps, dissonances and resonances, lapses and excesses of meaning when the constituent elements of anyone's gender, of anyone's sexuality aren't made (or can't be made) to signify monolithically" (Sedgwick 1993, 8). As an identity, it was embraced as a term of resistance by some gay- and lesbian-identifying people in the 1970s to proudly become legible or resist legibility, emerging as a theoretical and political lens in the late 1990s rejecting "minoritizing logic of toleration or simple political interest-representation in favor of a more thorough resistance to regimes of normal" (Warner 1991, 16; see also Jagose 1996). A body of work resisting naming but nevertheless identified as "queer theory" questions normative identities and even the concept of identity, acting to trouble binaries and phobias derived from the notion of a patriarchal hegemonic heterosexual family and protecting an essentialized gender binary (see Rubin 2006) but not just in sex, gender, and sexuality, also in intersections with race and class and institutions such as religion, family, schooling, and physical cultures such as surfing. Queering and querying surfing is an invitation to question/challenge the categories, question the positions and positioning constituted by the structures of patriocolonial "compulsive heterosexuality" (Rich 1993). As such, *queer* can mean many things, including a complex set of subject positions, sometimes an umbrella term for lesbian, gay, bisexual, transgender, queer, questioning, intersex, asexual, plus, and it can be used as an active verb, *queering*. Rather than discuss the description and potential of queering and querying surfing here, as that is done elsewhere (lisahunter 2018b), suffice to say, queering is all those practices that interrupt normativity, fixity, and dominance, whether rupturing heteronormative spaces, as in the work of Roy's research associated with lesbian surfers (2013a), or identifying queerly as nonnormative identities, both demonstrated in the radical cultures and countercultures described below. It is to these and other cultural artifacts that I turn to explore further the queer lines for surfing, where I suggest patriocolonial cishetnormativity is not only challenged but where a form of radical pedagogy is offering hope and belonging for previously absented, marginalized, or otherwise violated people.

Methodology: Documenting Lines of Change That Resisted Domination

Documenting cultural artifacts is useful in identifying what drives or illustrates change, such as artifacts that have resisted domination in modern surfing. As I have argued previously, *queer* has largely been absented from the epiphenomena of public and modern surfing, its media and its research, but early signs of queer lines of waves of change came through more recently in research (Comer 2010; Waitt 2008), in new media and social media (Evers 2008; Schumacher 2011), and when heteronormativity and homophobia in surfing was rendered more publicly visible by the release of the film *Out in the Line-Up* (Thomson 2014) and the book *Becoming Westerly* (Brisick 2015). These and the more recent #gaysurfweek (Castets 2018), Georgina Roy's doctoral thesis on the experiences of lesbians in surfing (2013a, b), and Keala Kennelly's World Surf League Awards acceptance speech (2019) signal a visibility and pride in queer identity groups who were previously/are marginalized, oppressed, and/or erased through modern surfing practices. The histories and historical artifacts constituted by modern surfing are evidence of the violences enacted on

First Nations people, women, Black people, people of color, and, among other identity categories and their intersectionalities, a diversity of categories relating to sex, gender, and sexuality (SGS). These include lesbian, gay, bisexual, transgender, queer, questioning, people with intersex variations, and many more collected together under the label, referred to sometimes as LGBTQQI+, the Rainbow Community, and more recently through the appropriation of what was historically a derogatory term, queer.[1]

This visibility that I explore in more depth below signals greater awareness of, and a challenge to, cisgender heteronormativity and SGS binaries, a radical opening of spaces for greater diversity and inclusion in societies and communities or cultures such as surfing. They are "radical" as they are self-determined and derived from lived experience, but they are also potentially a space for radical pedagogy that transforms social consciousness to support a move from dominating identities and spaces.

Resisting Domination and Normativity through Visibility

Whereas queer identities were previously kept secret for fear of violence or through experiences of violences, social media and the increased availability of technology to tell stories took queer and queering from secret to interest group collaborations and connections. Versed in structural feminism, Cori Schumacher, the first openly queer surfing world champion, used her visibility as an activist to raise issues of sexism, sexualization, and homophobia in surfing (2011). Responding to actions of the surfing industry and media more generally, but also an incident by an industry representative, she noted: "That three generations of female surfers have had to navigate the limitations of lesbian-baiting ought to bring us pause when considering the unapologetically sexualized image of female surfing we are currently receiving from Roxy and elsewhere in the surf industry. Reclaiming the narrative of women's surfing from that which is controlled by the surf industry, one that is constantly on the defence about sexuality, is the first step in truly advancing women's surfing" (Schumacher 2013).

Arguably, much of the media and industry in modern surfing had been engineered and produced by heterosexual men, maintaining the prominence of white Western male heterosexual surfing, and supporting binary cishet femininities over all other forms, and with queerphobias and biases central (see lisahunter 2016a, 2017a, 2017b for more discussion and references). Schumacher, leading activism with others, used a moment in time when a "visible trend of women and girls self-identifying as mermaids in the wider culture collided with the rupture in women's surfing of the Roxy feminine ideal, and a shift in perspectives on homosexuality in the wider culture" (2017, 295–96) to suggest a queer surfeminism. It embraced the mermaid, to go beyond the human, as well as embracing the waves of activism, change, and hope already achieved through surfeminism. At a similar time, Georgina Roy's attention to lesbians surfing in the United Kingdom was academically challenging the dominant male space and documenting the autonomy and spatiotemporality of surfing women who were collaborating to create a possible space in surfing, a space not publicly identified but one that was firmly established by lesbian surfers (lisahunter 2006). Visible narratives were political positions that were perpetuating and/or disrupting dominant and dominating narratives (lisahunter 2013, 2016b). Like Schumacher and Roy, I suggested that creating new spaces for queer and queering surfing, rather than penetrating the old, may disrupt practices and ultimately undo patriocolonialism's strength in maintaining the "old" modern spaces (lisahunter 2017b). Promoting multiplicities of difference in identities and subject positions seemed to be also creating possibilities to interrupt, dismantle, and disrupt fixedness of categories framed by patrio(colonializing) binary cishetnormativities.

Celebrating the achievements of athletes in the 2018 season, Keala Kennelly made some significant statements heralding two important milestones in surfing history:

> when I was twenty-five, I was hiding in the closet, soaked in shame, living in fear, and I hated myself because I didn't think you could be world champion and gay at the same time. I needed to dream bigger, because now I get to be the first openly gay world champion, and I

> get to be proud of who I am, and I get to love myself exactly as I am, not as people would want me to be. And it's my hope that I'm going to inspire other LGBT athletes that are suffering in silence to live your truth. And I needed to dream so much bigger, because when I was twenty-five, the difference in prize money between the men's and the women's was so radically different, and now I get to be world champion with equal pay. (from 0:49 to 1:42, Kennelly 2019)

Being a world champion as a "gay" athlete and getting equal pay to men was in the context of a big wave category of elite surfing competition. Like Schumacher in the longboard category, big wave surfing was/is not considered the pinnacle of surfing value, compared with the shortboard WSL Championship Tour. But female surfers have continued to break dominant barriers even more recently in that category, with elite surfer Tyler Wright identifying as bisexual.

In film, the "gay undertow" of the film *Newcastle* (Joyce 2008) seemed cause for public concern. The film focuses on three young brothers who surfed, and one commentary noted, "Its distributor is playing down the movie's gay following overseas for fear of frightening off mainstream audiences in Australia," mentioning the potential target audience as "surfers and teenage girls" (Joyce 2008). This film was featured at Outfest and the Los Angeles Gay and Lesbian Film Festival. In contrast, the very recent film *Girls Can't Surf* (Nelius 2020) also documents stories that until recently could not be told publicly in mainstream spaces. Like Kennelly's speech, one of several contemporary challenges to the male-dominated misogynistic and sexist professional surfing world, and in a small way to its homophobia, for the shared goal of equality and change, ex-professional surfer Jodie Cooper says, "The '80s were really hard. If you were gay, you were diseased." The documentary notes that the 1993 world champion, Pauline Menczer, was "the victim of maybe world sports' most brutal and blatant sexism. A world champ who could not raise a dime in sponsorship, who received a trophy that would not make the grade for the secondhand shop at the dump. Lesbian, when that was taboo, lacking the physical accoutrements that were classically assumed to stimulate the desire of a presumed male audience, and thus more or less discarded by the companies that largely funded the sport."

The film had a mixed following but was successful in entering mainstream film spaces. While other films (e.g., *It Ain't Pretty*, Soul 2017) have also broken into mainstream media to expose sexism and misogyny, *Girls Can't Surf* speaks more explicitly to homophobia. At the same time, the proliferation and expansion of outlets through new means of distribution has also meant greater visibility of what was once deemed invisible through structural blocks inherent in patriocolonial media. *Girls Can't Surf* is perhaps the first of its kind to directly challenge surfing's homophobia layered with misogyny and sexism in mainstream film cinemas and streaming, perhaps through the diversification of platforms such as Stan in this instance, but also with a greater awareness of such violences through nonmainstream productions and film festivals. One such example is Juul Hesselberth's *Just Go Fucking Surfing* (2021), in which gender, sexuality, sexualized bodies, and surfing were investigated and presented to diverse film festival audiences. The documentary captured how women outside cishet binary normativities were positioned and how they navigated their online and offline surfing culture and spaces to resist dominant narratives. Hesselberth herself was aware that she had become part of the change through making her documentary and disseminating the stories that resisted and spoke back to dominant narratives of women in surfing (pers. comm., July 16, 2019). Diverse representative and nondominant groups now have greater capacity to produce content, distribute, and follow, but not just in film, also in online/offline spaces such as websites. Two such cases are discussed in more detail below.

GAYSURFERS.NET: PROMOTING DIVERSITY AND INCLUSION IN THE LINEUP SINCE 2010

Talking about the rise of the queer surf community, Thomas Castets, the producer of *Out in the Line-Up* (2014) as well as the instigator/administrator of GaySurfers.net, noted, "Surfing is, unfortunately, primarily a male-dominated sport. And when you have all these men traveling together, hunting for waves, there is an element to the psychology that is about making sure there is no ambiguity between the men. . . . To prove your heterosexuality, you need to prove your skills in the water. There have never really been any gay surfers out there, so I would just call that ignorance and a lack of visibility" (Castets 2019). GaySurfers.net was created by Thomas Castets with a goal "Promoting diversity and inclusion in the lineup since 2010." The "Who We Are" page identifies, "First and foremost, we are passionate surfers! We represent a diverse range of individuals who are, or are supporters of, those who are gay, lesbian, bisexual and/or transgendered. GaySurfers.net offers a supportive community environment that focuses on building a positive image of gay surfers in the surfing world while encouraging a healthy, ocean-centered lifestyle for gays, lesbians, bisexuals and transgendered individuals within our own communities."

Thomas Castets recognized the homophobia in surfing, and he brought together his resources to work for his queer community in terms of the website and later film. The website now hosts eighty-one different groups, covering every continent from regions in Australia to Aotearoa New Zealand to Barcelona and Cataluña and Nouvelle-Aquitaine. It now also includes related physical cultures of skateboarding, bodyboarding, and kitesurfing, where skill set crossover often means someone who "surfs" does so in different ways (such as bodysurfing) and may use a different craft (e.g., kitesurfers). It acknowledges differences within queer identity groupings, hosts groups that pay attention to subidentity groups, such as North Orange County Women Surfers, Trans Surfers and those who support queer surfers such as gay-friendly surf schools.

In a 2019 article by Thomas Castets where he investigates the rise of the queer surf community, he captured the contemporary invisibility and lack of safety in being queer in the broader surfing community. At the same time, he suggested it is a "blossoming cottage industry of gay surf communities" for both queer surfers and potential queer newcomers to surfing. When interviewing viewers of the documentary he produced in 2014, *Out in the Line-Up*, he reported some being surprised by the toxicity of the surfing community and surprised that surfers were so homophobic, particularly at the professional level. While the surf industry had been called out for its sexism, more accurately, its binary cisgender normativity and sexism, there had been few challenges to its heteronormativity, binarism, and queerphobia.

The film opened up many online discussions about homophobia, and the website captured some of these. The website became a space for deeper discussions, connection to arrange surfing together, and stories, and it includes different groups within the queer community, not just gay and lesbian. It is also a space for different forms of surfing to be legitimized beyond singular focus or shortboard dominance. It facilitates connections across the globe and has significant membership.

As a website linking surfers identifying as queer, GaySurfers.net provides a member-driven public service to those otherwise invisibilized, wanting to connect locally but also normalizing language that is still often not seen by those identifying as queer, language such as GNC or genderqueer. GaySurfers.net also stimulated grassroots community development that further enhances visibility and belonging, providing not just an opportunity to belong but also an imagination to others on how to create belonging.

Work such as this offers radical learning to those open to listening, joining, or supporting. The website also connects community for holidays and surf trips and inspires new geographically localized communities to develop or connect, for example, North Shore Ko'olau Diversity Collective and Benny's Club.

BENNY'S CLUB

The online site of Benny's Club (https://bennysclub.com) is another illustration where those who felt marginalized and unsafe in surfing connected through GaySurfer.net and created space for people like themselves. Reaching others online, Benny's Club plays out in the physical world by bringing together two identity groups, queer and of color. Identifying that surfing is about fun, but that New York City Beach is "straight and macho," initiators Joanie and Momo set out to create a sense of community for others to be comfortable in their bodies. They want to be able to teach those outside dominant representations and identities in an environment that is not intimidating. They recognize it is possible in skate culture, but despite attempts by others in surfing, there is a lack of momentum and more "fronting" than follow-through. Using their online and surfing resources, they can control their site for safe discussion and their beach space for safe and joyful surfing (pers. comm., January 20 and February 8, 2022). This attention to intersectionality demonstrates the more radical awareness beyond single identity categories, an understanding of the nuances of how exclusion works, with an awareness of backlash from dominant groups.

Just as in feminism, backlash politics are certainly part of the fundamentalist right political complex. So too will any actions to challenge heteronormativity and cisgender norms in surfing be potential targets. Yet movements such as feminism provide clues for action. As noted by Comer (2019, 2), surfing already has ally groups in the form of surfeminism, which "focuses on access of women and girls to public ocean and beach spaces, environmental and ocean health, as well as issues of racial and economic justice, and physical liberation across the lifecycle." Building on McRobbie's (2008) warning about the dangers of "a re-patriarchalization" of Western gender orders, Comer adds, "In the dumbed down postfeminist public sphere of 2016, Trumpism capitalized on re-patriarchalized publics while fueling new ones"—a backlash caution to any who *do* challenge powerful norms.

What will it take to queer surfing from its (cisgender heteronormative patriocolonial) malaise? The illustrations above are examples of radical pedagogy; these are teaching and learning spaces within society that herald activism by queer surfers, and not just for queer surfers, but as queering surfing—with those with queer identities queering dominance. I suggest that while there may be a queer (re)turn, perhaps the most radical turn in surfing's history despite its many claims to counterculture, there is still great scope for surfing to be queered in the water, in the culture, and in its scholarship.

Surfing Queer Lines in Public Spaces (Queering Surfing)

One line of queering that is directing acts of unlearning cishetnormativity is in social media and film. As noted in its last post in *Surfer*, one of the surfing field's iconic magazines (and then online), a feature article called "How LGBTQ+ Surfers Are Creating a More Inclusive Surf Culture" (Prodanovich 2020), "Male surfers in the '80s were basically presented as rock stars, and at the same time, athletic female surfers were being castigated as lesbians." In the supporting YouTube for the feature article, Cori Schumacher talks about the policing in surfing, not just toward essentialized notions of femininity but also "making sure that we weren't hanging out with women who had been identified as lesbians on tour. . . . In fact, I was asked by a fellow pro surfer from here at home, a male, who I was hanging out with on tour. And when I gave the list of people, he nodded and said, "Good, those are the good ones to hang out with." In speaking about *Out in the Line-Up*, Cori Schumacher said the film opened discussions, but did not go far enough to address "the complex and systemic issue" (4:31, Prodanovich 2020).

For example, her parents told her that "those women" were holding back women's surfing as a whole, the implication being that if they just made themselves more desirable from the surf industry's dominant and dominating perspective, it would lead to more opportunity for all women in surfing. Such misrecognition (lisahunter 2017c) speaks to the importance of continuing the public pedagogy, not just in personal lives but also in systems, therefore targeting wider audiences and through different mediums to understand deeper issues holding practices such as homophobia in place.

Surfing as Public Pedagogy and/or Public Service

Addressing malaise, more explicitly, physical and symbolic violences, and/or inclusion for diversity and equity, requires not just queer members to be proactive but also those from the dominant group, be they cisgendered, heterosexual, white, male, on a shortboard, or intersections of such. GaySurfers.net is linking identities and linking beyond identities, educating for new possibilities to challenge domination in intersectional forms. As a website with new subcultural links to other ways of surfing, it affirms queer existence and complexity of membership across more than one group, within potential to fracture the notion of single identity groups, the members of which benefit from insider safety but are introduced to the possibility of excluding others in the act of being included. Marginalized identities of difference within a queer-identifying umbrella may come to understand the identity distinctions within and respect for those without. They may also appreciate homonormativity in operation and investigate its manifestations and effects, as well as understand and appreciate the relationships harnessed through already positive relationships within and beyond cishet. Here there are implications for research, to understand the reality of website usage for example, where one might feel they now belong due to the material-virtuality, but where online belonging fails to be manifested in offline activity.

I would argue that surfing activism, as lines of queering surfing, is working toward a radical pedagogy. Perception, language, membership, speech acts, activism, what we pay attention to, where we put our energies, dialogue, and support all cluster as radical pedagogies. Difference and diversity make for a richness of ecology, and humanity is just one part of that ecology, with its own internal diversity. While the outcomes that motivate human surfing, such as joy, challenge, beauty, companionship with other humans, and/or companionship with the sea might unite people to surf, we are obliged to embrace diversity as part of equity and inclusion. So the real challenge I see is how queer(ing) can surfing be? Like with many identity-based violences, there is need for more radical pedagogy to unlearning cishetnormativity, as one of many sources of dominance that blocks participation in surfing. Through formation of identity-driven virtual and physical groups, the visibilities of action also act to witness and document such action, giving inspiration and connection to others previously hidden.

Conclusion: Waves of Belonging, and Hope?

Previously, I drew on Australasian examples to document what might be a queer turn in surfing (lisahunter 2014a, 2014b, 2018b), including examples mentioned in this chapter. I argued that these Global South examples of "a hegemonic androcentric, patriarchal, (hetero)normative doxa that I term *patriocolonialism* facilitates an illusion of equitable participation for males and females, and therefore feminist victory, while symbolic violence reproduces a spectre of patriarchy, albeit in new or hidden forms" (2017b, 234–35). Five years on and this book's aspirational title, invoking waves of belonging, offers much hope for queer surfer visibility, celebration, connection, well-being, belongingness, and allyship that has been manifested quickly and in a relatively short period of time in modern colonialized surfing (history); that is, in the last decade. But not nearly enough to tick "inclusion," "diversity," or "equity" cards. To play with metaphors, perhaps the waves of change are more like wind-generated wave chop, as somewhat surface, isolated, small, and messy. Or perhaps the underlying groundswell that has been building for a long time is finally (able to be) surfacing as surfing culture matures. Chop can easily be met with winds or other forces that build to waves or cancel them out, as a metaphor for effects of support versus backlash. Groundswell and favorable weather conditions are far greater in ensuring a better ride for people who surf, and for many more who might be seeking access to such activity. It is clearly still not safe for some people who surf to be their "authentic" selves, in identifying as queer, and in some realms challenging (m)any of the normativities that surfing often embodies. Nor is it possible for queer-identified people who surf to be positioned as equal to others "choosing" cisgender heterosexuality—as demonstrated by queer worlds being largely absent(ed) or hidden in surf culture. This may be as simple as saying to them "don't (you dare) surf" or "queer people don't surf." There is much yet to understand about the more nuanced experiences of intersecting identity positions in relation to surfing. However, queerphobias, antiqueer practices, and binary cishetnormativities and their patrio(colonial) partners are under challenge on many fronts: by being rendered more visible, by being challenged and undone by allies, by queering or queer presence, by those identifying with queer identities being celebrated and supported, by careful affirmative action and creation of safe spaces. These challenges are waves of hope and belonging building for queer sexes, genders, and sexualities and also for other intersectional identities marginalized within queer worlds and the queer bodies they inhabit. Bring on the first WSL surfing championships final between all queer Indigenous competitors with a BIPOC CEO presenting the trophy, funding a worldwide set of sustained surfing clinics and access for marginalized groups, and hosting the annual activist and research conference on surfing's diversity, equity, and inclusion. What an exciting ride for marginalized identities and their allies until then. #queeringsurfing

Afterword

There have been significant discussions on the poor understanding, complexities, entanglements, miseducation, and conflicts with how "fairness," "equity," and fields such as sport interact with sexes, genders, and sexualities. Specifically, the case of the Western Australia State Championship win (2022) by longboarder Sasha Jane Lowerson was met with polarized (thoughtful and vitriolic) responses in the broader surfing community. Sasha is identified by some as the first transgender athlete in surfing or, as she says, "a proud woman with a trans experience," and her case to compete and win was embedded in Surfing Australia policy, ahead of World Surf League (WSL) or International Surfing Association (ISA) forming policies. The latter policy and WSL alignment with ISA were nevertheless pushed along by the 2022 case.

Citing the United Nations Educational, Scientific and Cultural Organization, International Charter of Physical Education, Physical Activity and Sport (1978) as part of the Universal Declaration of Human Rights, Surfing Australia's policy introduction stated:

> Participation in sport is a human right. We are all born free and equal in dignity and rights. Surfing Australia is committed to providing a safe, fun, and inclusive environment for all people, including

> transgender and gender diverse people. Being an inclusive organisation not only reflects our core values, but it also reflects the diversity of our local communities. We're passionate about helping people lead happy, healthy, and active lives. Surfing Australia celebrates diversity of sex, gender identity, gender expression, sexual orientation, intersex status, body, ability, skill, cultural background, ethnicity, location, religious or political beliefs, and life stage. There is a place in our sport for everyone, exactly as you are. (2022, 3)

The policy acknowledged partners as other important actors with power to sanction and inform, stating, "Pride in Sport, ACON Health, TransHub, State entities, members of the LGBTQ community, medical experts, athletes and administrators across Australia have aided and/or participated in consultations which informed the development of this work" (2022, 10). It also reflected the state of discussion structurally and nationally, nested in other laws such as the Sex Discrimination Act (1984) and the proactive nature and power of organizations such as Surfing Australia. But Surfing Australia's policy did not extend to ISA-sanctioned events or an elite or subelite competition, of which there was no policy for the Western Australia case.

The ISA Transgender Policy (2023), adopted by WSL, is considered as less aggressive in requirements associated with testosterone testing and limits for participation, as compared with other international levels of sports such as athletics. It is also open to change in light of further information and research. But such policies are also argued to be causing harm and fear about trans participation rather than supporting equity, fairness, or safety. Biomedical arguments and inadequate laws are in conflict with sociocultural arguments. Sociocultural understandings about fairness, sport, equity, and where inclusion leaves women's sport have led to significant discussions about definitions and understandings of sex, gender, and sexuality. However, this has also meant that mostly vulnerable people are being caught in the crossfire caused by insufficient understanding and dominance of binaried cishetnormativity.

It is important to note that transgender athletes/surfers have been present in surfing for a long time, but their visibility may not have been safe, celebrated, or noticed by certain forms of recordkeeping, such as the dominant (patriarchal-Christian-white) media/museums/memorials. Erasure and/or the need to remain hidden has made it less possible for clear discussions and decision-making in what is needed to ensure affirming and equitable spaces for a range of identities including trans*. Ensuing debates from the Australian case illustrate how far surfing more generally, sport, and many societies have yet to go for respectful, nuanced, and complex situations that to date have gone not only untested but also unconsidered in any deep way. Just which narratives were brought to the fore (see, for example, *Tracks Magazine* 2023) in arguments for and against were often missing the point that such discussions were all the poorer for the resistance to a more open understanding of the outcomes of marginalization and oppression. They also lack historical understandings of surfing outside dominant constructions of modern surfing tropes or understandings of sex/gender outside cishetnormativity.

Fairness, as an impossible but often used marketing of elite (and often not elite) sport, is a significant issue exposed in cases such as athletes shifting gender categories. The plea for fairness, equality, and equity is not new to many population groups. So too do such examples illustrate the illusions deeply embedded in society about who has access to which resources, whether in the name of bodily autonomy, identity categories, or in challenging the fixedness of categories and who can be, know, do, and be valued. Some bodies have had to, and will continue to, bear the weight of power imbalances embodied in acts of discrimination until societies and their groups enable equity for access to resources and in relation to affirmed identities. Of prime importance in cases such as this is the necessity for a deeper understanding of how sexes, genders, and sexualities operate to position people in ways, and as embedded in social spaces where power operates toward inclusion or exclusion. Of similar importance is listening to the lived experiences of those living in bodies and contexts where access to surfing is unimaginable or impossible and embodying the change needed for their inclusion.

Notes

This chapter is based on lisahunter, "Surfing Queer Lines in Public Spaces," paper presented at Impact Zones and Liminal Spaces: The Culture and History of Surfing, San Diego, April 26, 2019. Many thanks to elke emerald for valuable editing advice on drafts and to the editors who were patient and supportive to ensure this chapter was submitted in adverse COVID-19 times.

1 I acknowledge current debates with people with innate variations in sex characteristics mean some identify as intersex, some as queer, while others do not. I have included the *I* in this essay to bring attention to their absence in surfing literature.

References

Briggs, C. 2014. *The Journey Cycles of the Boonwurrung*. Melbourne: Victorian Aboriginal Corporation for Languages.

Brisik, J. 2015. *Becoming Westerly: The Transformation of Surfing Champion Peter Drouyn into Westerly Windina*. Crows Nest: Allen and Unwin.

Castets, T. 2018. GaySurfers.net. Accessed June 7, 2018. www.gaysurfers.net.

———. 2019. "The Rise of the Queer Surf Community." GaySurfers.net. Accessed July 1, 2019. www.gaysurfers.net/the-rise-of-the-queer-surf-community.

Comer, K. 2010. *Surfer Girls in the New World Order*. Durham, NC: Duke University Press.

———. 2019. "What Leisure? Surfeminism in an Era of Trump." *Palgrave Communications* 5, no. 1: 42. doi:10.1057/s41599-019-0250-9.

Evers, C. 2008. "Queer Waves." *Kurungubaa* 1, no. 2: 1–5.

Gilio-Whitaker, D. 2015. "Surfing and Indigeneity in the United States." RumiNative. November 10, 2015. https://dinagwhitaker.wordpress.com/2015/11/10/surfing-and-indigeneity-in-the-united-states.

Halperin, D. 1995. *Saint Foucault: Towards a Gay Hagiography*. New York: Oxford University Press.

Hesselberth, J., dir. 2021. *Just Go Fucking Surfing*. Private screening.

International Surfing Association. 2023. "ISA Transgender Policy Rule." Updated March 7, 2023. https://isasurf.org/wp-content/uploads/2023/03/ISA_Transgender-Policy_Updated_3_9_23.pdf.

Jagose, A. 1996. *Queer Theory*. Melbourne: Melbourne University Press.

Joyce, J. 2008. "Gay Undertow to Newcastle Surf Film." *Newcastle Herald*, updated

October 31, 2012. www.newcastleherald.com.au/story/487874/gay-undertow-to-newcastle-surf-film.

Kennelly, K. 2019. World Surf League Awards acceptance speech. SurferToday: The Ultimate Surfing News Website, April 2, 2019. www.surfertoday.com.

lisahunter. 2006. "'Girls Get Out There Day' and 'Surf Jam': Reinscribing Gender and Consumer Discourses or New Spaces for Participation?" Paper presented as the invited speaker for the Active '06: Making a Difference Conference. Western Australian Department of Sport and Recreation, Perth, September 2006.

———. 2013. "What Did I Do-See-Learn at the Beach? Surfing Festival as a Cultural Pedagogical Sight/Site." *Physical Culture, Pedagogies and Visual Methods*, edited by L. Azzarito and D. Kirk, 144–61. New York: Routledge.

———. 2014a. "Exploitation and (Unqueering) Public Pedagogy: Gender and Sex Parody in YouTube Surf Festival Promotion." Paper presented at Gender and Education. Melbourne, Australia.

———. 2014b. "She Was/Is Naked on a Surfboard: Making Sens* of Female, Surfing, and the Pacific." Paper presented at Contemporary Ethnography Across the Disciplines. Waikato, Aotearoa New Zealand.

———. 2015. "'Stop': 'No.' Exploring Social Suffering in Practices of Surfing as Opportunities for Change." *Pierre Bourdieu and Physical Capital*, edited by lisahunter, W. Smith, and e. emerald, 47–56. Abingdon: Routledge.

———. 2016a. "Desexing Surfing? (Queer)Pedagogies of Possibility." Paper presented at the Surfing Social Hui. Whaingaroa Raglan, Aotearoa New Zealand. February 11, 2016.

———. 2016b. "Becoming Visible. Visual Narratives of 'Female' as a Political Position: The History, Perpetuation, and Disruption of Patriocolonial Pedagogies?" In *Women in Action Sport Cultures: Identity, Politics, Experience and Pedagogy*, edited by H. Thorpe and R. Olive, 319–47. Basingstoke, UK: Palgrave Macmillan.

———. 2017a. "The Long and Short of (Performance) Surfing: Tightening Patriarchal Threads in Boardshorts and Bikinis?" *Sport in Society* 21, no. 9: 1382–99.

———. 2017b. "Desexing Surfing? (Queer) Pedagogies of Possibility." *Radical Politics, Global Culture: A Critical Surf Studies Reader*, edited by D. Z. Hough-Snee and A. Eastman, 263–83. Durham, NC: Duke University Press.

———. 2017c. "Positioning Participation in the Field of Surfing: Sex, Equity, and Illusion." In *Bourdieu's Field Theory and the Social Sciences*, edited by J. Albright, D. Hartman, and J. Wildin, 181–98. Singapore: Palgrave Macmillan.

———, ed. 2018a. *Surfing, Sex, Genders and Sexualities*. Abingdon: Routledge.

———. 2018b. "Queering Surfing from Its Heteronormative Malaise." In *Surfing, Sex, Genders and Sexualities*, edited by lisahunter, 168–89. Abingdon: Routledge.

McRobbie, A. 2008. *The Aftermath of Feminism: Gender, Culture and Social Change*. Thousand Oaks, CA: Sage Publications.

Nelius, C., dir. 2020. *Girls Can't Surf*. Australia, Madman Films.

Prodanovich, T. 2020. "How LGBTQ+ Surfers Are Creating a More Inclusive Surf Culture." *Surfer*. www.surfer.com/features/history-lgbtq-surfing.

Rich, A. 1993. "Compulsory Heterosexuality and Lesbian Existence." In *The Lesbian and Gay Studies Reader*, edited by Henry Abelove, Michèle Aina Barale, and David M. Halperin, 227–54. New York: Routledge.

Roy, G. 2013a. "Feminism in New Sporting Spaces: Gender, Subjectivity and the Female Surfer in Britain." Doctoral thesis, University of Brighton.

———. 2013b. "Women in Wetsuits: Revolting Bodies in Lesbian Surf Culture." *Journal of Lesbian Studies* 17, nos. 3–4: 329–43.

Rubin, G. 2006. "Thinking Sex: Notes for a Radical Theory of the Politics of Sexuality." In *Culture, Society and Sexuality: A Reader*, edited by R. Parker and P. Aggleton, 143–78. London: Routledge.

Schumacher, C. 2011. "Time for Surfing to Rise to Its LGBT Responsibility." *Guardian*, July 30, 2011. www.theguardian.com/commentisfree/cifamerica/2011/jul/30/gay-rights-surfing-sport.

———. 2013. "Lesbian-Baiting, a la Roxy Surfing." Accessed June 19, 2024. https://www.huckmag.com/article/cori-schumacher.

———. 2017. "'My Mother Is a Fish': From Stealth Feminism to Surfeminism." *Radical Politics, Global Culture: A Critical Surf Studies Reader*. Edited by D. Z. Hough-Snee and A. Eastman, 284–302. Durham, NC: Duke University Press.

Sedgwick, E. 1993. *Tendencies*. Durham, NC: Duke University Press.

Soul, D., dir. 2017. *It Ain't Pretty*. Candy Factory Film. http://itaintprettyfilm.com.

Stedman, L. 1997. "From Gidget to Gonad Man: Surfers, Feminists and Postmodernisation." *Journal of Sociology* 33, no. 1: 75–90

Surfing Australia. 2022. "Policy for the Inclusion of Transgender and Gender Diverse People in Community Surfing." https://assets.surfinginaustralia.com/wp-content/uploads/sites/12/2022/05/16070919/POLICY-Surfing-Australia-Policy-for-the-inclusion-of-transgender-and-gender-diverse-people.pdf.

Thomson, I., dir. 2014. *Out in the Line-Up*. Yellow Dot Productions.

Tracks Magazine. 2023. "Transgender Debate Divides Surfing." Accessed February 8, 2023. https://tracksmag.com.au/transgender-debate-divides-surfing.

United Nations Educational, Scientific and Cultural Organization, International Charter of Physical Education, Physical Activity and Sport. 1978. Art. 1; Universal Declaration of Human Rights, GA Res 217A (III), UN GAOR, 3r. November 21, 1978.

Waitt, G. 2008. "Killing Waves: Surfing, Space and Gender." *Social and Cultural Geography* 9, no. 1: 75–94.

Walker, I. H. 2011. *Waves of Resistance: Surfing and History in Twentieth-Century Hawai'i.* Honolulu: University of Hawai'i Press.

Warner, M. 1991. "Introduction: Fear of a Queer Planet." *Social Text*, no. 29: 3–17.

PART III

INTERSECTIONS AND RELATIONS

10

Being Good Relatives

A Story of Indigenous and Settler Surfeminist Collaboration and Legislated Land Acknowledgments

DINA GILIO-WHITAKER AND KRISTA COMER

Stories of effective political collaboration are stories of relationships and the motivations that keep people showing up for the work. To write about our collaboration is also to make public statements about who we are in our relationship and why we want to give to one another. As feminist scholars, one of us an affirmed Indigenous feminist, and the other a white settler feminist, we view our story as a living example of intersectional feminist collaborative work.[1] From an Indigenous framework, we see in our story the fulfillment of a cultural imperative centered around relationality or, as celebrated Lakota author Ella Deloria described it in her 1988 novel *Waterlily*, the obligation to be good relatives. Melanie Yazzie and Cutcha Risling Baldy write about *radical relationality* as a decolonizing Indigenous feminist project "which spans multiple institutional, grassroots, organizational, and government spaces."[2] How do we honor the shared value of being good relatives in an ethic of radical relationality, and what does it look like?

One shining example has meant joining forces at a choice moment in 2018 to help shape a bill in the California state legislature, AB 1782, designating surfing as the state sport. As we will show, the bill not only officially enshrines surfing as the state sport, it also amounts to what we believe is the first Indigenous land acknowledgment in any piece of state or federal legislation in the United States. This achievement is worth celebrating, and this essay tells the story of how that win came to be. Being good relatives is about more than a single example, though. Our relationship prior to that moment made the victory possible, and it continues and is alive in this moment of writing. We offer a reflection here in the hope that our story suggests strategies that help others to work across what so often seem like incommensurate differences and to help ourselves to stay close and keep at it.

The journey that led to the legislative victory began through our scholarly work in the realm of critical surf studies. It started in 2015, with the project Krista and others were getting off the ground, the Institute for Women Surfers (IWS). In 2015, the institute was in only its second year, and it met for a long weekend of surfing and mutual learning in Ventura, California, at the campus of the Brooks Institute, nestled in the coastal foothills. Dina was an invited speaker who worked with all of the participants on what she called "American Settler Colonialism 101."[3] She put together an interactive teaching exercise that helped us make connections between Native American history, surf culture, and narratives of discovery and conquest in surf media and tourism, and especially she taught about localism and territoriality in surfing. Very few people had linked settler colonial possessiveness to locals "owning" a surf spot. After the transformative impact of that lesson upon the gathered participants in Ventura, Dina joined the institute's steering committee and brought her leadership and vision of a decolonial future to the IWS Principles of Governance.[4] At the next institute meeting at Stanford in 2017, Dina continued to lead us in decolonial directions. We shared the stage at various other events, including a public event organized by Dina at San Onofre State Park and one for graduate students by Krista at Rice University's Center for the Study of Women, Gender, and Sexuality.

We also presented research to broad scholarly audiences in Estes Park, Colorado, at the Western Literature Association Conference 2019. In 2020, we came together in a new, non-surf-specific format as a small cohort of culturally diverse, multiracial women also including Priscilla Ybarra and Martha Pitts. We received funding from Rice University's Humanities Research Center to bring a symposium to Rice under a rubric we called

"Feminist Accountabilities." The project sought conversations across African American, Latinx, Indigenous, and white perspectives about women's accountabilities to each other as feminists in the context of the racial, settler colonial state. But the pandemic hit, the murder of George Floyd rocked our worlds, and massive protests in the streets transformed activist priorities. With the COVID lockdown in full force and the very communities we hoped to gather among the hardest hit, the symposium did not materialize. Our efforts did inform Krista's *Living West as Feminists* project, a remarkable series of dialogues focusing on questions about "the where of us"—the places that we love or belong, or don't belong, and who we are in them. Dina participated with an interview that took place, in fact, at Panhe, a place we will talk more about shortly. The work of this essay coincides with all the above energies to think through and define the contours of these commitments as we imagine them.

A unique offering of our work—embedded as it is in the practices of surfing and swimming and spending time in specific beach and water places—is it shows the possibilities for decolonizing the health and well-being of Indigenous bodies when physical activity aligns with Indigenous histories, ceremony, and community. This finding builds on the work of collaborators McGuire-Adams and Giles about decolonization, through running, for Anishinaabekweg women.[5]

Also important to the moment in which our work was being conceived and written is, as noted above, the fact of the COVID-19 pandemic, the murder of George Floyd, and the urgency surrounding climate crises in the midst of these other two crises. For some collaborators, those urgencies created a new resolve to address the painfully vexed relations and needed alliances between Indigenous activisms and African American activisms. A highly regarded example of this effort, Maynard and Simpson's *Rehearsals for Living*, suggests a path forward in which a politics of abolition emerges as a necessary framework for also thinking about land and sovereignty, justice, and world-building beyond the nation-state. *Rehearsals* develops an earlier conversation between McCabe and Finney about bridging Black/red divides that was important in the moment we were thinking through the forms our dialogue could take.[6]

Whether one embraces hopes for bridging as visionary or prefers to keep a focus on real-time laws and priorities in the now, all of these profound relational attempts show what it means to think together, and to imagine together a world that transcends seemingly intractable structures, across difference. For us, in doing this work, we did not skirt the fraught relation of Indigenous women to feminism as a history that arose in the United States from the social concerns of white middle-class women.[7] Instead, our focus as feminists has been and is on Indigenous priorities of unerasing Indigenous presence, decolonization, and land. Frameworks of sovereignty and real-time policy and legal contexts served these purposes and do so here.

DINA: As someone steeped in American Indian studies scholarship and as a longtime surfer, until these last few years I could never have imagined a serious, academically based conversation that brings the two topics together. The growing field of critical surf studies has opened up for me a whole new way of seeing surf history and culture that makes much more sense than the way it's been written for the last century. I started surfing in 1980, after I moved to the North Shore of O'ahu, the global epicenter of the surf world. I became obsessed with surfing Pipeline as one of the very few women to do so at the time. A few years later I relocated to Northern California, where the ocean is really cold, and I fell out of the sport for about twenty-five years. I started surfing again in 2009, after returning to Southern California, where I grew up, settling in San Clemente, ground zero of the surf industry. In those years surf culture had changed dramatically. I became aware of this growing surf scholarship, where people were bringing critical and hard-hitting analyses to the table, disrupting all the feel-good, tunnel-visioned, and inaccurate historical perspectives that white settler men had been writing for a century.

I first encountered critical surf studies with Kristen Lawler's amazing book *The American Surfer: Radical Culture and Capitalism* around 2014. The very next book in the critical surf studies canon I found was Krista's *Surfer Girls in the New World Order*. It blew me away to see Marxist and feminist analyses of surf culture, and from there it became obvious to me that surfing as a place-based phenomenon existed not only within the structures of heteropatriarchal neoliberal capitalism but the settler colonial state as well. But no one was writing about it through that lens yet. I started writing social media and news articles, then a chapter for *The Critical Surf Studies Reader*.[8] *The Critical Surf Studies Reader* roughly coincided with other critical surf studies projects, including a 2016 conference in New Zealand and the Institute for Women Surfers. I had become connected to Krista and the institute one day after randomly meeting Cori Schumacher, three-time women's longboarding world champion. She told me about the Institute for Women Surfers and suggested I reach out to Krista. It was kismet.

KRISTA: When I was first getting to know Dina in the wintertime of 2014, I was still astonished that surfers were reaching out to me after reading *Surfer Girls*. Cori Schumacher and I had done the pilot institute, and I did not know then that that work would become transformative for me as a researcher and lead to an agenda of publicly engaged research and writing. Nor did I know how much that transformation would bring to the fore the fact that the more I grew into university life, the more my own water life had grown distant. I did not want to completely lose the call of the water. I had points of connection with Dina's work in Indigenous studies. I had heard of her as a journalist and read with admiration "Surfing as Sovereignty" in *Indian Country Today Media Network*. I had talked about Panhe in *Surfer Girls* and highlighted the partnership between Native peoples and Surfrider Foundation during the famous Save Trestles campaign. But I did not know about Dina's extensive MA work yet. I attended the Native American and Indigenous Studies Association (NAISA) in 2014, the year Dina and I met, which was early in NAISA's history. A few scholars of Native and Indigenous literatures whom I had known for years from the Western Literature Association were founders and ecstatic the organization was getting off the ground. It turned out Dina in her work for the Center for World Indigenous Studies had presented a paper that year. I did not present because I was too aware of myself as a settler woman from the US West; I was too nervous. I would not have told her that then.

I was also questioning myself, after the surf book. What was I doing?

I had written the book in isolation in Houston, though the research was international, and I wanted to think about a next project. There was not yet a surf studies field and certainly no sense of a "critical" surf studies. My closest colleague friends were working on the US/Mexico borderlands and anticapitalist labor movements. I had been invited by Alex Young, a scholar of settler theory and then a grad student, to be a symposium speaker about a year earlier at "The Significance of the Frontier in an Age of Transnational History," hosted by USC Center for the West and the Huntington Library. There I heard Patrick Wolfe speak for the first time, and Jodi Byrd. It was world-changing. I knew my thinking about feminist critical race theory would never be the same.

I say the above to say that Dina's work as it was developing and who she was, herself, suggested some of the ways forward. Her work with me, and with the institute women, was a leap in ways to be together. We seemed to stumble onto a new surfeminist relationality. The meeting in Ventura where Dina taught us all how to rethink localism as possible only because of established masculine settler prerogatives was where we started to talk about the institute not as an "it" but as an "us." The institute was our relations; it was dynamic. Building momentum in this direction, we heard from another invited guest, the Latinx scholar Michelle Habell-Pallán, from Southern California and a professor at the University of Washington who co-runs the public humanities project Womxn Who Rock.[9] She urged us to remember the preciousness of "co-vivencía," of our living together-ness, our worldmaking, and to take to heart the small achievements of our new communal life, not to overlook what we accomplish, even when it falls short of our hopes.

AB 1782 and Histories of Surfing in California

DINA: Critical surf studies works to dismantle and reconstruct misleading and harmful surfing narratives. The goal is to accurately depict history and the social processes that have shaped the sport and its subculture, including its dark underbelly of sexism, racism, and other isms. Just as Krista's book showed that global surf economies tie women's second-rate status and hyperobjectification to the way the sport and industry is male dominated (and men make the big money), seeing surfing through the frameworks of Indigeneity and colonialism casts an entirely different light on surf history and culture. Because of the work of Isaiah Walker, John Clark, Patrick Moser, and earlier contributions of Ben Finney, scholars now know the ways that surf promoter Alexander Hume Ford and his accomplice Jack London narrated early twentieth-century surfing in Hawai'i in historically biased and white supremacist terms. Scott Laderman's work in *Empire in Waves* as well as Krista's work help us understand surfing in a broader context of transnational colonial, post–World War II militaristic and political processes. Looking at the ways early surf history in California has been written, one finds a similar historical blindness, divorced from the actual historical foundations of the state. History in the settler state always begins with settlers, whitewashing and downplaying the brutality toward American Indians that was committed with the founding of the country and state. This process of disavowing Indigeneity to maintain state-sanctioned willful ignorance is what Kevin Bruyneel calls "settler memory." Settler memory reinforces fantasies of settler innocence as it constructs legitimizing narratives of belonging on stolen Indigenous lands. Certainly, one sees these patterns of settler memory at work in California surfing historiography.

As Kristen Lawler showed, surf culture is far from the apolitical, radical but innocent community on the fringes of American society it has fancied itself. On the contrary, when one thinks of the period when surfing took hold in Southern California, with the arrival of George Freeth in 1907, a disturbing picture emerges. California had been a state for only five decades. Beginning in 1851 with his State of the State address, Governor Peter Burnett explicitly declared a war of extermination against the California Indian population, which was already in precipitous decline due to the violence of the Spanish missions and the introduction of foreign diseases. For the next two to three decades, as a matter of policy and funded with federal dollars, the state employed citizen militia groups to systematically hunt down and kill California Indians. This is a history well-documented by Brendan Lindsay (*Murder State*) and Benjamin Madley (*An American Genocide*) and California Indian scholars before them who laid the foundation for understanding California history as genocidal. At the same time, a history of Indian slavery started by the Spanish lasted until the turn of the twentieth century, as the work of Andrés Reséndez (*The Other Slavery*) shows. The California Land Act of 1851 then intentionally defrauded former Mexican citizens out of the (stolen) Indian lands they received as land grants from the Spanish and Mexican governments, in violation of the Treaty of Guadalupe Hidalgo. Within just a few decades, virtually all the land—especially coastal land—had fallen into white ownership. I did a survey of all the land grants in Orange County, for instance, and discovered that land transfers into white ownership were complete only thirty-seven years after the treaty. The net result of processes of ongoing invasion and violence is that the California Indian population fell from a precontact number of three hundred thousand to one million to between ten thousand to twenty thousand people. This is a genocide of a staggering 97–99 percent within less than a century and a half.

What you have, in other words, is an ethnically cleansed landscape as the condition of possibility for surf culture to become embedded as a sport in California. Yet the way the history of surfing has been written starts with empty beachscapes into which legendary Hawaiian surfer and lifeguard George Freeth steps in order to help developers Abbot Kinney and Henry Huntington sell their newly acquired coastal properties. Even the work of Peter Westwick and Peter Neushul, in an otherwise wonderful book, *The World in the Curl: An Unconventional History of Surfing*, gets this important history wrong. It casts too narrow a net, failing to inquire about how these business magnates came to possess all that land. Settler memory means that history tales begin with assumptions of land as legitimately acquired and never implicates settlers in the dispossession of the Tongva, Chumash, Acjachemen, Kumeyaay, Payómkawichum, and other coastal California Indigenous people and their thousands-year-old tenure. This classic example of how popular surf historians have whitewashed American historical narratives and erased Indigenous presence is why it became my mission to do the work I call "unerasing" in my surf and broader research, a perspective I brought to the first workshop at the Institute for Women Surfers in 2015.

When I first heard of California Assembly Bill (AB) 1782, to make surfing the official state sport, I immediately knew it was an opportunity to do the work of unerasing Indigenous people in the history of California and of surfing. AB 1782 was sponsored by State Senator Al Muratsuchi, a surfer from the South Bay. In its original skeletal form, the language of the bill simply focused on surfing as an iconic history and image of California culture as well as its importance as an economic driver in the state. As it was then written, the language was typical of histories that erase Native people in California. Moreover, it ignored the fact that surfing is an Indigenous sport brought to the world and to California by the Kanaka Māoli (Native Hawaiians). I saw AB 1782 as an opportunity to create a broader legislative discussion and recognition of the historical context of surfing and enter it officially into the state record.

Initially, the bill mentioned the names of some of California's most popular surf breaks, including Malibu, Huntington Beach, Trestles, Maverick's, and Steamer Lane. I inserted what I believed would be the most important amendments, including a reminder about surfing as an Indigenous Hawaiian sport (section 1[b]), that the most beloved and renowned surf breaks today are Indigenous homelands that California Indian people still live on in the present, and that the protection of an ancient Acjachemen village site called Panhe upon which Trestles is located was instrumental in the years-long battle to "save Trestles" from potential ruin due to a proposed six-lane toll road. I researched the original place names of the surf breaks and the tribes associated with them and wrote them into the bill (section 1[c]). My master's thesis on the protection of Panhe, which serves as an initial case study for what environmental justice looks like when it is "Indigenized," ended up being the seed for *As Long as Grass Grows.* I applied that research in section 1(d), which acknowledges the importance of Panhe in the story of the Save Trestles campaign.

KRISTA: In February 2018 Dina and I began conversations about the bill and included Jennifer Savage, who at the time served as Surfrider Foundation's communications director. Jennifer was known to all of us through her powerful presence at the Institute for Women Surfers 2017 meeting at Stanford University. At the time I was spending a sabbatical as a visiting scholar at the Lane Center for the American West. The 2017 institute meeting deepened the understanding among participants of decolonial perspectives on surfing and on beach spaces begun the previous year with workshops Dina led. The meeting was in fact the first time we began with a land acknowledgment, as Dina offered a group gratitude to the Ohlone peoples on whose lands we met the first night, which present-day Pacifica occupies. Jennifer Savage, as an IWS member, became a quick and knowledgeable ally to various projects, suggesting speaking engagements for participants to present material on environmental racism as it was evident in surfing. The IWS meeting had forwarded, through participants' own histories, the complexity of "environmental access," and we wished for those perspectives to become part of Surfrider legal strategy and to take advantage of California Coastal Act law, which favors a very broad definition of accessibility. As Jamila Hubbard of Brown Girl Surf and others made clear, barriers to access include more than physical restraints like fences or roadblocks. The assumption that "Black people don't swim" can be reinforced by recreational spaces that are historically and unwelcomingly white. Jennifer Savage took it upon herself as a Surfrider leader to bring awareness to the intangible barriers of race, gender, language, and economic difficulties in getting to the coast. Using these competing meanings of access, the IWS research report "Beaches as Spaces of Democracy" teased out research and action recommendations.[10] Immediate speaking engagements and action events came out of that weekend and put many of us in Sacramento in late 2017 and 2018.

DINA: Coincidentally, I had traveled to the state capitol on Oceans Day, in February 2018, and met Matthew Hurley, a legislative aid for Assemblywoman Sharon Quirk-Silva. In March I attended the California Democratic Convention in San Diego, where I tracked down Senator Muratsuchi during a session on environmental issues to have a conversation about the language revisions in AB 1782. He listened as I lobbied him about why it was important to recognize Indigenous aspects in the bill. Meanwhile, Jennifer Savage organized several events in which women surfers spoke out about barriers to access on the coast. One brought both Jennifer and

Krista to Sacramento for a panel at the California Green Summit with Marley Reynosa of Brown Girl Surf, an Afro-Latina; Olivia VanDamme of City Surf Project, a Latina; and Dionne Ybarra, of Project Wahine/ El Proyecto Wahine, also a Latina. The panelists spoke to the barriers of access they faced and gave examples of interventions into environmental racism and sexism.

KRISTA: Serendipitously, Jennifer and I were in town and were enthusiastic about lobbying for changing the bill's language at Dina's request. Everybody on our California Green Summit panel was on board, and so were their organizations. We talked about it the whole weekend. Jennifer set up the meeting; she is experienced in working with elected officials. I had not been in meetings before with a legislative aide, and Jennifer knew the ropes. We had our talking points in order, the rationale for why the changes should be adopted, and she let me take the lead as a researcher making a case in the meeting. In an email thread coordinating this beforehand, we were connected with Senator Muratsuchi's legislative aide, Brady McCarthy. Brady was the link to Senator Muratsuchi, and that connection advanced the conversation Dina had begun with him at the Democratic convention. I had written a letter of support on behalf of IWS to Muratsuchi and Assemblyman Ian Calderon, cosponsor of the bill. I had been leafleting the California Summit panels we attended with a handout that urged others' support on behalf of Native peoples and histories. The meeting was friendly, with a sense the cosponsors supported the changes. We left believing it was likely the changes would be adopted.

DINA: Krista and Jennifer really went out of their way to make that meeting happen, and it's hard to know how things might have turned out without their support and influence. I couldn't do it alone. It's situations like these when people show up for you in ways that are meaningful and effective, especially when they don't personally benefit from it, that demonstrate relationality as a verb. Whether within or outside a tribal context, this is what relationality looks like in action, not as a fancy ideal or academic concept. For a few weeks after their meeting with Brady, there was a flurry of back-and-forth communicating as the legislature circulated the bill through committees and markup processes. Throughout May, June, and July the bill had continued through readings and amendments, and by August the governor signed it into law. The language changed somewhat from the original, but it was still very strong, and it was amazing that it didn't get eliminated altogether. To understand how pleased and surprised I was, we need to take a longer view of how embattled the concept and practice of land acknowledgments is, and why.

Land Acknowledgments

KRISTA: In the fall of 2020, in consultation with Dina, I asked my graduate student research assistant, Zainab Abdali, to do some searches into legislated land acknowledgments. None of us was aware of any federal, state, city, or even local government legislation that did, or encouraged, land acknowledgments. The goal was to search out any kind of legislation that includes such language or whose sole purpose deliberately acknowledges or encourages the acknowledgment of the Indigenous peoples of any given place in the United States as the Original Peoples. This would be different from laws, bills, or resolutions that impart rights. Zainab used the website LegiScan to search for any relevant state and federal bills, including proposed bills, whether the bill passed, whether it was a partisan or bipartisan bill, and whether amendments were made.[11]

The general findings of Zainab's research showed nothing close to a land acknowledgment in older resolutions, with the well-known exception of the 1993 Hawaii Apology Resolution, acknowledging the illegal overthrow of a sovereign monarchy and the ruination of a harmonious social and natural ecosystem, as well as the 2009 HJ Resolution 46.[12] Resolution 46 acknowledges "a long history of official depredations and ill-conceived policies" by the US government, explicitly naming treaty violations, policies of termination, extermination, forced removals, the criminalization of Native religions, and destruction of sacred lands. Toward hopes for reconciliation between Indigenous peoples and the United States, and for healing of the land itself, the resolution offers an "apology to all Native Peoples." Zainab also noted in her research that resolutions often contain disclaimers that release the United States from any responsibility for land claims. Resolution 46, for instance, contains such a disclaimer.

The language of recent resolutions from 2019 and 2020 is much stronger, many of them from state resolutions establishing Indigenous Peoples' Day in the place of Columbus Day. The 2019 DC Emergency Resolution, for instance, notes both that Columbus never set foot in what is today the United States and moreover that he "enslaved, colonized, mutilated, and massacred thousands of Indigenous People in the Americas."[13] The Pennsylvania HR 508 acknowledges as original inhabitants the Erie, Iroquois, Lenape, Munsee, Shawnee, and Susquehannock and recognizes as well that "more than one highway in this Commonwealth follows an original Native American Indian trail."[14] Vermont Bill S0068 notes that the original inhabitants were the Abenaki people and "honors them and their ancestors."[15] But as Zainab observes, the bill goes on with the highly problematic and offensive suggestion that, in the wake of displacement and forced assimilation, "Vermont's recognized tribes . . . [might] move forward and formulate positive outcomes, from the history of colonization." It should be noted here, however, that Vermont's state recognition of four self-proclaimed Abenaki "tribes" is highly contested, as the groups are viewed as illegitimate by federally recognized Abenaki in Canada and many members of the Wabanaki Confederacy tribes of the Passamoquoddy, Penobscot, Maliseet, and Mi'kmaq in the United States.[16]

To be sure, resolutions can be significant documents. Nonetheless, resolutions and land acknowledgments are not the same kinds of gestures toward decolonial futures. Resolutions most often acknowledge Indigenous presence and claim to land in the past tense, implying that colonization is over and does not persist in the present. The DC resolution, for instance, characterizes "Native American Indians who *were* the original inhabitants, explorers, and settlers of the United States." Land acknowledgments perform a different kind of work. And that's what makes AB 1782 as a "legislated land acknowledgment" so relevant.

DINA: From my perspective, AB 1782 is remarkable for three key reasons. First, as a surfer I appreciate that the sport is recognized for its importance in shaping California history and culture, as do most other surfers I've talked to. It substantiates and brings to life the arguments that Westwick and Neushul made in *The World in the Curl*, that surfing was not just incidental or peripheral to California history and culture but central to it. Second, with support from organizations like Surfrider Foundation, the bill also recognizes the increasingly important role that sustainability, environmental protection, and stewardship plays in surf culture (section 1[k]), which benefits everyone, surfers and nonsurfers alike. This section of the bill effectively enshrines these concepts as a statement of values and purpose of the state legislature.

Finally, and perhaps most obviously, the language about the Indigeneity of surfing not only reinforces respect toward Kanaka Māoli people as the creators of the sport as we know it, it also restores the historical reality of California Indian people as the *still existing* Original Peoples of California's coastal land and seascapes. It reminds us that like the rest of the continent where American Indian people tended the land for thousands of years (reservation or not), in what we today call "California," its beaches, too, are Indian Country, even if current state structures still sever Native jurisdiction over those lands. They are places of sacred significance to the tribes that originated in them and whose worldviews and cultures are shaped by them, even for tribes who were assigned to reservations inland or who have no reservations at all but who historically occupied coastal lands. This gets to the heart of why land acknowledgments are important, and here I draw from the land acknowledgment toolkit we created on our campus in American Indian studies at Cal State San Marcos in collaboration with the California Indian Culture and Sovereignty Center and Southern California Tribal Chairman's Association.[17] Land acknowledgments are first an opportunity for people to learn whose Indigenous homelands they reside or work on, undoing patterns of intentional erasure. They are opportunities for settler people to acknowledge—especially in California—that Native people never ceded their lands. They are thus moves toward settler responsibility.

The danger of land acknowledgments is that they can function as a kind of "settler move to innocence," in Tuck and Yang's formulation,[18] where the statement helps settler people feel good about having acknowledged painful histories of dispossession but then ultimately does nothing to rectify ongoing injustices. Land acknowledgments without meaningful action thus only serve settlers. As Zainab noted in her research, land acknowledgments are the opposite of resolutions and bills that portray Indigenous claims to land as past tense, complete with their disclaimers. They are statements that affirm the contested nature of land, centering Indigenous perspectives where land is claimed in the present despite ongoing juridical dispossession. Although a legislated land acknowledgment like AB 1782 does not attempt to restore land to Native communities, it does represent a fundamental shift in perspective without reverting to disclaimers that foreclose any acts of real justice. Land acknowledgments reject disclaimers that reinforce state hegemony and dispossession.

Looking Forward

In the few years since that flurry of AB 1782 activity, both of us have been doing new writing, and speaking, and as the world opened after the worst of the pandemic, traveling. We have stayed connected with one another. After our meeting at Stanford, the Institute for Women Surfers created two new chapters, one in Europe, one in Oceania, and to be sure, the institute travels with principles of the decolonial vision Dina brought and encounters those of others. We learn from the surf worlds and lifeways of Indigenous peoples in Oceania and the South Pacific. Dina is at work on two new books with Beacon Press, one tentatively titled *Illegitimate Nation: Privilege, Race, and Belonging in the U.S. Settler State*, and the other, *Who Gets to Be Indian: Ethnic Fraud and Other Difficult Conversations about Native American Identity*. Krista has been posting to a blog, and an interview with Dina is part of the *Living West* book, which is in press.[19]

As noted already, there is social momentum gathering around land acknowledgments in universities and in cities. In March of 2021, an article in *Stateline* from the Pew Foundation reports, "A Growing Number of Cities

Weigh 'Tribal Land Acknowledgements,'" including Denver, Portland, Eden Prairie in Minnesota, and Phoenix and Flagstaff in Arizona.[20] In California, so often a national trendsetter, Assembly Bill 1968, the Tribal Land Acknowledgement Act of 2020, cosponsored by the California Indian Culture and Sovereignty Center and California Indian Museum and Cultural Center, offered a wide-reaching and hard-hitting statement about the political and social value and need for land acknowledgments.[21] Though AB 1968 passed in the Assembly, it failed in the Senate. But in local contexts of city councils, school boards, and citizen-run civic organizations, land acknowledgments are increasingly present in civic life. In Sacramento, the city council has reprioritized its ritual opening and, before pledging allegiance to the American flag, meetings commence with recognition and honoring of those who came before and "still walk beside us today on these ancestral lands," including the Nisenan people, the Southern Maidu, Valley and Plains Miwok, Patwin Wintun peoples, and the people of the Wilton Rancheria, Sacramento's single tribe with federal recognition.[22] Though this ritual act falls short of AB 1968, which would have encouraged statewide statements in public schools, parks, and libraries and at public events, the city council moves speak toward a growing consciousness of Native history and survivance. As Dina notes above, such moves reframe interactions between Native peoples and settlers, offering a glimpse that better relationships are possible.

KRISTA: When Dina talks about relationality as a verb, I listen. For me, it is a way of being and doing, together. I take Tuck and Yang's assertion that decolonization is not a metaphor seriously; it involves land repatriation and the recentering of Indigenous life and knowledge. It is not so unsupple that it inverts power dynamics in order to dominate settler people. It is not one size fits all. It is also, for me anyway, about my own path toward those goals, what being an ally possibly can mean, and it's about people as much as projects. This essay is focused on action and thinking and teaching, all of which are the topics at hand. But let me say, too, I feel the presence of times Dina and I swam, sat on the beach, sat together at sunset at Panhe, ate family dinner together, went out for Mexican food, commiserated about motherhood and entering elderhood as women of the same age. I feel a history of listening, and of being listened to. I feel Dina as a woman who is mature and experienced, which is a crucial kind of friend to have. So reaching toward decoloniality for me has been textured inside of all of these behaviors. It is not transactional. It involves a politics of attentiveness, attunement, of attempting accountability as a white settler woman to Indigenous histories, yes, but not abstractly, since it must be in the form of showing care to people whom I am lucky to know. If relationality is not simply reduced to an elite or academic theory, as Dina says, I also have understood relationality as a form of collaboration and as a feminist methodology in real time, a way to enact our intentions now in the worlds we occupy in the meanwhile.

DINA: In closing I'd like to say it's not difficult to see the world in relational terms, and all cultures do to one extent or another. But for Indigenous people, it is an animating principle that defines what it means to live correctly in the world. While colonization and capitalism have disrupted these value systems, our job is to identify these disruptions and do the reparative work. Indigenous feminism is one such intervention and is truly decolonizing when settlers and Native people engage together to affirm a relational ethic that centers Indigenous futurity.

POSTSCRIPT

We would like to thank Jennifer Savage for her relationality and contribution to making AB 1782 what it was in its final form. We would like to thank Zainab Abdali for her crack research and perceptive understanding of the stakes of her work.

Appendix

TEXT OF AB 1782

THE PEOPLE OF THE STATE OF CALIFORNIA DO ENACT AS FOLLOWS:

SECTION 1.

The Legislature finds and declares all of the following:

(a) Surfing is an iconic California sport.

(b) It is important to recognize that surfing traces its origins to the Polynesian people and was imported into California from indigenous Hawaii. Since its arrival in California, surfing has been embraced by the state and many Californians have made important contributions to the sport as we know it today.

(c) California is home to a number of world-famous surf breaks like Malibu, Trestles, Mavericks, Rincon, Steamer Lane, and Huntington, which are destinations for both domestic and international surfers. It is important to remember that California's coastline is not only home to these surf breaks, but is also the ancestral homeland to indigenous peoples like the Chumash in Malibu, known as "Humaliwu" in the Chumash language, and Rincon, the Acjachemen in Trestles, known as "Panhe" in the Acjachemen language, the Amah Mutsun in Steamer Lane, the Ohlone in Mavericks, and the Acjachemen and Tongva shared territory in Huntington Beach, known as "Lukupangma" in the Tongva and Acjachemen language. These indigenous people continue to live in these ancestral homelands today and have embraced the sport of surfing in these areas.

(d) It is important to acknowledge that the Acjachemen were instrumental in saving Trestles from potential destruction by a proposed toll road in 2008, due to Panhe's recognition as an ancient Acjachemen village site by the California Coastal Commission.

(e) Every year, California surf breaks host numerous domestic and international surf events, including the International Surf Festival in the Cities of Hermosa Beach, Manhattan Beach, Redondo Beach, and Torrance, the US Open of Surfing in Huntington Beach, the Mavericks Big Wave Surf Contest in Half Moon Bay, and the Founders' Cup of Surfing in Lemoore.

(f) California is home to the Surfers' Hall of Fame, the International Surfing Museum, and the California Surf Museum.

(g) California's coastline spans 1,100 miles and its beaches and coastal areas generate $1.15 trillion in economic activity annually.

(h) California is the heart of the surfboard building industry, which has innovated surfboard technology and pioneered sustainable manufacturing practices and techniques.

(i) The world's first neoprene wetsuit, a modern staple of surfing, was invented in California's San Francisco Bay area.

(j) California pioneered the science of surf forecasting at the University of California's Scripps Institution of Oceanography. Surf forecasting allows surfers around the world to predict when and where to go surfing.

(k) California's surfing culture is taking a national and global leadership role in promoting sustainability as a core value, while also placing a high value on environmental protection and stewardship, in order to preserve the ocean, waves, coastline, and wildlife that make the state such a unique place to surf, live, and visit.

SEC. 2.

Section 424.7 is added to the Government Code, to read:

424.7.
Surfing is the official state sport.

Notes

1 Huhndorf and Suzack note that there is not one Indigenous feminism but do recognize the shared colonial history and imposition of patriarchy that allows us to "understand the changing situations, the commonalities, and specificities of Indigenous women across time and place." Huhndorf and Suzack, "Introduction," 3. For more about whiteness in relation to feminism, please see Comer, "Staying with the White Trouble."

2 Yazzie and Baldy, "Introduction," 7.

3 "2015 Curriculum," updated July 2018, www.instituteforwomensurfers.org/summer-institute-2015/2015-curriculum.

4 "History, Charge, and Principles of Governance," updated July 2018, www.instituteforwomensurfers.org/about-us/iws-steering-committee.

5 McGuire-Adams and Giles, "Anishinaabekweg Dibaajimowinan (Stories) of Decolonization through Running."

6 See Woman Stands Shining (McCabe) and Finney, "Conversation at the Crossroads."

7 Many have written on this topic. One earlier example is Huhndorf and Suzack, "Introduction."

8 Hough-Snee and Eastman, *The Critical Surf Studies Reader.*

9 See tab "Speaker Michelle Habell-Pallán" at www.instituteforwomensurfers.org/summer-institute-2015, updated December 2023. For more information on Womxn Who Rock, see https://womenwhorockcommunity.org.

10 Comer, "Beaches as Spaces of Democracy."

11 LegiScan, accessed July 7, 2024, https://legiscan.com.

12 See US Public Law 103–50, "The Apology Resolution," November 23, 1993, www.hawaii-nation.org/publaw.html, and 2009 HJ Resolution 46, April 30, 2009, www.congress.gov/bill/111th-congress/house-joint-resolution/46/text.

13 Washington, DC, Council Resolution 230500, October 22, 2019, https://legiscan.com/DC/bill/PR23-0500/2019.

14 Pennsylvania HR 508, September 19, 2019, https://legiscan.com/PA/text/HR508/id/2054194.

15 Vermont Senate Bill 68, May 8, 2019, https://legiscan.com/VT/text/S0068/id/1883456.

16 Leroux, "State Recognition and the Dangers of Race Shifting."

17 *Land Acknowledgement*, www.csusm.edu/cicsc/land.pdf.

18 Tuck and Yang, "Decolonization Is Not a Metaphor," 9.

19 For the blog site, see https://feministwests.blogs.rice.edu.

20 Caitlin Dewey, "Growing Number of Cities Weigh Tribal 'Land Acknowledgements,'" Stateline, March 17, 2021, www.pewtrusts.org/en/research-and-analysis/blogs/stateline/2021/03/17/growing-number-of-cities-weigh-tribal-land-acknowledgements.

21 AB 1968, August 8, 2020, https://openstates.org/ca/bills/20192020/AB1968.

22 Andrews, "Land Acknowledgment in the State Capital."

Bibliography

Andrews, Emily. "Land Acknowledgment in the State Capital for Indigenous People—A Step towards Widespread Change." The Davis Vanguard Organization. December 21, 2021. www.davisvanguard.org/2021/12/land-acknowledgement-in-the-state-capital-for-indigenous-people-a-step-towards-widespread-change.

Bruyneel, Kevin. *Settler Memory: The Disavowal of Indigeneity and the Politics of Race in the United States*. Chapel Hill: University of North Carolina Press, 2021.

Comer, Krista. "Beaches as Spaces of Democracy: Center Hosts Women Surfers Conference." Stanford University, The Bill Lane Center for the American West, December 15, 2017. https://west.stanford.edu/news/beaches-spaces-democracy-center-hosts-women-surfers-conference.

———. *Living West as Feminists: Conversations about the Where of Us*. Lincoln: University of Nebraska Press, 2024.

———. "Staying with the White Trouble of Recent Feminist Westerns." *Western American Literature* 56, no. 2 (2021): 101–23.

———. *Surfer Girls in the New World Order*. Durham, NC: Duke University Press, 2010.

Deloria, Ella. *Waterlily*. Lincoln: University of Nebraska Press, 1988.

Gilio-Whitaker, Dina. *As Long as Grass Grows: The Indigenous Fight for Colonization to Standing Rock*. Boston: Beacon Press, 2019.

———. "Surfing as Sovereignty: How Native Hawaiians Resisted Colonialism." *Indian Country Today Media Network*, November 14, 2014, updated Sept. 13, 2018. https://indiancountrytoday.com/archive/surfing-as-sovereignty-how-native-hawaiians-resisted-colonialism.

Hough-Snee, Dexter Zavalza, and Alexander Sotelo Eastman, eds. *The Critical Surf Studies Reader*. Durham, NC: Duke University Press, 2017.

Huhndorf, Shari M., and Cheryl Suzack. "Introduction. Indigenous Feminism: Theorizing the Issues." In *Indigenous Women and Feminism: Politics, Activism, Culture*, edited by Cheryl Suzack, Shari M. Huhndorf, Jeanne Perreault, and Jean Barman, 1–20. Vancouver: UBC Press, 2010.

Laderman, Scott. *Empire in Waves: A Political History of Surfing*. Los Angeles: University of California Press, 2014.

Land Acknowledgement: You're on California Indian Land, Now What? Acknowledging Relationships to Space & Place Toolkit. California Indian Culture and Sovereignty Center, California State University San Marcos. www.csusm.edu/cicsc/land.pdf.

Lawler, Kristen. *The American Surfer: Radical Culture and Capitalism*. New York: Routledge, 2011.

Leroux, Darryl. "State Recognition and the Dangers of Race Shifting." *American Indian Culture and Research Journal* 46, no. 2 (2023): 53–84. https://doi.org/10.17953/aicrj.46.2.leroux.

Lindsay, Brendan C. *Murder State: California's Native American Genocide, 1846–1873*. Lincoln: University of Nebraska Press, 2012.

Madley, Benjamin. *An American Genocide: The United States and the California Indian Catastrophe*. New Haven, CT: Yale University Press, 2016.

Maynard, Robyn, and Leanne Betasamosake Simpson. *Rehearsals for Living*. Chicago: Haymarket Books, 2002.

McGuire-Adams, Tricia D., and Audrey R. Giles. "Anishinaabekweg Dibaajimowinan (Stories) of Decolonization through Running." *Sociology of Sport Journal* 35, no. 3 (2018): 207–15. https://doi.org/10.1123/ssj.2017-0052.

Resendéz, Andrés. *The Other Slavery: The Uncovered Story of Indian Enslavement in America*. New York: Houghton Mifflin Harcourt, 2016.

Tuck, Eve, and K. Wayne Yang. "Decolonization Is Not a Metaphor." *Decolonization: Indigeneity, Education and Society* 1, no. 1 (2012): 1–40.

Walker, Isaiah Helekunihi. *Waves of Resistance: Surfing and History in Twentieth-Century Hawai'i*. Honolulu: University of Hawai'i Press, 2011.

Westwick, Peter, and Peter Neushul. *The World in the Curl: An Unconventional History of Surfing*. New York: Crown Publishers, 2013.

Woman Stands Shining (Pat McCabe) and Carolyn Finney. "Conversation at the Crossroads: The Intimacy of Right Relations." Franklin Environmental Center at Hillcrest, Middlebury College, November 17, 2020. www.youtube.com/watch?v=tDlJXxcN5UU.

Yazzie, Melanie K., and Cutcha Risling Baldy. "Introduction: Indigenous Peoples and the Politics of Water." *Decolonization: Indigeneity, Education and Society* 7, no. 1 (2018): 1–18.

11

In the Name of Public Safety

Gendered Surveillance and Sexual Violence within Southern California Beach Lifeguarding Culture

ASAKO YONAN

"I bet he's been watching you all day, just staring at your ass," a male coworker said to me about my supervisor, who was sitting in the lifeguard headquarter building directly behind my tower, beneath tinted windows. It was the summer of 2015, and I was a California State beach lifeguard working in Southern California at the time. Being one of the only female-identified lifeguards in my particular district, let alone one of the only women of color, and queer, I was acutely aware of the fact that I was being watched. And often. Not only by my coworkers, but by the beach-going public as well (the majority of whom were white, male, upper-middle-class surfers). I didn't need him to remind me.

A few months later, I was sexually assaulted by a beachgoer while on duty. That same coworker came to the tower I was working at after his shift ended. "I heard what happened earlier today through the radio," he said. He went on to use words like *brave* and *bold* to describe the person who assaulted me, given that the assault had occurred in broad daylight and to someone wearing a uniform. After my shift ended, I went to speak to the head of the department about what had happened even though he was already aware via the radio channels because as a supervisor, it was his job to know. He said, "You need to be aware that you work in an environment where you're not wearing a lot of clothing." He was simultaneously blaming me for the sexual violence that I experienced and, like the previous coworker, attempting to inform me that I was being watched. I didn't need him to remind me.

In a way, they were right. I *was* being watched all day. My supervisors were watching me all day because it was their job to do so. Lifeguarding *is* surveillance. It's embedded in the militaristic "chain of command," which I learned about more deeply when I was fired a few months later for "insubordination" after I had filed several complaints against my supervisors with the Equal Employment Opportunity Commission (EEOC). Whether it was through radio channels, tinted windows, or the jeeps patrolling the shoreline, I was always being watched. And their justification for watching me rested upon the fact that the main job of a lifeguard was to save lives.

Whether it was to drop off medical supplies, provide backup on a rescue, or simply to give someone a break on a busy day, any act of surveillance could and would be written off as them simply doing their jobs. I spoke with other women that I was working with at the time, in addition to some who were long retired. I heard horrific stories: women being ordered to take off their clothes in exchange for receiving their paychecks, underage lifeguards being approached alone in their towers only to be asked how old they were and if they had boyfriends. One lifeguard was told by her supervisors over the phone to "get a big rock" as a solution to the sexual harassment that she was experiencing from beachgoers. All part of the job. All in the name of public safety.

Introduction

Much of the recent scholarship about beach and surf culture addresses the regimenting of water spaces in relation to policies and/as tools of oppression such as environmental policy, economic policy, race and Indigeneity, gender inequality, et cetera. What is missing from this work is that there are institutions in place (and on the beach) with the purpose of regulating and enforcing these policies and systems. Lifeguards have been a prominent feature of coastal spaces since the early 1900s and are inherently connected to the beach and its associated cultures.[1] Scholars in Oceania like Douglas Booth and Edwin Jaggard have written about "surf lifesaving" in Australia as a culture of hegemonic masculinity and militarism, yet there remains to be a substantial research gap to fill about lifeguarding in the United States.[2]

Heralded as heroic figures, lifeguards present a cultural image that embodies care and valor, imbuing them with a sense of moral authority and assumed integrity that can often shield them from a critical lens. Their authority is not often questioned, and lifeguards hold a great deal of social capital and power, which is exercised through a militaristic style and structure that is closely adhered to. Whether it's standing up when the truck drives by to show respect and vigilance or wearing a uniform, these characteristics frame lifeguarding as an institution bound by values and traditions modeled after the US military and law enforcement entities. These adopted structural regimes include but are not limited to the chain of command, a culture of silence surrounding sexual violence, and gendered surveillance. I have coined the phrase *patch privilege* to illustrate the way in which lifeguards become institutionally shielded from accountability, particularly in relation to sexual assault/harassment, through the California State lifeguarding patch, which, as cultural myth, designates them as public saviors.[3] I make connections between the infrastructures of lifeguarding and the US military in relation to sexual violence, contexts of impunity, and an implied code of silence mired in these patriocolonial systems.[4] Through an autoethnographic lens, this chapter presents a queer of color feminist critique arguing that beach lifeguarding is a state-sponsored site of gendered and sexualized surveillance where sexual violence thrives. The autoethnography that I employ draws from my experiences of sexual violence and harassment working as a California State beach lifeguard in Southern California and the four-year labor lawsuit that ensued as a result of my being terminated promptly after filing a formal complaint with the EEOC. This chapter contextualizes these experiences within larger frameworks of US militarism, feminist surveillance studies, and white supremacy while speaking to lifeguarding culture through my concept of "patch privilege."

Given the importance of patch privilege to upholding the institution of lifeguarding, the following sections trace the cultural and historical backgrounds of lifeguarding, particularly in relation to other institutions oriented toward public safety. For example, the legal protection that lifeguards are given is the same as that for US police officers. After all, the California State Parks lifeguard patch can be found on "Hero's Pride," a website that sells gear for law enforcement and military officers such as magazine holders, handcuff pouches, and baton holders. Professional California State lifeguards, called "peace officers,"[5] are technically law enforcement officers with jurisdiction on the beach. Their relationship to policing and the status of being an officer is significant, particularly because there are legal caveats in place that protect law enforcement officers from being convicted of crimes.[6] Indeed, the heavily armed "peace" officers patrolling the shores fully equipped with guns, tasers, and batons contradict the proliferating cultural image of a lifeguard as a bronzed, bikini-clad figure. But how did lifeguards become known as bronzed saviors? In the following sections, I will be detailing these historical/cultural myths that are associated with public safety and the ideologies that undergird them.

Lifeguarding as Cultural Myth

The bronzed, red-trunk-wearing beach lifeguard has become synonymous with irreproachable hero as the dominant cultural representation of lifeguards as a savior symbol, or what Roland Barthes calls a "cultural myth." Through this cultural myth, the lifeguard becomes a "sign" that signifies heroism and public saviorism. A myth, as Barthes argues, does "not deny things . . . on the contrary . . . it purifies them, it makes them innocent, it gives them a natural and eternal justification, it gives them a clarity which is not that of an explanation but that of a statement of fact."[7] In this application, lifeguards are a "sign" that signifies them as public saviors, when in fact, lifeguarding's origins are intimately linked to surfing's entanglements of imperialism, Indigenous erasure, and settler colonialism. Indigenous scholar Dina Gilio-Whitaker importantly points to a genealogy of California surf and beach culture rooted in settler colonialism and imperialism: "Understanding surf history in the context of imperialism helps to shed the veneer of innocence undergirding these cultural narratives. . . . The narrative of the surfer as social pariah within the counterculture is part of what scholars of settler colonialism term 'moves to innocence,' where complicity in an oppressive society is denied. Because oppression is consigned to the past, no longer existing in the present, no one is responsible for their roles in maintaining the system."[8]

The more accurate history of California surf/beach culture, she explains, involves land developers Abbot Kinney and Henry Huntington hiring Hawaiian lifeguard/waterman George Freeth in 1907 to give surf demonstrations as a "marketing tool to entice the sales of coastal properties."[9] As a result of Spanish and US colonialism, the genocide of Indigenous peoples living in those coastal communities has been removed from the Southern California coast, which "fell into predominantly white ownership within a few short decades after California statehood in 1850. . . . Beneficiaries of this land-clearing process, Kinney and Huntington could cultivate the new beach-culture they envisioned, with the help of George Freeth. Unwittingly part of this colonial project, Freeth is also famous for single-handedly pioneering the art of lifeguarding, necessary for the beach lifestyle that now characterizes Southern California and surf culture."[10]

Connecting this back to Barthes, "The function of myth is to empty reality: it is, literally, a ceaseless flowing out, a hemorrhage, or perhaps evaporation, in short, a perceptible absence."[11] In this employment, beach lifeguarding becomes a tool to maintain settler colonial order/ideology, which has been masked through the mythological "naturalization" of lifeguards as "saviors." "Founded on a history of Indigenous erasure," beach culture, and by extension, lifeguarding culture, becomes a site where settler colonialism becomes eclipsed through the function of myth. It is these myths that create and sustain patch privilege.

Baywatching Bodies

In my cultural analysis of patch privilege, it would be remiss of me to exclude *Baywatch* since it is arguably the most prevalent and culturally significant representation of lifeguarding in American culture. So significant, in fact, that spell check corrected my initial misspelling of "Hasselhoff." The various stereotypes represented in *Baywatch* are essential for framing the subsequent cultural symbolism and power dynamics that materialize through patch privilege. Through Stuart Hall's framework of representation and stereotyping, "(a) the construction of otherness and exclusion; (b) stereotyping and power; (c) the role of fantasy; and (d) fetishism,"[12] I examine the ways in which race, gender, and sexuality are depicted in various episodes of *Baywatch*.

Baywatch remains notorious for the infamous slow-motion running montages featuring David Hasselhoff, Pamela Anderson, and other white, bronzed, heteronormative bodies as the valiant (and always sexy) beach lifeguards of Los Angeles County. Pointing to the sexist and hypersexualized representations in *Baywatch* may seem like an obvious observation to make, but it is important to put the overt sexism of the show in context with what beach lifeguards are experiencing on the ground, specifically in the contexts of sexual violence and white supremacy.

The image of Pamela Anderson running on the beach in a high-cut red bathing suit has become synonymous with *Baywatch* and its cultural depictions of what a female-identified lifeguard looks like and does. Dripping with misogyny and sexism, this objectification of women (most of whom are white) is pervasive, and the subsequent stereotypes are established through these cultural depictions. The female-presenting beach lifeguard is almost always a white, thin, nondisabled, hypersexualized object. Recalling Hall's schema of stereotypes, we can identify fantasy and fetish as defining associations with female lifeguarding.[13] Through fantasy and fetish, the female lifeguard becomes the objectified symbol of sexual desire—she is the socially acceptable object onto which the expression of desire is placed. This image then gets translated to popular culture as a hegemonic blueprint for who/what lifeguards represent: a white, heteropatriarchal institution where heroic, sexy, sanctimonious white men and their white, sexualized objects save lives. Lifeguarding becomes a place where white bodies are seen as superior. BIPOC bodies, then, become figures that do not belong.

Stuart Hall explains how stereotyping "*deploys a strategy of 'splitting.'* It divides the normal and the acceptable from the abnormal and the unacceptable. It then *excludes* or *expels* everything which does not fit, which is different."[14] In a YouTube clip of one of the earlier *Baywatch* episodes, a Black LAPD officer named Garner Ellerbee is seen chasing two men whom he witnessed stealing on the beach.[15] In the scene, Ellerbee jumps off his horse and tackles the pair, and he proceeds to make growling noises while biting the tank top of one of them. Lifeguard Mitch Buchannon (aka David Hasselhoff) enters the scene, pulls Ellerbee off of them, and proceeds to taunt Ellerbee, saying that people will start calling him "Cujo." This can be seen as an example of Hall's notion of "binary oppositions," in which racialized discourse becomes structured. Hall argues, "There is the powerful opposition between civilization (white) and 'savagery' (Black)."[16] In this scene we see the binary as Buchannon, the "civilized" white lifeguard, versus Ellerbee, the "savage" Black LAPD officer who, we realize through another episode, has been sent to patrol the beach as "punishment," when he really belongs (as Hasselhoff points out) in the "inner city." This racial binary gets emphasized later in a scene where Ellerbee and Buchannon are exiting the locker room shower while discussing their day at the beach. Buchannon is shown wearing a solid-color black speedo, while Ellerbee is wearing a leopard print speedo, amplifying the "civilized/savage" racist binary. As seen in just these two examples, white supremacist ideology is starkly illustrated, resulting in a clear delineation of what Hall calls "the maintenance of social and symbolic order" by defining who the savior is and who needs saving.[17] And while *Baywatch* is often regarded as a shoddy, over-the-top caricature of beach lifeguarding, the show's cultural and hierarchical values are reverberations that reflect and influence the ways in which lifeguarding culture is produced and maintained.

Lifeguarding as an Institution

Thus far, this chapter has worked to dispel the myths associated with lifeguards and lifeguarding that proliferate within dominant cultural depictions of them. In the following sections, I extrapolate on how lifeguarding operates as an institution heavily influenced by US militarism. Excerpts from the depositions that were conducted for my legal case confirm that some highly ranked lifeguards in the institution understand it to operate as a military structure. One of the most crucial passages from the depositions in my legal case is from the lifeguard superintendent III, who said simply,

"We work in a paramilitary organization."[18] This frames the lifeguarding institution in relation to militarism as a parallel/inspirational ideology, despite prevailing cultural myths of lifeguards as wholesome saviors. In this section I discuss how militarism is represented through the chain of command and upheld by notions of safety, which highlight the use of *paramilitary* in this context.[19]

THE CHAIN OF COMMAND

Orange Coast South Sector Chain of Command

State Park Superintendent V

|

Lifeguard District Superintendent III

|

Lifeguard Supervisor II

|

Lifeguard Supervisor I

|

Lifeguard Permanent

|

Seasonal Lifeguard II

|

Seasonal Lifeguard I[20]

The California Department of Parks and Recreation defines the "chain of command" as "the reporting structure that extends from the employee up through district/office management, division management, department management, agency management and eventually to the Governor's office."[21] The chain of command is much more than a simple reporting structure. It is a hierarchy and power system, adopted from the military, that is both endlessly resourced and surprisingly hard to pin down. It is a chain of authority and power through which each link on the chain has more authority, the higher ranked they are, and gives orders from the top down. So rather than simply being a "reporting structure," as the state likes to call it, it is more widely utilized as a command structure similar to the modes in which the military operates. Orders are given from the top down, and they must be followed, never questioned. The way that the power dynamic of the chain plays out discourages reporting from lower-ranking members. In fact, the chain of command is structured particularly so that low-ranking members do not get the opportunity to ask questions at all. As a lower-ranking member, your job is to simply follow orders: "If you are involved in a situation where you question an order by the Permanent Lifeguard, complete the task, and at an appropriate time ask your Lifeguard Supervisor about the incident. Failure to follow an order constitutes insubordination, and is grounds for separation."[22] In this framing, asking follow-up questions becomes grounds for termination, demonstrating the unquestionably patriarchal ideology of the chain of command.

With this protocol, even the circumstances surrounding if or when the question will be asked are left up to the supervisor, or higher-ranking member, to decide. If your supervisor decides that it isn't an "appropriate time" to discuss an issue, they have the authority to delay it for as long as they see fit. And even if the question does reach your supervisor, the chain of command has plenty of time. If you can be patient long enough, what the chain of command considers to be your unsubstantiated allegations might make it all the way to the governor's desk. In the case of my termination, it took four years to exhaust the chain of command through legal discovery, depositions, and mostly waiting. Waiting days, weeks, months, and years to get a shred of news. So, in short, rest assured. Should you have a complaint, simply follow the procedure:

> To resolve a problem or issue using the chain of command, start by talking to your supervisor about the problem and trying to resolve the issue at that level. If working with your supervisor is unsuccessful, inform the supervisor, either verbally or preferably in writing, that you are going to bring your second-level supervisor into the process. Meet with the second-level supervisor or advise him/her of the issue in writing with a cc to your supervisor. Continue this process, moving up the management ranks to the District Superintendent,

Division Chief, etc., until a solution has been reached or until you have exhausted the chain of command. As you contact each new level, provide the person at that level with documentation of the Steps you have already taken to attempt resolution.[23]

Exhausting the chain of command implies that if you have gone through every supervisor in the chain and a solution has not been reached, then a conclusion actually *has* been reached: the conclusion will likely be that your "claims are not substantiated" and that the supervisors in question are supported, leaving the subordinate vulnerable and at the will of the state. This procedure also implies the notion that the supervisor above you, or even the supervisor to your supervisor, will listen to, trust, or believe you, when in reality, the chain of command is already set up so that the more "trustable/believable/reliable" employees are supposedly ranked higher up on the chain, so really there is no reason to listen to an inferior-ranking lifeguard because your rank has already predetermined your credibility and privilege.

In the *Lifeguard Operation Field Book* for the state of California South Sector, the authority of the permanent lifeguards is detailed as follows: "The Permanent Lifeguards are an integral part of the chain of command. Even though the permanent lifeguard may have specific assignments and duties unrelated to the aquatic program, they are essential players in the visitor safety program. Their requests and opinion will be respected by all Lifeguard II (seasonal) and Lifeguard I (seasonal) employees."[24] In this context, the phrase *visitor safety program* is used as a way of framing the job of the LG Is and IIs around the notion of safety and protection of the general public, and in the event that the safety of the public becomes jeopardized, the "requests and opinions" of perms become the only ones that matter.

Gendered and Racialized Surveillance

The chain of command has been established as the central operating system of the lifeguarding institution that not only allocates power but also determines the level of privacy that one is afforded or not afforded. I will start with the most fundamental rule of lifeguarding: "Watch the water." It is the ubiquitous phrase that is considered paramount in the lifeguarding community. It is the unwritten, number one rule of the job that isn't included in any handbook or state document. It is drilled into us from the moment we start our training that above all else, our job is to "watch the water." In this way, lifeguarding in its essence *is* surveillance: to monitor the beach under the structural dominance of the chain of command. In the Lifeguard Operation Field Book, these practices are outlined under the Lifeguard Duty Statement for the lifeguard I (seasonal). In the subsection "Aquatic Safety," these duties are listed out:

- Watches designated sections of water from an assigned station to detect persons in distress
- Maintains telephone and/or radio communications with headquarters regarding all rescues. Notifies adjacent towers regarding rescues when needed.
- Monitors adjacent tower activity and provides backup as required.
- Remains in constant contact with dispatch throughout shift.
- Does not leave patrol area without receiving authorization from a supervisor.[25]

Terms such as *monitor* and *constant contact* illustrate the level of surveillance that is happening on the job to the extent that there is literally no point during the day when you are not being watched or communicated with. Using Foucault's panopticon as a literal and figurative structural analogy, we can understand the lifeguard tower that the lifeguard I inhabits as the centrally surveilled/surveilling structure. Since the lifeguard I's job is to watch the water, they are not allowed to turn around, and even if they do turn around, the headquarter buildings behind them are covered in heavily tinted glass. The "headquarters," as mentioned in the field book, is always positioned behind the lifeguard towers on the sand because their job is to watch and monitor the lifeguard towers and the trucks that patrol the beach (and the lifeguard Is). The heavily tinted glass is used to allow the supervisors to survey the beach without the harsh glare of the sun, but it also conveniently affords the supervisor a level of privacy. The power dynamic, and by extension the chain-of-command hierarchy, is enhanced when the supervisors can watch the lifeguard Is but their behavior is completely mystified and protected by the heavily tinted glass. In addition to the surveillance from the headquarter building, the rescue boats and trucks drive back and forth, patrolling both the water/beach and the lifeguards in the towers. After "watching the water," the second biggest rule relayed to me was to always stand up on the balcony when the truck or boat passed by your tower. This was for two reasons: to display vigilance and to communicate respect. In a variety of ways, we can see how surveillance is what's happening *to* the lifeguard I but is also what the lifeguard I represents and *is*.

As a queer woman of color, this became something that I was constantly experiencing. White male coworkers would call me incessantly on the phone, asking me what I was doing, if I had a boyfriend, and other intrusive inquisitions. I had been reduced to a sexual object of voyeuristic pleasure through institutionalized invasiveness, all falling under the protected category of "supervision." In Yasmeen Abu-Laban's "Gendering Surveillance Studies: The Empirical and Normative Promise of Feminist Methodology," she calls for a gendered approach to surveillance studies along with feminist methodology in order to have more in-depth conversations about surveillance and how it can "create new possibilities for enhanced attention to difference and identity."[26] Abu-Laban begins by unpacking surveillance studies and its roots, including the work of Michel Foucault and his focus on the connection between social control and surveillance represented in his panopticon and his lack of applying gender. This aspect of her analysis helps to theorize about lifeguarding and its relationship to sexual assault, specifically in terms of the panopticon and the idea of self-surveillance, stating, "Contemporary Surveillance Studies, following often in the tradition of work established by Michel Foucault, puts a decided emphasis on the role of surveillance in relation to social control. . . . An additional insight coming from the fledgling work on gender and surveillance draws attention to the gendered assumptions underpinning forms of external control."[27]

In relation to lifeguarding, the external control could be framed as both the literal structure and location of the lifeguarding buildings and the chain-of-command hierarchy, while the internalized self-regulation stems from gendered sociocultural norms exemplified in the culture of lifeguarding. In linking this section to lifeguarding, I interpret the panopticon in a very literal way and consider how surveillance operates not just to discipline women, but to watch them as objects of sexual pleasure, incorporating elements of voyeurism. At every beach there is a lifeguard HQ building that sits behind the towers and behind the sand. The perms and the LG IIs sit in the HQ building and watch the watchers. Those who do the watching in the HQ look at women (lifeguards and beachgoers alike) through their binoculars, all while sitting high up in a window-tinted building. It allows them free rein on watching your every move, and it is in their job description to do so. The LG IIs and perms "train" the new lifeguards by putting them in towers where they can more easily be watched. If you "miss a rescue" (aka don't see a rescue that's happening in front of your tower), they call you on the phone line (all towers have phones that link to headquarters). If they're bored and want to talk to you, they call you. If you do not answer the phone, you get written up. If they want to ask you inappropriate questions, they wait until you're alone, and they drive down and sit in your tower and ask you how old you are and if you have a boyfriend. This position of power (both the literal vantage point and the chain of command) amplifies the male gaze while not only allowing but encouraging predatory behavior. Through the white, heteronormative male gaze, women become designated as objects of sexual pleasure for the male viewer.[28]

Gendered surveillance also operates by twisting notions of privacy in ways that ultimately undermine feminist goals while upholding gendered hegemonies. For instance, Toby Beauchamp's *Going Stealth* highlights the gendering of surveillance studies, particularly looking at its relation to the surveillance of trans bodies. Although my work does not include trans bodies as a particular example, there are concepts around privacy and deception that can be dovetailed in relation to my own experiences with sexual assault while I was lifeguarding. In the introduction, Beauchamp states, "As scholarship and activism in areas such as reproductive justice and disability justice maintain, and as the chapters in this book show, privacy is not a default status but an exceptional one, granted largely on the basis of wealth and racial privilege."[29] In other words, framing public safety around questions of the "right to privacy" may not be the most salient for feminist work, when not all subjects are afforded the status that gives access to this right. Particularly relating to a response in justification of my sexual assault, and how it related to the assault itself, is the comment that the chief permanent lifeguard made. The logic being that I was not owed privacy given what I was wearing. In other words, a woman of color in a bathing suit represents something overtly sexual that invites attention, therefore it should be expected that I would have lost my privacy (this is assuming that I had privacy to begin with). Furthermore, it implies the notion that I should have practiced self-regulation in order to have privacy by the act of covering myself, even though I was in my lifeguard uniform.

Public Safety

As demonstrated throughout this chapter, the obligation to follow orders via the chain of command is justified based on the concept of public safety. The "Lifeguard Duty Statement" for a seasonal lifeguard I states, "This position is responsible for the front-line defense of both aquatic and non-aquatic emergencies. A Lifeguard I will understand that visitor safety and service to the public is the key objective, with *Aquatic Safety* being the priority."[30] As shown through this specific example, the use of terms like *defense* and *service* is reminiscent of militaristic ideologies of self-sacrifice and protection. Even the term *lifeguarding* ingrains the message that lifeguards are guardians of "public safety," which, according to the field book, makes up 75 percent of the job description. This reiterates that if orders are not followed via the chain of command, then public safety will be compromised, and it suggests that ultimately, people will die.

This framing is crucial in understating how the chain of command is utilized in the context of the lifeguarding institution through narratives of safety and care. The chain of command is used to implement power, or in other words, the chain of command gives supervisors overarching power and authority, all in the name of public safety. For example, when asked about the general patterns and practices that are punishable when disciplining a lifeguard I, one permanent lifeguard stated in his deposition, "General behaviors that would compromise public safety, such as not showing up on time, not having the—not showing up on time, not making rescues, professional appearance, incorrect uniform etc."[31] According to this logic, institutionalized rules and regulations such as donning an "incorrect uniform," which according to the handbook could be anything from not having a black pen to wearing the incorrect hat, would inevitably compromise public safety. Public safety then becomes a means of controlling the behavior of and practicing surveillance on the subordinates, aka the lifeguard Is. In the LG superintendent III's deposition, for example, we can see how public safety becomes the justification for "supervision":

Q: Is supervision of a Lifeguard I important?
A: Yes.
Q: Why is that?
A: Because they are out there saving—safeguarding the public.[32]

Breaking this down further, the policies about uniform, being on time, et cetera, get connected to public safety, and, in turn, public safety becomes the excuse for a certain kind of supervision/surveillance to be practiced.

Feminist scholars have articulated the hegemonic masculinity that structures the military as a heteropatriarchal, violent institution.[33] Elizabeth Mesok argues that "military sexual violence, like discrimination based on race or sexuality, is understood as solvable through the extension of military equality—treating all individual soldiers as equal in their capacity to labor."[34] These frameworks can be applied to lifeguarding and its assumed "equitable space" (i.e., everyone is placed in the same environment with the same equipment under the same structure). Mesok further dismantles these structures by pointing out how liberal feminism places women in the position of having to "choose to struggle for recognition for full personhood, which is always already gendered male, or for 'recognition as women, as a difference that cannot be equality, a difference that is an ideologically ontologized division of labor."[35] These patterns are shared in the lifeguarding institution in the sense that the job itself, the space that it inhabits, and the values associated with it are already gendered as male, in which women are placed in a position where "equality" is not possible.

The values inherent in this structure can be directly linked to the institution of lifeguarding in a multitude of ways. I analyze the operating system of the lifeguarding institution, which is structured by the chain of command and upheld by notions of public safety.[36] A main tenet of these operating systems are the cultural logics that underpin them: one example being the US military's historical roots in orientalism, in which anti-Asian racism and xenophobia play a crucial role in the framing and justification of the US military.[37] In addition to the dehumanization of Asian people, Marie Myung-Ok Lee argues, "Gender and misogyny enter this mix of intentional psychological warping that the government institutes and rationalizes as one of the necessities of war. For instance, while decrying the sex slavery WWII Japan instituted on its Korean subjects—kidnapping and forcing young girls to serve in military brothels euphemistically known as 'comfort stations'—the US military ended up repurposing this system and even some of the same women for US soldiers during the Korean war."

These examples demonstrate how the US military commits racialized and gendered sexual violence and reframes it as a necessity for supporting the war effort, which would ultimately result in keeping US public "safe." This logic is reminiscent of how lifeguarding institutions employ the idea of public safety and the warping of care in order to exercise power through the chain of command. Essentially, imperialism, colonialism, and gendered violence are the foundations and sustenance of the US military, and by extension beach lifeguarding, and are embedded within the chain-of-command operating systems that they deploy. As institutions, both the US military and lifeguarding like to present themselves as isolated from sociocultural realities through the operating system of the chain of command based on notions of uniformity (i.e., everyone gets the same uniform, the same training, and the same equipment), when in reality their histories of imperialism, colonialism, sexism, et cetera, remain deeply embedded in these ideologies. This links back to Lee's article, where racism, specifically in this case anti-Asian dehumanization, becomes an eclipsed cornerstone of US militarism: "Beyond these flashpoints centered in Vietnam, or Atlanta, our entire cultural training tells us to avert our eyes, to not think of murdered Asian men, women, and children as people who love and have dreams and faces. Doing so would disturb our narrative as a great nation, one where white people cannot really do wrong; that there is always an explanation."[38]

In order to justify military operations, both racism and settler colonialism are erased in order to preserve a narrative of what Teju Cole calls the "White-Savior Industrial Complex."[39] I use Cole's analysis here as a framework that is used to justify US militarism and related institutions like state beach lifeguarding. Like the US military, the lifeguarding institution becomes seen as a domestic symbol of a heteropatriarchal colonialist savior ethic. These ideologies cross over into the lifeguarding institutions through US beach culture's history of military presence and settler colonialism in Hawaiʻi and Southern California, and become the justification for the violence that they enact, which are not, as these institutions would like us to believe, separate from their operating systems.

Conclusion: Alternative Concepts of Care

In this chapter I have analyzed the California State lifeguarding organization as a "paramilitary" institution through a queer of color lens. I make critical interventions in surf studies that are crucial to understanding how lifeguards operate as protectors of not just swimmers at the beach but oppressive structural regimes through the militaristic frameworks and modes of operation that are foundational to them.

By introducing lifeguards and their histories of militarism and settler colonialism, I frame much of my analysis on Barthes' concept of the cultural myth while interweaving the concept of patch privilege to demonstrate how lifeguards are protected from accountability through their public persona as saviors—accountability particularly in relation to sexual violence, because after all, who would want to accuse the "hero" of sexual harassment? As shown in this chapter, there are many structures in place that create an atmosphere that protects and encourages sexual violence, such as the chain of command and the intrusive surveillance of the job that is not only allowed but required. And it is all performed in the name of public safety and, ultimately, care.

I would like to end with chapter with a more radical form of care. Inna Michaeli positions radical care as a way of understanding "a self which is grounded in particular histories and present situations of violence and vulnerability."[40] Refuting notions of care drenched in individualism and capitalism, this definition names care as a sometimes gritty reckoning, naming systems of violence through vulnerability. This chapter speaks to a narrative that has been systemically silenced through "care" and bears a relationship to the vulnerability of testifying, not in the way that the US legal system calls for, but one that works outside of these systems toward accountability. In this chapter these gritty reckonings are made visible and refuse the violent frameworks of the California State lifeguarding institution: An institution that claims to both exercise and be rooted in care.

Notes

1 Mike Brousard, *Warm Winds and Following Seas: Reflections of a Lifeguard in Paradise* (self-published, Lulu Publishing Services, 2018).

2 Douglas Booth, "The Dark Side of Surf Lifesaving," *Journal of Sport History* 29, no. 1 (2002): 7–13; Edwin Jaggard, "'Tempering the Testosterone': Masculinity, Women and Australian Surf Lifesaving," *International Journal of the History of Sport* 18, no. 4 (2001): 16–36. Australia's lifeguarding institutions are called "surf lifesaving" organizations and differ from lifeguarding in the United States in that they are nonprofit organizations. Though Booth describes lifeguarding in an Australian context, Booth's observations about lifeguarding's "military-style attitudes" and "institutional structures" are applicable to the US context in various ways, as these sentiments are echoed throughout lifeguarding spaces across the Pacific: "Surf lifesaving was very much a male institution and the lifesaver the epitome of Australian masculinity. Discipline, military-style attitudes and single-sex clubhouses shaped the institutional structure of lifesaving clubs and nurtured a particularly raw

form of masculinity." Douglas Booth, *Australian Beach Cultures: The History of Sun, Sand and Surf* (London: Routledge, 2001), 79–80.

3 Asako Yonan, "Patch Privilege: A Queer Feminist Autoethnography of Lifeguarding" (master's thesis, San Diego State University, 2021).

4 lisahunter argues, "Sex has defined surfing, and its current form continues to rape participatory subject positions. . . . Here, a hegemonic androcentric, patriarchal, (hetero)normative doxa that I term *patriocolonialism* facilitates an illusion of equitable participation for males and females, and therefore feminist victory, while symbolic violence reproduces a specter of patriarchy, albeit in new or hidden forms." lisahunter, "Desexing Surfing? (Queer) Pedagogies of Possibility," in *The Critical Surf Studies Reader*, edited by Dexter Zavalza Hough-Snee and Alexander Sotelo Eastman, 265 (Durham, NC: Duke University Press, 2017).

5 Peace officer is the designation of a certain rank of state lifeguards who go through police academy and wear a police uniform fully equipped with guns, tasers, etc. My research suggests that California State lifeguarding institutions are also closely related to the military. While there is scholarship regarding the heavy militarization of law enforcement entities in the United States, this is not the focus of my work. Both law enforcement entities and the US military are deeply embedded within lifeguarding culture. I discuss militarism more specifically due to the way in which the chain-of-command system operates, as well as the ways in which California State lifeguards have defined themselves through my lived experience as a California State lifeguard. Moreover, my scholarly analysis draws on the Australian-based academic research on the discursive inflection of the military modes and epistemologies into lifeguarding/saving. See Jaggard, "'Tempering the Testosterone'"; Booth, "The Dark Side of Surf Lifesaving"; and Aileen Moreton-Robinson, *The White Possessive: Property, Power, and Indigenous Sovereignty* (Minneapolis: University of Minnesota Press, 2015).

6 "Qualified Immunity," Legal Information Institute, accessed June 20, 2024, www.law.cornell.edu/wex/qualified_immunity.

7 Roland Barthes, *Mythologies*, selected and trans. by Annette Lavers (New York: Hill and Wang, 1972), 225.

8 Dina Gilio-Whitaker, "The Complicated History of Indigenous Knowledge and Colonial Entanglements in Surfing" (PBS SoCal, www.pbssocal.org/shows/earth-focus/the-complicated-history-of-indigenous-knowledge-and-colonial-entanglements-in-surfing, 2017).

9 Gilio-Whitaker, "Complicated History."
10 Gilio-Whitaker, "Complicated History."
11 Barthes, *Mythologies*, 25.
12 Stuart Hall, ed., *Representation: Cultural Representations and Signifying Practices* (Thousand Oaks, CA: Sage in association with the Open University, 1997), 36.
13 Hall, *Representation.*
14 Hall, *Representation*, 258.
15 *Baywatch*, "BIG LAPD Police Chase on Horseback on The Beach! Baywatch Remaster," YouTube video, 2:04, January 10, 2020.
16 Hall, *Representation*, 22.
17 Barthes, *Mythologies*, 37–38.
18 *Yonan vs. California Department of Parks and Recreation.*
19 The chain of command is a concept borrowed from the US military and is outlined in the *Lifeguard Operation Field Book* used in this chapter.
20 This chain of command can be found on page 9 of the *State of California Department of Parks and Recreation Orange Coast District/South Sector Aquatic Service Lifeguard Operation Field Book*, which is an operations manual pertaining to the South Sector of the California State lifeguarding institution and was also one of the many documents of discovery for my legal case.
21 *Lifeguard Operation Field Book*, 76
22 *Lifeguard Operation Field Book*, 14.
23 Page 52 of DPR discovery document.
24 *Lifeguard Operation Field Book*, 14.
25 *Lifeguard Operation Field Book*, 17.
26 Yasmeen Abu-Laban, "Gendering Surveillance Studies: The Empirical and Normative Promise of Feminist Methodology," *Surveillance and Society* 13, no. 1 (2015): 44–56.
27 Abu-Laban, "Gendering Surveillance Studies," 47.
28 John Berger, *Ways of Seeing* (London: BBC, 1972).
29 Toby Beauchamp, *Going Stealth: Transgender Politics and US Surveillance Practices* (Durham, NC: Duke University Press, 2019).
30 *Lifeguard Operation Field Book*, 17.
31 Deposition DPR discovery.
32 Deposition DPR discovery.
33 For example, Cynthia Enloe, *The Curious Feminist: Searching for Women in a New Age of Empire* (Berkeley: University of California Press, 2004).

34 Elizabeth Mesok, “Sexual Violence and the US Military: Feminism, US Empire, and the Failure of Liberal Equality,” *Feminist Studies* 42, no. 1 (2016): 41–69.

35 Mesok, “Sexual Violence and the US Military.”

36 In her article “Queer OS,” Kara Keeling references McPherson’s analysis in relation to these cultural logics, stating, “Queer OS would take seriously McPherson’s suggestion that the cultural logics of the early operating system Unix embed some of the racial logics of the post-World War II era in which Unix (and the modern civil rights movements) were developed.” Kara Keeling, “Queer OS,” *Cinema Journal* 53, no. 2 (Winter 2014): 154–57.

37 Asian American scholar Marie Myung-Ok Lee references these connections between US militarism, anti-Asian racism, and the fetishization of Asian women. She states, “This systematic dehumanization was not inadvertent, and it continues to eat away at American society today. The release of *This is Korea* was just one of the ways the American public has historically been groomed to see Asians as less than human. In 1974, in the Oscar-winning documentary *Hearts and Minds*, the commander of American military operations during the Vietnam War famously said, ‘The Oriental doesn’t put the same high price on life as does a Westerner. Life is plentiful. Life is cheap in the Orient.’” Marie Myung-Ok Lee, “The US Military’s Long History of Anti-Asian Dehumanization,” Medium, March 21, 2021.

38 Lee, “The US Military’s Long History of Anti-Asian Dehumanization.”

39 Teju Cole, “The White-Savior Industrial Complex,” *Atlantic*, March 2012.

40 Inna Michaeli, “Self-Care: An Act of Political Warfare or a Neoliberal Trap?” *Development* 60, nos. 1–2 (2017): 50–56.

12

Totally Tubular Aesthetics

Surfing, Seafaring, and Storytelling in News from Native California

LYDIA HEBERLING

the gift of watching children grooving with the ocean was tubular

L. FRANK MANRIQUEZ, "Second Serving" (Winter 2009/2010)

There is truly something delightful about watching children play in the ocean, splashing at the shoreline, playing tag with the waves, shrieking in glee as they bellyboard for the first time, flowing with the ebbs and flows of tides. It is nothing short of magic, it seems, watching children navigate the dynamic energy of the world's largest bodies of water as they play, their bodies meeting and matching the energy along the shoreline. Maybe you remember your own first experience at a beach—the briny smell of salt, the gritty touch of sand, the whooshing brush of wind, the icy chill or tepid warmth (depending on which ocean and which time of year) of water. Maybe that memory is sweet, and maybe it is one of terror—the ocean is, after all, an unruly and powerful relative.

For those of us fortunate enough to know what it is to "groove" with the ocean, as Acjachemen and Tongva writer, artist, and activist L. Frank Manriquez (who often goes by L. Frank) suggests in the epigraph above, it is likely that we know something about feeling like our time at and with the ocean is a gift. Potawatomi botanist and writer Robin Wall Kimmerer defines a gift as something that "comes to you through no action of your own, free, having moved toward you without your beckoning. It is not a reward; you cannot earn it, or call it to you, or even deserve it. . . . Your only role is to be open-eyed and present."[1] Any surfer or surfing-adjacent reader may experience this, an intimate, embodied experience of humility and mystery when approaching the ocean.

In line with the themes of hope and belonging throughout this collection, the idea of the gift, especially articulated through Indigenous epistemologies, affirms relationship and reciprocity between the recipient and the giver.[2] When that exchange occurs between Indigenous peoples and other-than-human relations, such as between a human and the ocean, as Frank suggests, it animates long-standing connections between peoples and places. These connections encode potentially powerful decolonial possibilities that resist and refuse Indigenous erasure from coastal spaces. In the context of this particular essay, this connection between a people and the ocean is mediated through the twinned Indigenous technologies of surfing and storytelling. What, then, might it look like to "read" this act of surfing?

This essay draws on discourses in both Indigenous literary studies and critical surf studies to argue for the generative possibilities that emerge when we examine surfing in literary analysis. It insists on rigorous, critical engagement with the innovative, adaptive poetics of California Indian writers and artists, who have for millennia lived in intimate entanglements with coastal and oceanic ecologies. As an Indigenous decolonizing methodology, surfing helps process a world that lacks predictability and serves as both metaphor and embodied practice for navigating the chaos of tidal uncertainties. It draws together the scholarly projects of literary mapping—understanding how stories are encoded in lands and waters—with the concept of "boarderlands" relationalities—relationships that occur in the liminal space between the shoreline and the ocean and affirm social, ecological, and political relationships between Indigenous people, settlers, and other-than-human relatives.[3] To situate surfing as a methodology and reading practice, I unsettle it from its contemporary position as a predominantly white, settler sport and resituate it as an Indigenous Polynesian practice.[4] When surfing appears in literatures, especially in the literatures of Indigenous peoples who are not Polynesian, it invites us as readers to draw a productive comparison *across* Indigenous epistemologies and narrative practices—what literary scholar Chadwick Allen calls a "trans-Indigenous" methodology.[5]

The epigraph of this essay comes out of Frank's semiregular column titled "Second Serving" in the winter 2009/2010 issue of the quarterly publication *News from Native California*, published through Heyday Books. "Second Serving" can best be described as a kind of travelogue, a scrapbook of short narrative quips recounting and recollecting Frank's experiences on the road, in community, both near the ocean's shore and beyond. These loosely related personal narrative stories, or fragments, are organized and formally structured with a DIY or collage-style aesthetic.[6] In the winter 2009/2010 "Second Serving," Frank includes eight short stories visually arranged as horizontally layered strips down the page, with a hand-drawn single-line borderline around each typed short story. Several color photographs and images accompany the text-based stories, enhancing the stories' meaning through purposeful juxtaposition of multiple kinds of media. Some of these images are contained within the borders of a story, while others transgress the borderline, straddling two stories at a time.

Out of this collection of eight stories and thirteen images, I focus on the seventh, or penultimate, story, with its accompanying single photograph. In this story Frank recounts being invited to watch a young Karuk and Pomo boy named Bert participate in a surfing competition in Crescent City, California. Crescent City is located along the northern coast of California, in Tolowa and Yurok territories. In this story, relationship and reciprocity are grounded in a California Native youth's connection with the ocean—the Pacific is, in this case, a relation, rather than an object, engaged in an exchange with the youth.[7] The surface-level interpretation of Frank's story seems simple: she was invited to watch this young person surf and bears witness to the gift that comes with connecting to the ocean in that way: a happy experience unearned, undeserved, somewhat mysterious, and often full of joy.

This, I will note, is the only story about surfing that shows up in any "Second Serving" publication.[8] In spite of California's reputation as a surf state, California Indians have not adopted surfing as a central community-building cultural practice in the same way that skateboarding has been adopted across Indian Country, for example.[9] The instances of California Natives surfing remain anecdotal yet significant: Luiseño artist, poet, and activist James Luna, and Luiseño and Cahuilla activist, educator, and Alcatraz occupier Ed Castillo, for example, were both surfers who began surfing in the 1960s, within and through the counterculture surf scene.[10] In the contemporary moment there is Andy Nieblas, world-famous longboard stylist and 2018 Vans Duct Tape Invitational champion, who does not politicize his identity in person but whose Instagram biography, where, as of 2024, he currently has over fifty-one thousand followers, nonetheless simply states "Ajachemen Nation."[11] There are also relocated Native surfers in California, such as our own Colville scholar and activist Dina Gilio-Whitaker.[12] In these anecdotal instances, I would argue that surfing is a trans-Indigenous water technology and an embodied practice that affirms long-standing oceanic relations that predate colonialism and affirms a vast network of Indigenous relations. Surfing demonstrates how Indigenous peoples employ a diverse range of activities, traditional and borrowed, to (re)build a rooted interconnection between people and place that becomes a means by which Indigenous struggles are expressed. It turns out that surfing has been, and continues to be, an important through line in Indigenous acts of resurgence, including in California.

So, while Frank does not center surfing as a major theme in this edition of "Second Serving" (or anywhere else, particularly), Bert's surfing story nonetheless articulates an important relationship between literary form, oceanic relationalities, and cultural thrivance that can be seen elsewhere in other acts of California Indian revitalization, such as around seafaring canoe cultures. In other words, Frank's representation of surfing in this column animates how to understand why the ocean and coastlines of what is now California are significant sites of cultural revitalization.

The way that it does this is best understood in the context of the full story about Bert, and so I will include the entire narrative here:

> surfing. bitchen. being a so.cal.ndn, I am so stoked when my karuk, pomoan friend little bert invited me to head up to crescent city for a

surf contest. i was there! always, supporting youth is sweet, but, again for me, the gift of watching children grooving with the ocean was tubular. the water was sooo cold, and the sky threatened a cold rain, but those kids hit the waves like pros. little bert has two loving parents and a surf mentor. How funny that I think he is privilaged. privilaged to have what all children deserve. love.

In this short story Frank watches from the beach as a young Karuk and Pomo boy surfs in a youth surfing competition. The text is accompanied by a color photo of Bert, the subject of the story, who looks to be about seven years old, with his surf coach. They stand at the shoreline, both in wet suits and holding up a *shaka*, a Kanaka Māoli hand gesture of greeting. Bert's hood is pulled up over his head and ears, affirming Frank's description of the "sooo" cold water. The coach holds the longboard diagonally behind them, and viewers can glimpse the cold, rugged, and undeveloped Northern California coastline behind man and boy. The smiles on both their faces radiate toward the viewer.

Like the ocean, Frank's story appears visibly navigable and straightforward but contains unseen profound depth and energy. As a California Indian person from two of California's Pacific coastal tribal nations—the Acjachemen trace their ancestral homelands to what is currently known as Dana Point in Orange County, and the Tongva Nation to what is now known as Los Angeles—Frank is a known language activist whose artistic works often center the trickster figure, Coyote.[13] In this story Frank uses linguistic puns, misspellings, allusions, and formal innovations to unsettle easy assumptions about California and surfing within the story. In doing so, she unsettles usual reading practices to make readers aware of themselves in the act of reading, inviting space for multiple interpretations into these moments of disruption.[14] From small disruptions such as refusing to capitalize several proper nouns, such as Karuk, Pomoan, Crescent City, and the name of the surfer, Bert, to larger ones I will momentarily address, these aesthetic and formal manipulations act as a decolonial literary project that provokes settler surf culture structures and celebrates California Native coastal peoples' long-standing relationships to each other and the ocean.

Frank invokes the playful jargon of "surf speak," such as *bitchen* and *groove* and *tubular*, to convey her enthusiasm and delight at the entire surfing event. Surfers' jargon like this emerges out of the 1950s and 1960s era of the Beach Boys and *Gidget* and a predominantly white and male surfing culture in Southern California.[15] Frank, however, deftly dislocates surf jargon from its work of reifying settler surf cultures and redeploys these terms, along with other subtle rhetorical and linguistic manipulations, to articulate California Native presence and belonging on ancestral coastal homelands. Her opening declaratives, "surfing. bitchen," affirm Frank's general feelings about surfing: *bitchen* is a phrase commonly deployed to convey excitement and enthusiasm about an activity or accomplishment or generally "cool" things. This two-word, coupled exclamation is followed by Frank locating herself in the context of surfing culture: by identifying as "a so.cal.ndn" she most obviously locates herself as someone who comes from Southern California—or So Cal—which is where Frank was born and raised and where her tribal affiliations locate her.[16] Southern California is also the epicenter of contemporary settler surf culture, implying that Frank is therefore naturally well-versed in all things surfing related, as its visual, mediated, linguistic, and performative cultures saturate coastal Los Angeles. But calling herself a "so.cal.ndn" also might just as easily assert that she is SO California Indian, with an emphasis on the *so*, affirming a claim to California Indian presence and vitality within, in spite of, and beyond any other claims to Southern California identities and belongings. As a "so.cal.ndn" from Southern California who is SO California Indian, Frank reinserts herself into dominant assumptions and stories about Southern California and its surf culture, repurposing surf lingo as a site of linguistic resistance.

She is struck by the fact that Bert surfed (like a pro!) in spite of the cold and threatening weather conditions, and by her own surprise at his "privilage" for having a supportive intergenerational community of California Indians (including her, whom he personally invited to the competition). Within Indigenous communities, these intergenerational relationships are crucial for connecting younger generations to long-standing knowledges and customs that have survived colonialism. She is not primed to enter this experience at a surf contest (of all things) and recognizes it as a vital relational system that is generating real-world, Indigenous alternatives to colonial formations of California Indians and human-ocean relations. (And, her insinuation that it looked like it was going to rain, that the environment was dark, might mirror this.) Her intentional misspelling of *privilege* evokes the word's potential homophonic pun on the word *village*, underscoring the network of strong California Native connections present at this unique event in which she has now found herself entangled.

And I return now to the emphasis in the epigraph on idea of "tubular" gifts. Frank's deployment of the term *tubular* once again unsettles popular surfing discourse. *Tubular* is another expression of enthusiasm that derives from the hollow tube-like shape that some waves make as they break.[17] While it means awesome and conveys excitement, in "Second Serving" it also hooks into imagery of the materiality of waves, as circular, hollow, repetitive, and continuous—in other words, as tube-like. Departing from common understandings of the term as well as the material shape, structure, and movement of a wave, this statement also encodes the idea that this surfing Karuk and Pomo boy is drawing on a deeper, long-standing, circular, ancestral link between California Native coastal peoples and the ocean.

More than a delight for Bert, the young surfer, or for Frank, then, this experience is a "tubular" gift. The ocean, via surfing, continues to animate and reinforce this Karuk and Pomo youth's ancestral relationship to lands and waters in spite of hundreds of years of brutal settler colonialism. Although Karuk territory is more inland and Pomo territory is further south, these California Indian communities, lands, rivers, and the ocean have been and remain intimately linked for millennia via vast interconnected networks. Frank finds herself entangled in this network of relations at the California coast, and this surprises her. This surfing boy embodies futurity for Karuk and Pomo Nations, and for California Indian peoples more broadly; surfing is a vehicle for connection, belonging, and relationship between a young boy and his ancestral homelands. The entire statement, then—"the gift of watching children groove with the ocean was tubular"—is a powerful decolonizing statement that unsettles surfing discourse and asserts and affirms California Indian belonging in coastal spaces from time immemorial.

Surfboards and Canoes: Voyaging through Story

The form and content of "Second Serving" work together to encode Indigenous knowledges that generate creative solutions to the pernicious and ongoing problem of Indigenous erasure in California. As previously mentioned, this story is the seventh of eight short narrative fragments collected into a single edition of the semiregular column "Second Serving" that is loosely organized around the theme of love. The autobiographical nature of the column offers readers a snapshot of Frank's framework of love—and, I argue, ideas of belonging and hope. This "Second Serving" column opens with an acknowledgment of two recent weddings between California Indian people and Frank's observation that "these unions spelled home." The next narrative short abruptly transitions to the stark and austere halls of the US Congress building in Washington, DC, where several young California Indian activists navigate the performative and rhetorical dynamics of what Frank calls "bill language" to "ma[k]e themselves visible to these people who saw nothing" as they fought to accredit Indigenous languages in California. From the halls of Congress, Frank moves next to the Pride parade in San Francisco, California, and she expresses pride in two young allies marching with and for Frank—herself a public two-spirit figure.[18] Frank then describes traveling to Australia for a language-revitalization conference and then tells a story about watching *Australia*, the 2008 feature film starring Nicole Kidman, linking experiences of Indigenous Australians being cast out and alienated from each other to "Ajachmem" practices of disenrollment, a practice of which Frank is herself a victim. She returns again to a long-standing and well-known California language-revitalization conference called "Breath of Life," a three-day conference where language learning is "fuel for the soul" when the constant work of cultural revitalization "can be quite frustrating and lonely." Here, then, the story about Bert and the surfing competition arrives, and against the narrative backdrop of Frank's broader cultural efforts and the challenges she encounters in this, her surprise at Bert's easy belonging, his intergenerational support network, and his intimacy with his ancestral coastal lands and waters emerges as a gift—one in which being open-eyed and present is enough to see the mystery. The final narrative of the column celebrates the diverse and multifaceted work of cultural resurgence and links it to the intimacy of her own romantic relationship, writing, "tongva, luiseno and desert cahuilla in d.c. wappos at pride, karuks in oz and karuks in the ocean. we lead interesting lives while working for our cultural futures. we ca. ndn activists have become family." In this final narrative fragment, Frank deftly links the communities, themes, locations, and relations of the previous seven stories into a brief expression of gratitude for the gift of community and care, affirming hope for California Indian and other Indigenous cultural futures as she affirms her own belonging. Bert's single story, which performs surfing and surf culture and celebrates the way they connect Native youth to the ocean and to community, gathers strength and significance through the undercurrent of abundance that collectively surges out of this issue of "Second Serving."

Frank has been a semiregular contributor to *News*, which since 1987 has been dedicated to the publication and circulation of literary and artistic works by California Indians.[19] She is perhaps best known for her Coyote cartoons, a series of single-panel comics depicting a Coyote trickster figure unsettling dominant assumptions about California's missionization and the colonization of California tribal nations, which began in 1769 and is still ongoing. The title, "Second Serving," refers to the single-panel Coyote cartoon series, which she collected and published through Heyday Books as *Acorn Soup* in 1999. *Acorn Soup* derives *its* name from the food that is traditional to many California Native tribal communities and thus puns on the idea that the content of the book is rich in nutrition and good for the body. "Second Serving" in this context can mean several possible things: It could suggest the scraps of the leftovers, as in, second servings are often scraped together out of whatever was left after the initial meal. It could also suggest excess, or plenty, as in there was such an abundance that there is plenty for seconds. The juxtaposition of the possible interpretations of the title also shows the enriching and provocative tension between lack and excess, because this is the case in the ongoing and real-time process of cultural revitalization in Native California. There is certainly lack, as in a lack of cultural continuity, access to traditional lands and waters, knowledge of languages, food traditions, and technologies. But there is also certainly abundance, if you know where to look and how to locate the archives, the knowledges, and the memories. I suggest that the column is best read as both: As fragments, the individually collected stories and images testify to a certain form of lack and fragmentation. But collectively, the fragments work together, and an abundance of new forms of knowledge emerges.

Frank was born in 1952 in California. She is a descendant of peoples who survived the California mission era, the period of Spanish settler colonialism between 1769 and 1830 during which the Spanish violently enlisted the enforced labor of California's Indigenous peoples to construct twenty-one missions along California's coastline between what is now San Diego and San Francisco. The Spanish missionaries and military forcefully imposed religious social order on California's tribal nations, fundamentally reorganizing political, social, and ecological life for California's Indigenous peoples, particularly along the coastline. Spanish missionization was the first of three waves of settler colonialism in California that occurred in quick succession. Following the secularization of the missions in 1830, the Mexican government occupied the region until the US-Mexico War and the signing of the Treaty of Guadalupe Hidalgo in 1848, turning control of California over to the United States. Within these waves of settler colonization, California's Indigenous nations experienced disease, dispossession, and a legal policy of genocide whose impact on the population and the cultures cannot be understated.[20]

Within and against these structures of settler colonialism in California, California Indian nations have always resisted and persisted, creatively transmitting cultural knowledges and practices through time and generations. Frank is a dynamic activist whose multifaceted work carries her around the globe to connect with other Indigenous people in projects of cultural revitalization. Frank works on and in many interrelated aspects of cultural resurgence, from language revitalization to photography, storytelling, and two-spirit activism, and utilizes Indigenous technologies—

specifically the form of the *ti'at*, a plank canoe—to affirm tribally specific knowledges while also linking Indigenous communities from across California and throughout the Pacific together. Her work models the fact that Indigenous acts of cultural revitalization—the reclamation of Native spaces, technologies, languages, and identities—do not happen exclusively in tribally specific, isolated, or individualistic ways: they happen in community, collectively, and often *across* communities, technologies, and stories. Her work emphasizes the importance of the personal, the tribal, and the local, as well as the inherent integration between these and the global and the trans-Indigenous.

Frank has been central to the revitalization of the Tongva *ti'at*. The *ti'at*, like the Chumash *tomol*, is a seafaring plank canoe built to paddle from California's mainland out to the Channel Islands through the Pacific. With the help of Chumash *tomol* knowledges and the support of Indigenous peoples across Turtle Island and the Pacific, Frank with other Tongva tribal members reconstructed their first *ti'at* in the 1990s. *Ti'ats* are constructed by sewing together wooden planks (historically planed from foraged redwood trees that drifted down the coast from Northern California; contemporarily these planks are acquired otherwise, perhaps through a relational exchange with the Karuk Tribe of Northern California. It is strongly preferred that the wood for these canoes is not purchased, if possible).[21] The planks are sealed with an asphalt made from asphaltum, which occurs naturally along California's coastline, as well as pine resin.[22] Finally, the *ti'at* includes decorative mosaic-like abalone designs that signify the canoe's name or perhaps its relation to a family or community.

Revitalization of *ti'at* construction and culture began in the 1990s and relied heavily on relationships between Tongva, Chumash, and other Pacific Indigenous canoeing peoples, as knowledges of seafaring material culture had been scattered as a result of settler colonialism. As Deborah Miranda writes in her 2013 book, *Bad Indians: A Tribal Memoir*, one Chumash informant named Fernando Librado kept knowledge of how to construct *tomols* over the generations and shared this with salvage anthropologist John Peabody Harrington in the early 1900s. It was through Librado's documented knowledges that Chumash and Tongva Tribes were able to begin building canoes again. The first *ti'at* built in the 1990s was named *Moomat Ahiko*, or "breath of the ocean."[23] This group of Tongva, Chumash, and Acjachemen canoe builders emphasize that this canoe family is a people who are reconnecting with the ocean and with the material, spiritual, and cultural practices of their ancestors. Indeed, these practices are central to who California Native peoples are. In California Indian creation stories, the world almost always "begins on the water."[24] In the Concow creation story, the world is water and Earth Maker floats "in a boat on a vast sea."[25] In the Yuki creation story, Taikomol, or "he who walks alone," emerges out of sea foam. All first beings necessarily have to construct a livable relationship to the water, and as in the Concow story of Earth Maker, constructed technologies such as boats are integral to worldbuilding. As the Earth was formed, coastlines necessarily took shape as well. Bauer Jr. explains, "California Indians understood themselves as a people of place. Creators made the world for a certain People and a unique People for a specific place."[26] The peoples who live in the coastal places of California necessarily understand themselves as from and of the coast, with relationships and responsibilities to the ecologies and relationalities embedded in the stories and in the land and waters. This is a form of intimacy that situates a relationality with water at the center of California Indian existence in the world.

Tongva *ti'at* builders acknowledge a deep interdependence between themselves and other voyaging nations in California and across the Pacific, a connection many California tribes acknowledge through oral tradition and contemporary responsibilities.[27] Whether it is sourcing the redwood from the Karuk Tribe, harvesting asphaltum outside of traditional home territories, greeting the Hawaiian *Hōkūle'a* when it arrives on the California coast, or participating in the Coast Salish canoe journeys, the *Moomat Ahiko* has voyaged across and through Pacific Indigenous communities, forging dynamic connections between traditions, stories, peoples, and cultures. Tongva tribal member Valerie Arias explains, "It doesn't matter if you don't know anything other than how to hammer a hammer. It doesn't matter if you don't know anything other than how to cook some food. It doesn't matter if you don't know anything other than how to sing. As long as you come together as a community and you give that little bit of what you learn . . . you're still giving something of yourself and you're still learning as well."[28]

Frank's involvement in the revitalization of Tongva *ti'at* culture raises productive possibilities for thinking with the *ti'at* and literary form. The collage-style DIY aesthetic of "Second Serving" serves to visually replicate the form of the Tongva *ti'at*. The column juxtaposes narrative fragments in a horizontal format down the page; that is, each of the eight stories is transformed into one of the planks that, collectively, compose the body of the canoe. Thinking with "Second Serving" in this way invites readers to reimagine the relationship between the seemingly disparate stories; separately each plank is limited in the kind of work it might accomplish, but when hewn together, the stories transform into a vessel. As a published text, that vessel then voyages (or circulates) broadly across communities, affirming long-standing connections between Indigenous Pacific peoples and beyond. The photos and images that accompany the textual narratives then function like the abalone inlay—they are strategically laid out within and across the "planks," signifying multiple, rich possible interpretations of each written anecdote. The photos and images also help visually signify relations, connections, and responsibilities, affirming the *ti'at*'s kinship ties. When the individual works are juxtaposed and circulated together, they assert abundance, not scarcity.

If Frank's column is like a Tongva *ti'at*, then the possibilities of "reading" surfing in this literary context are rich. One might say that the anecdote about little Bert's surfing competition found in the winter 2009/2010 issue functions as part of the resin that helps fill the gaps between the main hewn planks: the anecdote is the adapted technology that has been added along with pine pitch to patch the canoe. By this I mean that while surfing has not been a central cultural or material practice within coastal California Indian communities, it nonetheless is a Pacific Indigenous built technology that animates cultural and social lives and entangles humans with waters. Little Bert's surfing competition on the Northern California coast animates a depth of meaning for California Indian people like Frank who are invested in the future of their peoples and lands. Surfing may not be the typical way that Karuk and Pomo Nations have connected with, or been in relation to, boarderlands in coastal Northern California from time immemorial. But as an adapted Indigenous technology, it is one method of filling in the gaps, rendered by settler colonialism, between peoples and homelands.[29] And, Bert excels at it! Frank reminds readers that these kinds of events encode deep significance, especially for coastal California Indian peoples; watching Bert surf in his ancestral homelands surrounded by an intergenerational community of support is a testament to the vibrant possibilities of a California Indigenous future. This, as Frank states simply, is a gift.

By linking both the processes and the aesthetics of canoe building and storytelling, Frank animates multiple forms of Indigenous knowledges in a powerful decolonial practice. Her inclusion of surfing opens up productive possibilities for understanding how Indigenous material cultures, from seafaring to surfing, can be encoded in literary form to rides waves and voyage through diverse readerships. As a methodology and value, survivance in California depends on a trans-Indigenous network of individuals and tribes doing the work to reclaim culture, tell old and new stories, and combat the evil spirits of colonialism. When that methodology expands outward to integrate adapted Indigenous technologies such as surfing and the surfboard, those dynamic trans-Indigenous relationships enhance place-based, tribally specific anticolonial work.

As it circulates in the quarterly periodical, this canoe travels and connects readers and knowledges. In this text, a California Indian author engages in a form of aesthetic activism that draws together a diverse range of voices and forms to affirm tribally specific knowledges that support sovereignty and survivance.

Notes

1 Kimmerer, *Braiding Sweetgrass*, 23–24.

2 The values of respect, relationship, reciprocity, and responsibility are foundational in Indigenous communities, and they form the bedrock of Indigenous research methodologies as well. See Wilson, *Research Is Ceremony*, as well as Archibald, *Indigenous Storywork*.

3 Here I utilize the term *boarderlands* as Kanaka Māoli historian Isaiah Walker does in his 2011 book, *Waves of Resistance*. Punning on Chicana scholar

Gloria Anzaldúa's figuration of borderlands, the geographical area between what is now the United States and Mexico where identity and power become muddled, and reorganized, in the ambiguity of these border regions, Walker extends the idea of these spaces and applies it to the surf zone.

4 I originate my readings of surfing from Goenpul scholar Aileen Moreton-Robinson's claim, "Surfing was and continues to be a native Hawaiian cultural practice introduced to the West by Duke Kahanamoku. Native Hawaiians' form of surfing was to flow with the waves, adhering to an ideal of soul surfing, which was part of their culture for more than fifteen hundred years." Moreton-Robinson, *The White Possessive*, 41.

5 Allen's conceptualization of the trans-Indigenous involves the way one Indigenous worldview, ontology, or cultural/material practice helps us examine a different Indigenous cultural practice by asserting and affirming Indigenous critical methodologies rather than applying Western frames of understanding onto Indigenous relations and practices. Allen, *Trans-Indigenous*.

6 "Second Serving" actually only appears three times between 2008 and 2010—once in the spring 2008 issue of *News from Native California*, once in the fall 2008 issue, and once in the winter 2009/2010 issue.

7 For Indigenous peoples, water is a relative rather than an object. Animate, not inanimate, it evokes a sense of knowing, relating, respect, responsibility, and reciprocity. See Leonard et al., "Water Back."

8 I mention this because I want to emphasize here that surfing, ultimately, plays only a minor role in Frank's broader projects as a California Indian activist and community organizer.

9 See Kamper, *Rez Ballers, Skate Elders, and Joyful Futures in Indian Country*.

10 The late Luiseño artist James Luna was a surfer, as noted in McHugh, "Profane Illuminations." Castillo remains committed to surfing even though he is now in his eighties, acknowledging that although he recently had a stent placed in his heart he demanded that the doctors place it in a way that would not interfere with lying on a surfboard while paddling (2018 personal interview).

11 Nieblas is now featured in a 2024 documentary titled *Haagua*, a surf film produced by the organization Native Like Water that features Indigenous surfers and surfing practices in California. Also note the variation in Nieblas's spelling of *Acjachemen*. Although this spelling is missing the *c* at the beginning of the word, I am quoting the way Nieblas spells it on his Instagram page as of June 2024.

12 Indeed, Native people all over the world engage in surfing. I know several young Makah surfers who surf their traditional waters in the northwest corner of the Olympic Peninsula in Washington State. I met two Sea Sámi surfers in northern Norway in 2018 who surf in spaces where the Sea Sámi are barely recognized as still existing, even by other Sámi peoples.

13 More than the common trickster figure who appears in tribal literatures across Turtle Island, Coyote is a tribally specific First Being and Creator grounded in creation narratives and traditions. By making the important distinction between Coyote as a literary trope and Coyote First Person as a tribally contextualized Being, Hupa scholar Cutcha Risling Baldy argues that "Coyote First Person is not only a trickster, but also a complex embodiment of Indigenous decolonizing methodologies." Risling Baldy, *We Are Dancing for You*, 2.

14 I like to think that these disruptive reading moments feel like catching your fin on a clump of kelp while riding down the face of a wave—that is, the kelp disrupts your speed and momentum, often requiring you to catch your balance and restabilize without falling. Non-Native literary scholar Susan Bernardin has claimed that Frank's literary aesthetic and formal practices—especially those that disrupt how readers read—"[coax] active collaboration" because they require that we readers slow down and think critically about the text. Bernardin, "Acorn Soup Is Good Food," 15.

15 See Krista Comer's work in *Surfer Girls in the New World Order* for a more in-depth understanding of the role *Gidget* plays in producing social and gender relations in California surf culture in this era.

16 American Indian peoples often utilize the shorthand *ndn* or *NDN* to refer to themselves. While this term, shorthand for *Indian*, circulates within American Indian discourses and rhetorics, non-Natives and settlers should not use the term *Indian* or its shorthand *ndn* when referring to or about American Indian peoples. Driftpile Cree writer Billy-Ray Belcourt explains in the epigraph to his book *NDN Coping Mechanisms*, "NDN is internet shorthand used by Indigenous peoples in North America to refer to ourselves. It is also sometimes an acronym meaning 'Not Dead Native.'"

17 Waves that create tubes are the dominant image that people call up when they think about surfing. Waves such as Pipeline on O'ahu's North Shore create this shape and dominate surf visual media and culture.

18 The term *two-spirit* is a contested term that broadly refers to the expression of gender and sexuality according to Indigenous cultural practices, particularly

as they deviate from Western expressions and constructions of the same. As Andrew Jolivétte writes, the term is not a broad umbrella or "catch all" term but rather "a relatively recent phenomenon" that "exists because some of our people, from some of our tribal communities and urban pan-Indian communities, remember another way of being—one that is expansive and open, rather than reductive and closed." Jolivétte, *Indian Blood*, 11.

19 Indeed, *News* has published "many of the top California Indian artists, photographers, and writers: Deborah Miranda, Darryl 'Babe' Wilson, Judith Lowry, Dugan Aguilar, Julian Lang, Greg Sarris, Harry Fonseca, Frank LaPena, and Janice Gould, among others. Their poems, stories, paintings, and photographs appear alongside articles on politics, education, law, land, foods, and language." Bernardin, "Acorn Soup Is Good Food," 4. This vibrant publication is a significant site of California Indian knowledge production and circulation and has long served as a space that affirms California Indian survivance.

20 A vast and diverse range of California Indian scholars have constructed a rich archive of California Indian scholarship that addresses this history and cultural survivance. Within California Indian studies, one must read Cutcha Risling Baldy (Hupa, Yurok, and Karuk), historian William Bauer Jr. (Wailaki and Concow), writer and literary scholar Deborah Miranda (Chumash and Esselen), literary scholar Mark Minch-de-Leon (Pomo), and many more. For a more complete list of California Indian scholars working on constructing a robust discipline, you can visit the California Indian Studies and Scholars Association web page at www.californiaindianstudies.org/current-members.html. Additionally, texts such as settler historian Brendan Lindsay's Murder State: California's Native American Genocide, 1846–1875 have provided crucial historical context on settler colonial violence in what is now California.

21 *Tending Nature.*

22 *Tending Nature.*

23 Frank, "Second Serving" (Spring 2008), 49.

24 Bauer, *California through Native Eyes*, 10.

25 Bauer, *California through Native Eyes*, 10.

26 Bauer, *California through Native Eyes*, 28. Canoes were also spaces of diplomatic and political encounter and exchange during early contact with Europeans. As Damon Akins and William Bauer Jr. write in *We Are the Land: A History of Native California*, many tribal nations engaged new European arrivals via watercraft. Tongvas paddled *ti'ats* out, from what is now Oxnard and from Pimunu (Catalina), to meet European explorers. Coast Miwok

peoples canoed out in what is now Bodega Bay to meet Sir Francis Drake in 1579. The Pomo and Tongva again paddled out to meet the Spanish explorer Vizcaino, in 1602 and 1603. Akins and Bauer, *We Are the Land*, 37–39.

27 For example, Darryl Babe Wilson recounts an Achomawi and Atsugewi oral narrative in *The Sound of Rattles and Clappers: A Collection of New California Indian Writing* (1994) about the time the Hawaiian peoples canoed to the coast of Northern California, crashed their canoes into the rocks, and stayed, intermarrying with California Indian peoples, for a while (143–49). Such stories affirm a relational knowledge of Pacific Indigenous peoples and their technologies prior to European contact and resituate transpacific knowledges within Indigenous narratives rather than European ones.

28 Tending Nature, season 2, episode 1, "Rethinking the Coast with the Ti'at Society," directed by Anna Rau and Corbitt Jones, aired 2019, PBS SoCal, www.pbssocal.org/shows/tending-nature/episodes/rethinking-the-coast-with-the-tiat-society.

29 In fact, the focus on Indigenous youth-led activities and actions that support tribal sovereignty is especially important, especially since these installments of "Second Serving" have been published. Youth organizations such as Ríos to Rivers are organizing events like Paddle Tribal Waters that invite young Indigenous paddlers to kayak the entire stretch of the Klamath River for the first time since the dams came down. These paddles are meant to connect stolen histories with vibrant futures for these Indigenous youth.

Bibliography

Akins, Damon B., and William J. Bauer Jr. *We Are the Land: A History of Native California*. Los Angeles: University of California Press, 2021.

Allen, Chadwick. *Trans-Indigenous: Methodologies for Global Native Literary Studies*. Minneapolis: University of Minnesota Press, 2012.

Anzaldúa, Gloria. *Borderlands/La Frontera: The New Mestiza*. San Francisco: Aunt Lute Press, 1987.

Archibald, Joann. *Indigenous Storywork: Educating the Heart, Mind, Body, and Spirit*. Vancouver: University of British Columbia Press, 2008.

Bauer, William, Jr. *California through Native Eyes: Reclaiming History*. Seattle: University of Washington Press, 2016.

Belcourt, Billy-Ray. *NDN Coping Mechanisms: Notes from the Field*. Toronto: House of Anansi Press, 2019.

Bernardin, Susan. "Acorn Soup Is Good Food: L. Frank, News from Native California, and the Intersections of Literary and Visual Arts." *Studies in American Indian Literatures* 27, no. 3 (2015): 1–33.

Castillo, Edward. Interview by Lydia Heberling and David Kamper, November 12, 2018.

Comer, Krista. *Surfer Girls in the New World Order*. Durham, NC: Duke University Press, 2010.

Frank Manriquez, L. *Acorn Soup*. San Francisco: Heyday Books, 1999.

———. "Second Serving." *News from Native California* 21, no. 3 (Spring 2008): 49.

———. "Second Serving." *News from Native California* 22, no. 1 (Fall 2008): 49.

———. "Second Serving." *News from Native California* 23, no. 2 (Winter 2009/2010): 42–43.

Haagua. Directed by Octavio Coutiño Aceves and Marc Antony Chavez. Native Like Water, 2024.

Jolivétte, Andrew. *Indian Blood: HIV and Colonial Trauma in San Francisco's Two-Spirit Community*. Seattle: University of Washington Press, 2016.

Kamper, David. *Rez Ballers, Skate Elders, and Joyful Futures in Indian Country*. Lincoln: University of Nebraska Press, 2024.

Kimmerer, Robin Wall. *Braiding Sweetgrass: Indigenous Wisdom, Scientific Knowledge and the Teaching of Plants*. Minneapolis: Milkweed Press, 2015.

Leonard, Kelsey, D. David-Chavez, D. Smiles, L. Jennings, R. 'Anolani Alegado, L. Tsinnajinnie, J. Manitowabi, R. Arsenault, R. L. Begay, A. Kagawa-Viviani, D. D. Davis, V. van Uitregt, H. Pichette, M. Liboiron, B. Moggridge, S. Russo Carroll, R. L. Tsosie, A. and Gomez. "Water Back: A Review Centering Rematriation and Indigenous Water Research Sovereignty." *Annual Water Alternatives Review* 16, no. 2 (2023): 374–428.

Lindsay, Brendan. *Murder State: California's Native American Genocide, 1846–1875*. Lincoln: University of Nebraska Press, 2012.

McHugh, Kathleen. "Profane Illuminations: History and Collaboration in James Luna and Isaac Artenstein's *The History of the Luiseño People*." *Biography* 31, no. 3 (2008): 429–60.

Miranda, Deborah. *Bad Indians: A Tribal Memoir*. Berkeley: Heyday Books, 2013.

Moreton-Robinson, Aileen. *The White Possessive: Property, Power, and Indigenous Sovereignty*. Minneapolis: University of Minnesota Press, 2015.

Risling Baldy, Cutcha. *We Are Dancing for You: Native Feminisms and the Revitalization of Women's Coming-of-Age Ceremonies*. Seattle: University of Washington Press, 2018.

Sarris, Greg, ed. *The Sound of Rattles and Clappers: A Collection of New California Indian Writers*. Tucson: University of Arizona Press, 1994.

Tending Nature. Season 2, episode 1. "Rethinking the Coast with the Ti'at Society." Directed by Anna Rau and Corbitt Jones, aired 2019, PBS SoCal, www.pbssocal .org/shows/tending-nature/episodes/rethinking-the-coast-with-the-tiat-society.

Walker, Isaiah Helekunihi. *Waves of Resistance: Surfing and History in Twentieth-Century Hawai'i*. Honolulu: University of Hawai'i Press, 2011.

Wilson, Darryl Babe. "Gedin Ch-Lum-Nu/'Let it Be This Way.'" In *The Sound of Rattles and Clappers: A Collection of New California Indian Writers*, edited by Greg Sarris, 143–49. Tucson: University of Arizona Press, 1994.

Wilson, Shawn. *Research Is Ceremony: Indigenous Research Methods*. Nova Scotia: Fernwood Publishing, 2008.

13

"This Is Like a Renaissance"

The Making of Surfing's Oppositional Culture in the Age of Black Lives Matter

ELIZABETH SINE

The summer of 2020 marked a remarkable moment in the history and racial politics of surfing. Beginning the first week of June and continuing throughout the rest of the summer, thousands of people at beaches across the globe paddled out for Black lives, participating in a ceremony that has roots in Indigenous Hawaiian ritual practices and that was organized in this historic moment to support the Black Lives Matter movement.[1] On one level, the paddle-outs were memorials honoring the lives of African Americans lost to police violence—including George Floyd, Breonna Taylor, Ahmaud Arbery, and others. Yet, they were also expressions of political solidarity with struggles for racial justice in a much broader sense. In addition to the paddle-outs, expressions of antiracism reverberated across major channels of the surf industry. Many professional surfers across the globe used their public platforms, on social media and beyond, to express outrage at the realities of anti-Black violence and structural racism in the United States and to support the Black Lives Matter movement. *Surfer* magazine chief editor Todd Prodanovich penned an article urging, "Now's the Time for Surfers to Prove We Really Are Anti-establishment."[2] The World Surf League (WSL) declared its stance "in solidarity with Black Lives Matter, against racism, police brutality and discrimination of any form, [along with a commitment] to championing social justice."[3] Two-time surfing world champion Tyler Wright devoted the first 439 seconds of her heat in the Tweed Coast Pro to kneeling beside her board with "BLACK LIVES MATTER" emblazoned across the bottom, as she commemorated the 439 Aboriginal people that had died in Australian police custody over the past thirty years.[4] When criticism flooded in from her detractors, Wright's sponsors and the WSL affirmed their support for her action.[5] In these and other expressions, people across the surfing world positioned themselves in more public and explicit ways than had been previously seen on the side of antiracism. When surf broadcaster and action sports icon Selema Masekela joined the founders of Textured Waves for the virtual premiere of their short film *Sea Us Now* that summer, he reflected on the palpable reckoning that had shaken the surfing world, noting what a departure it represented from the norms he had experienced in his twenty-five-year career in the surf industry. "I never thought that I would see that," he remarked. "It feels like this could be a turning point."[6]

The upheaval within the surfing world channeled a political energy that was in tune with and, in significant ways, an expression of the wider upwelling of grassroots protest that had swept the nation and the world in the same moment. It was a few months into the COVID-19 pandemic. Overlapping crises of public health, the economy, politics, the environment, and race relations laid bare long-standing inequalities across the globe. Within the United States, the coronavirus disproportionately devastated communities of color, not least of all those composing a large part of the essential workforce and those residing in tribal nations, immigrant detention centers, migrant camps along the US-Mexico border, and jails and prisons across the country. Against this background, a string of highly publicized police killings of unarmed African Americans sparked a massive surge of grassroots uprisings nationwide. All of this drew issues of racial injustice, state violence, and the intertwined imperatives of systemic transformation and racial liberation into the center of popular discussions. Sports were no exception. Although major currents of the surf industry and wider surfing population had historically insisted on the sport's existence outside politics, surfing was not immune.

While the level of public attention to issues of racism in surfing was new, the reality of those issues, and an awareness of them by the people and communities of color who were impacted most directly by them—including Masekela, the women of Textured Waves, and other surfers of color the world over—was not. For many within these segments of the surf community, the broader cataclysms of the historical moment signaled not the introduction but the continuation of long-standing hardships and generations-old struggles. Rather than illuminating the unfamiliar, the reckoning that now coursed through surfing's mainstream reflected the surfacing of deeply rooted patterns of exclusion in the sport that they knew all too well. To the extent that the upheavals disrupted prevailing discourses that had long cast surfing as a sanctuary from the wider world's political tribulations in general and from the trappings of racism in particular, they also presented an opening. In that opening lay fresh possibilities for advancing alternative visions of what surfing was and ought to be—visions that were anchored in efforts that had been long in the making.

This essay explores the roots of the recent upsurge of antiracist expression across the surfing world by examining the crystallization of the movement for a more inclusive surf culture in the years that preceded the 2020 uprisings. I focus particular attention on an array of initiatives that took shape across the continental United States—a major zone of global surf industry activity and a critical engine driving the production of a whitewashed heteropatriarchal surf culture—during the decade leading up to the Black Lives Matter paddle-outs. I trace how in different ways, in different geographic locations, and with different strategies and priorities, Black, Brown, and Indigenous surf communities together have contributed to the making of an oppositional surf culture that challenges dominant patterns of settler colonialism and racial capitalism within the sport. I examine how this oppositional culture has formed across multiple planes of activity, including within the surf industry, in a growing web of nonprofit and community-based organizations, and in the realm of visual culture and media representation.[7] I also illuminate how the movement has generated its own field of knowledge about surfing as a generative site of liberatory struggle. Framing surfing's oppositional culture as a "movement of many movements," I shed light on its multifaceted, multifronted, multiracial character, and on the dynamics of difference, interconnectivity, and interdependence that animate it.[8] I ultimately argue that for the communities of color at the helm of its construction, the oppositional culture taking shape in the surfing world is more than a movement for diversity and inclusion; it is an avenue for advancing expansive and wide-ranging struggles against dehumanization and for dignity. For them, building a surf culture more embracing of difference is not an end goal but an avenue for nourishing the self-actualization, self-definition, and self-determination of aggrieved and historically marginalized populations, and for charting the way toward a more sustainable existence on this planet.

Race and Resistance in the Surf Zone

While the scale of antiracist expression that coursed through the surfing world in summer 2020 was unprecedented, the existence of such expression and the desires that it reflected were not. These developments built on a longer history of struggle in which people of color in coastal areas have worked to define their own relationship to the ocean and to challenge forms of subordination, exclusion, and erasure they have experienced within surfing for generations. As historian Isaiah Walker has underscored, *ka poʻina nalu*, or the "surf zone," has long been a battleground on which patterns of colonization, nation building, and racial hierarchy have been fought over and contested. In addition to being critical targets of Western-led settlement and development since at least the late nineteenth century, surfing and the spaces in which it occurs have proven to be crucial sites of resistance.[9]

Against the many forces militating against their engagement with the sport, aggrieved and racially marginalized communities have long contested the hegemony of whiteness on the beach and in the lineup, refusing the marginal place that white-led surf culture has reserved for them, while recreating their relationships to the ocean and to surfing on their own accord. From Indigenous peoples who have kept alive ancestral knowledge about their connections with the sea and who have asserted themselves at the helm of movements to protect coastal ecologies and surf spots to Black beachgoers who built thriving beach cultures at "Inkwells" in the age of Jim

Crow and wade-in protestors who turned beaches into sites of civil rights confrontation to individuals like Nick Gabaldón, who went to great lengths to ride waves at a world-class point break customarily reserved for white surfers, or like Mary Mills, Andrea Kabwasa, and Sharon Schaffer, who helped inspire a whole generation of women of color surfers, to the Black Surf Association (BSA), which Tony Corley founded in 1975, providing an early model of nonwhite surf community organizing on the US mainland, surfers of color have long demonstrated possibilities for reclaiming the spaces and sport of surfing to support their own needs and aspirations.[10] For them, the stakes of struggles over surfing have always been about much more than surfing itself.

The early twenty-first century marked a new chapter in this longer history of resistance. New departures in the globalization of the world economy, the restructuring of the US political order to support the demands of capital over the needs of people, and the dismantling of the social safety net that had represented the hard-won gains of labor and civil rights movements all created new vulnerabilities for people in and beyond the United States. With the ending of long-standing racialized immigration restrictions and the demands for cheap, flexible pools of labor within the shifting economy, the United States became both more diverse and more unequal than ever. California became a majority-minority state by the year 2000, and the United States is on its way to following suit.[11] These demographic shifts have sharpened anxieties among many who harbor concerns about maintaining a racialized sense of social order in the country. Increasingly, ramped up efforts to enforce "law and order" and the expansion of carceral systems reflect growing efforts to resolve the nation's "social problems" by caging them.[12] All the while, new levels of wealth concentration and the expansion of neofascist political currents have heightened the forms of deprivation, neglect, abuse, and terror that people experience in their daily lives. The perils that confront aggrieved populations within this context have made sites of play and recreation, sites of healing and rejuvenation, into critical veins within the circulation of wider struggles for dignity.

Building an Infrastructure of Opposition

If developments preceding the 2010s created the conditions for the oppositional culture's emergence, they did not make it inevitable. Rather, the movement grew most directly from the determined actions and relentless creativity of surfers of color refusing to accept hegemonic constructions of surf culture as is. Across the surf industry, a network of surf-oriented nonprofit and community-based organizations, and a grassroots-driven visual culture, people and communities with widely different backgrounds and identities have rejected the very idea of a singular surf culture imposed from the top down, and have gone about building their own cultural worlds around surfing from the bottom up.

As a set of institutions that has arguably done more to reinforce white patriarchal dominance within the sport than to challenge it, the surf industry may seem like an unlikely arena for oppositional cultural formation. Yet, some individuals within industry channels have found ways to leverage their platforms and build conversations about race and surf culture that many would prefer to ignore and have long worked to repress. The contributions of surfer, sport broadcaster, and commentator Selema Masekela are especially significant in this respect. A self-described "only" within the action sports industry—that is, one of the only Black-identified people in that space for decades–Masekela ushers forth a radical tradition of struggle in which his father, South African jazz musician and anti-apartheid freedom fighter Hugh Masekela, was a pivotal figure.[13] In a career that has carried him from TransWorld Surf to ESPN, the X Games, ASP (later WSL), and beyond, Masekela has challenged narrow definitions of such categories as "Black" and "surfer," including popular assumptions that have regarded these categories as separate and distinct.[14] On the global stage, he has opened up dialogues about racism and colonialism in surfing on which surf media was otherwise virtually silent.[15] He has also utilized his platform to direct resources and build institutional spaces supporting the self-expression of populations largely neglected by the industry's main channels. In 1998, he cofounded Alphanumeric, a Black-owned action sports–inspired streetwear brand.[16] In 2004, he cofounded Stoked Mentoring, a nonprofit that utilizes surfing, snowboarding, and skateboarding as avenues for supporting underserved youth.[17] From expanding the soundscape we associate with surfing through his band Alekesam's "surf R&B" to cofounding the South African–based surf lifestyle brand Mami Wata in 2017 to coediting the book *Afro Surf* in 2020, Masekela has contributed to the advancement of an oppositional narrative about surfing that decenters whiteness and honors the multiplicity of grassroots surf cultures across the globe.[18] Importantly, even as he has modeled ways in which industry channels can be made to nurture alternative visions of the sport, he cautions against any potential overemphasis on the industry per se as a source of change. "The industry will choose to get on board if it feels like financially they have no choice," Masekela notes. Ultimately, though, in terms of substantive, lasting transformation, "I don't expect anything from the industry."[19] Rather, he clarifies, "What I expect," and where he expects change to come *from*, "is us taking things into our own hands, and creating new brands, and storytelling it according to our experiences, and providing space for people who would like to hear a new song . . . a new song in the hallowed halls of the ocean."[20]

Indeed, the surf industry's limitations as a site of change deepen the significance of work that has been occurring beyond it. Over the same decades that saw the unfolding of Masekela's career, an array of community-based and nonprofit organizations sprouted up, in different localities along both coasts of the continental United States, with aims of widening access to the sport and (re)building connections between displaced and historically marginalized populations and the ocean. Building on the groundwork laid by early groups like the BSA, the organizations that formed in the early twenty-first century carried the approach of grassroots-level organizing into new locations and new directions. In 2000, Marc Chavez began bringing Native youth to San Diego County's beaches, reconnecting them with coastal homelands and Indigenous maritime and wave-riding traditions, as part of the broader efforts of his organization Young Native Scholars (later InterTribal Youth) to "Indigenize education." As the years went on, the connection of Indigenous people to water became increasingly central to Chavez's efforts, inspiring him to refine his focus and formally reestablish his organization as Native Like Water (NLW) in 2014.[21] During the years leading up to Chavez's formalization of his focus on Indigenous-aquatic interconnections, as Masekela's Stoked Mentoring expanded its reach from New York to Los Angeles, Farhana Huq was building the foundations of Brown Girl Surf, which she founded in Oakland in 2012. As she joined forces with cofounder Mira Manickam-Shirley, what began as a place where what Huq described as the "misfits of surfing" could connect, share their stories, and find affirmation in community evolved into an engine for the production of an alternative surf culture in its own right, combining surf programming with environmental stewardship in ways that centered and amplified the creativity of girls, women, and nonbinary people of color.[22] In 2014, Rhonda Harper founded Black Girls Surf from her home in San Jose, California, establishing what would become a transnational network that would stretch from California to Jamaica to Senegal, building connections among Black female surfers and broadening attention to the challenges confronting girls and women of color within the sport.[23] Around the same time, Vanessa Yeager was busy shuttling students from her PE classes in Santa Ana to Newport Beach, marking the informal beginnings of what would become the Latinx Surf Club. In 2017, Yeager met Giselle Carrillo and Cassie Comley and together the three of them expanded the club's reach and also established the Latinx youth–focused Los Courage Camps. Through Los Courage Camps, Carrillo and Comley have continued to provide surf lessons to diverse youth from across the greater LA and Orange County areas.[24] Meanwhile, Kayiita Johansson launched his Black.Surfers platform from his home base in Santa Cruz, opening up a new avenue for Black surfers across the globe to connect with each other in digital space as well as in person within the localities in which they lived and traveled. With time Johansson's aims expanded to include efforts to address institutional inequities that limit access to beaches and surfing through public policy.[25] In 2018, GiGi Lucas's Jacksonville Beach–based Surfear Negra began providing financial support to girls of color across the country who wished to attend surf camps within their home communities. Since then, the group has also begun sharing the fundamentals of surfing with young people geographically removed from the beach, an added expression of its commitment to "make surfing accessible to any girl anywhere."[26] Also in 2018, in Far Rockaway, Aydon Gabourel's initial imperative to nurture his daughter's desire to surf provided the heartbeat for what grew into the Laru Beya Collective, which he runs alongside his nephew Warren Sampson to foster the empowerment of underrepresented youth through surfing.[27] Anchored in and animated by the locally based communities they work to serve, all of these organizations have been creating new surf communities of their own and providing surf instruction not simply as a way of imparting the skills of the sport to new or aspiring surfers but as an avenue for fostering the autonomy, empowerment, and self-definition of populations who are often denied these things.

If surfing's oppositional culture has been making it possible for the surfing world to "hear a new song," to borrow from Masekela, it has also been enabling the world to see surfing in new ways, specifically through the production of a vibrant, variegated visual culture. From the women-centered surf photography of Sachi Cunningham to the street art–inspired painting of DJ Javier to films like Ted Woods's *White Wash* (2011) and Monica Medellín's *Water Warrior* (2018), the years that preceded the 2020 uprising saw the early flourishing of cultural expressions by and about surfers of color, utilizing the arts to reshape the narratives we inherit about surfing and to imagine a new future. Importantly, for the movement's cultural workers, the transformative potential of visual media is not reducible to the role of imagery alone or to the aim of increasing representation of historically underrepresented communities. Rather, for them, the possibilities of new imagery and representations are contingent on, and must go hand in hand with, a fuller production process that engages, respects, and supports the self-determination of the communities they seek to represent. As Medellín emphasizes in her own work, it is vital not only "to diversify stories in front of the camera, but also to make sure behind the camera it [the film's production team and process] is still reflective of those communities and stories. You need both."[28] Medellín identifies this principle as the "true essence and mission" of her work, one that guided her formation of the women-led film collective Gnar Gnar Honeys in 2018, and that continues to drive her involvement in projects ranging from the docu-series Surf Girls:

Kaikaina to her production company Waves Made.[29] A relatable priority drives the work of Textured Waves, which Danielle Black Lyons, Chelsea Woody, and Martina Duran formed in 2018. The group began with a website and Instagram account focused on sharing imagery of female surfers of color in an effort to "propagate the sport of women's surfing toward women of color and underrepresented demographics."[30] As Black Lyons explains, "Basically we didn't see ourselves in the surf world represented in a way that we wanted, so we decided to create this platform to showcase the unsung heroes of surfing, women of color that we admire, and put them on a platform, which in this case was social media."[31] Since that time, the group has created multiple short films and expanded the reach of their platform and influence across the broader circuitry of surf media. But increased exposure alone has never been the group's priority. As they put it, "The driving force behind Textured Waves is sharing OUR story in our voice, through a lens of our choosing. We are invested in being the ones in control of our narrative because for so long, our story has not been accurately represented, if at all." The group adds that in addition to producing imagery resonant with their vision of the sport, "It's equally important to us that the production process, the team behind the lens, is selected by us and the story we conceptualize comes from our perspective—which is why we seek creatives within the Black and Brown community when we can to help tell these stories authentically."[32] Acutely aware of the dangers of a narrow focus on the politics of representation per se, in an economy where tokenizing efforts to commodify "diversity" abound, Textured Waves, Medellín, and other creatives across surfing's cultural front are utilizing existing platforms and creating new ones to amplify alternative visions of the sport while underscoring the vital necessity of creative autonomy to the possibilities of wider social and structural change.

Together, the individuals, communities, and organizations that compose surfing's oppositional culture form a multifronted, multiracial, interethnic movement to redefine what surfing is about and who it is for. Their efforts to expand access and inclusivity in surfing not only challenge exclusionary, settler-led constructions of surf culture that have historically bolstered wider structures of domination; they are actively expanding the horizons for reimagining surfing as a site where wide-ranging grassroots struggles for survival and humanity can flourish.

Another Horizon

Just as imperatives of grassroots dignity and autonomy have guided the movement-building activity of surfers of color in recent years, so too have they provided the pulse for the movement's production of knowledge about surfing as a site of liberatory struggle. Against the dominant insistence on treating surfing as an apolitical, postracial arena of pure fun, surf communities of color over the past decade have contributed to a field of oppositional knowledge about the sport's radical potential to nurture the well-being and worldbuilding of communities most threatened by the overlapping crises of our current conjuncture. Exploring the range of meanings that surfing holds for surfers of color within the movement helps shed light on the scope and stakes of the movement itself and on the political possibilities of surfing more generally.

For surfers of color at the helm of the making of surfing's oppositional culture, part of what makes surfing a generative avenue of liberatory struggle has to do with what occurs at the level of the individual, at the juncture of time and space, in the actual experience of surfing itself. Surfing's temporal orientation around the present moment and its place-based connection to the physical environment of the ocean together form some of the sport's most distinguishing characteristics. From the moment of setting foot in the water while en route to the lineup to the process of attuning to the ocean's rhythms while awaiting an incoming set to the embodied experience of wave riding itself, surfing has been widely recognized for its capacity to open up a sense of time and space in which the constraints of the past and pressures of the future are loosened, where one's immersion in and synchronization with the energy and elements of the natural world move to the foreground of consciousness. Surfers, observers, and scholars alike have variably hailed this temporal-spatial dimension of surfing for its therapeutic potential, its spiritual quality, and its contributions to personalized pathways of self-actualization.[33] As commonly remarked upon as that celebrated "feeling" that "only a surfer knows" is, much less attention has been given to how varied actual experiences of the "feeling" can be, how it is accessed within a wider field of power relations, and what particular meanings those experiences have for and among surf communities of color.[34]

For surfers of color—whose place in the present and in relation to the ocean have been structured, at least in part, by the long histories and persistent perils of colonialism, slavery, and the myriad forms of dislocation, denigration, deprivation, and devastation that accompany them—being in the moment, in the space of the ocean can be an act of insubordination.[35] In the spirit of what longtime surfer and Black surfing advocate Rick Blocker calls "Blacksurfing," it can be an embodied refusal of the impingements of settler colonialism and racial capitalism on their lives. It can be a way of suspending the pressures of everyday life, however temporarily, creating space for alternative ways of being, on their own terms.[36] Mira Manickam-Shirley has described the actually lived experience of "freedom and liberation" that surfing represents particularly for people living at the intersection of overlapping forces of racial, gender, sexual, and class oppression. "Our bodies are so regulated and gazed upon and assessed and judged," Manickam-Shirley remarks. "Especially for adolescent girls of color . . . there's so much weight" to bear in the work of navigating everyday life. Within this context, surfing offers what she describes as "a lifting" of that weight and a "liberation of the body and spirit."[37] Addressing her own experience as a Black woman who took up surfing in adulthood, GiGi Lucas recalls, "The ocean was the only place where I felt like my mind could rest." In her words, "I had been through some serious trauma in terms of being the only one in a lot of spaces, the only woman, definitely the only Black woman . . . having to navigate [what are now commonly called] microaggressions" along with the added challenge that "so much in life as a woman of color your feelings [are treated as if they] don't matter." Lucas explains that "when I connected with surfing, I was able to breathe and start to make sense of how I felt . . . getting some clarity around what I wanted in life."[38] Whether framed as a lifting or liberation as Manickam-Shirley characterizes it, or as breathing room in the way Lucas describes, the practice of surfing holds an important place in the lives of surfers of color in no small part because of the sense of autonomy it nurtures, despite and against prevailing social demands and expectations.

As fleeting as the experience of liberation-through-surfing might be, surfers of color recognize its potential for supporting an expanded sense of physical, mental, and emotional health, and well-being in general. Giselle Carrillo frames surfing's importance, particularly for the Latinx community she serves and of which she is part, as a "health practice" with life-buoying potential. Like Jiu Jitsu and other athletic activities that she coaches through her El Barrio Athletic Club, which she founded when the pandemic put Los Courage Camps on hold, Carrillo sees surfing as a valuable component of a routine that can help "take care of your mind and your heart and be healthy."[39] As seemingly straightforward as the concept of surfing-as-health-practice may be, Carrillo underscores its profound significance in the context of prevailing health disparities. As she puts it, "My mantra right now is health is a human right. . . . Health is a human right, and it's been denied to so many people."[40] Marc Chavez carries the point even further. As he puts it, "Surfing saves lives. . . . It's saving lives, and it's staying alive."[41] To be sure, Chavez's statement carries particular gravity with respect to the Indigenous communities who are the focus of much of his work, whose elimination has been constructed as a condition of Western-led modernity and whose erasure is imbricated in the structural forces of everyday life. As Chavez acknowledges, in different but relatable ways, the forms of dehumanization that confront differently racialized non-Indigenous populations make surfing an important vehicle for supporting Black and Brown survival and humanity as well. To the extent that "the solution [to the problems wrought by colonization] is just showing up and being present and surviving," Chavez remarks, "I want to get more people surfing," including more Indigenous people surfing as well as "more Brown people surfing and more Black people surfing."[42]

The forms of survival that surfing supports are not merely matters of individuals in the present; they are cross-generational and cultural. For some, surfing is a way of carrying on the legacies of ancestors, continuing the work of earlier generations who nurtured and regenerated traditions in the face of colonialism's atrocities. As Aydon Gabourel conveys, his work in Laru Beya is intimately shaped by his connection to the Afro-Indigenous Garifuna people in Belize, where he was born, from where he migrated, and where he maintains strong cultural and kinship ties. Laru Beya, after all, is Garifuna for "on the water," or "by the water." For Gabourel, sustaining the relationship of the Garifuna with the ocean—as a source of food, place of play, and life source—serves as an active reminder of his people's resilience and resistance in the face of uprooting, enslavement, and devastation. For Laru Beya's participants, including those with ancestral ties to the Garifuna and those of different backgrounds, anchoring the experience of surfing and other forms of ocean engagement in the frame of knowledge about the "roots and routes" of their ancestors can be a source of affirmation.[43] It is a way of reminding people, "You are special. This is you. This is your culture. . . . You know, hold on to that, regardless of what you're facing out there, regardless of when somebody's telling you can't do something."[44] A relatable practice of honoring Indigenous inheritance and identity through surfing plays into the work of Chavez's Native Like Water. For the Native Like Water community, surfing is part of a wider field of exploration into the intertribal legacies of local and transpacific Indigenous maritime histories—legacies that hinge on intricate knowledge of, embeddedness in, and reverence for the ocean and all of the natural world. Native Like Water's curriculum highlights how Indigenous peoples not only rode waves but crossed oceans, built transoceanic relationships, and engaged in cross-cultural exchange with seemingly disparate and far-flung populations well before the arrival of Europeans.[45] On one level, learning about this history is a way of honoring the deep-rooted relationships of Indigenous peoples with water. On another level, it breathes life into Indigenous lifeways while shifting the lens for understanding the interconnections linking Indigenous people, surfing, and modernization more generally—reframing Native peoples not as outsiders to the sport but as its originators, not as ethnic minority within the culture but as part of a global social majority.

Surf communities of color further acknowledge the sport's value as a mode of play and source of joy, a practice that affirms the wholeness of the humanity of populations who confront varying forms of dehumanization in their daily lives. Indigenous studies scholars Caleigh Cornell and Lydia Heberling have described surfing's capacity to serve as a conduit for "healing, trans-Indigenous expressions of cultural 'thrivance,'" linking Native peoples across different localities and tribal identities in a collective assertion of visibility over erasure, cultural affirmation over deracination.[46] The founders of Textured Waves similarly underscore how the joy and play of surfing help to decenter trauma and counter its fetishization within dominant narratives and representations of Blackness, as Chelsea Woody puts it, "portray[ing] our humanity beyond just our ability to feel pain."[47] In Martina Duran's words, "As Black people there is this unspoken trauma that we all share . . . that unspoken language that I think we all have, born out of the traumas that we've faced, and the generational traumas we face." But at the same time, she remarks, "It's not all heavy. . . . The Black experience is always portrayed as something very heavy, but we do have a lot of light and joy."[48] For Woody, "Capturing our joy in the sea and on beaches is not radical or rebellious in and of itself; it is a state of our existence that has yet to be fully documented, creating a radical rebellion in context."[49]

Surfers of color highlight how the physical and technical elements of surfing can fuel a sense of confidence and empowerment that has particular significance for communities of color. Giselle Carrillo explains that surfing is "the master teacher in every human emotion: peace, adventure, mystery, joy, ego, tranquility, and for me," she emphasizes especially, "fear and courage."[50] According to Vanessa Yeager, "At the root of it, it's not all about surfing. . . . It's about doing something that scares you, knowing that you have power and that you can do things that make you feel a little bit uncomfortable sometimes."[51] She highlights how surfing reinforces a broader lesson for Latinx community members: "Don't let being Mexican, don't let being Latino, don't let being a woman stop you from doing things, because we've been told it's a white man's world."[52] Mira Manickam-Shirley points to surfing's capacity to carry people "a little step forward on the path [toward feeling] that, 'oh this is something that I can do. If I start with this [one thing], I can do this [other thing].' Just knowing that is super powerful, I think."[53] GiGi Lucas, who was thirty-five when she started surfing, described the sense of confidence and independence that she gained from surfing as a kind of "rebirth." She reflects, "Had I known about surfing when I was like thirteen, fourteen, [in those] formative years when I was making decisions about who I am as a woman, man, I would have made some different decisions. . . . Had I had the confidence that surfing gives me? Man . . . "[54]

Beyond defying the limits of dominant social forces and representations, surf communities of color are actively building forms of social connection that challenge the divisions that structure much of the world around them. "It's about belonging and truly feeling that," Monica Medellín asserts.[55] Kayiita Johansson explains how his own efforts to foster such a feeling of belonging within the Black.Surfers community hinge on a distinctive notion of "positive community." For Johansson, the idea of a positive community stands in contrast with the competitive ethos of what he characterizes as a "negative mindset, or maybe crabs in a barrel mindset." In a positive community, like that which Johansson has worked to foster, "it gives you a place to feel like you belong . . . having that sense of other folks that not only accept you in this space, but actively encourage you, and are interested in and pulling you into that space, to give you a sense of belonging, a sense of confidence that you wouldn't have otherwise."[56] A similar spirit characterizes Gabourel's description of the Laru Beya community as "a family." As he puts it, "You don't 'join' Laru Beya, you know . . . [just as] you don't join a family. . . . You don't have to take a test to become a part of it. . . . You can let your guard down. . . . It's community, it's grassroots, it's family."[57] As patterns of surf community organizing link racialized populations across differences of ethnicity, nationality, gender, tribal affiliation, and sexuality, they also challenge broader ethnic, national, and social divisions. Reflecting on the experience of overhearing a conversation among white men in the lineup about how the implementation of then-President Trump's vision for the US-Mexico border wall "could not come soon enough," Yeager says of her work in the Latinx Surf Club, which includes surfers with ethnic ties to Mexico, Guatemala, and elsewhere across Latina America, "I feel like I'm breaking down the wall, little by little."[58]

Importantly, many within surfing's oppositional culture see the work they are doing within the surfing world as intimately related to change they wish to see in the wider world. As surfing's movement builders recognize, the communities and connections they are fostering around surfing carry the potential to provide a structural foundation for more overtly political, coalitional activity. Mira Manickam-Shirley says of her organization, "I've always thought about Brown Girl Surf as a social movement."[59] She explains, it is "more than just a program. . . . It's a community, and the community is a basis for a movement and a basis for culture shift." When issues arise that call for a direct-action response, she emphasizes, "The community shows up."[60] Brown Girl Surf has been involved in efforts to impact policy and public access along the coastline in Northern California, with particular attention to changing the permitting process for surf instruction to allow for a wider diversity of surf schools, and surfing populations, in Pacifica.[61] Kayiita Johansson, too, emphasizes the political aims that intertwine with his community-building efforts in the Black.Surfers platform. "Community and self organization is not enough in my mind," Johansson asserts. "We actually require policy changes. Affordable coastal housing, universal water safety, parking changes and so much more."[62] Aydon Gabourel sees the building of an inclusive surf community and political organizing in other arenas of life as mutually constitutive. Whether it be around policies mandating water safety education across the state of New York or in response to police killings of African Americans or the upsurge of anti-Asian violence that swept the country amid the COVID-19 pandemic, Gabourel emphasizes the importance to him of "getting these kids involved in everything that's going on with social justice. . . . When you run a nonprofit . . . you don't want to get political, right, but I don't think it's politics per se," at least not in the conventional sense of the term. "It's right or wrong," he stresses. "So we've taken them to different functions, where they could learn about these things. We've taken them out to a few of the protests." Describing an event that Laru Beya organized with the multiracial, queer-affirming surf collective Benny's Club after an Asian-descent family member of one of the group's volunteers was attacked in Flushing, Queens while attending a wedding, he says, "We just want them to understand these things and to know that you have to stand up and fight for these things. . . . Some people say, well, that's not happening to me, that's happening to [somebody else]. . . . No, no, no, it's happening here today. Tomorrow, it's gonna be [closer to home], and we have to stand up for things."[63]

Altering the Alchemy

By the end of the 2010s, the oppositional cultural currents that surfers of color forged across the surf industry, organizational networks, and visual media presented radical alternatives to the white heteropatriarchal norms that had long dominated the sport, particularly on the US mainland. Although none could have anticipated the surge of antiracist expression that coursed through the surfing world in summer 2020, it is difficult to imagine what scale or forms any sort of reckoning within the sport might have taken in that moment without the social, cultural, institutional, and intellectual groundwork that had been laid by surfers of color in the decade prior. Of course, the uprisings of 2020 also reshaped the terrain on which surfing's oppositional culture continues to evolve. New players, organizations, and media outlets have entered the landscape, and new relationships continue to crystallize between and among surfers of color across and beyond the United States. Meanwhile new levels of public attention to the movement all present new challenges as well as possibilities for movement builders. While the oppositional surf culture's formation is ongoing and its future remains actively under construction, there is clear continuity between past and present efforts by surfers of color to advance a vision for the expansion of inclusivity within surfing that is not an end in itself, but a necessary, constitutive part of a wider movement for social and cultural transformation. For these communities, changing surf culture is as much about altering the alchemy of how people relate to each other and the environment as it is about riding waves. It is as much about access to life—life lived with wholeness, wellness, and dignity—as it is about access to a place in the lineup.

Among the many new leaders that have emerged within the movement in more recent years is Brick Howze. Along with Tre'lan Michael and Gage Crismond, Brick cofounded Black Sand in the fall of 2020 as a surf-and-art collective, which the group reestablished as Ebony Beach Club in 2022, naming it after the Black beach club that was preparing to open its doors in a Santa Monica–based building in 1957 when it was seized by the city and subsequently leveled.[64] With an eye on the long arc of movement formation, Brick describes what is taking place in the surfing world as a "renaissance." He says that if there was "only one word that can characterize any of these things" taking place within surfing currently, "It's not *movement*. It's not *collective*. It's not even *group*. It's not even *organization*. To me, this is like a renaissance."[65] Reflecting on the contributions of earlier generations of Black, Brown, and Indigenous surf communities, he underscores that the movement has little to do with short-term gains that might be won through political gamesmanship or short-sighted maneuvering. Rather, "This is a hundred-year project."[66] Brick explains, "We're fully unlearning, relearning, rethinking everything that has been what we know as 'surf culture,'" in fact, he says, "x-ing out surf culture" and doing away with the very idea of surf culture as a singular, monolithic construct altogether, forging in its place a new relationship between "'surf' and 'culture'"—one that centers multiplicity, multivocality, and grassroots dignity and self-definition.[67] In working to make surfing a site on which a multiplicity of cultural currents can thrive, engage, and enrich each other, the many players involved in the ongoing movement are working to reclaim surfing as a terrain on which the seeds of a new world can be sown. To the extent that surfing's oppositional culture is helping to shed light on a world worth building and a future worth seeking, then we would do well to pay attention.

Notes

The author extends their gratitude to all who interviewed for, discussed, and offered input on this essay along the way. Special thanks to Rick Blocker and Natalie Bowers for their close readings and feedback on early drafts, and for the generosity of time and spirit that each of them lent to engaging with this project.

1 On the paddle-outs of summer 2020, see, for example, Bryan Benattou, "The Surfing Community Paddles Out for Equality," World Surf League, June 3,

2020, www.worldsurfleague.com/posts/452545/the-surfing-community-paddles-out-for-equality-and-justice; Dashel Pierson, "Memorial Paddleouts for George Floyd: A Running List of Events Showing Surfers in Support of Racial Justice," Surfline, last modified June 4, 2020, www.surfline.com/surf-news/memorial-paddleouts-george-floyd/87148. Literature on the paddle-out tradition and its history is limited, but the evidence suggests it is a modern adaptive ritual brought into practice by Native Hawaiians during the 1920s. See Margaret Gibson and Mardi Frost, "Surfing and Ocean-Based Death Ritual," *Mortality* 24, no. 3 (2019): 304–18.

2 Todd Prodanovich, "Now's the Time for Surfers to Prove We Really Are Anti-establishment," *Surfer*, June 9, 2020, www.surfer.com/features/opinion-surfing-and-racial-justice-counterculture/.

3 World Surf League (@wsl), "Surfing Is for Everyone" Instagram, June 20, 2020.

4 Tyler Wright (@tylerwright), "Before I'm an athlete, I'm a human being . . . " Instagram, September 12, 2020; Tyler Wright (@tylerwright), "Reflect, Listen, Acknowledge, Learn, Change . . . " Instagram, September 13, 2020. Also Alyssa Roenigk, "How World Champion Tyler Wright Came Back from a Crippling Virus to Change Surfing Forever," ESPN, March 7, 2021, www.espn.com/espnw/story/_/id/31010434/how-world-champion-tyler-wright-came-back-crippling-virus-change-surfing-forever.

5 Roenigk, "How World Champion Tyler Wright Came Back"; "Congratulations Tyler Wright—2020 Tweed Coast Pro Champion," Rip Curl, September 15, 2020, www.ripcurl.com/us/blog/tyler-wright-2020-tweed-coast-pro-champion.html.

6 Selema Masekela, panel discussion with Danielle Black Lyons, Amanda Chinchelli, Martina Duran, GiGi Lucas, Bethany Mollenkof, and Chelsea Woody, "Sea Us Now Film Premiere," YouTube, 1:05:00, July 16, 2020, www.youtube.com/watch?v=liSf7KrVqqQ.

7 This is not to suggest these are the only arenas in which surfing's oppositional culture has been taking shape. For instance, the scholar-activism reflected in the growing field of critical surf studies, and the currents of dialogue and community of which this collection is part, in many ways form an additional pillar of movement activity. For an analysis foregrounding the interface between surf-oriented scholarship and activism, see, for example, Krista Comer, "What Leisure?: Surfeminism in an Era of Trump," *Palgrave Communications* 5, no. 42 (2019): 1–6.

8 My framing of surfing's oppositional culture as a movement of many movements draws on the theoretical contributions of late twentieth- and early twenty-first-century antiglobalization movements. See, for example, Tom Mertes, Walden F. Bello, Bernard Cassen, and Jose Bove, et al., *A Movement of Movements: Is Another World Really Possible?* (New York: Verso, 2004).

9 Isaiah Helekunihi Walker, *Waves of Resistance: Surfing and History in Twentieth Century Hawai'i* (Honolulu: University of Hawai'i Press, 2011), esp. 10–11. Also see Alison Rose Jefferson, *Living the California Dream: African American Leisure Sites during the Jim Crow Era* (Lincoln: University of Nebraska Press, 2020), chaps. 2–3; Scott Laderman, *Empire in Waves: A Political History of Surfing* (Berkeley: University of California Press, 2014).

10 I thank Rick Blocker and Andrea Kabwasa for their contributions to the mapping of this history. In addition to her prominence in the LA surf scene, Mills wrote a blog, "Black People Don't Surf," beginning in 2005, http://surfandthefury.blogspot.com, accessed August 24, 2022. Schaffer is the first African American female professional surfer. For more on the overlapping historical currents referenced here, see, for example, Walker, *Waves of Resistance*; Jefferson, *Living the California Dream*, chaps. 2–3; Dina Gilio-Whitaker, *As Long as Grass Grows: The Indigenous Fight for Environmental Justice, from Colonization to Standing Rock* (Boston: Beacon Press, 2019), esp. chap 7.

11 US Census Bureau, "Census 2000 Profile: California: 2000," US Department of Commerce, August 2002, 2.

12 Kelly Lytle Hernández, *City of Inmates: Conquest, Rebellion, and the Rise of Human Caging in Los Angeles* (Chapel Hill: University of North Carolina Press, 2017); Michelle Alexander, *The New Jim Crow: Mass Incarceration in the Age of Colorblindness* (New York: New Press, 2010); Ruth Wilson Gilmore, *Golden Gulag: Prisons, Surplus, Crisis, and Opposition in Globalizing California* (Berkeley: University of California Press, 2007).

13 Selema Masekela, interviewed by Rich Roll, host, "Episode 594: Selema Masekela Is the Action Sports Evangelist," *Rich Roll* podcast, podcast audio, https://podcasts.apple.com/us/podcast/selema-masekela-is-the-action-sports-evangelist/id582272991?i=1000516761906.

14 Selema Masekela, video chat interview with the author, December 7, 2021; Selema Masekela, interviewed by Sandy Clunas, "Episode 38: Authenticity, with Selema Masekela," *The After Hours Lounge*, podcast audio, November 25, 2020, https://podcasts.apple.com/gb/podcast/authenticity-with-selema-masekela/id1503664779?i=1000500210450. Also see Elizabeth Sine, "'Yeah,

I Lived That': Selema Masekela Breakdances on Water," *Emocean*, no. 3 (July 2022): 88–105.

15 See, for example, "The Visible Man: Sal Masekela Gives a Face to Race Relations in the Surfing Community," *Surfer*, September 1998, 99; "Sal Masekela on Racism in Surfing," YouTube, 9:23, *The Inertia*, November 19, 2014, www.youtube.com/watch?v=5Lu4cMsItUA; Zach Weisberg, "Sal Masekela Recalls a Disgusting Encounter the First Time He Surfed in Post-Apartheid South Africa," *The Inertia*, October 24, 2018, www.theinertia.com/surf/sal-masekela-recalls-a-disgusting-encounter-the-first-time-he-surfed-in-post-apartheid-south-africa.

16 Cofounded with Alyasha Owerka-Moore and Mirko Mangum.

17 Cofounded with Steve Laroseliere. "Stoked History," Stoked Mentoring, accessed July 12, 2021, www.stoked.org/about.

18 Mami Wata, *Afro Surf* (Berkeley: Ten Speed Press, 2021; originally published by Mami Wata, 2020).

19 Masekela, video chat interview.

20 Masekela, video chat interview.

21 "Our Story," Native Like Water, accessed July 12, 2021, www.nativelikewater.org/our-story; Marc Chavez, video chat interview with author, March 29, 2021.

22 Farhana Huq, video chat interview with the author, January 28, 2021; Mira Manickam-Shirley, video chat interview with the author, January 14, 2021, and January 21, 2021.

23 J. D. Simkins, "Surfing for 'Something Positive': Black Girls Surf and the Rising Ride of Equal Representation," *Sunset*, July 16, 2020, www.sunset.com/travel/wild-lands/black-girls-surf-rides-wave-equal-treatment.

24 Vanessa Yeager, video chat interview with the author, February 2, 2021. Notably, Comley's contributions to surfing's oppositional culture extend into the realm of scholarship as well. See, for example, Cassie Comley, "'Mexicans Don't Surf': An Intersectional Analysis of Mexican Americans' Experiences with Sport," in *Surfing, Sex, Genders, and Sexualities*, ed. lisahunter, 91–109 (New York: Routledge, 2018) and "'We Have to Establish Our Territory': How Women Surfers 'Carve Out' Gendered Spaces within Surfing," *Sport in Society* 19, no. 8–9 (February 2016): 1289–98.

25 Kayiita Johansson, video chat interview with the author, April 7, 2021.

26 GiGi Lucas, video chat interview with the author, January 13, 2021.

27 Aydon Gabourel, video chat interview with the author, April 7, 2021.

28 Monica Medellín, video chat interview with the author, December 7, 2021.

29 Monica Medellín, "Surf Girls: Kaikaina," accessed July 19, 2022, https://monicamedellin.com/portfolio/surf-girls-kaikaina; Waves Made, accessed July 19, 2022, www.wavesmademedia.com.

30 Textured Waves, accessed July 12, 2021, www.texturedwaves.com/about.

31 Danielle Black Lyons, with Chelsea Woody and Martina Duran, interviewed by Jo Carberry, "The Ladies of Textured Waves Talk about the African American Surf Experience," The Inertia podcast, season 1, episode 11, podcast audio, September 20, 2020, https://podcasts.apple.com/us/podcast/ladies-textured-waves-talk-about-african-american-surf/id1491836972?i=1000492197653.

32 Textured Waves, email interview with the author, May 3, 2021.

33 On the healing/therapy potential of surfing, see David Fleischmann, Betty Michalewicz, Eric Stedje-Larsen, et al., "Surf Medicine: Surfing as a Means of Therapy for Combat-Related Polytrauma," *Journal of Prosthetics and Orthotics* 23, no. 1 (January 2011): 27–29; Margarida Gaspar de Matos, Anabela Santos, Cristiana Fauvelet, et al., "Surfing for Social Integration: Mental Health and Well-Being Promotion through Surf Therapy among Institutionalized Young People," *Journal of Community Medicine and Public Health Care* 4, no. 1 (June 2017): 1–6; Roger H. Charlier and Marie-Claire P. Chaineux, "The Healing Sea: A Sustainable Coastal Ocean Resource: Thalassotherapy," *Journal of Coastal Research* 25, no. 4 (July 2009): 838–56. On surfing and spirituality/religion, the seminal resource is Bron Taylor, "Surfing into Spirituality and a New, Aquatic Nature Religion," *Journal of the American Academy of Religion* 75, no. 4 (December 2007): 923–51. Also see "Nature=God; It's Official: Surfing Is a Religion," *Surfing*, July 2008, cover story; Eileen Luhr, "Seeker, Surfer, Yogi: The Progressive Religious Imagination and the Cultural Politics of Place in Encinitas, California," *American Quarterly* 67, no 4 (December 2015): 1169–93. On surfing and self-actualization, see Richard Bennett, *The Surfer's Mind: The Complete, Practical Guide to Surf Psychology* (self-published by the author, 2004), 2–3.

34 The popular phrase "only a surfer knows the feeling" was emblazoned, for example, on a Billabong ad that appeared in the fall 2010 issue of *Surfer's Journal*, pictured in Tim Cooley, *Surfing about Music* (Berkeley: University of California, 2014), 5.

35 On the cultural politics of time and place, see J. Judith Halberstam, *In a Queer Time and Place: Transgender Bodies, Subcultural Lives* (New York: New York University Press, 2005). On the relationship between temporality, racial capitalism, and settler colonialism, see Arun Saldanha, "A Date with Destiny:

Racial Capitalism and the Beginnings of the Anthropocene," *Environment and Planning D: Society and Space* 38, no. 1 (September 2019): 12–34; Anna M. Agathangelou, "On the Question of Time, Racial Capitalism, and the Planetary," *Globalizations* 18, no. 6 (April 2021), 811–20; Jessica Ty Miller, "Temporal Analysis of Displacement: Racial Capitalism and Settler Colonial Urban Space," *Geoforum*, no. 116 (November 2020): 180–92.

36 Rick Blocker, in *White Wash*, directed by Ted Woods (2011). Also see Krista Comer, "'We're Blacksurfing': Public History and Liberation Politics in *White Wash*," *Journal of American Ethnic History* 35, no. 2 (Winter 2016): 68–78. On the politics of refusal and autonomy, see John Holloway and Eloína Peláez, "Introduction: Reinventing Revolution," in *Zapatista!: Reinventing Revolution in Mexico*, ed. John Holloway and Eloína Peláez (London: Pluto Press, 1998), 14–17; John Holloway, *Change the World without Taking Power* (London: Pluto Press, 2010).

37 Manickam-Shirley, video chat interview, January 21, 2021.

38 Lucas, video chat interview.

39 Giselle Carrillo, phone interview with the author, April 29, 2021.

40 Carrillo, phone interview.

41 Marc Chavez, "Pacific Surfing Traditions and Water Access of Indigenous Communities: Short Film and Panel Discussion," Vimeo, 1:37:12, https://vimeo.com/514128344.

42 Marc Chavez, "Pacific Surfing Traditions."

43 My reference to "roots and routes" draws on James Clifford, *Routes: Travel and Translation in the Late-Twentieth Century* (Cambridge: Harvard University Press, 1997) and Paul Gilroy, *The Black Atlantic: Modernity and Double Consciousness* (Cambridge: Harvard University Press, 1995).

44 Gabourel, video chat interview.

45 Chavez, video chat interview.

46 Caleigh Cornell and Lydia Heberling, "The Politics of Play: Surfing as a Trans-Indigenous Expression of Thrivance," Boarder X, March 20, 2017, https://boarderx.wag.ca/blog/display,article/7/the-politics-of-play-surfing-as-a-trans-indigenous-expression-of-thrivance.

47 Chelsea Woody, "Before You See Our Pain," *Emocean*, no. 1 (2021), 26.

48 Martina Duran, panel discussion with Danielle Black Lyons, Amanda Chinchelli, Martina Duran, GiGi Lucas, Bethany Mollenkof, Selema Masekela, and Chelsea Woody, "Sea Us Now Film Premiere," YouTube, 1:05:00, July 16, 2020, www.youtube.com/watch?v=liSf7KrVqqQ.

49 Woody, "Before You See Our Pain."

50 Giselle Carrillo, "Giselle Carrillo," The Ocean Is Female: Stories of Sistas in the Surf and Sea, 2020, https://theoceanisfemale.com/giselle-carrillo.

51 Yeager, video chat interview.

52 Yeager, video chat interview.

53 Manickam-Shirley, video chat interview, January 21, 2021.

54 GiGi Lucas, in Fat Tony, interview with GiGi Lucas, Sharon Schaffer, and Mary Mills, "Volcom Presents True Conversations, Season 1, Episode 6: Black Women in Surfing," *Volcom*, podcast, November 9, 2020, https://podcasts.apple.com/us/podcast/s1-e6-black-women-in-surf-gigi-lucas-sharon-schaffer/id1531779884?i=1000497780289.

55 Medellín, video chat interview.

56 Johansson, video chat interview.

57 Gabourel, video chat interview.

58 Yeager, video chat interview.

59 Manickam-Shirley, video chat interview, January 14, 2021; Huq, video chat interview.

60 Manickam-Shirley, video chat interview, January 14, 2021.

61 Manickam-Shirley, video chat interview, January 14, 2021.

62 Kayiita Johansson, email to the author, June 26, 2022.

63 Gabourel, video chat interview.

64 Jefferson, *Living the California Dream*.

65 Brick Howze, video chat interview with the author, April 28, 2021.

66 Howze, video chat interview, April 28, 2021.

67 Howze, video chat interview with the author, June 18, 2021.

Contributors

J. PETER BROSIUS's research has been engaged with issues related to the political ecology of environmental degradation, Indigenous rights, and conservation in Sarawak, Malaysia (Borneo). His research in Sarawak initially focused on the international rainforest campaign centered on Penan hunter-gatherers, and he continues to be involved in efforts to seek acknowledgment of Penan land claims in oil palm plantations and national parks. From 2004 to 2010 he participated in the MacArthur Foundation initiative Advancing Conservation in a Social Context, which led to the creation at the University of Georgia of the Center for Integrative Conservation Research and the Integrative Conservation PhD program. He also played a key role in the development of collaborative event ethnographies of major conservation meetings. In addition to recent research on bioenergy in the American South, he has ongoing research on the Tolak Reklamasi movement in Bali, Indonesia, and the political ecology of real estate in occupied surfscapes in the Global South. He is currently working on a book on the concept of race in the history of anthropology.

CHASE BUCKLEW is an independent researcher based in Los Angeles, where she graduated from CalArts with master's in aesthetics and politics in 2018. Her writing has been featured in *Zérodeux* contemporary art review, *Herein* arts journal, and the edited volume *Serial Killing On-Screen*. Her research interests include true crime media, film and television studies, popular culture, contemporary art, and apocalypse studies.

KRISTA COMER is a professor of English and women's studies at Rice University in Houston, on the Gulf Coast South. In 2014 she cofounded the Institute for Women Surfers, an international grassroots educational initiative in the feminist public humanities. She writes for scholarly as well as nonspecialist audiences. She has written many essays, and her books include *Landscapes of the New West*, *Surfer Girls in the New World Order*, and *Living West as Feminists: Conversations about the Where of Us*. She is at work on *Feminist Surf Life in an Age of Climate Change* as well as on a memoir.

CASSIE COMLEY holds a PhD in sociology, from the University of Oregon, in the field of gender and race/ethnicity. She works for the Department of Justice, California, as a research associate in the Department of Justice Research Services. Additionally, she works as a sociology instructor in the Sociology Department at Loyola Marymount University in Los Angeles. Generally, her academic work focuses on social inequalities, sociology of gender, critical race theory, and women in sport.

KEVIN DAWSON is lifelong surfer and historian of the African diaspora at the University of California, Merced. His scholarship considers how enslaved Africans recreated and reimagined Atlantic African aquatic traditions in the Americas, including swimming, underwater diving, surfing, canoe-making, and canoeing. He has published numerous articles, and his book, *Undercurrents of Power: Aquatic Culture in the African Diaspora*, was awarded the 2019 Harriet Tubman Prize from the Schomburg Center for Research in Black Culture at the New York Public Library.

DINA GILIO-WHITAKER (Colville Confederated Tribes descendant) is a renowned Native American studies scholar and journalist, focusing on the topics of environmental justice, Indigenous knowledge, and identity. She is lecturer faculty in American Indian studies at California State University, San Marcos, where she co-founded the Indigenous Climate and Environmental Collaborative, advising researchers and conservation and other organizations on Indigenous engagement and other policy-based protocols. Her most recent book is the award-winning *As Long As Grass Grows: The Indigenous Fight for Environmental Justice, from Colonization to Standing Rock* (2019), and her forthcoming book *Indians for Sale: Pretendians, Disenrollment, and Native American Identity in Late Capitalism* is scheduled for release in 2025.

LYDIA M. HEBERLING is an assistant professor in the Ethnic Studies Department at California State Polytechnic University, San Luis Obispo. She holds a PhD in English from the University of Washington. Her areas of expertise are American Indian literatures, with a focus on the literatures from Indigenous California, as well as the field of critical surf studies. She has published in *Studies in American Indian Literatures* and *Zocalo Public Square*. With Nicholas Reo, she organized the inaugural Indigenous surfers' symposium, "Surf Sovereignty: Coastal Stewardship, Embodied Activism, and Indigenous Wave Riders" in 2024 in San Luis Obispo. She loves to longboard and her favorite surfing spots are Tourmaline Beach in San Diego and Hobuck Beach on Makah Nation in Washington State.

JAIMIE ISAAC (she/her/hers) is a curator and interdisciplinary artist, Anishinaabe member of Sagkeeng First Nation, and is of British heritage. She was the chief curator at the Art Gallery of Greater Victoria from 2021 to 2023 and advisor from 2023 to 2024. As the curator of contemporary and Indigenous arts at the Winnipeg Art Gallery, from 2015 to 2021, she was awarded the Canadian Museums Association's outstanding achievement award in exhibitions category with the *Boarder X* exhibition. Isaac has a degree in art history and a master of arts from the University of British Columbia focused on decolonizing gallery/museum practices. Through academic, curatorial, consulting, collaborative, and artistic projects, she engages in areas of reconciliation, resistance, decolonization in art and in sport, Indigenous feminism, environmental justice, language, and cultural resurgence. Isaac has lectured, curated internationally with research trips and residencies in Norway, Finland, Italy, Australia, New Zealand, Chicago, and New York. With published work, Isaac has contributed to scholarly collections of writing within textbooks and journals.

DAVID KAMPER is a professor of American Indian studies at San Diego State University. He is a settler scholar whose people are Bundist from The Pale. For the last fifteen years he has been working with skaterboarders and basketball players on Turtle Island witnessing the joy these activities bring to Indian Country. His forthcoming book *Rezballers and Skate Elders: Joyful Futures in Indian Country* will be published in 2025. He is also the associate director of SDSU's Center for Skateboarding, Action Sports, and Social Change and the academic advisor for the sport and society minor. He is grateful to currently live and surf in the Kumeyaay homeland.

LISAHUNTER (all one word and lowercase, pronouns they/it) lives and works on unceded Boonwurrung Country, researching bluespaces and greenspaces as places of learning, teaching, regenerating, and envisioning better ways for planetary health. In 2018 after seeing a need (still) for surfing spaces to better contribute to planetary health (in this instance for attention to sexes, genders, and sexualities as one of many social spaces that undermines "better ways") they edited and contributed to *Surfing, Sex, Genders and Sexualities*. Their work beyond surfing includes ethnograpies, digitial storymapping, queering as methodology, field theory, informal education spaces, and equity for diversity and inclusion as part of planetary health. They pay attention to First Nations–settler/colonial (re)conciliation through caring for country, BSLGBTQIA+ intergenerational learning, health and physical education, sexuality education, and teacher education for ecosocial justice. They love to surf and be with the wildness.

JESS PONTING specializes in the use of sustainable tourism for community development. He has been particularly active as a researcher/consultant in equatorial Asia-Pacific, most recently as a member of the World Commission on Protected Areas and as a consultant for Fiji's Tourism Master Plan. His areas of interest include sustainable tourism, surfing tourism, cross-cultural interactions in tourism, the social construction of tourist spaces, and volunteer tourism. He is currently researching peak experiences in surfing tourism, hermeneutic circles of representation and surfing tourism, volunteering as a decommodified tourism experience, and the interface between traditional systems of reef resource ownership and sustainable marine tourism in the Pacific Islands.

NICHOLAS REO is an Anishinaabe teacher-scholar and an enrolled member of the Sault Ste. Marie Tribe of Chippewa Indians. He uses Indigenous methodologies to study and participate in Indigenous knowledge practices, Indigenous land and sea tenure, and Indigenous language revitalization. Reo also works to create spaces for Indigenous international knowledge exchange and expansion of Indigenous kinship networks. He is a faculty member in the Department of Indigenous Studies at Simon Fraser University and holds a Canada Excellence Research Chair (2023–2031) focused on coastal regeneration and relationalities.

TARA RUTTENBERG is a free surfer, researcher and instructor with a PhD in development studies (Wageningen University, 2022), specializing in political ecology, sustainable tourism, and critical surf studies. Her research explores decolonial approaches to surf tourism, surfeminism, and alternatives to development in Global South surfing destinations. Tara is seminar leader and lecturer for global environmental studies (Kultur-Studier/OsloMet), lead instructor for conservation ecology and sustainable development in southern Costa Rica (wildlands studies), teaching assistant and program coordinator for Surfing and Sustainability: Political Ecology in Costa Rica (University of Georgia), and member of the Community Economies Research Network.

ELIZABETH SINE is a lecturer in history at California Polytechnic State University, San Luis Obispo. Her research and teaching examines the histories of race, labor, culture, and social movements in California and the broader US. She holds a PhD in history from the University of California, San Diego, and is the author of *Rebel Imaginaries: Labor, Culture, and Politics in Depression-Era California* (2021) and co-editor of *Another University Is Possible* (2010).

Born and raised in Keaukaha, Hilo, Hawaiʻi, ISAIAH WALKER is a professor of history at Brigham Young University–Hawaii on O'ahu's North Shore. Walker earned a PhD in history from the University of California, Santa Barbara, and a master's degree from the University of Hawaiʻi at Mānoa. He is the author of *Waves of Resistance: Surfing and History in Twentieth-Century Hawaiʻi*, an award-winning book where he illuminates the interwoven relationship between surfing and Hawaiian culture, identity politics, and American colonialism. Walker poignantly recounts examples of Hawaiian surfers successfully resisting colonialism and flipping hierarchies upside down. Additionally, he has published several academic articles and book chapters and frequently consults as a historian for documentaries and various media outlets. He also serves as a regular commentator at professional surfing competitions.

ASAKO YONAN (she/they), earned her master's degree in women's studies at San Diego State University located on Kumeyaay land. Her thesis examined the California State Beach lifeguarding institution as a state-sponsored site of gendered surveillance and sexual violence toward women of color. She is currently a PhD student in the Indigenous, Race, and Ethnic Studies Department and a new media and culture certificate recipient at the University of Oregon located on Kalapuya Ilihi. Her research interests include race and technology, comparative ethnic studies, and queer of color critique.

Index